The Place of Value
in a World of Facts

Nobel Symposium 14

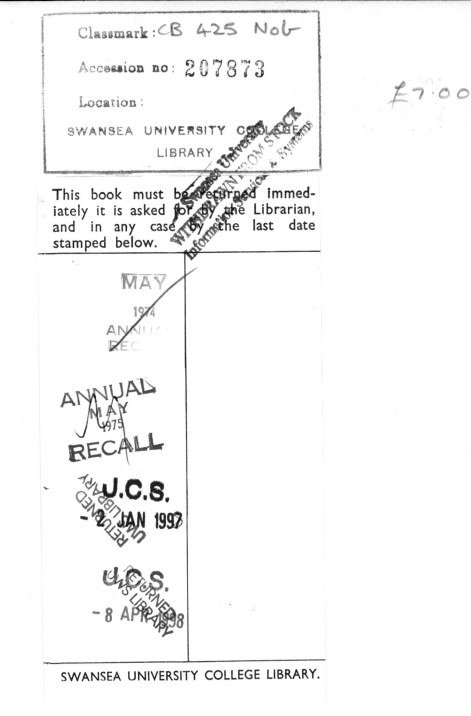

The Place of Value in a World of Facts

Proceedings of the Fourteenth Nobel Symposium
Stockholm, September 15–20, 1969

Edited by

ARNE TISELIUS and SAM NILSSON

Professor, Head of the Nobel
Institute of the Royal
Academy of Sciences, Sweden

Dr. Techn., Stockholm,
Sweden

WILEY INTERSCIENCE DIVISION

John Wiley & Sons, Inc. *New York, London, Sydney*

ALMQVIST & WIKSELL *Stockholm*

Printed in Sweden by
Almqvist & Wiksells Boktryckeri AB, Uppsala 1970

Contents

The menace and the promise of science

The teaching of knowledge and the imparting of values

The new republic—Scientist, humanist and government

Free or directed research—A choice for the individual and for society

Strategy for survival

Nobel Symposium Committee

N. K. Ståhle (chairman), Executive Director of the Nobel Foundation

L. Hulthén, Professor, Member of the Nobel Committee for Physics

A. Tiselius, Professor, Chairman of the Nobel Committee for Chemistry

B. Gustafsson, Professor, Secretary of the Nobel Committee for Medicine

K. R. Gierow, Dr.Ph., Secretary of the Swedish Academy (literature)

A. Schou, Director of the Norwegian Nobel Institute (peace)

Organizing Committee of Nobel Symposium 14

A. Tiselius (*chairman*), Professor, Head of the Nobel Institute of the Royal
Academy of Sciences

K. R. Gierow, Dr.Ph., Secretary of the Swedish Academy

A. Schou, Director of the Norwegian Nobel Institute

C. G. Hedén, Professor, Bacteriological engineering, Karolinska Institutet,
Stockholm

S. Nilsson (*secretary*), Dr. Techn.

List of participants

H. D. AIKEN, Brandeis University, Dept. of Philosophy, *Waltham,* Mass. 02154, U.S.A.

W. H. AUDEN, 77 St Mark's Place, *New York,* N.Y. 10003, U.S.A.

HARRISON BROWN, California Institute of Technology, Dept. of Geological Sciences, *Pasadena,* Calif. 91109, U.S.A.

J. S. BRUNER, Harvard University, Center for Cognitive Studies, William James Hall, 33 Kirkland Str., *Cambridge,* Mass. 02138, U.S.A.

F. CASTBERG, 7de Juni Pl. 1, *Oslo* 1, Norway

C. CHAGAS, 38 Francisco Otaviano, ZC-37-*Rio de Janerio,* Brazil

C. A. DOXIADIS, Doxiadis Associates, 24 Strat Syndesmou, *Athens* 136, Greece

V. A. ENGELHARDT, USSR Academy of Sciences, Leninski Prospect 14, *Moscow,* USSR

K. R. GIEROW, Swedish Academy, Börshuset, Källargränd, 111 29 *Stockholm,* Sweden

E. H. GOMBRICH, The Warburg Institute, Woburn Square, *London* W.C. 1, England

W. GUTH, Deutsche Bank AG, *Frankfurt am Main,* Västtyskland

Y. HAYASHI, Tokyo Institute of Technology, 4-12-5, Nukui, Minami-cho Koganeishi, *Tokyo,* Japan

C.-G. HEDÉN, Karolinska Institutet, Bakteriologiska Institutionen, 104 01 *Stockholm* 60, Sweden

A. KING, OECD, 2 Rue André-Pascal, *Paris* 16ᵉ, France

O. KLINEBERG, International Center for Intergroup Relations, 4 Rue de Chevreuse, *Paris* 6ᵉ, Frankrike

A. KOESTLER, 8 Montpelier Square, *London* S.W. 7, England

T. A. LAMBO, University College Hospital, Dept. of Psychiatry and Neurology, *Ibadan,* Nigeria

H. D. LASSWELL, Yale University, Law School, *New Haven,* Conn., U.S.A.

J. LEDERBERG, Stanford University, School of Medicine, Dept. of Genetics, *Stanford,* Calif. U.S.A.

K. LORENZ, Max Planck Institut für Verhaltensphysiologie, 8131 *Seewiesen,* Germany

I. MALEK, Institute of Microbiology, Czechoslovak Academy of Sciences, *Praha* 4 — Kvc, Budejovicka 1083, Czechoslovakia

M. MEAD, American Museum of Natural History, Central Park West, *New York,* N.Y. 10024, U.S.A.

M. D. MILLIONSHCHIKOV, USSR Academy of Sciences, Leninski Prospekt 14, *Moscow,* USSR

J. MONOD, Institut Pasteur, 25 Rue du Docteur Roux, *Paris* 15ᵉ, France

G. MYRDAL, Institute for International Economic Studies, Wenner-Gren Center, Sveavägen 166, 113 46 *Stockholm,* Sweden

S. NILSSON, Incentive AB, Arsenalsgatan 4, 111 47 *Stockholm,* Sweden

L. C. PAULING, University of California, Dept. of Chemistry, Revelle College, *La Jolla,* Calif. 92037, U.S.A.

J. R. PIERCE, Bell Telephone Lab., Mountain Avenue, *Murray Hill.* N.J. 07974, U.S.A.

B. PREGEL, World Academy of Art and Sciences, 630 Fifth Avenue, Suite 627, *New York,* N.Y. 10020, U.S.A.

A. SALAM, International Center for Theoretical Physics, Prosecco-Miramare 21, 34100 *Trieste,* Italy

A. SCHOU, Norwegian Nobel Institute, Drammensveien 19, *Oslo* 2, Norway

G. T. SEABORG, U S Atomic Energy Commission, *Washington* D.C. 20545, U.S.A.

T. SEGERSTEDT, University of Uppsala, Box 256, 751 05 *Uppsala,* Sweden

J. R. D. TATA, Tata Industries Private Ltd., Bombay House, Bruce Str., Fort, *Bombay* 1, India

J. TINBERGEN, Haviklaan 31, *The Hague,* Holland

A. TISELIUS, University of Uppsala, Box 531, 751 21 *Uppsala,* Sweden

C. H. WADDINGTON, Institute of Animal Genetics, West Mains Road, *Edinburgh* 9, Scotland

Opening Address

By Arne Tiselius

Head of the Nobel Institute of the Royal Academy of Sciences

On behalf of the Nobel Foundation and of the Organizing Committee I wish to extend to all of you a hearty welcome to this Symposium. A welcome also to Södergarn, where most of our activities during this week shall take place. Several Nobel Symposia have been held here. We have found that Södergarn has many advantages for a gathering of this kind. It is far enough from Stockholm to create a quiet atmosphere for our deliberations and also to make it easier to resist an eventual temptation to sneak out into the turmoil of the big city. It is close enough, however, if some of you sometimes would find it difficult to resist such a temptation—we may then even help you with the transportation.

We in the Organizing Committee are aware that this Symposium is an ambitious undertaking—perhaps even an overambitious one. Some believe that nowadays there are too many meetings, also on the international level, of which some deal with subjects closely related to ours. This, however, can be interpreted as a growing awareness among people of all nations that something is wrong with the world and that there is an urgent need to come together to see what should be done. Nobody expects that such a meeting will solve the problems, but there is a hope behind these efforts that we shall thus gradually approach certain measures to be recommended. Already the fact that people representing widely different nationalities, political and religious orientation, and a diversity of fields of human endeavour, can come together and frankly discuss the situation is a gain in itself.

As you know the Nobel Symposia so far have been organized to cover subjects and problems in each of the five Nobel Prize fields. Thus they have dealt with questions which have been considered to be of great actual interest in either physics, chemistry, medicine—physiology, literature or peace. The scientific symposia have naturally mostly been highly specialized and technical. The meetings are closed and limited to invited participants and some observers, but papers presented and part of the discussion are published.

It has been our experience so far that the informal and intimate character of these gatherings has stimulated a frank and therefore fruitful discussion. Unhampered by the presence of a large audience people may tell the conference not only what they have thought and what they have achieved, but also what occupies their minds to-day and perhaps even what they hope to do in the near future. The Nobel Symposia have not yet found their final form, we are constantly trying to find our way. We are experimenting and modifying as we collect experience. Perhaps the discussions are the most valuable results. If so, the papers should rather serve as an introduction and stimulus to an exchange of views than as a mere presentation of facts and results which may have been published elsewhere and may be known to many among the participants. In any case we hope that the Nobel Symposia will find a character and a form which will serve the scientific and cultural community of the world, to promote mutual understanding and collaboration.

This, we believe, would be in accordance with Alfred Nobel's ideals. Even if the awarding of Nobel Prizes must be the main duty of the Foundation and of those institutions who have the immediate responsibility for this, other activities are by no means excluded.

The idea of trying to organize a kind of "cross-cultural" symposium, covering all five Nobel Prize fields and being of sufficiently general interest, came up several years ago. In part it was the result of some letters—both from leading scientists and from laymen—which I received particularly when I served as president of the Nobel Foundation. The consensus of this correspondence was an appeal to the Foundation to use its international status and its prestige to do something more, to contribute in some way to the welfare of mankind, other than by each year distinguishing a selected few with Nobel Prizes. The idea appealed very much to me personally, as I have long held the opinion that distinctions involve obligations, that prestige among individuals or organizations should be spent for a useful purpose instead of sometimes leading to a rather unfruitful overrating of oneself or even to conceit.

I remember in this connection particularly some stimulating letters from my friend Joshua Lederberg. He and a few others have helped us as the plans took form, by encouragement and by advice in the selection of topics and participants. Besides Joshua Lederberg also Ralph Bunche, Arthur Koestler, Ivan Málek, Jacques Monod, Abdus Salam have provided valuable help as "international advisers". We are very much indebted to these "wise men" for their stimulating collaboration.

We have chosen as title of this symposium "The Place of Value in a World of Facts". This may be interpreted as based on a feeling that our world to-day superabounds with facts—and still we are unable to use all this knowledge in an optimal way to relieve mankind of its sufferings. As Frank Borman, the captain of Apollo 8, expressed it when returning from his flight round the moon "Man can now do anything he wants to technically". The question is, however, what do we want?

Valuations are necessarily highly subjective but should be influenced by correct information about facts. But isolated facts or specialized knowledge are not enough. It is the interrelation between facts, the integration of knowledge in different fields, relevant to the problem, which may help us. If we can not agree about values we may at least facilitate mutual understanding by clearly stating the facts on which our evaluation of values is founded.

I referred to the abundance of facts—but is there an abundance of *true* facts? In science and technology—yes. In some other fields of research—perhaps. But the rest, the facts which influence our daily decisions, our valuations, our political attitudes? Facts can be and are distorted, people are purposely excluded from certain facts which may influence their attitudes. Distortion of facts in mass communication media are tragically one of the most efficient means of ruling the world to-day. By mixing true and false one can make a terrible brew to manipulate the minds of the uncritical, and not only of these.

Especially to a scientist—like myself—such a situation is unbearable. In scientific research there is a clear distinction between false and true. Any attempt to manipulate this is deemed to be a failure. True, wishful thinking or, even worse, human weaknesses may often lead us astray. But if we insist, Nature will sooner or later strike back—and it hits hard. The experiment will answer yes or no, whatever we hope for or wish. And if Nature answers "perhaps" it just means that we shall have to sit down again to think more.

Research workers all over the world of many different races, nationalities, religions and political creeds are aware of this. They can speak and listen to each other and become friends. This is one of the very few remaining fields in which people can agree or at least arrive at a mutual understanding. Maybe we have here a nucleus for such an understanding also in non-scientific and even political questions. And if the problems are too difficult or if factual information insufficient, why not then resort to the scientist's method: make experiments. Or, in other words, accept a peaceful but competing coexistence of different ideological, political and economic systems and let a comparison of the results be our judge.

These considerations may appear naive, especially to politicians, but some among these do not realize that in the long run facts can *not* be manipulated to serve some purpose. But, alas, there may have to be enormous sufferings before the world by realization of this fact is set to right again—if the world remains.

I have spoken of values and facts—but are these enough in themselves if we wish to achieve what we hope for? Man is an irrational creature and ever so convincing arguments may not reach him so that he really becomes *engaged*. Something more is needed to find the way to his mind. Religion, philosophy, literature, and the arts have known some of these ways for centuries. But also in technical and scientific matters we have similar experiences. I shall refer to only one recent example. The growing risks involved in the misuse of our natural resources and in the contamination of our surroundings were realized rather late, although the facts were there. Still, I believe that the major break-through in engaging the minds of people came first with Rachel Carson's book *The Silent Spring*. Is it that people are engaged first when they feel an immediate threat or even begin to suffer? We know of course ways and means with the help of mass communication media. But we must not be tempted to flavour the facts to an extent which would disagree with our conscience. Nor do we want to scare people to death with our message.

Nevertheless I hope we shall be able to discuss here also the problem of imparting facts and values to the man in the street. I have already mentioned that this meeting is not unique in its character or in its purpose. Many similar manifestations have taken place recently in different countries and more are likely to follow. If I may express a wish here I would desire a greater continuity in all these activities, so that one conference may benefit from the previous ones and those to follow could further pursue the matters discussed earlier. When dealing with difficult and controversial matters a gradual approach is unavoidable, a step-by-step procedures as we see for example in the Geneva discussions of possible disarmaments. These and also for example the Pugwash movement illustrate what is required. It is true, of course, that some individuals represent such a continuity in what they are writing—some of these are present in this room to-day. But still a continuity in the *debate* would be highly desirable. In planning this Nobel Symposium we have studied reports from a number of earlier conferences and discussions of similar aims, and, as you may have seen in the program, we have indicated some possibilities of a continuation, at least in certain fields. This again, I hope will be discussed further during the week.

We have been somewhat concerned about the proper form for an eventual summing up at the end of this Symposium. Should there be a "message" in the form of a declaration, a manifest or something on which we all could agree? There is the risk that this would become too weak and too dilute, as too many controversial matters are involved. Another possibility

THE MENACE AND
THE PROMISE OF SCIENCE

would be to let the summing up contain essentially a number of individual statements. I shall leave it to you to advise us while we are together which of these alternatives—if any—would be preferable. I believe, however, that we would make it too easy for us if we only recommended measures which are too general, too world-embracing to be realistic just now. This may look impressive on paper but would dilute our efforts and probably lead to nothing.

In one respect this symposium is unique, as far as I know. As you may have seen in the program there is a group of young students who have followed the development of our plans with great interest. We have tried to help them with material and in other ways and I can assure you that they have worked very hard. Their ideas may not always agree with ours, and they will probably let us know why. You will find them around here and they may wish to approach some of you to ask questions. I hope you will find it worth while to listen to them. Also I believe they have prepared some surprises for us.

We must remember that in 10–15 years these young people will take over. They belong to that future which we are going to discuss. And some of them may eventually some time wish to organize a Nobel Symposium.

On Values in the Age of Science

By Jacques Monod

Collège de France and Institut Pasteur, Paris, France

A cet instant subtil où l'homme se retourne sur sa vie, Sisyphe, revenant vers son rocher, contemple cette suite d'actions sans lien qui devient son destin, créé par lui, uni sous le regard de sa mémoire et bientôt scellé par sa mort. Ainsi, persuadé de l'origine tout humaine de tout ce qui est humain, aveugle qui désire voir et qui sait que la nuit n'a pas de fin, il est toujours en marche. Le rocher roule encore.

Je laisse Sisyphe au bas de la montagne! On retrouve toujours son fardeau. Mais Sisyphe enseigne la fidélité supérieure qui nie les dieux et soulève les rochers. Lui aussi juge que tout est bien. Cet univers désormais sans maître ne lui paraît ni stérile ni futile. Chacun des grains de cette pierre, chaque éclat minéral de cette montagne pleine de nuit, à lui seul forme un monde. La lutte elle-même vers les sommets suffit à remplir un cœur d'homme. Il faut imaginer Sisyphe heureux.

Albert Camus. Le Mythe de Sisyphe.

In the present paper I wish to summarize the following simple and radical theme: the traditional concepts which provided the ethical foundation of human societies from time immemorial, all consisted of imaginary onto-genies, none of which remains tenable in the face of scientific enquiry. Modern societies, technically based on science, still attempt to withhold the traditional views, or some modernized version of them. This contradiction creates intolerable tensions under which these societies will collapse, unless a radically new foundation for their value system can be defined, accepted and respected.

The most significant, the most profound, the most disturbing (and to many the most frightening) consequence of the development of Science lies not in the industrial and technical revolution, but in the agonizing reappraisal, which Science forces upon Man, of his deepest rooted concepts of himself and of his relationship to the universe.

The urge, the anguish to understand the meaning of his own existence, the demand to rationalize and justify it within some coherent framework has been, and still is, one of the most powerful motivations in the human mind. This profound urge which has given rise to all the myths and religions of humanity and to the great philosophical concepts, also is, of course, at the root of the discovery of the scientific method. But while the myths, religions and philosophies did bring positive answers to the problem of meaning, and while it was believed for a long time that Science would bring the final, definitive solution, we now realize, at last, that the problem of meaning is the one to which no scientific answer ever could be provided.

Science, in its development, has gradually attacked and dissolved to the core the very foundations of the various value systems which, from pre-historic times, had served as ethical framework for human societies. I believe that most social anthropologists would agree with the statement that the structure of virtually all ancient or primitive myths, as well as of more advanced religions, is essentially ontogenic. Primitive myths provide his-tories which almost invariably refer to one or several god-like heroes, whose sagas both account for the foundation of the group and imperatively govern its social structure and traditions, that is, its basic ethical system. The great religions may be regarded as generalizations, attempting to embrace the whole of Mankind in a similar, except much wider, interpretative ontogeny, whose recognized function is to provide a transcendent and therefore perma-nent and indisputable basis for a system of values. Most of the great philoso-phical systems, from Plato to Hegel and Marx may also be regarded as attempts to establish on an ontogenic basis an untouchable, irrefutable basis for a system of values, in turn serving as foundation of the social system.

Whether an ethical structure is justified by reference to a founder-hero, to a universal god, to an absolute idea, to the "laws" of history, or to some "natural" foundation for human rights, all such systems, from the concepts of Australian aborigenes, to the ideas of Rousseau or Marx, share one es-sential characteristic: namely that values and ethics are not a matter of human choice. Whether they are supposed to stand on divine, or "natural" foundations, they are beyond the realm of human freedom. Reason or faith may serve to identify and recognize values, but not to define or alter them. To Man, Ethics and values do not belong; he belongs to them.

It is indeed easy to see the psychological purpose and the social function of raising these concepts on to so high a pedestal as to put them beyond human reach and make them untouchable. The psychological purpose is to abate and perhaps satiate the hunger for meaning; for the meaning of such absolute realities as life and death. The social function is one of stability: no social structure could survive whose very foundations could be ques-tioned, denied or dismissed by anyone at any time. The foundations of a value system therefore must appear not only unquestionable, but as it were, inaccessible.

The invention of Myths and Religions, the construction of vast philosophical systems, thus may be regarded as the price that Man had to pay for surviving as a highly social animal. As is well known, of course, other social animals, such as bees, ants or termites, have had recourse to a much more reliable method of insuring the stability of their social institutions: namely genetic determination of behavior through proper embryological wiring of their nervous system. Man in fact, is the only highly social animal whose code of conduct is largely transmitted culturally rather than genetically. Hence the fact that human societies have histories, while animal societies could only claim a paleontology.

Genetically coded traits are not immune to change, as we know. They are however off limits and beyond reach to the species itself. Once stabilized by selection, they may survive, unchanged, for hundreds of thousands or millions of years. In spite of all the efforts of priests, statesmen and philosophers, cultural codes are not untouchable. They have changed through prehistoric and historic times, at a rate that no biological, genetic evolution could have approached. In spite of all these changes however, one concept remained, up to recent times, invariant: namely that *some* immutable foundation of the value system did exist, and could be found or recognized.

It is this concept, the most essential within any ethical system, the cornerstone of any social structure, the sole (even though unreliable) substitute for genetic coding, that science now has destroyed, reduced to absurdity, relegated to the state of nonsensical wishful thinking.

Many may not agree with this last, somewhat radical statement. There has been as we all know, an enormous amount of benevolent, systematically optimistic talking and writing about Science, presenting it as an exclusively constructive and creative activity. The phenomenal destructive potential of the scientific method has largely been ignored, in part I believe, not from ignorance but from fear of facing it. (I am referring of course exclusively to the destruction of ideas or concepts, not to the Bomb). That the ideas or concepts that Science has proved to be untenable indeed were wrong or meaningless from an objective point of view does not imply that they were subjectively meaningless and served no function. The reverse is obviously true. Let us however see, briefly, how and how far, the traditional concepts which lent "meaning" to man's existence, have all become more and more untenable in the context of modern science.

The core of the matter may, I believe, be put as follows:
In virtually all the mythic, religious or philosophic systems, Man's existence receives its meaning from being supposed part of some general purpose which accounts for the whole of nature and creation. The "purpose" may be naïvely attributed to a mythic founder-hero, or more grandiosely (albeit

less poetically) to some abstract divine intention; or it may be assumed that the "laws of nature" are such that the universe in its evolution, could not fail to produce Man and history, inevitably leading eventually to the class-less society. The structure and the social function of these systems, diverse as they are, remain the same. They all assume between Man and the Universe, between Cosmology and History an unbroken continuity, a pro-found immanent alliance, wherein Man and Nature together serve the universal purpose or the inevitable outcome of the whole of creation. Such views necessarily imply also the assumption of a certain identity of essence between Man and Nature. And since the essence of Man, as he cannot fail to experience it, is his own consciousness, his subjective knowledge of him-self and of his own dialectical thought-process, the same "essence" is attributed to Nature itself. These assumptions of course are most precisely and clearly expressed in primitive animist Myths. But the initial, basic animist assumption, the interpretative projection into Nature itself of Man's conscious essence is equally basic to certain modern Philosophies. The most revealing example may be Dialectical Materialism whose cornerstone (even though actually a late addition to an already largely erected edifice of social philosophy) according to Engels is the recognition that the three "dialectical laws" of Hegel are the general laws of Nature itself.

That the fundamentally very same assumption had to be introduced into their system of the world by Engels and Marx as well as by Indian Tribes-men, would prove, if necessary, how essential to Man it always has ap-peared, and still does, to discover in Nature his own "meaning" and in himself the "meaning" of Nature.

It is precisely this initial assumption, this idea perhaps as old as Man, of a two fold relationship based on a community of purpose between Nature and Himself, that Science has utterly destroyed. This it has done in two ways.

To begin with, the adoption of the scientific method, defining "true" knowledge as having no possible source other than the objective confronta-tion of logic and observation, eliminates *ipso facto* the animist assumption of the existence of some kind of subjectivity in nature. The absolute *objec-tivity* of Nature is the basic postulate of the scientific method, initially grounded in the formulation of the concept of Inertia, by Galileo and Descartes, which eliminated once and for all the teleological physics and astronomy of Aristotle. The church would have been wise to condemn Galileo for this ominous discovery, rather than for his defence of the Coper-nician system.

This basic postulate however, was for a long time used mostly in the physical sciences. The enormous complexity of living beings, and more than anything else, the fact that in their structure, development and behavior one can immediately see their obviously purposeful "essence", appeared to estrange them, and Man, from the physical world. Indeed how could a postulate of objectivity apply to the interpretation of such evidently intentional creatures? As more was learnt of the structure and physiology of living beings, this apparently valid objection to the Cartesian views appeared to make them less and less tenable.

Thus, the animist assumption was eliminated from the study of physical phenomena, while it could, and did, remain in Biology in one form or other of vitalism. Vitalism indeed can take many aspects, some subtle enough to pass as expressing an objective approach. The formulation of the theory of evolution, first by Buffon and Lamarck, then much more forcibly and demonstratively by Darwin, did not interrupt this current of thought. In some ways it reinforced it: evolution in the biosphere appeared to testify to the existence of some ascending driving force, necessarily and unfailingly leading from the physical to the biological world, and through it to its crowning achievement, Man himself.

This idea, which in fact reinstated in an apparently "scientific" form the old animist alliance, is not only clearly present in Engels and Teilhard de Chardin. It in fact subtends much of XIXth Century "progressist" positivism. The theory of selection as the one driving force of evolution, due to Darwin's genius, should have cautioned against this kind of wishful thinking. Actually, while evolution was enthusiastically accepted by progressists of all kinds, and furiously rejected by all types of reactionaries, the theory of selection was neither fully understood, nor widely accepted. The main reason was that, while the concept of "survival of the fittest" was easy enough to comprehend, it could not fail to shock the moral code of heirs to the American and French Revolutions. Moreover Darwin had not, and could not have, formulated with any precision the mechanism of the initial events wherein lay the ultimate source of evolution, these "sports" which, of course, had to precede selection. Indeed Darwin himself did not reject Lamarckian adaptationism, which to many appeared as a "natural", easily acceptable mechanism, and of course pleased the progressists much better.

It remained for modern Biology, beginning with classical genetics, and blossoming into Molecular Biology, to discover the ultimate source of both stability and evolution in the Biosphere, and thus blow to its last shreds the myth of the old alliance.

I may perhaps be allowed to simply summarize without proof or illustration, the main conclusions of Modern Biology which are relevant to this discussion:

1. The one universal and essential characteristic of living beings is the

conservativity of the chemical structure (DNA) wherein the genetic code is written.

2. Evolution is not an inherent tendency of living beings. Quite the reverse: their whole structure is intensely conservative, mostly resisting successfully any alteration.

3. The ultimate and only source of true novelty in the biosphere are random perturbations within the conservative machinery. Perturbations such as any physical object shall inevitably be subject to. These perturbations affect *single* molecules, and are, therefore, fundamentally unpredictable and uncontrollable.

It should perhaps be pointed out that the concept of a strictly random source for Evolution does not stem from or express ignorance of the intimate mechanism itself. Quite the reverse: it is because the nature of these mechanisms is clearly understood that one is led to the conclusion that they can only be purely random in origin. Thus the appearance of life itself and, within the biosphere, the emergence of Man, can only be conceived as the result of a huge Monte-Carlo game, where our number eventually did come out, when it might as well not have appeared and, in any case, the unfathomable cosmos around us could not have cared less.

From these conclusions there is no escape, nor any prospect whatever that they might be radically altered as a result of future scientific progress. One hardly needs to insist on the absolute incompatibility between this scientific view of Man and his origin and the traditional concepts upon which values, ethics and societies were founded. The scientific approach reveals to Man that he is an accident, almost a stranger in the universe, and reduces the "old alliance" between him and the rest of creation to a tenuous and fragile thread. None of the gracious or frightening myths that he had dreamed, none of the hopes he had tenaciously entertained, none of the certainties that had formed the structure of his moral and social life for thousands of years, can stand anymore.

Science, as it emerged and developed, has shaped the modern world, given modern nations their technology and power. Yet these societies have failed to accept, hardly have they understood the most profound message of science. They still teach and preach some more or less modernized version of traditional systems of values, blatantly incompatible with what scientific culture they have. The western, liberal-capitalist countries still pay lipservice to a nauseating mixture of Judeo-christian religiosity, "Natural" Human Rights, pedestrian utilitarianism and XIXth Century progressism. The Marxist countries still throw up a stupefying smoke-screen of nonsensical Historicism and Dialectical materialism.

They all lie and they know it. No intelligent and cultivated person, in any of these societies can really believe in the validity of these dogma. More sensitive, more impatient, the youth perceives the lies and revolts against them, forcefully revealing the intolerable contradictions within modern societies. Let us not live with the illusion that it always was more or less so, in previous times. Primitives do believe in the Myths which guide their whole life; Medieval societies did believe in Paradise, Hell and Sin; French revolutionists did believe in Natural Human Rights; Lenin and Trotsky had absolute confidence in Historical Materialism and in its formal promise of a classless society, free of contradictions.

No society can survive without a moral code based on values understood, accepted, respected by the majority of its members. We have none of this kind anymore. Could modern societies indefinitely master and control the huge powers which they owe to science on the criterion of a vague humanism admixed with a sort of hopeful materialistic Hedonism? Could they, on this basis, resolve their intolerable tensions? Or shall they collapse under the strain?

I believe they will, except perhaps at the price of a profound reappraisal of human values, of their true nature, of their source; beginning with the recognition of Man's strangeness in the cosmos, of his absolute loneliness. Then he may realize that there is, that there can be outside or beyond himself no source, no criterion, divine, historical or natural for his values. That he alone creates, defines and shapes them. This is to say that, in order to reconstruct the foundations of a system of values upon which social, political and personal life might be based in the age of Science, we must start from an absolute *Tabula rasa*; we must go further and deeper than Nietzsche's prophetic "Gott ist tod", for, not only is God dead, but also his various romantic, historicist and progressist substitutes. Nor can we, as Nietzsche did, followed by some of the modern French existentialists, proclaim the "absolute" freedom of Man. No biologist could accept such a view; we know that we are made up of the same amino acids and nucleotides, and that we carry the same genetic code as any bacterium, plant, or fish. We would have to be blind not to recognize our close similarity, not only structural, but behavioral to our first cousins, the great apes. And we had better listen attentively to the ethologists pointing out, as does Professor Lorenz, that many genetically determined behavioral attitudes of mammals, birds, or fishes, could be described as obeying strictly certain commandments of the Decalogue. One need not look for a transcendent basis for the categorical imperative: its biological source is clear enough in many instances.

This profound, demanding, biological heritage is part of Man's essence. It would be just as foolish to disregard it, as it would also be to deny that his "essence" also partakes of another realm, which transcends the physical and even the biological, I mean the kingdom of ideas and knowledge, the "Noosphere", to use Teilhard's word. The noosphere exists as a partially autonomous realm, because, in the Hominid family, a form of communication was developed, which is unique to that particular family. Undoubtedly selected and developed, primitively, for its survival value, it must have also (by introducing new selective pressures), influenced the physical evolution of Man, I mean the development of his cortex which it is reasonable to consider as "prewired" for the acquisition of language. Thus language is, simultaneously, inseparably, a physiological trait and a cultural development, and partakes most intimately of the dual nature of man's essence.

It has recently become fashionable, in certain French philosophic circles, to deny any meaning, any value, to the concept of a human "essence". No biologist could consider such a statement as anything but sheer nonsense. The concept of a human essence signifies, to my mind, the most important, the most fascinating of all problems, embracing genetic, embryological and physiological questions as well as cultural, linguistic, psychological and aesthetic aspects.

A rational reconstruction of our values system will have to take all these aspects into account, and be prepared for evolution and alteration, as our insight into Man's essence becomes more profound. But it must be fully understood and recognized that even in the age of Science, moral philosophy could not rely simply on some sort of biological essentialism, for no value system, no Ethics, could ever be based on a purely objective analysis of Man as he is. By definition, by function, a value system, an Ethics must define an "ought" not an "is", a high ideal, a goal to be pursued *which cannot be Man himself*. No ethical system can be purely utilitarian: this is a psychological error, a contradiction in terms, a denial of the very function of Ethics.

It follows that, in the age of Science, when none of the traditional transcendent assumptions is tenable anymore, whose function it had been to define a superhuman goal or command, we must do the same, except for the fundamental departure that we will know and proclaim our choice to be deliberate; that is, in fact and intention, axiomatic. I believe it can be done, that such a system could be taught, understood, and would be respected to the very extent that it defined the loftiest values as measure and criterion of all values, of social and personal Ethics.

And what other ultimate values to choose then, than those creations, born from Men, yet transcending their creators, as existing in the Kingdom of ideas, richer and wider in content than any single man nor even all men at any one time, can perceive? I mean of course the great, ever unfinished, monument of creation and knowledge, that is, of Art and Science.

Ethics and values have, since Man started enquiring into the meaning of his own existence, always been based on some essential relationship assumed to exist between him and the universe. We now know that the only authentic relationship goes through that abstract kingdom, the noosphere; that man, the stranger in the cosmos, can conquer the universe only through knowledge. Art and Science express two complementary aspects of human knowledge, one synthetic and partially subjective, the other analytic and strictly objective. A society that would accept these transcendent values as the ultimate standard of all, more immediate, human values, and designed itself deliberately to serve them, would have to defend intellectual, political and economic freedom; to foster education, both extensive and intensive, as its primary task; and it would also have to develop the welfare state, not as an end in itself, but as a means towards more freedom, creativity and knowledge, that is, towards serving Man in his most unique and precious essence.

Orthobiosis: The Perfection of Man

By Joshua Lederberg

Stanford University, Stanford, Calif. U.S.A.

My assigned task is to comment on the promise and the menace of futuristic advances in biological research.

This is a hazardous course.

A great deal of recent discussion about "genetic engineering" should be mentioned only to be deplored, for it gives a distorted view of the present status and ultimate purposes of research on molecular biology. Nevertheless, it would be obtuse to deny the ultimate revolutionary importance of developments that bear on the further course of human evolution. By replacing blind fate with human reason, they may place a crushing burden of responsibility for the assignment of goals for man. Many people react with dismay that knowledge is coupled with such a responsibility. Failing to accept it is also a decision, and one that has its own consequences.

This is an old story, one that links Prometheus to Adam. Once man knows that he can know, and that he can judge good and evil, his acts have a moral significance whether he chooses to learn or to deny.

There are other problems, for example of time-scale. Twenty years is a long time in the growth of science, and the fifty years of an adulthood are too long for reasonable extrapolation. In such an interval, *anything* might be possible, even the most lurid titillations that the popular press advertises about humanoids of either mechanical or biological provenience. In refusing to dwell on such extreme speculations, I do not deny the technical possibility of their accomplishment. I merely point out that so much else will have happened in every other sphere of human concern that it would be foolish to concentrate on very specific forecasts. The forecasts will be objectively faulty, and more important, the context in which future events will be judged will have changed more than we can foresee. (In 1920, contraception was a dirty word, and who would have dared discuss voluntary abortion, much less advocate it!)

The critic of "biological engineering" should also be careful to deal with the contemporary aspects of his subject in context, for which reason I prefer the phrase *orthobiosis* (the correction or perfection of life and of man). Orthobiosis is already implemented on a very large scale—constructively, in the practice of medicine and hygiene; negatively via a global system that ensures that hundreds of millions of underprivileged children will be mentally retarded owing to malnutrition and virus infection. The drastic extension of the average human lifespan during the past century is itself a major orthobiotic influence. Apart from all the changes in the human environment, the quality of a life is very different with the average prospect of 60 as compared to 20 years after adolescence. The side-effects of infant-death control, without the balance of birth control, hardly need to be elaborated. The prospect that death can be postponed, without the means to retard senescence, may be an equally painful technological disharmony of the next few decades.

Some examples of orthobiosis may be unduly traumatic to the layman who has had insufficient experience of human pathology to appreciate the gravity of some of the ills that cry out for help. No procedure could be more intrusive than the surgical modification of sex, and it would hardly be condoned anywhere without the knowledge of the suffering that results from gender-confusion. An awareness of the chromosome abnormalities, chimeras, hermaphrodites and congenital abnormalities that are nature's experiments with man is prerequisite to understanding research in embryology that may lead to interventions in human development. Man's evolution from and biological affinities to other primate species must also be perceived as an objective fact, not a literary allusion. This is not a demand that these matters be left to experts; to the contrary, it is a plea to broaden the base of public understanding for intelligent participation.

The techniques of *biology* cannot be fairly judged without comparing them to those of *education* and of the multitude of other ways by which normative behavior is shaped by the cultural milieu—by just such institutions, for example, as the Nobel prizes and this very series of symposia. The understanding by the reader that the very act of perception both actively alters and is modulated by his own neurobiological structure is another sine qua non for an informed perspective on orthobiosis. (Professor Bruner will speak to this in detail.) This term, then, describes the whole category of influences on the quality of the human organism—an enterprise in which religion, politics, education, medicine and mass advertising converge with the evolutionary endowment of the individual human being.

Antithetical reactions to the concepts of orthobiosis can be expected from various people, depending on their accustomed ways of coping with difficult problems. The scientist asks for more fundamental facts and is sceptical about mere speculations; the philosopher resonates with issues bearing on the nature of man; the legalist may already have proposals for regulation and control. The poet may understand best of all that many of our discussions of orthobiosis are a metaphor, even a parody of existing institutions. The greatest merit of talking about "genetic engineering" may be the light it throws on the de facto patterns of human evolution; about euphenics for the exposure of the brutally dysphenic effects of our present environment; about sex control to illuminate the disparate value our culture puts on the sexes. It is also important that we understand social control in much broader terms than the compulsions of criminal law. To install a policeman in the bedroom is not a promising approach to questions of population control, whether we think of mere numbers or more subtle questions like "who shall decide who is to be born?"

Value judgments inevitably play an important part in the implementation of any programs of orthobiosis. Applied genetics in particular is so laden with religious implications about the nature of man that some question the morality of even investigating the scientific bases of human nature, just as others challenge the basic commitment of western culture to scientific enquiry. This was once called the work of the devil (as in the Faustian legend); the counter-cultures today denounce science simultaneously as a toy of the intellectuals and a tool of class oppression. Since Galileo (or might we say, Prometheus) the Establishment has also feared the revolutionary impact of objective scientific inquiry on the mythologies which sustain the status quo.

At this symposium we have been taxed to make an explicit formulation of a pro-scientific ideology. In general, I have been very leery of such enterprises, and particularly of any claims that a particular ethical system can be validated by a direct application of scientific reasoning, i.e., that morals can be proven by science. Attempts to base ethics on evolutionary biology have been conclusively criticized by Simpson and Dobzhansky[1] as examples of circular reasoning: "How do you prove from what we know of evolution that human individuality is more important than human society? And yet we do feel that individuals should not be sacrificed for attainment of social ends."

Ideology, furthermore, tends to degenerate into a set of wooden formulas susceptible to self-serving rationalizations of the ideologists' established pattern of conduct. It is beyond doubt that more human misery has been inflicted in the name of public ideals, myths, gods, and altruistic interventions, than through the sum total of private venality. Furthermore, the individual ego-ideal is often quite unconscious. The complexes that reconcile the ego-ideal with professed ideology, on the one hand, and actual behavior, on the other, are even more obscure and self-reports about them most unreliable.

Few of us here have digested the vast literature on ideology and on value systems from the different standpoints of religion, economics, history, politics and psychology. It is delightful to contemplate the creation of the perfect slogan which might mobilize the disorganized efforts of the rest of the world and perhaps even provide a convincing personal cause. In practice, we know that any group of intellectuals needs little license to produce a number of precepts which is some higher power of the size of the group. The "end of ideology" then comes forth as one of the major ideologies of the current era.—The sources of "moral character and moral ideology" are, nevertheless, amenable to scientific investigation as illustrated by the studies of Lawrence Kohlberg[2] on the stages of their development in children. The capacity to defer gratification, which he emphasizes, can be translated as a measure of the scope of the personality. This can, as most religions teach us, be extended in space (empathy or vicarious gratification) as well as in time (investment for larger, future goals).

Science relates to ethics in many ways more defensible than claims on its behalf for ultimate verification.[3] Logical argument can expose inconsistencies within and between posture and behavior. It often brings unwelcome news about the consequences of an action that we might prefer to ignore. (Unfed children will starve to death even if they live in Biafra or India.) Technology which creates many ethical dilemmas can also make for evasions of others: the American ethos has taken pride that an overall glut in total production might soften the inequities of the relative distribution of wealth. If kidney machines or artificial hearts can be made cheap enough we can evade the problem of choosing "who shall live?" now thrust upon us. We already face so many difficult moral decisions that we ought to be glad of any we can defer and keep our strength for the others.

This cautionary preamble still does not deter me from casting a tentative vote in the direction of evolutionary humanism. Julian Huxley was, I believe, an accurate reporter in suggesting that self-admiration was the most pervasive of human ideologies, and that no serious scientist doubted that evolution, in the large, was *good progress*. Even the cynic must respect his own uniquely human capacity for cynicism; the physicist for physical cerebration; the biologist can add an informed wonderment about the actual process of evolution itself and its culmination in man.

At one time I may have scoffed at the efforts to dignify evolutionary humanism as a religion—but the very convening of this session persuades me that Huxley was quite right in his perception of the depth of the religious instinct. If we distill the convergent essence of the beliefs of scientists, we probably will not go far from the doctrines he suggested in his manifesto upon the founding of UNESCO,[4] the working hypothesis of a scientific, evolutionary humanism in which man is dignified as "the sole trustee of further evolutionary progress".

My main complaint about humanism is the quibble that we do not quite know how to define a man (i.e., to identify which bodies are inhabited by souls). No other religion has solved this problem much better. The biologists at least face a more manageable debate on where to divide a concensual line, knowing that life and death, human and animal, are regions on a continuum. My quibble is then a sectarian dissent, not basic schism.

In recent years, man-baiting has become a fashionable literary sport—all our troubles come, we are told, from man's implacably hostile and aggressive character, inherited from his animal ancestors. I know too many good men to accept such a generalization about man. If the trouble were merely in man's genes, we would have a relatively easy task assigned to us, and a full license for the practise of eugenics. We must not overlook the vastness of his task, the perfection of a culture to colonize the whole planet, with no tools other than his wits.

One failing still stands out. Our imperfect solutions aggravate every problem. In contrast, the computer memory can be totally erased; its task is hardly altered by successive iterations, and programs can then be gradually perfected. We must always build on the sins, mistakes and hatreds of every step on the way.

I may, then, summarize my conception of evolutionary humanism with the conclusion that it depicts *man as the historical animal.* Our evolution has reached the point that progress is far more a function of our traditions and our social forms than our biological functions. As part of the world-mind,[5] with a unique consciousness of past and future, each individual should be less jealous of the life of his own body, and more protective of every other one, than a purely zoological ideology would encourage.

Molecular biologists are often slapped with a red herring, the imputation that they degrade man into a mere machine. We do in the main insist on "mechanism", mainly as a reaction to the pessimists who have disparaged and who discouraged research on the frontiers of biochemistry.[6] (The recent elucidation of the mechanism of DNA replication counts for more than all the verbiage that has ever been expended on this debate.)

To insist on the inherent inaccessibility of other processes, like the brain or feeling, to analyses of mechanism remains as much a mistake as to boast of accomplishments whose realization is still remote and may never be complete at the hands of finite human intelligence.

The attribution that man is *merely* anything is merely an idiosyncratic misanthropism.

In the rapture of self-exaltation, many humanists may nevertheless forget that evolution is a continuing process.

The perfectibility of man and the corollary of his present imperfection, should stand out as one of the most precise implications of the evolutionary outlook.[7] We should be optimistic (and humble) that our posterity will progress beyond our capabilities, even for moral judgment, to the same degree as our own proudly proclaimed emergence from apedom. We have then one precept about values—that we ought to guarantee that there will be a posterity, and that we take care not to foreclose the options available to it. The ravaging of the earth, of primitive peoples, of our wild life, of one another, and even our carelessness about the planets, are our cosmic sins.

This humility supports the policy of pluralism—that the state must not intrude in the intimate lives of citizens except for the most inescapable needs of public order. This principle must be renewed and reinforced to stem the temptations of totalitarian exploitation of techniques of biological engineering, just as the constitutional protection of free speech is the only defense against mind control by the techniques of communication engineering.

"Orthobiosis" has the etymologically obvious meaning "right living". Before discussing orthobiotic innovations—the possibilities of human improvement from new knowledge of molecular biology and genetics—we ought reflectively to ask "what are man's real problems in biological perspective?" We do better to look for solutions to real problems, if we can, than invent problems for our new tricks and techniques.

Uppermost is the avoidance of war, or rather the positive promotion of world harmony and economic development and integration. These are manifestly not problems of biology, at least not human biology; for the political reaction would engulf any effort at biological change. (What could be more hostile than to attack a neighbor with a pacificatory virus? For the tanks would surely follow!)

Economic productivity, especially in tropical and semi-arid habitats, clearly does have a biological basis about which we know very little. The potential for biological innovation in tropical agriculture is now hinted at by the "green revolution" of recent years. These improvements in wheat and rice strains were brought about rather traditional methods; modern molecular genetics is just now being discovered by plant breeding specialists.

The escape of world population growth rates, a byproduct of modern medicine, is a well documented threat to the survival of the species. It is primarily a problem of self-aggravating poverty, i.e., failure of economic development, rather than of the technical potential for food production. Proposals for biological solutions, e.g., by the use of environmental sterilants (antidotes by prescription requiring a license to bear a child) are, fortunately, pure fantasy. Quite apart from the political problems of obtaining public acquiescence to such schemes, they could never be guaranteed to be safely reversible so as to avoid sterilizing the species.

On the other hand, the present patterns of growth and urban concentration and poverty, are ideal for fulminating epidemics of virus diseases[8] that may spontaneously solve the population problem in the harshest way imaginable.

Poverty, hunger, pestilence, pollution are beyond doubt the further problems that this generation must face, or there will be no posterity. No one of us here would hesitate to abandon every other commitment if he knew any effective route to answer their challenges—and I offer my deepest respect to men here who have had the wit and the power to make important contributions in these spheres. But the paths are tortuous, and the main problems are unabated.

Certainly it would be short-sighted to redirect all our resources into the panaceas for instant relief of global problems. We need to maintain constant vigilance that our remedies do not have side-effects as portentous as the original disease—consider the history of DDT as a rather stark example.

Basic scientists who have worked in the genetics of bacteria and viruses believe that these discoveries have ever growing importance for the prevention and healing of serious human diseases. We live, in the present era, in an incompletely justified optimism about having "conquered infectious bacterial disease" as the fruit of the development of the antibiotics. However, viruses are in general still beyond the reach of antibiotic therapy. Even bacteria, believed to be under firm control with antibiotics, are continuing their own evolution and continue their assaults upon human health with renewed vigor. In the long run, only our continued vigilance over bacterial evolution can justify our hope of maintaining a decisive lead in this life and death race.

However, whatever pride I might wish to take in the eventual human benefits that may arise from my own research is turned into ashes by the application of this kind of scientific insight for the engineering of biological warfare agents. In this respect we are in somewhat the same position as the nuclear physicists who foresaw the development of atomic weapons.

There is, however, a crucial difference. Nuclear weaponry depends on the most advanced industrial technology. It has then been monopolized by the great powers long enough to sustain a de facto balance of deterrence and to build a security system based on non-proliferation. Nuclear power has thus, ironically, become a stabilizing factor tending to reinforce the status quo in parallel with established levels of economic and industrial development. Germ power will work just the other way.

The United Nations Study Report on chemical and biological weaponry has summarized some infectious agents that have served as points of departure for the development of biological weapons. Any knowledgeable virologist could suggest many more. I will not repeat these technical details, nor will I bludgeon you with the horrible diseases that some of these agents provoke. I will also leave to your own conscience the burden of moral judgements about using these kinds of weapons. Most civilized people would be repelled by the thought, but perhaps no less by exposure to the human realities of any other form of warfare. Overriding such comparisons should be the grave moral issue in a policy that risks the lives of a world of innocent bystanders. Fortunately, these concerns actually converge with our self-interest in calling for a halt to BW before it becomes established in the arms-traffic of the world. (This discussion of BW was written from the standpoint of a U.S. citizen just prior to President Nixon's announcement (Nov. 25, 1969) of the U.S. renunciation of BW.)

My main fears about BW are to do with the side-effects of its proliferation 1. as a technique of aggression by smaller nations and insurgent groups and 2. by the inadvertent spread of disease.

If the great powers could actually protect the secrecy of their BW work I would be much less alarmed. The chance of BW ever being used in a major strategic attack is essentially negligible in the face of the nuclear deterrent. The suggestion that we need BW or CW weapons for specific retaliatory purposes in order to deter their use aims at a ridiculous kind of precision. Will our deterrent missiles have to follow the same trajectories as those that might potentially attack us? Will they have to be launched at the same time of day? Will they have to have the same mix of explosive energy and radioactive fallout? If we are attacked with anthrax strain B27 must we reply with anthrax B27?

On the other hand, if I were a Machiavellian adviser to a would-be Hitler I might indeed advocate a considerable investment in biological weaponry as a desperate approach to the cheap aquisition of great power even if at a very great risk. And, of course, the first thing I would do would be to plant my intelligence agents in the existing BW establishments of the high-budget powers in order to get the necessary scientific information at the lowest possible cost.

However, if I were patient I would not bother to do even that. No security system, no counter-intelligence system in the world expects more than a delay of 5 to 10 years in the leakage of vital information. We do not have, and I presume do not contemplate, security reservations like war-time Los Alamos for the containment of BW research. If a high level activity is to be maintained there will be frequent turnover of personnel. It is unreasonable to expect a tighter security barrier here than has prevailed in any other area, given the problems of reconciling security with a free society. Besides these channels for diffusion of information, there are also bound to be Pueblo-like incidents, and finally calculated leaks in the budget competition of the services. The American people might be the last to know. But we can hardly rely on more than a ten year delay between many important discoveries in BW research laboratories and their availability to hostile and irresponsible forces outside.

As a matter of prudent self-protection, BW research laboratories in the U.S. and the U.K. have pioneered in the technology of containing dangerous microbes. I have great respect for the technical capabilities of the senior civilian management of these laboratories. They should be credited with the outmost diligence in protecting both their personnel and the surrounding community. They have also published a great deal of their work in the engineering of such protective facilities and this experience is unquestionably of great value in public health work. For example, the British laboratories at Porton were acclaimed for the safe handling of the very dangerous Marburg virus upon its first outbreak in Europe two years ago.

In spite of these precautions, disease organisms have nevertheless escaped from time to time and inevitably will do so in the future. Such escapes already constitute a breach of security. They also compromise public health, which is further complicated by keeping civilian physicians in ignorance of potential agents that might fulminate into large scale epidemics. The intentional development of virulent strains resistant to conventional antibiotics obviously worsens the problem. We simply have no way of assuring ourselves that a BW development activity will not eventually seed a catastrophic world wide epidemic that ignores national boundaries.

On the immediate horizon are modern developments in molecular genetics. These undoubtedly point to the development of agents against which no reasonable defense can be mounted. Because of the uncertain danger of retro-action, such agents are hardly likely to be used in consequence of any rational military decision, but would obviously play into the hands of aggressive insurgence and blackmail.

Finally, even the publication, albeit as a positive contribution to humanity, of the technology of safe containment insidiously helps solve a problem that might have hindered a potential insurgent from dabbling in BW.

The problem of containing infectious agents being manufactured and stockpiled in large quantities, or tested in the open air, is a much more difficult technological challenge; and it is encumbered with even more official secrecy than the laboratory work. The main effect of security has not been to deny information to an enemy but to protect an establishment from both destructive and constructive criticism at home. In this case, more open constructive criticism would be crucial for assurance that procedures for containing microbes are well conceived and correctly implemented.

BW agents for use against man can be expected to be far more capricious than any other form of weapon. For any strategic purpose they are essentially untestable since large populations would have to be held to an uncertain risk. With nuclear weapons we can at least be confident of the laws of scaling. The destruction of targets can be calculated from simple physical measures like the energy released. Nothing comparable to this can possibly apply to BW agents. For this reason again the United States and other nuclear powers have absolutely nothing to lose in disavowing their use in war. Our continued participation in BW development is akin to our arranging to make hydrogen bombs available at the supermarket.

Microbiological research must be expanded in programs of public health research for defense against our natural enemies. In fact, the public health bureaucracy has refused to give prudent thought to the recurrence of major pandemics of human disease, be they of spontaneous or human-intelligent origin. Perhaps this is simply a consequence of their sense of futility about mobilizing the necessary measures of global health needed to protect the species. If we add to already urgent concerns the spread of dangerous diseases from large foci of infection established by BW attack, the prospects become even gloomier.

Our self-interest as human beings urgently calls for the institution of improved measures of world public health and of international controls on the development and use of BW agents. Research related to BW perhaps should continue; but it is of the first importance that this be fear-reducing rather than fear-generating, for the latter can only lead to mutual escalation of anti-human developments.

It is difficult at this stage to detail the texture of new agreements subsequent to our ratifications of the Geneva protocol. We cannot suddenly impose unilateral decisions on the international community; but no other issue can evoke such a unanimity of world opinion. New agreements probably should include (1) public legal commitments against secret BW research; (2) the establishment of central, international laboratories to monitor the occurrence of threatening organisms and to help develop generally available means of protection against them; (3) a legal system to protect the freedom of information and communication of data on disease organisms to such central authorities; (4) a general acceleration of research and health services to minimize the incidence of infectious disease, particularly in underdeveloped countries. No situation could be better designed for the evolution of serious new viruses than the existence of crowded, underfed human populations in which foci could develop and spread with a minimum of medical control; (5) treaty commitments on BW analogous to the nuclear non-proliferation treaty; (6) pre-agreed sanctions by the civilized world against the release or development of BW agents, clearly invoking international law against such "offenses against mankind" as akin to war crimes.

If political wisdom can dispel the threat that molecular biology will be harnessed to the task of global suicide, the most important challenges to applied biology are (1) monitoring and managing the threats of world-wide epidemics from the spread of old viruses and the evolution of new ones even worse; (2) world nutrition; (3) the understanding of the human consequences of environmental degradation; and (4) efficient ways of assessing side effects of drugs, food additives and substitutes and other consumer products of vital importance in a crowded world.

The progress of science would in fact be paralyzed if its practitioners took an all-or-nothing approach in the selection of problems for attack, and the patient exploration of the possible must be weighted at least as dearly as the pursuit of iconoclasms.

In this light, there remains some justification for saving some of our energies to deal with some longer range problems like those pertaining to man's evolutionary future. These are also very immediate in the context of family life, which counts for an important part of human concerns, even while the storms of geopolitics rage.

The doctrine of pluralistic choice dominates my own prescriptions for ethical policies in the general field of human reproduction. This is in part an attempt to evade the external imposition of moral principles on others; but it is also a constructive attempt to preserve the fluidity of human options in facing rapid change in the physical and socio-technical environment. For example, the time is not far off, we hope, when soldiering will be an obsolete profession and commitments by martial states to combat-adapted genotypes would be grossly malfunctional. Almost every other aspect of human value, except the elusive one of intellectual breadth and flexibility, is subject to the same reservation, which undermines the utility of any comprehensive long-term eugenic schemes beyond the minimization of undoubted defects. Even here we may expect ironic discoveries, for example, that some "defectives" are the most amenable to specific treatments with drugs or hormones that will more than restore "normal" capabilities. Certainly we must be quite cautious about plans to "eradicate" *genes* which make defective homozygotes (like cystic fibrosis) before we understand the biological advantages of the heterozygotes that supposedly maintain the gene in the population. The target of such programs should be the disease itself, the immediate cause of human distress.[9]

"Individual choice" faces an inevitable paradox in this field: whose choice, and when? For the child does not make himself—in many different ways he is the creature of his parents and of his culture. The newborn cannot have decided by and in whom he was conceived, and carried, and to rely upon his choice about his early care would stand as criminal neglect. The parents must undertake the systematic manipulation of their child's development—presumably in his own interests, and certainly constrained by many realities of their particular culture. We call this, without irony, the *humanization* of the child, for his acculturation is as indispensable to his human functioning as is the biological substratum that makes it possible.

There are many compromises here, in different styles, between the varying interests of the community and of individual families; which change from one polity and time to another. I propose that parents assume the same kinds of responsibility in their wider orthobiotic choices as they now do in the education and family discipline of the child. Indeed, they cannot rationally be separated from one another. The traditions of political freedom that minimize the intrusion of political and religious sectarianism in the schools are precisely those that can protect the autonomy of the family at home.

This approach is not free of patent ethical hazards—we must condemn excesses of paternal authority, but within broad limits the children themselves will find more effective remedies than we would have the sophistication to apply by legal sanctions.

This discussion can only begin to open the issue of the meaning of manipulation. The generation gap shows how urgently we must work on our confusions, even before we face new problems of conscious orthobiosis.

The technology of orthobiosis differs from medicine only in its greater breadth. Medicine is usually thought of as a *reparative* rather than *constructive* art, but this simply reflects an arbitrary definition of abnormal and diseased. Thus, in the field of mental health, we see an unlimited range of sources of distress that the therapist will aim to relieve; nor can we find any sharp boundary between mental health and education. Medicine is also abutted by nutrition and physical exercise, the traditional arenas of domestic orthobiosis, whose importance to health is being rediscovered by contemporary medicine.

In fact, biological engineering is merely speculative medicine—as theoretical promises are realized, they will and should be assimilated into the framework of medical practice. This is important to insure not only technical competence but also the ethical tradition of commitment to the needs of the individual patient.

For the sake of orderly classification, orthobiosis can be classified into *eugenics, euphenics* or *euthenics,* depending on whether the target for improvement is the DNA of the germ cell(s), the somatic characteristics of the individual, or the environmental scene. Eugenics implies an influence on the genetic endowment of future generations; euphenics does not. As far as euthenics is concerned, this paper will concentrate on those aspects of the environment that most directly influence the characteristics of the individual. Plainly, genes, soma and environment are intimately connected through channels like natural selection, environmental hygiene and economic opportunity.

Especially with respect to psychotropic influences, euthenics is the input, euphenics the output of the same process. I can speak with less authority on these most important forms of human manipulation (education, mass communication, language, the popular arts, explicit psychotherapy, and all the subtleties of group behavior). For that reason only, an undue weight of my remarks will be a technical exposition of processes which may have only ancillary importance. These are, however, compressed in tables I and II, with a few additional notes.

My purpose in this exposition is to share my expertise with a wider community, so that the issues of orthobiosis may be ventilated, understood and rationally decided. I hope this caveat is unnecessary, but it comes from weary dismay at having advocacy for wide and intrusive applications thrust at me for the sake of a critic's rhetorical shorthand. I do however advocate responsible, carefully thought out, and humane experimentation.

Euphenics. This term was coined[1] as a counter-slogan to eugenics, to parallel the antinomy of phenotype and genotype. It was intended to suggest that new knowledge of molecular genetics would be as powerful for medicine as for direct genetic intervention. In fact, euphenics is simply medicine, stressing the outlook on this as the modulation of developmental processes towards the restoration of health, or some other optimum.

As indicated in table I, euphenics is widely practiced already, but with few exceptions, its purpose is the restoration of normal health. Those who would seek super-normal nutrition are likely to be labelled food-faddists, insofar as an "optimum" nutrition has already been assimilated into our norms for health. Nearly the same applies to education, although a wider variety of styles is practised in the privacy of the home nursery than in the public schools.

We know less than most people think about the norms for fetal and new-born nutrition. The former are a matter of current controversy. The prevalent style of emphasizing control of the pregnant mother's weight and fluid accumulation has been sharply attacked by Brewer[10] as neglecting the

Table I. *Euphenic (and dysphenic) influences on human nature by period of life.*[26]

The entires in the table refer to important (□) or incidental (●) influences having particular impact on the stage indicated.

The table emphasizes effects that are likely to persist for long periods after the evoking stimulus is removed. The "euphenic" effect is, in many cases, figurative, and may be implied mainly by the remedial measures taken to prevent or repair injury.

Form	Fetus	Prem.	New Born	Youth	Adult	Age
Growth of brain						
Dysnutrition	□	□	□	□	□	
Specific regulation (hormones)*	□	□	□	□	□	
Induced tolerance to grafts	□	□	□			
Teratogenic drugs, radiation & infections/prophylaxis	□	□	●	●	●	
Induced abortion/therapy for threatened abortion	□	●	●			
General control of organ differentiation with inducers and repressors**	□	□	●	●	□	●
Surgical repair of congenital and other defect		□	□	●	□	□
Transfusion; organ transplant		□	●	●	□	□
Critical dietary (MSG) & hormonal (estrogen, steroid) triggers			□	□	□	●
Hypoxia; oxygen poisoning			□	□	●	
Sensory stimulation			●	□	●	
Virogenic therapies**		□	●	●	□	●
Vaccination				□	□	●
Dietary & hygienic habits established				□	●	
Psychotropic & other drugs, including addiction & other side-effects				□	□	●
Hormonal, surgical mod'n of sex				□	□	
Artificial organs				□	●	●
Environmental pollution	□	□	□	□	□	□
Sonic habituation; deafness				□	●	
Psychodynamics & psychotherapy	?			□	●	●
Popular culture; music	?			●	□	□
Education; letters; arts				□	□	□
Propaganda				□	●	□

* Known from animal experiments, but not observation on man.
** Speculative possibilities under laboratory investigation in animals.

fetus' need for protein. Nor do we have the faintest idea as to the level of early nutrition that would sustain the best vigor of the fully developed youngster, in mind or in body. Now ancient experiments have shown that rats lived longest when somewhat "undernourished" with respect to calories; experiments like these are rare in man, for the political system tends to produce kwashiorkor (protein malnutrition) instead.

Recently, Olney[11] has shown that newborn mammals can be altered by large doses of MSG (monosodium glutamate) with lifelong effects. The furor that these findings have raised with respect to formulas for baby foods may obscure the deeper interest of the finding. Evidently the neonatal hypothalamus can be injured by otherwise non-toxic doses of a normal nutrient, with subsequent failure of appetite regulation. This suggests that a wide range of nutrients can influence the setting of chemosensors that signal important homeostats. Few other compounds have been studied so far. There is little doubt, however, that our styles of baby-feeding have amounted to considerable, if unconscious, developmental manipulation.[27]

Hormones. The most potent regulators of organ development and function are the "hormones". We now have substantial information about the natural systems involving such organs as the gonads, secondary sex apparatus, thyroid and adrenal, and have some insight into the regulators of the muscle and red cell mass, skeleton, kidney and liver. This knowledge now has definite application mainly in replacement therapy to remedy obvious failures of the natural endocrines, or to inhibit the unwanted growth of tumors derived from some of these tissues. With farm animals, the use of sex hormones for fattening or improving food yield is a well-established euphenic practice. One also hears that masculinizing hormones have been used to promote muscular prowess in women competing in athletics—a rather pointed illustration of the extrapolation of restorative medicine, which has raised perplexing questions of criteria for, and means to enforce, social controls. Is there much logic in prohibiting the use of a hormone to help achieve the same ends that we encourage by physical exercise? It is, of course, the possibility of insidious and irreversible side effects that elicits the deepest concerns, though specific evidence for such side-effects may bear no relationship to the social revulsion against the drugs.

We know the least about the regulation of the most important organ, the brain. The extent to which its growth is regulated in part by external hormones is beginning to become a popular research area.[12] We have long known that the thyroid hormone is indispensible for maturation.

Zamenhof[13] has demonstrated that the pituitary growth hormone can influence the size and cell number of the brain of the newborn rat when administered to the pregnant mother. This effect may, however, be an indirect one, mediated through dietary behavior, since prenatal insufficiency of amino acids limits brain size. A hormone has already been described that regulates the growth of nerve cells of the sympathetic ganglia. Since antibodies to this hormone will inactivate the sympathetic nervous system of the intact animal, the hormone is important in the normal functioning of these neurones.

One can visualize that similar hormones operate on the central nervous system, and even that some forms of mental retardation may be attributed to auto-antibody formation. The elucidation of such a hormone may be the

Table II. *Methods of eugenics, existing and prospective.*

I. *Genetic hygiene*—controlling the environment to minimize germinal exposure to mutagenic chemicals, radiation, and virus infections.

Effects of temperature are theoretically suspect but have not been satisfactorily assessed.

II. *Selective mating*

1. By phenotype of parents (assisted by biochemical and cytological assay)
   (a) negative—distracting, discouraging or sterilizing the "unfit".
   (b) positive—
     i. encouraging select pairs.
     ii. with artificial insemination, donor ("rational germinal choice").
     iii. with oval or ovarian transplant.*
     iv. both, or fertilization in vitro, followed by implantation.*
     v. extracorporeal gestation (est tube baby)—see also euphenics.**
     (i–v are not very different in their *genetic* consequences).
2. By genotype of parents—as above, with deeper analysis of parental constitution. Except for specific aberrations very little can be said at present about genetics of *desirable* traits.
3. By relationship of parents.
   (a) inbreeding. The main impact is to expose recessive, usually deleterious genes; increase phenotypic variability of F_1; decrease the genotypic variability of later generations.
   (b) outbreeding—antithesis of (*a*). Most cultures strongly encourage outbreeding.
4. By age of parents—to forfend accumulation of deleterious mutations and chromosome anomalies which increase with parental age.
5. By phenotype or genotype of the zygote or of fetus (antenatal diagnosis and voluntary abortion). Earlier selections would avoid the trauma of aborting an established fetus.
6. By genotype of the gametes, e. g. separation of X from Y, or normal from defect-bearing sperm.**
7. With sperm of other species (compare 1. (*b*)iv). Nothing is known of the consequences among primate species. All contemporary races of man appear to be freely interfertile.*

III. *Innovations in zygote biology*

Vegetative (asexual) propagation. Cloning.

1. Parthenogenesis—development of an unfertilized egg. (This might be genetically identical to the mother, or might be a product of meiosis, which would be an intense form of inbreeding.)*
2. Regeneration—development of whole individual from somatic tissues (as in some plants and lower animals like earthworms).**
3. Differentiation of gametes from somatic tissues previously subject to extensive genetic manipulation.**
4. Somatic reduction in gamete-forming cells in culture (somatic inbreeding)—would allow predictable outcome of further matings from a given parent which is not now assured.**
5. Nuclear transplantation—renucleation of a fertilized, enucleated egg. Genetically equivalent to cloning from the source of the nucleus.*
6. Embryo—splitting to produce twins or multiplets, not to be confused with multiple ovulation (occasionally induced by fertility-promoting drugs.) About 1/3 of spon-

taneous twins are monozygotic, i.e. arise from the splitting of one embryo.*
Note also the opposite phenomenon.

7. Embryo fusion (chimerism) so that one individual comprises 2 or more genotypes. This grades into tissue transplantation at later stages. It should allow different genotypes a new latitude for mutual complementation, e.g. mens sana in corpore sano. Somewhat less than 1/1 000 live births are spontaneous chimeras, but some of these arise by other mechanisms.*

IV. *Adjuncts from somatic cell biology*

For eugenic applications these would be coupled with procedures like III 5. For euphenic effects, altered cells can be grafted back to a host or some manipulations done directly on his tissues.

1. Algeny—directed alterations of genes
   (a) Controversial claims of effects of DNA uptake in mammalian cells following a long tradition of genetic work with DNA in bacteria.
   (b) Incorporation of viruses.
      i. Experimental tumor viruses.*
      ii. Use of specially modified viruses
         1) Vaccination to induce immunity to viruses.
         2) Virogenic therapy to replace missing genes.**
         3) Virogenic enhancement for superior performance—if we but knew the biochemistry thereof.**
   (c) Specifically induced mutations. No plausible approaches are now apparent.**
2. Random mutation and specific selection of cells with altered properties—has full precedent in strain selection in microbes. Many uncertainties relating to possible cancer potential of such implants.*
3. Cell fusion to form somatic hybrids. These cells may then lose various chromosomes to give many new forms. Extends scope of 2. Can be readily applied to fuse cells from "distant" species, e.g., fish and human.*
4. Development of symbiotic strains of lower species, with habitats that grade from the external world (e.g. crops) to internal to intracellular. Parasitic worms in man have evolved in this direction with the help of adaptations to thwart immunological rejection. In principle they might be domesticated. So also might algae be trained to an intracellular habitat in man where they might photosynthesize essential nutrients, if not bulk calories, as they already do in primitive animals.**

---

* Known from animal experiments, but not observation on man.
** Speculative possibilities under laboratory investigation in animals.

next major turning point in the progress of human mental capacity. We might find, for example, that it bridges the main gap between man and the other apes. It may also pose dilemmas on the social regulation of its use, analogous to those concerning the use of masculinizing hormones. If the "norm" for cerebral capacity were suddenly open to a substantial jump, what place would be left for vestigial imbeciles like ourselves? Or will we therefore take every means to be sure this never happens?

It is not clear whether or how purified repressor proteins could be introduced into target cells from outside, but when this step is also achieved, we will have the tools for the most comprehensive regulation of gene functions. This would be tantamount to instructing undifferentiated cells to co-operate, say, to reform a liver or heart to replace a failing organ, or to produce totally new kinds of tissues and organs.

Needless to say, we spend enormous effort at "manipulating" the development of the child's brain through mental exercise, i.e., education, though the principles of action in wide use are too numerous for them all to be well-founded.

The concept of hormonal regulation has also been expanded by studies on gene action in bacteria, which have culminated in the isolation so far of two specific "repressor" proteins, a prelude, without doubt, to many more. The repressor interferes with the initial transcription of a specific segment of DNA, in the formation of the RNA messenger, thereby regulating the function of that gene. The role of repressors in mammalian systems is a subject of hot controversy, and there is indeed good evidence that regulation can (also?) occur at the level of the differential translation of existing RNA messengers.

To summarize, it is enough to predict that the obstetrics-pediatrics (the hyphenation, i.e., the gulf between the specialties, hints at part of the problem) of the new future will include respectful attention to hormones and other growth regulators, as it now does in principle to nutrition and vaccinations.

Vaccination and virogenic therapy. Since 1798, vaccination has exemplified the use of viro-genic information in medicine, though its practitioners to this day are often oblivious to it. Jenner found that inoculation with cowpox (vaccinia) caused a mild disease immunity which also protected against the dangerous smallpox.

Many aspects of vaccination are still scientifically obscure; but we can now describe the process in terms of molecular genetics. The DNA of the cowpox virus is purposely introduced into certain cells which adopt the genetic information contained therein. These cells thereupon produce new gene products, encoded by the viral DNA, which stimulate other body cells to produce antibodies against them. The cross-immunity is then a byproduct of the virogenic alteration of some cells of the host.

Live viruses are now widely used for vaccination against many other diseases, including polio, measles, and in special cases or in the near future, rubella, mumps, rabies, and so on.

Vaccination can be regarded as if it were a therapy to replace the functions of hypothetical genes not normally present in the human organism, those that would endogenously stimulate the formation of antibodies. This idea can be extended, in principle, to other gene products, for example enzymes that may be missing in certain gene-defect diseases like phenylketo-nuria and perhaps diabetes. Laboratory models for this kind of virogenic therapy are well established; there is good reason to expect trials for human disease in the near future.[14] Although basic genetic principles underlie this technique, and the genetic apparatus of somatic cells is altered, it is classi-fied as euphenic because the germ cells are left unchanged and there should be no effects in future generations. This is matter of empirical observa-tion, rather than necessary principle in biology, and it is quite conceivable that some inoculated virogenes might also be inherited, as has already been postulated for certain tumor viruses in rodents. This reservation applies with equal force to vaccination against infectious diseases, about which we have little information in proportion to the enormous numbers of children involved.

As applies to euphenics generally, the main limitation to broader applica-tions is not in the detail of the technique. It is in the biochemistry of trait whose modification is in question. When we know enough about the bio-chemistry of brain development to make sensible statements about which genes might be involved and how, a variety of approaches will be open to reparative or constructive changes in that biochemistry. The poverty of present knowledge is illustrated by our helplessness (late 1969) about dis-eases like Huntingdon's chorea, despite rather precise knowledge about its mode of inheritance.

The practical application of virogenic therapy might lie in enzyme re-placement. For example, a gene for phenylalanine hydroxylase (missing in PKU) might be isolated from human DNA by an extension of techniques successfully applied to bacteria.[15] It would then have to be grafted on to the DNA of some carrier virus already well authenticated for use in a vaccine. After inoculation, some infected cells would be expected to have restored the necessary function. Plainly, many further refinements, especially in the cell-specificity and the regulation of enzyme levels, are also called for—not to mention the most careful tests for the harmlessness of the carrier virus.

The same criteria, may it be repeated, deserve to be applied to con-temporary vaccines designed for immunization against virus infection.

Transplantation. The potentials for transplantation as a means of replacing worn-out organs have already been too well advertised to warrant much more comment. There remain serious problems of supply and allocation of vital organs, like hearts, but a socially acceptable market has been organ-ized after some early tribulations. Nevertheless, there will probably never be enough suitable hearts to meet the demand, especially as the procedure is technically perfected. The heart transplants may, however, serve an important way station in the development of artificial hearts, and for example as an ethically acceptable backstop to their early trials, as well as a source of important physiological information.

The augmentation of the brain has also been accomplished—in fish—by the pooling of primordia from two embryos into a single hatchling. These fish evidently were able to make good use of their enlarged cerebrums, at least from a man's-eye view of their behavior.[16]

We should not, however, confuse any *organ* with *personality,* which is a complex *process* that functions through a variety of tissues, and in a larger sense, even of many extensions of the body in the form of machines (clothing, automobiles, telephones and radio communication, computers, etc.)

The problem of graft-rejection by the immunological defenses of the host remains unsolved at a fundamental level. However, so much important theoretical as well as empirical information is being accumulated that this must also be surmountable. We will then find that the spectacular, life-saving accomplishments of heart-and kidney-transplantation will be much more mundane, but equally important life-enhancing procedures, involving many other tissues. Even cosmetic transplants of skin and hair should not be shrugged off as a humanly important application.

The prime hint to an answer to graft-rejection is the phenomenon of induced tolerance, obtained by exposing the fetus to graft antigens before the stage of immunological reactivity. The antigen-specificity is then treated as part of the "self-identity" of the host, and later grafts of tissues from related sources will be accepted. (The phenomenon also sheds indispensable light on the diseases of "auto-immunity" and some on the prevention of cancerous growths.) If other methods fail, we could envisage the precautionary injection of pooled, purified human tissue antigens as a kind of vaccination during fetal life.

The experiment has, in fact, been done with other intentions—namely the transfusion of a fetus mortally afflicted by RH-disease with fresh blood from another donor. Unfortunately, viable white cells in the donated blood, now protected against rejection by the infant, survived to react instead against him. The result nevertheless verified the theory of induced tolerance as applied to man.[17]

Eugenics. Selective breeding; selective abortion; algeny.
Having domesticated his food crops and animals, and his pets, man has speculated at least as far as his knowledge of heredity permits about influencing his own progeny by the wise choice of genetic "stock". Optimism

may be the most responsive trait, for there is little else to support the tenability of such experiments over any period of time: the recombination of genes that accompanies sexual reproduction is an almost insuperable barrier to eugenic progress by selection alone. The farmyard domesticators have the additional advantage of inbreeding (incestuous matings) to stabilize the genetic characteristics of a given breed. Wisely, even the most enthusiastic eugenicists refrain from this breach of custom—for its short term consequence to human viability would be disastrous. The corn breeder is after all quite willing to sprout and discard millions of seeds in order to select an advantageous genotype—a price no one could negotiate for human improvement.

A specific approach to selective breeding, "germinal choice", has however been strongly advocated by the late Herman J. Muller and by Julian Huxley.[18] Their scheme would provide for the banking of sperm from individual men in cold storage for later voluntary use in artificial insemination. They suggest that a considerable period of time elapse to allow a calm retrospective judgment of which men carried the most useful set of genes. The problems so far of promulgating such a scheme are all social, not technical. So far there is little evidence that "rational germinal choice" has become a household phrase. It is hard to see any fundamental objections to discreet small-scale experiments along these lines: legal recognition of artificial insemination is needed to prevent the hardships that arise from confusion about proper procedures of parental consent and anonymity. We have ample experience with adoption to use as a precedent.

Real problems arise, of course, in the identification of preferred males, even some years posthumously, and the advertisement of the qualities of potential sires probably should be confined to professional journals, package inserts, and a physicians' desk reference.

More recently, a genetic engineering mania, algeny, has been advertised as an aftermath of research on DNA as the chemical embodiment of genetic information. "We have merely to specify the optimum sequence of some 5 billion nucleotides—the DNA information of the fertilized egg—and we can define the ideal man." This fantasy has elicited dark anxieties about "genetic control", in an absurd misunderstanding of the metaphor "specify the sequence". This of course already happens to some degree by the voluntary sexual coupling of two parents. They have thereby decided that a child will be formed, specified as a Mendelian sample of each of their chromosomes.

At the present time, we have no plausible approach to the use of "synthesized" DNA that could begin to match fertilization as a way of "specifying" the DNA of the zygote. And if we did, it could hardly differ from the act of choosing a particular sperm and an egg from specified parents. Some lay readers have unfortunately misread these fantasies to occasion a worry that "their own genes" might be controlled from without. We should reassure them that this is the least of their legitimate worries, if for no other reason than the redundancy of their DNA in trillions of different cells.

What of the future? The main impact of the fruition of algeny would be to reduce the relevance of the genetic constitution as the seat of destiny. When the genes are so easily changed, this deep knowledge of genetics cannot be developed without the means to divert the action of the genes in specific developmental pathways—i.e., the full realization of euphenics. Finally, algeny will hardly be possible before the materialization of other manipulations of the germ cells, for example the renucleation of egg cells with nuclei taken from somatic cells of an existing individual or in cell culture.

This technique has already been worked out in frogs by Briggs and King; Gurdon and others.[19] Their experiments were intended to determine whether tissue differentiation is invariably associated with a permanent loss of developmental functions in the cell nucleus. Apparently this is not always true, for some nuclei of adult tissue cells are capable of supporting the total development of a new frog from a re-nucleated egg. From a genetic point of view, however, the new frog was vegetatively propagated from the mature tissue since it carries exactly the same set of genetic information.

Groups of individuals derived by vegetative propagation and having identical genetic constitutions are called clones. The propagation of new plants from cuttings is such a familiar experience in horticulture that the term "vegetative propagation" is used generally for the by-passing of sexual reproduction. In lower animals like the earthworms, cloning is a common occurrence with the spontaneous regeneration of "whole animal from cuttings" of the previous individual. (There is no theoretical argument against this kind of regeneration in mammals, but no experimental evidence for it either.) The most immediate implication of cloning is the production genetically homogenous groups of individuals, and particularly of propagating a genotype already tested in one generation for further trial in a second.

We already have a foretaste of the properties of a clone in the behavior of identical twins. Twins are commonly recognized as having an unusual psychological relationship to one another, and in that sense, differing already from non-twin individuals. There has, however, been relatively little critical psychological study of twins, particularly from the point of view of objectively testing their capacity to communicate with one another more efficiently than obtains for randomly chosen individuals. These observations would be very difficult to control for the usual reason that the hereditary similarity between twins will often be confounded with the empirical fact of their having been reared together and treated nearly as identical individuals during their early development. One can argue on purely theoretical grounds, however, that at least some twins will have a great advantage in mutual communication (and this, of course, also means education) just by virtue of the similarity in their blueprints for their central nervous systems. Since the thread of culture is what binds the human experience, the mere fact of their homogenity may make clones more efficient in intellectual cooperation and educational advance. This hypothesis is independent of the opportunity to select those genotypes for clones which already manifest outstanding capabilities.

The chief human motivation for taking advantage of clonal reproduction would, undoubtedly, be in the quest for some kind of immortality, which plainly has a deep influence in the direction of human affairs. Quite apart from this, clonal propagation would afford an otherwise unavailable opportunity for certain humanic "experiments", in the same sense that efforts to optimize a child's education are an experiment. It is unlikely that we will otherwise ever be able to know the extent which the performance of acknowledged geniuses or athletic stars are manifestations of unusual genetic endowment.—The technical limitation to cloning by renucleation, is mainly the much smaller size of mammalian eggs by comparison with the frog's egg, but this is almost certainly not an insuperable difficulty. There may be other obstacles based on differences in the biology of the frog egg as compared to that of the human which are unknown to us at present.

What are the real hazards of cloning? The shock of such a large deviation in the fundamental biological system may cloud clear thinking; it is of the same magnitude as the institution of voluntary reproduction, which depends on human knowledge of the relationship of sex to pregnancy. We may not be able to ignore incidental aspects of the technique that may be quite crucial to public acceptance. There are not many arguments *for* bypassing sexual reproduction, but they might include (1) parental narcissism, and instinctive attachment to some form of personal immortality; (2) some social and familial interest in the perpetuation of unique genotypes, for their own sake, and to improve our educational methods; (3) the wish of some couples to have "their own" children when this is frustrated by some forms of sterility or risk of genetic disease that would be unmasked by sexual reproduction, and (4) social need or other dynamic encouragement to produce many similar individuals of a specific genotype, e.g., an elite guard, an SS, or a suicide squad who could be relied upon to end the world in a national interest.

The trap of over-specialization is indeed the main hazard that the evolutionary biologist would warn about. World-enders are all too easy to produce without orthobiotic innovations, but a society might well trap itself into staking its genetic resources to meet more legitimate short-term challenges, and find itself unable to adapt rapidly enough to change. This is a general objection to any scheme for genetic commitment, and to institutional rigidity overall. Cloning has the advantage of retaining the latent variability of heterozygotes, which can be re-expressed in future, sexual generations.

A vegetative progeny suffers from another hazard, the accumulation of new mutations without the constant filtering of natural selection against homozygotes. A commitment to cloning will then require a new level of vigilance about reducing the hazards from mutagenic pollutants of the environment (an important element of any eugenic program).

Biological theory offers no basis for opposing vegetative propagation on a modest scale, as an option to isolated families, so long as the population processes most of its genetic heritage through the sexual mechanism. We have to fear the social hazard that cloning may become *too* attractive,[20] that no parent will again care to face the hazards of bearing a randomized child. However, some of the more serious perils of that gamble can be countered by prenatal diagnosis and abortion (discussed hereinbelow).

Cloning will surely reawaken the zeal of the eugenicists, which is now dampened by the sheer inefficacy of their proposals.[21] It is easy to see how a totalitarian government might wish to add imposed clonal propagation to the repertoire of its techniques for homogenizing its subjects and minimizing dissidents. Legally enforced pregnancy of any kind is an abhorrent violation of human rights.

This is not to exclude the interest of the community in, say, discouraging the birth of a repeated series of defective children who are burdens to themselves as well as the group. However, these incidents are so rare that we ought to exhaust non-compulsive solutions before inviting a massive intrusion of the authority of the state into reproductive decisions.

The deepest and most irrational fears about the abuse of scientific knowledge are fueled by anxieties that some external authority might succeed in dominating our lives through control of the mechanisms of genetic control. Every advance, major or minor, in experimental molecular genetics is followed by editorializing on this theme, rarely spelled out explicitly enough to be answerable.[22] The main thrust is that the state might acquire the means to turn reproduction from a family avocation into an assembly-line for manufacturing loyal citizens, along the lines of The Republic, or Brave New World.

In all candor, this outcome cannot be dismissed but it must be viewed as a political rather than a technological disaster. One should ask more concretely, just which traits is the state likely to impose involuntarily? And how could it enforce unpopular edicts without already having enslaved the population? If there is to be a "correct" skin color or shape of nose, does the totalitarian state—by historical evidence—not already have ample technology to achieve these among its citizenry, at the point of a gun?

These anxieties are in fact promoted, or ought to be, by another movement that holds it necessary to impose legal controls in order to confine population growth. The bureaucracy that administers such controls plainly would have a leverage on the life of the community that would be vulnerable to the most flagrant abuses. (Fortunately, no such involuntary atmospheric contraceptive can now be forecast; we have enough trouble authenticating the safety and wide use of acceptable, voluntary ones. Besides the obvious need for better techniques of contraception, we have the most urgent need for social inventions that can press the needs of the community for population limitations, without destroying personal freedoms.) A well established totalitarian society might, indeed, try to assure its own perpetuation by genetic technology, as further support to its existing apparatus of thought control. The most obvious step would be to encourage the uniformity of outward appearance (which all more primitive cultures have done spontaneously) as a way of bolstering Groupthink or distinguishing Ins from Outs.

More realistic moral problems arise in the area of the proper social controls over the use of new techniques, even as experiments, by individual family units. Should the community have any concern about isolated trials of cloning, artificial insemination, oval transplantation, or similar techniques, if these are done with an obligation and intention of responsible care for the human individuals born as a consequence? The community does, however, insist that every child be a potential citizen, and therefore invokes such laws as compulsory vaccination and schooling. Its requirement that a child be taught English (in the U.S.) might be regarded as barbarous by any objective onlooker, but we do not usually indict this as an unwarranted intrusion.

It is certain then that the community will properly set bounds on the characteristics of individuals produced by any kind of rational design. If the technical power now existed, it would probably vent its wrath on any person who, for example, intentionally and knowingly produced an idiot. Laws for compulsory sterilization have wisely been held in abeyance mainly out of scientific uncertainties and the difficulties of fair enforcement, not a constitutionally protected privilege to make any kind of monster one pleases. The same principles will undoubtedly evolve in our adjustment to genetic innovations. In fact, the moral issues that attach to the problems of new genetic technology are fully foreshadowed in our present customs of public health and education.

An interesting variant arises, however, in the speculation that sub-human races might be evolved, like Aldous Huxley's "gammas". This is plainly a vicious parody on the institutions of race prejudice. Szilard has stated the speculation in a possibly more confusing way: what if we were to discover that the dolphins were (or could be altered to be) at least as intelligent as humans? Would we not have to tax them, restrain their movements by requiring visas, conscript them and offer other privileges of human dignity?

It has been answered that the world will continue on its dubious course so long as the scientists and the politicians shuttle the responsibility to one another about these central problems. The definition and nurturing of personal freedom is one of the most difficult and most important that we face. In a non-ideal world, the responsibilities and the temptations of new powers may be more than the system can bear.

The suppression of knowledge appears to me unthinkable, not only on ideological, but on merely logical grounds. How can the ignorant know what they should not know? We can, however, try to play the other game better, to use our scientific skill and artistic intuition to forecast some glimpses of the future, and in particular of the worst paths to be avoided.[23] That prevision may help to plan the compensatory institutions, the public education, or the balancing research to regain the harmony that is the best measure of human progress.[24, 28]

Appendix

Does modern science dehumanize man?

It is easy to find deeply ambivalent feelings about science among intellectuals (even including some scientists), in Congress, among alienated youths and among bewildered citizens. We live in a scientific age whose glories and terrors are both credited to science. At this level, we can hardly deny that our ever-growing scientific mastery over the forces of nature imposes an almost unbearable responsibility on political authority and on a democratic electorate to learn about, think about, plan for, and use these forces for real human benefit.

In this climate, many people have become highly sensitized to more ethereal questions that are raised by the scientific study of man. One such question is the doctrine of mechanism. Dr. D. E. Wooldridge, a well-known physicist and systems engineer and a successful industrialist—formerly president of TRW (Thompson–Ramo–Wooldridge) Inc.—has written several excellent syntheses of present day thought in biology. His latest work, *Mechanical Man—the Physical Basis of Intelligent Life,* concludes "that a single body of natural laws operating on a single set of material particles completely accounts for the origin and properties of living organisms. Accordingly, man is essentially no more than a complex machine."

A few eccentrics aside, the whole community of contemporary science shares the view that the same laws of nature apply to nonliving and living matter alike. All of us who investigate the chemistry and physics of living organisms pursue our work as if organisms were complex machines, and we find man to exhibit no tissues or functions that would except him from this way of analyzing human nature.

Nevertheless, we are or should be careful to state just what we mean before we assert that "man is a machine," and much more so before using the phrase "merely a machine". The statement that man is "a mere machine", or a mere anything, is a needless irritant to precise communication between scientists and laymen. (We might better proclaim that "man is merely the most complex product of organic evolution on earth, the only organism whose intelligence has evolved to the point that his culture far transcends his biological endowment.")

The "mere machine" phrase is usually a retort to the claim that there are mysteries of human nature that are, in principle, beyound the reach of scientific investigation. Scientists would do better to save their breath quarreling about what they can analyze in principle; in their own work, they are mercilessly pragmatic about confining their conclusions to what they can examine in practice.

There are, in fact, theoretical limits to scientific analysis that may justify men in repudiating Dr. Wooldridge's assertion that "the concept of the machine-like nature of man is incompatible with a long-cherished belief in human uniqueness". There is nothing "mere" about a machine as complex as a man; the word "machine" is just a manner of speaking about the scientist's faith in a universe ordered by natural law. That faith was expressed most eloquently by the French philosopher the Marquis de Laplace, who averred that, given complete knowledge of the universe at one instant, the scientist could in principle compute all of its future states in infinite detail.

In practice, we must now remind ourselves, the scientist and his computers are machines that occupy space and consume energy. Dr. Rolf Landauer of IBM has pointed out that the process of calculation itself soon reaches fundamental limits. If the whole visible universe were one gigantic computer, made of components at the theoretical lower limit of size and energy consumption, it would still be insufficient for some problems that are soluble "in principle".

Far short of the complexity represented by a human being, some mere machines called computers nevertheless have already reached the point where their actual behavior is predictable only to a rough approximation, and we must be careful to program internal checks to detect when these highly individualized robots deviate from *their* intended instructions. (*Washington Post,* 28.12.68.)

Notes

[1] Dobzhansky, T. *Mankind Evolving.* New Haven and London: Yale University Press. 1962, page 342; Simpson, G. G. *The Major Features of Evolution.* New York: Columbia University Press. 1953.

[2] Kohlberg, L. "The development of moral character and ideology." in M. Hoffman (Ed.), *Review of Child Psychology.* Russell Sage Foundation. *Vol. 1* 1964.

[3] Haldane, J. B. S. *The Inequality of Man and Other Essays.* London: Chatto and Windus. 1932. Chapter Three, "Science and Ethics".

[4] Huxley, J. UNESCO: *Its Purpose and its Philosophy.* Washington: Public Affairs Press. 1948.

[5] Muller, H. J. "Mankind in Biological Perspective." in The Centennial Review, *Vol. X,* No. 2, Spring 1966, pages 163–213; Thorpe, W. H. *Science, Man and Morals.* Ithaca, N.Y.: Cornell University Press. 1965; Haldane, J. B. S. *The Inequality of Man and Other Essays.* London: Chatto and Windus. 1932. Chapter Three, "Science and Ethics".

[6] Koestler, A. and Smythies, J. R. *Beyond Reductionism.* The Alpbach Symposium 1968. London: Hutchinson of London. 1969. See Appendix to this article for the view of the present author on the mechanistic theory of man.

[7] Lederberg, J. "Experimental genetics and human evolution." in Bulletin of the Atomic Scientists. *Vol. XXII,* No. 8, October 1966.

[8] Dorolle, P. "Old plagues in the jet age." in WHO Chronicle, *Vol. 23,* No. 3, pages 103–111.

[9] Fraser, G. R. and Motulsky, A. G. "Genetic effects of selective abortion for inherited diseases." in *Program and Abstracts.* American Society for Human Genetics. Annual meeting, October 10–13, 1968. Austin, Texas.

[10] Brewer, T. H. *Metabolic Toxemia of Late Pregnancy: A Disease of Malnutrition.* Springfield, Illinois: Charles C. Thomas. 1966.

[11] Olney, J. W. "Brain lesions, obesity and other disturbances in mice treated with monosodium glutamate." in Science, *Vol. 164,* pages 719–721, May 9, 1969.

[12] Hamburgh, M. "The role of thyroid and growth hormones in neurogenesis." in Moscona, A. A. and Monroy, A. *Current Topics in Developmental Biology.* New York: Academic Press. 1968. *Vol. IV,* Chapter Two.

[13] Zamenhof, S., *et al.* "DNA (Cell Number) and protein in neonatal brain: alteration by maternal dietary protein restriction." in Science, *Vol. 160,* pages 322–323, April 19, 1968; Zamenhof, S., *et al.,* "Stimulation of proliferation of cortical neurons by prenatal treatment with growth hormone." in Science, *Vol. 152,* page 1396, 1966.

[14] Rogers, S. "Skills for genetic engineers." in New Scientist. *Vol. 45,* No. 686, pages 194–196, January 29, 1970.

[15] Shapiro, J., *et al.* "Isolation of pure *lac* operon DNA." in Nature. *Vol. 224,* pages 768–774. November 22, 1969.

[16] Bresler, D. E. and Bitterman, M. E. "Learning in fish with transplanted brain tissue." in Science. *Vol. 163,* pages 590–592. February 7, 1969.

[17] Naiman, J. L., *et al.* "Possible graft-versus-host reaction after intrauterine transfusion for Rh erythroblastosis fetalis." in The New England Journal of Medicine. *Vol. 281,* No. 13, September 25, 1969, pages 697–701.

[18] Muller, H. J. "Human evolution by voluntary choice of germ plasm," in Science, *Vol. 134:* page 643+, September 8, 1961. Reprinted in Young, Louise B. (Ed.) *Evolution of Man.* New York: Oxford University Press. 1970, page 530.

[19] Harris, M. *Cell Culture and Somatic Variation.* New York: Holt, Rinehart and Winston. 1964.

[20] Brunner, J. *Stand on Zanzibar.* New York: Ballantine Books. 1969 (Fiction).

[21] Haller, M. H. *Eugenics.* New Brunswick, N. J.: Rutgers University Press. 1963; Osborn, F. *The Future of Human Heredity.* New York: Weybright and Talley. 1968; Pickens, D. K. *Eugenics and the Progressives.* Vanderbilt University Press. 1968.

[22] Taylor, G. R. *The Biological Time-Bomb.* New York and Cleveland: The World Publishing Company, 1968; "The gene: iolated—for good or evil?" *The New York Times.* November 30, 1969; "Genetic tampering." *Washington Post.* November 3, 1967; "Genetic warnings." *The Christian Science Monitor.* January 8, 1970; "Voice fears on possible uses; Scientists isolate single gene." *The Palo Alto Times.* November 24, 1969.

[23] Popper K. *The Open Society and Its Enemies.* Princeton, N. J.: Princeton University Press. 1950.

[24] Tiselius, A. "Balance and unbalance in scientific progress." Address to the Athens Meeting 1964. The Royal National Foundation. Elsevier Publ. Comp. 1966.

[25] Lederberg, J. "Humanics and genetic engineering." in 1970 *Yearbook of Science and the Future.* Encyclopaedia Britannica. Metz, C. B. "Gamete surface components and their role in fertilization." in Metz, C. B. and Monroy, A. (Eds.) *Fertilization. Comparative Morphology, Biochemistry and Immunology.* New York: Academic Press. 1967. *Vol. 1*; Harris, H., *et al.* "Suppression of malignancy by cell fusion." in Nature *Vol. 223.* No. 5204. Pages 363–368. July 26, 1969; Gurdon, J. B. "Transplanted nuclei and cell differentiation." in Scientific American. *Vol. 219.* No. 6, pages 24–36. December, 1968.

[26] Eichenwald, H. F. and Fry, P. C. "Nutrition and Learning." in Science. *Vol. 163,* page 645–648. February 14, 1969; Shooter, E. M. "Some aspects of gene expression in the nervous system." in Schmitt, F. O. (Ed.) *The Neurosciences: Second Study Program.* New York: Rockefeller University Press. in press; Scott, J. P. "Critical periods in behavioral development" in Science, *Vol. 138,* No. 3544. Pages 949–958. November 30, 1962; Levine, S. and Mullins, R. F., Jr. "Hormonal influences on brain organization in infant rats." in Science. *Vol. 152.* Pages 1585–1592. June 17, 1966. Denenberg, V. H. and Rosenberg, K. M. "Nongenetic transmission of information." in Nature. *Vol. 216,* pages 549–550. November 11, 1967; Mintz, B. "Gene expression in allophenic mice." in "Symposia of the International Society for Cell Biology". *Symposium on Control Mechanisms in Expression of Cellular Phenotypes.* New York: Academic Press. in press; Altman, J., *et al.* "Behaviorally induced changes in length of cerebrum in rats." in Developmental Biology. *Vol. 1* (No. 2), pages 112–117. March 1968.

[27] A recent report suggests that rats reared on cyclamates suffer from an irrever-

sible induced hyperactivity. (The effect was initially interpreted as an augmentation of "intelligence")—see Stone, D., E. Matalka, and J. Riordan "Hyperactivity in rats bred and reared on relatively low amounts of cyclamates." in Nature. *Vol. 224,* page 1326. 1969.

[28] The general subject of value questions in relation to science is the subject of several comprehensive studies, including the Harvard University Program on Technology and Society, and the Columbia University Institute for the Study of Science in Human Affairs. At Indiana University, the Program in Public Policy for Science and Technology of the Department of Government has published an unusually extensive annotated bibliography, so far in two volumes, 1968–69.

Possibilities and Pitfalls in Electronic Information Transfer

By John R. Pierce

Bell Telephone Laboratories, Murray Hill, New Jersey, U.S.A.

Electronic information transfer has no value in itself, no justification as a final good. The technology of communication and information processing is a tool of man's devising, a tool increasingly swift, flexible and powerful. In various countries, to varying degrees, man has made this technology an essential part of his life and work, that is, of his culture. Its value is its value in man's life.

Electronic technology is advancing rapidly. The transistor, invented in 1948, and ensuing solid-state art have reduced the size, power consumption and cost of electronic apparatus and systems and have vastly increased their reliability. These changes have already been revolutionary. We now have solid-state devices for all ranges of frequency up to some 100 GHz (corresponding to a wavelength of 3 millimeters). We can produce tiny complicated silicon integrated circuits at a cost comparable to that of producing single transistors. Along with solid-state devices we have magnetic cores and films for information storage. These resources have not all been fully realized or exploited, but we can see what sorts of possibilities they afford.

The invention of the maser in 1955, which led to the laser, has opened up other possibilities. The laser generates and amplifies coherent light. Along with other ingenious devices, the laser will make it possible to carry out at optical frequencies all of the complicated functions we can now carry out at radio frequencies. Potentially, the laser offers greatly increased speed and communication capacity. Practically, various technological advances must be made before the potentialities of the laser can be exploited effectively.

What I want to convey is that we have in our hands powerful technological resources with potentialities far beyond those yet realized, and that progress is very rapid. The particular modes of electrical information transfer which these resources will provide will be a matter of complex technological choice. Certainly, they will include electronic switching systems more capable, flexible and economical than those we now have. They will include many communication satellites, some providing millions of telephone circuits or an equivalent amount of other communication. They will include waveguide systems in which hundreds of thousands of telephone conversations will be transmitted through a two inch pipe by means of millimeter waves. They will include optical transmission systems using the coherent light of lasers. They will include more powerful and economical wire, coaxial cable and microwave transmission systems. And, they will include, not only huge and powerful electronic computers, but small and powerful electronic computers no larger than a stack of books.

In the next decade we will have many if not all of these instrumentalities of communication. How will these resources be used; how will they affect our lives? Of what pitfalls should we beware? Here we can best ask, what has electrical communication done for and to us in the past?

While numbers are often thought of as being cold and impersonal, when numbers are about people and about the things that people use this need not be so. We can learn a great deal about the world by considering what such numbers tell us.

There are around 100 million telephones in the United States and around 200 million in the world. I think that it is more meaningful to consider the number of telephones and the number of telephone calls per person in various countries. These data are shown in Figs. 1 and 2.

The United States and Sweden are examples of technologically advanced and very prosperous countries. We see that the number of telephones and calls per person is about the same in each country—about one telephone for every two people and about 600 calls a year per person. The rate of growth of telephones and telephone calls in Sweden is a little higher than that in the United States, and although the numbers are smaller, Sweden is catching up. I don't know why this is; perhaps it is because there are few if any poor people in Sweden.

It is obvious from Figs. 1 and 2 that technological progress in Japan is rapid. While the Japanese standard of living is lower than that in Sweden or the United States, it is rising rapidly, as is their gross national product. Here we have a country which has been far behind America or Sweden in standard of living, but which is catching up.

France is a rather different case. Japan was a feudal country a hundred years ago, with little trace of contemporary technology. France has been among the leading nations of the world for many centuries. Yet we can see from the small number of telephones and of telephone calls per person and the moderate rate of growth that France must be a very different country from Sweden or the United States. Indeed, I once asked some visitors from France, who had spent a year in the United States, in what respects life in the two countries differed. One thing that they had noticed was that life in

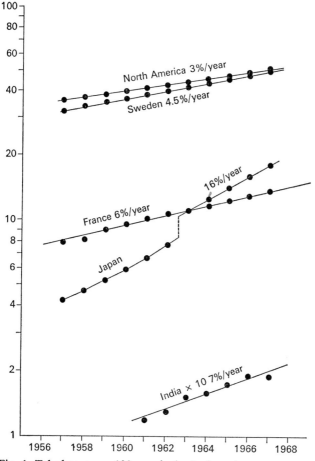

Fig. 1. Telephones per 100 people (end of year).

the United States is more informal, more spur of the moment, than life in France. Social engagements, parties, activities, are organized quickly in my country. They are planned over a longer period in France. Perhaps this is because the availability of good telephone service in the United States has made a different sort of life possible.

When we look at the figures for India we see that we have to multiply the number of telephones and telephone calls per person by 10 even to get the points on the graph. A few in India may rely on the telephone. The telephone has no place in the lives of the vast majority.

Would giving everyone in India a telephone change their manner of life? Certainly not immediately. We use the telephone socially to keep in touch with friends and associates who live at some distance. The Indian, without a telephone, is in touch only with those who live close by, with his neighbors. He has no friends and associates who live at a distance. It used to be that

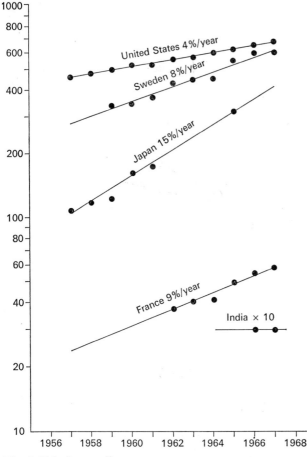

Fig. 2. Telephone calls per person.

way in my own country. Today we can order things by telephone. We can consult the doctor by telephone. We can transact business by telephone. All of this is completely foreign to the way of life of the vast majority of people who live in India. Their life is qualitatively different. Partly, it is different because they have not lived with the telephone, as well as with many other products of technology, over many years; indeed, over generations.

People sometimes idly and thoughtlessly say that technology fills needs people already have. This may be true in some special cases. I think, however, that it misses the most important point concerning the place of technology in man's life. Technology changes the world and man's way of life in it, so that he comes to have a need for devices and services without which he had lived a different sort of life for millenia.

There was no widespread need for the telephone when Alexander Graham Bell invented it. Life was organized in such a way that people lived and worked satisfactorily without the aid of the telephone. Once the telephone was invented and put into service, people found uses for it. Through these uses, their way of life changed. Now people have come to depend on the telephone. A failure of telephone service would be disastrous.

Of course the telephone is not the only thing that has changed our world. So have the automobile and the airplane, and electric power. Together, these technologies have created an entirely new environment and an entirely new sort of life. People live further apart than they used to, yet their activities are more coordinated and interdependent. The medieval manor with its fields, serfs and craftsmen could be nearly self-sufficient. No present-day small community is self-sufficient to that degree, nor is any larger city.

Technology has changed the world into one in which there are demands for telephony, for automobiles, for air travel. These demands are outgrowths of the existence of the technologies and their exploitation by man. Larger demands for these things come into being only through a gradual change in the way people live and have dealings with one another.

We can see this process at work today. Life in Japan appears to be moving rapidly in the direction of life in Sweden and the United States. Life in France is different from life in the United States or in Sweden. The use of the telephone is consonant and consistent with this difference. This does not mean that life is better or worse in France. One can argue ways of life forever without coming to any conclusion. There is no question, however, as to the reality of the difference. Life in India is even more different. Telephone usage is miniscule and the rate of growth is not high.

For many many years life in India will be very different from life in the United States or in Sweden or in Japan. Will life in India ever change in its nature through the impact of technology, so that it will be similar to life in the United States? We cannot know, but we can see that any such change would take a very long time.

The data I have used show that in the United States the number of telephones per person and the number of calls per person grow rather slowly. Does this mean that electrical communication has played its part, that it is now growing only slowly, that it will have no new dramatic impact in the future? I don't think so. Although telephone service is growing at a moderate rate as a whole, some aspects of telephone service are growing more rapidly.

While local calls in the United States are growing at a rate of about 5% a year, long distance calls are growing at a rate of about 10% a year, and calls to other countries are growing at a rate of over 20% per year. This is consistent with a real change in our life, an interdependence not only among people in one city, but among people in the whole country, and indeed, an interdependence among people of the whole world.

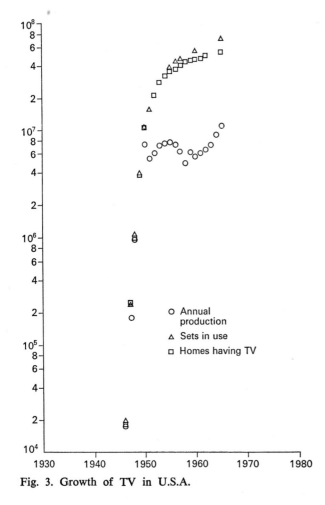

Fig. 3. Growth of TV in U.S.A.

Such interdependence is a part of one of the most startling aspects of modern technological civilization. People and industries are spread over the United States and over the world far more than they ever were before. Industry is no longer clustered near one city or near a few cities. Yet industry and all aspects of our lives are more closely interrelated than they ever were before. This interrelation has been brought about and made possible by improvements in transportation and improvements in communication.

Even the rapid growth of long distance and transoceanic telephony is not as spectacular as the growth of a totally new service which finds acceptance with the public. Fig. 3 shows the growth of television in the United States, now largely accomplished. Instead of a smooth curve which has a constant slope on semilog paper, as we have seen in the earlier plots, the number of television sets and the number of families with television sets

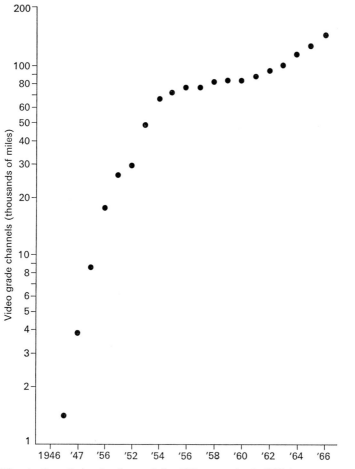

Fig. 4. Growth in circuits used for TV networks in U.S.A.

increased extremely rapidly over a surprisingly small number of years. While growth has not levelled out completely, it has decreased drastically. Here we see a real revolution in a way of life.

The growth of television was accompanied by, and indeed made possible by, a growth in the circuits used for television network programming, as we see in Fig. 4.

Did the rapid growth in television come about because people suddenly wanted it? No. It came about because at a particular time technological advances made television possible at a price that people could afford to pay. In the same way, the circuits that made networks possible did not come because of sheer hunger. They came because, through years of research and development in the field of communication, people finally succeeded in devising new means of transmission, such as coaxial cable and microwave radio relay which were capable of carrying television signals.

The growth of television in the United States, Europe and Japan has been phenomenal. Partly, this has been possible because television is simpler than telephony. Television makes use of one-way broadcasting from the few to the many. Each user buys and owns a television set. Telephony requires multitudes of individual circuits, complex switching and transmission systems and a highly integrated and interdependent organization of such subsystems and of operating procedures into one overall, complex communication network.

Partly, however, television can grow rapidly because it is easier to add to life than is telephony. Technologically, we can imagine bringing television to the villages of India, perhaps by broadcasts from satellites. We can also imagine the villagers as eager to hear and view entertainment, comments and information about common problems, and the surprising news that they are citizens of a huge nation which has a central government whose policies may affect their own village life.

Television might have a quick and profound influence in a country such as India, while telephony could have a profound influence only through a drastic but necessarily slow change in the country's life.

Whatever influence television might have in a country such as India, its influence in technologically advanced countries has been profound. I don't mean merely the decline of the motion picture as mass entertainment. I think more about how we apprehend the world. In my country, advertising on television has given a compellingly believable picture of affluent middle-class life to all of America, including those in the poorest ghetto. Other programming affects us as well. Surveys indicate that people rely more on news by television than on news from newspapers, and that they trust TV news more. This doesn't mean that newspapers no longer have a function. It merely means that a new function has arisen which affects newspapers.

This new function has various aspects. Partly, I suppose, people get news by television merely as a substitute for newspaper news. But television gives them a different picture of the world. Newspapers have space for explanations of the world, for telling a story about how things fit together. The impact of television is greater in showing what actually happens to people. We may continue to rely on newspapers and magazines for theories and explanations of community, national and international events, but we can check these theories and explanations against firsthand knowledge of individual incidents—in Vietnam, Czechoslovakia, Biafra, Paris or Chicago. This can have a power similar to that of the ugly fact which destroys a beautiful theory.

The explosive growth of television is a thing of the past. Again I can ask, is electronic communication somehow exhausted, or may we expect explosions with revolutionary effects on our lives in the future, comparable with those of the past? I believe that we can.

A revolution which may be in progress today is wired television, usually called cable television or community antenna television. Its growth has been somewhat retarded in the United States by regulatory and legal obstacles and uncertainties, but it holds promise of being qualitatively different from broadcast television.

The difference is partly, of course, in the quality of the signal. Signal quality is becoming increasingly important as we go to color television. Even more than this, however, is the difference in the number of channels available. Frequencies for broadcasting television are a limited resource. One can have only a rather small number of television stations in one area. Channels are perhaps ample near a few large cities, but they are scanty elsewhere. Further, television stations are expensive.

The number of channels that one can bring into a home by cable is not limited in this way. Twelve is easy; 20 have been tried, and more could be made available. This means that it will be possible to supply to the home, not only the most popular programs, which compete for a limited number of channels in prime time, but many other programs of local or even of trivial interest, programs which will appeal to only a small fraction of viewers. The cost of the wired system, which in a suburban area is about that of putting a good antenna on the top of each house, can be borne by the access it affords to popular programs. Thus, one doesn't have to reach a large percentage of viewers with every program in order to justify the cost of program generation and transmission.

Cable television can give television something of the qualities of newspapers and magazines. It can make possible programs which appeal to smaller interest groups among the audience—those interested in local affairs, in a variety of sports, in gardening, in cooking, in something other than what the networks now supply. While an explosive growth and consequent change in national life have not yet come through cable television, they may in the near future.

We have noted that mass communication is only a part of communication. Mass communication is communication directed from the few to the many. Personal commmunication, of which telephonic communication is an example, is directed from one individual to another or, sometimes, from one individual to a machine. Will there be revolutionary changes and revolutionary growth in personal communication? I think that there will be.

One prospect for this is *Picturephone*® service, or two-way video transmission with telephony. About eight years ago a colleague and I had a video telephone system installed between our offices, about 30 miles apart. In those days of the vacuum tube, video telephony could not succeed. The equipment was too bulky and expensive. It was unreliable. The thing that I remember most about this experiment is how frequently service broke down.

Today I have an experimental "Mod 1" *Picturephone* terminal in my office. It connects me with about 50 other people, some at the Bell Laboratories at Murray Hill, some the Bell Laboratories at Holmdel, about 30 miles away, and some at the AT & T Headquarters in Manhattan. This *Picturephone* terminal is practical because a revolution in technology has made it practical. That revolution is the transistor and the solid-state art inspired by the transistror.

In the days of the vacuum tube, the video telephone could not have succeeded. In the day of the transistor it is a possibility. The Bell System proposes to offer *Picturephone* service in selected localities in the early 1970's.

Picturephone service is not the only form of communication that may grow so rapidly as to have revolutionary effects. Another sort of new service may involve computers.

The growth of computers has been spectacular. Fig. 5 shows the growth in the cumulative number of computers. Fig. 6 shows the cumulative cost of computers sold.

We see that the growth in cumulative cost of computers is perhaps a little less rapid than the growth in number of computers. This is because transistors and integrated circuits are making computers, not only bigger and better, but smaller and better as well. The solid-state art is making possible a computer that will give computing service more and more cheaply.

Computers have to do with communication because increasingly we are able to consult and to use computers at a distance by means of communication facilities. We can gain access to a computer by means of a teletypewriter connected to a telephone line through a *Data-Phone*® set. A number of companies offer the remote use of computers through such facilities. We have a large number of such remote computer terminals, using commercial computer services, at the Bell Telephone Laboratories.

Sometimes we may want to get from the computer, not tables of numbers, but drawings or diagrams of one sort or another. A number of experimental terminals have been produced which have a cathode ray tube for display of graphs, charts and drawings as well as a keyboard. The user communicates with the computer, directing it, or questioning it, by means of a teletypewriter keyboard. Such terminals are not as yet in wide use.

When we consider the various sorts of communication which we have today, we see that they are serving us increasingly well. Further, we may

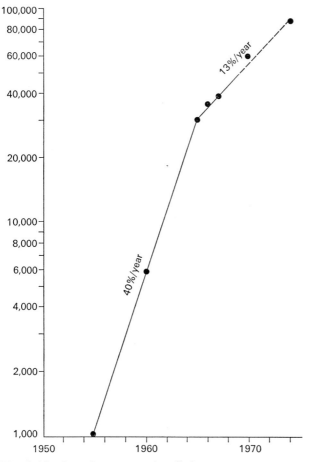

Fig. 5. Number of computers installed.

expect revolutionary advances in our use of communication. These, like present uses, can profoundly affect our lives.

I expect that in developing countries it will be the mass communication of broadcast radio and television that will grow most rapidly and will quickly affect the lives of large numbers of people.

In technologically advanced countries, the sorts of communication which I expect to grow very rapidly are cable television in the field of mass communication, and in the field of person-to-person or person-to-machine communication, *Picturephone* communication and communication with computers. These latter two forms of communication may affect us in a variety of ways. I think they are related, because the *Picturephone* terminal may be an effective means for communication with computers.

Already, communication with computers is very important in our society. Airline reservations are made through the remote use of computers, as one

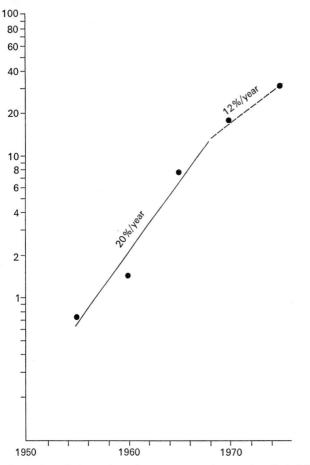

Fig. 6. Cumulative value of computer equipment installed, billions dollar.

can see in any large airport. Stockbrokers have quotation services involving a computer and a local terminal. Computers are increasingly used in banks and businesses in connection with various transactions.

For the office or the home, I can imagine a number of computer services. One would be merely storing text in computers and using the computer in editing the text and in printing out a final corrected copy. Other uses fall under the general heading of business, information and teaching services.

It is impossible to predict in detail exactly what new computer services will be used for. Shopping by computer, scheduling deliveries by computer, credit transactions by computer, getting skiing weather information or sports information or business information from computers are possibilities. So is learning French or algebra by computer.

At present, the cost of the terminals alone is enough to prevent wide-spread use of many proposed computer services. Communication costs are not negligible. Terminals will get better and cheaper, and communication costs will go down as larger volumes of communication are called for by *Picturephone* service and other new services. We will really know the effects on our lives of *Picturephone* service and computers only when *Picturephone* service and remote access to the computers are in wide use.

So far, I have dwelt on possibilities. Many others have pointed out obvious pitfalls.

Mass communication, and especially television, can be constructive in opening a new world to people, in welding them into a nation and in teaching them a common language, a common purpose and a common course of action. Television could be dangerous in inciting national, class or race distrust or hatred. This danger is particularly great in societies without a highly developed, much used and untapped telephone system. In the United States the telephone enables groups to organize meetings, demonstrations and confrontations within hours of viewing some event on television.

The content of television is different from that of books, newspapers, plays and motion pictures. Some bemoan this. I believe that the difference is a necessary result of a large and volatile audience, high cost, and a limited number of channels. I have suggested that by making channels plentiful and cheap, cable television may make a qualitative as well as a quantitative change in television programs.

Various people have been concerned with the threat to privacy posed by computer information systems. The threat is real. Computers are increasingly useful in storing information, and it is increasingly easy to obtain access to such information, legitimately or illegitimately, by electrical communication. Alan F. Westin has discussed this better than I could in his book *Privacy and Freedom*.

Some have envisaged a society in which "intelligent" machines will enslave man. I think that this is nonsense.

The two pitfalls to which I wish to call attention are different. I find them both very alarming.

The first and perhaps the lesser has to do with the growing portion of our technology which lies in what is commonly called the public sector. This embraces all services for which we pay, not directly, but through taxes.

When a man spends his money directly for products or services, he makes some sort of individual choice among alternatives. In my country, a negligible number of people would buy an Edsel, and manufacture of that car was discontinued. In contrast many have bought Mustangs, and that car has been widely sold and widely imitated.

In a broader way, individuals make choices in which travel, housing, household applicances, servants, cars, boats, entertainment, and even cities, suburbs and states as places of work and residence, are weighed against one another.

Whatever one may say concerning such individual choices, collective decisions, in which the individual may have a voice at the polls but no choice thereafter, seem to me to be made far less well. While great and useful public works are certainly accomplished, ineffective, expensive, and abortive public programs are conspicuous by their presence. Further, while the way some men treat their fellows in a ghetto is shocking, the way in which nations composed largely of respectable, well-intentioned citizens treat segments of their own population and some inhabitants of other lands is far more shocking.

Such collective action by respectable nations is shocking because of the disparity between proclaimed ends and the real ends, which, a wise man has observed, *are* the means. As in the functioning of a legal system, it is what happens to a man, not what words are uttered about it, that reveals the true nature of the law of a land.

Like all other technologies, the technology of electronic information transfer is a potential source of benefits and a potential area of expenditure of man's effort, which we commonly measure in money spent. The technology of electric information transfer could be an expensive and unrewarding area if a nation chose to make large expenditures in the public sector as unwisely or as ineffectively as many such expenditures have been made in the past. The pitfall of large, unwise, unproductive public expenditures is not unique to electrical communication, but is very important to it.

The other pitfall I foresee as increasingly dangerous is what might be called abnegation of self. It is the very opposite of being enslaved by an intelligent machine. It is hiding behind a stupid machine.

This did not come into the world with advanced technology. The bureaucrat who heeds not how his actions may help or harm his nation or his neighbor, but rather seeks safety in irresponsibly fulfilling his narrowest and most mechanically prescribed duties, must be as old as government itself.

Today, the increasing complexity of life and the increasing power of machines make it easier and safer to forego one's human nature and responsibilities and to act as an irresponsible machine.

Consider a salesman of the past, who made out a sales slip and added up the figures himself. Such a man might plausibly feel an obligation to discuss a possible error with a customer, and even an obligation to see that an actual error was rectified.

Consider a programmer of today who misprograms the computer in a mechanized occounting system so that it misfunctions. Is he likely to feel sympathy for a defrauded individual, whom he never meets face to face? Is he likely to admit his error to his superior? Is he not more likely to blame the machine, which has no feelings, especially if his superior is ignorant and can be gulled?

In common with others of my countrymen, I have dealt painfully with computerized companies seemingly devoid of responsible individuals, and I have always lost. This need not be so. Telephone companies have used complicated machines for years and know that they are senseless and fallible. Commonly, telephone company employees will heed complaints and rectify errors.

The problem of abnegation of humanity, of hiding behind the machine which we have misused, is not unique to electrical communication. A man who could not bring himself to kill ten individuals by burning them with a blow torch is quite capable of roasting tens of thousands by releasing an atom bomb.

The problem of abnegation of one's humanity, of hiding behind a machine and becoming a machine, is increasingly important in many areas of life, including the electronic transfer of information. Computer stores of information, accessible remotely by electrical communication, can increasingly involve our privacy and safety as well as our pocketbook. We hope that such stores of information will be designed, operated and controlled by responsible human beings.—These two problems: ineffective expenditure of public funds, and irresponsibly hiding behind a machine, are both widespread and disastrous in their consequences. If there is anything that can help to solve them, perhaps it is electrical communication and electronic information processing.

Computers and communication are making it increasingly practical and easy to collect, store, process, summarize and display data from large bodies of information. Some corporate executives now have prompt and meaningful access to operational information which reflects the effects of their policies and decisions. If they wish, the heads of government departments and the heads of nations can in time have quickly available to them data reflecting the condition, woes and resources of a nation and of the nation's policies.

Such resources might also help in improving each individual's picture of his country. But here, the particular is as important as the mean or the deviation. I know that what I see done by or to an individual on television, moves me more powerfully than pages of statistics or piles of tracts and theories. Electrical communication can make it possible to see the world beyond our homes and offices first hand and to appreciate the lot of individual men in that world. And we ourselves are all men in a wide and interdependent world. The lot of man is affected by what we do.

Man is highly adaptable. Perhaps seeing what is unpleasant, stupid and painful will merely accustom us all to unpleasantness, stupidity and pain. But perhaps men may remain human enough to care, even in a world which teaches us the safety and rewards of hiding behind and imitating machines.

Notes

The numerical data in Figs. 1 and 2 was obtained from *The World's Telephones,* published yearly by the American Telephone and Telegraph Company: that for Fig. 3 from *Statistical Abstract of U.S.* (1966), *The Economic Almanac,* the Conference Board (1964), *Information Please Almanac* (1967) and (1959), *World Almanac* (1941) and (1965) and Clure H. Owen, Television Broadcasting, Proc. IRE, vol. 50, p. 818 (1962): that for Figs. 5 and 6 from *The State of the Information Processing Industry,* a report of the American Federation of Information Processing Societies based on a study completed in late 1965 and updated early in 1966.

The general ideas expressed have come to be my own over many years, through personal experiences and observation as well as through reading. However, I wish to acknowledge two general sources:

Alan F. Westin: *Privacy and Freedom,* Athaneum Press, 1967.
Lee Loevinger: "Reality in a Dream World", a talk republished as an advertisement in the *New York Times,* April 24, 1967, p. 25 and in substantially the same form as "Games People Play Over Television" in *Television Magazine.* May 1967, vol. 24, p. 28. Commissioner Loevinger called attention to the effect on the poor of advertising which gives a compelling picture of affluent, middle-class life.
"The Reflective-Projective Theory of Broadcasting and Mass Communications", the *Journal of Broadcasting,* vol. 12, p. 97, spring, 1968.
"The Government of Utopia", commencement speech given at the University of Minnesota Law School, June 7, 1968. In this talk Loevinger says in substance that in the world of government the means are the ends.
"Sociology of Bureaucracy", the *Business Lawyer,* November, 1968, p. 7.

Priorities in Science

By Carlos Chagas

UNESCO, Paris, France

Introduction

Priorities proceed from criteria previously established. The choice of criteria may be difficult when dealing with problems related to social evolution and development. A great number of disparate variables, the urgency to act at once in relation to some of them, the rate at which others are evolving, make the establishment of criteria a troublesome task. It is in this complex framework that the question of priorities in science takes shape. In an individual perspective, this query may be answered in a rather simple way. The activities of a scientist have primordially, as a goal, the satisfaction of his intellectual curiosity. In a social perspective, however, this picture changes as scientific work may—and should in many instances—be influenced by diverse factors emerging from the world the scientist lives in.

One of the most significant of these factors is the need that compels mankind to defeat the challenges it faces. Thus, when speaking on priorities in science, we have to enter the domain of broad intellectual interests and material needs, of economic conditions and development, and of cultural and social processes, leaving behind that of scientific research "per se".

This paper does not aim at producing a list of priorities, even incomplete. It will try to present criteria. With this restriction in mind, it will attempt to focus some of the most significant aspects of modern thought and of those trends of science policy that have a world-wide reflection. This may sound as an over-ambitious approach, but any sectorial one would certainly be too limited, and would conceal the fact that the benefits of scientific progress should not be limited to particular regions of the world, in which case it would only increase the disparity of wealth and the sense of defeat which are overshadowing the future of mankind.

The three criteria chosen may seem at the first approach to be of a competitive or excluding character. A closer analysis, however, will show them to be closely knit together.

The *first criterium* to be discussed has to do with the significance of basic research for the present and for the next decades. The *second* is related to the ideas which arise nowadays from the study of the interaction

of Man and his environment, a study which touches one of the most significant trends in the evolution of modern thought. The *third* one, more closely
related to social evolution, depends on how we equate the problem of
priority on a basis of a world divided between developed and underdeveloped countries.

Basic research

There is no need to stress the fact that basic science has paved the way
to scientific and technological progress. The question one asks now relates
to the role we expect it to play in the future and to its importance in the
global perspective of development.

To take basic research as a criterium to decide about priorities may
be criticized. As a matter of fact, it is unanimously accepted that today's
most momentous world problem is the abyssal difference between the developed or industrialized countries, and the underdeveloped or poor ones;
we are consequently anxious to reduce this gap by increasing the economic
status of underdeveloped countries. We know, however, that one of the
most important elements responsible for this gap is the fact that basic research is confined—for obvious reasons—to the specialized centers existing in developed countries. Every result they produce, and every progress
they achieve, brings about an enlargement of this split. Hence, if we are
searching for solutions of world-wide dimensions, it may seem contradictory
to emphasize a field which, in the minds of many, should be considered
only in the prospect of developed countries, a field the strengthening of
which only enlarges the "malaise" mankind is confronted with.

Basic research, however, is an important element in science planning
for all countries, in any state of development. This point is worth to be
dealt with at some length.

In developed countries, at present, the place and priority of basic research in science policy is challenged, so much so that in many of those
nations where, up to now, a heavy support has been given to basic research,
this attitude is being reconsidered and attempts are being made to build
up a different policy based on a more "utilitarian" type of activity. Against
this tendency, one needs only to stress the fact that basic research will
lead, over a long-term period, or even a short-term one, to technical contributions which will produce quantitative results many times superior to the
initial investment. This is indeed a truism, and as such should not even
be recalled here. Only the hope to reach those who, politically, determine
the scientific policies of a country, justifies our mentioning it.

On the other hand, in developing countries, basic research has been considered by many as a luxury, if not as a hindrance to their proper development. This is an unfounded assumption. On the contrary, the gap between developed and developing countries will increase if this assumption is accepted, as we will try to prove later on, when discussing the science policy those countries must adhere to in order to attain their own development.

However, the direct bearing of basic research on technological development has no need to be presented in detail. It has been already well-publicized: only emotional or purposedly misdirected reasons have been given for its non-recognition.

Basic research is part of Man's intellectual trust, and it satisfies the human desire for progress. Science has yet a great deal to achieve before reaching a complete understanding of some of the fundamental problems that surround us, problems that span, in a "pascalian" frame, from the unknown of cosmogony to the reconnoitering of the mechanisms which preside over cerebral activity, and to the inquiries on the ultimate constitution of matter. Those problems are still surrounded by a veil of mystery which stimulates Man's curiosity and prompts his unending search for truth.

However, it is not only on the merit of its validity for technology, or of its significance to the advancement of knowledge, that basic research should be emphasized as the first criterium where from priorities should be derived. There is still another of its traits which may have a particular influence on human behaviour, and from which, as a matter of fact, no direct priority can be drawn.

Basic research is conducted, as a rule, in obeyance to a certain number of rules which turn out to be of an utmost value in an ethical contexture. The rules which constitute the ethics of scientific research are simple: objectivity and veracity of information, respect of the fellow-scientist, cooperation in unselfishness, independence of judgment free from any pressure, be it economic, political or social.

These rules may be found in the ethical behaviour of others groups, like the religious ones, but these groups are not associated with the image of progress and development, and are less glamorous for men fascinated by our technological evolution. It is on this account that the ethics of scientific research may have a more important role to play in the new world that has to be built.

But independence of judgment, respect for fellow men, cooperation, objectivity and veracity, are also the necessary composite elements of the true democratic process. For this reason, fundamental research is vital to any country, in its fight for economic independence, social justice, peaceful progress, goals unattainable outside the democratic process. Basic scientists form one of the few social groups which may resist political pressures, internal or external, any country has to overcome in its way to social progress.

It is true that scientists, like other men, are subject to errors and pitfalls, but the fact remains that their sectorial ethics—if such an adjective can be used—may exert a great and justified influence on human ethics.

Jacques Monod has stressed this quite clearly in his inaugural lecture at the Collège de France.[1] It is rather puzzling, however, to see that Monod's idea of extrapolating from the ethics of experimental research to human ethics—of which in any case it constitutes a fraction—has raised such a negative repercussion. His objectors probably think that the scientist, having reached certain achievements—spectacular at times—in his search, wants to impose upon mankind a new attitude, if not new rules. Far from it. The scientist feels that by dealing with Nature, he has not only gained a new knowledge, but also a new thinking attitude, both of which may give to the whole mankind a new demeanour, that in turn will improve Man's collective life, giving him a better understanding of his problems, and an increased sense of responsibility in his dealings with the world's problems.

Only scientists have the ability to perceive and promote changes which may affect Mankind in the evolution of our society. Man, in his search for progress, has to defend principles, even if he may surrender positions in the pursuit of the reconsideration of his present system of values; the scientist, who is changing the shape of our civilization, believes he is able to guide him in this path. Certainly, he cannot complete this task alone, but he will probably play a major role in its success.

It is important to remark that the opposition to the scientist playing a role in shaping a new code of ethics, is but a part of a very dangerous anti-scientific feeling—fashionable in many circles—which is spreading and has already penetrated the ideas of some members of the younger generation. This mood is reflected in some of the most daring "avant-garde" thought, that comprises the leading trends of "gauchisme", taken from the writings of some of the political or philosophical leaders of our days, like Adorno, Marcuse or Mao Tsetung. This trend reflects the naive concept that, as our present civilization, based on the application of science, has not produced the grade of fruitfulness one could expect from it, it follows necessarily that science is responsible for man's present unhappiness. This tendency must be fought very vigorously. Basic scientists thus have a mission. They have to prove the unreality of this antiscientific feeling and show to those who are suffering that their world is conducted in a sense of responsibility for Mankind, and not for the selfish purpose of satisfying their personal interests and curiosity.

From this discussion, it may be ascertained that basic research continues to be a need for social development. Progress in knowledge and in technological evolution can be sustained only if the place basic science has at present is maintained, if not upgraded. It must be stressed, however, that basic research plays fundamentally the same role in developed countries as in developing ones, even if their impletion has to be undertaken under different perspectives.

As much as an overall basic research development should be underlined for rich countries, chosing priorities in the realm of basic research is a matter of strategy in less-developed ones, where this choice should be coupled to certain fields more closely connected to the national development needs. However, this is not a unique role, as the value of basic research overpasses this concrete approach.

Man and his environment

Man's idea of his position in the Universe, as much as his attitude towards Nature, has changed and is still moving. This is the basis for a second criterium from which priorities are to be chosen.

One may say, shortly, with reference to the position of Man in the Universe, that human thought, from the end of the XVth Century, has gradually passed from a theological phase to a rational one, in which the universe looses its supernatural character, and acquires an anthropocentric one, man being the dominant element and the beneficiary of the environment in which he lives, and which he aims to subdue.

A subtle change is occurring now, and as Man's supremacy is being blurred, it appears that three elements, at least, may be responsible for this change.

The first one is the influence exerted in modern thought by the philosophy of Heidegger, and by the evolution of his philosophic thought, which has been developed, modified and diffused by the existentialist trend which occurred after the second world-war. This has given rise to what may be called an "anthropophagic" philosophy. Man has been downgraded and become an instrument of his sensorial experiences, his language, and his reason, no longer being his own master. He, who was The Being, became The Existant. A quotation from Michel Foucault illustrates this tendency: "In our days, one cannot think but on the vacuum left by the disappearance of Man. This vacuum does not mean an absence, it does not determine a void that must be filled. It is nothing more, and nothing less, than the deployment of a space where it is at last possible to think anew".[2] Michel Foucault is not an isolated esoteric French philosopher. His thought is much more a reflection of modern thinking than the origin of a new turn in philosophy.

If one comes to the area of morals, the new trend is steered by the gradual disappearance of the respect for human dignity and for human life, which began at the period of "l'entre-deux-guerres" so deeply resented by the desperate music that echoes through the poetry of T.S. Eliot. This is shown by the existence of concentration camps, where human experiments were undertaken, "in anima coacta", by the existence of tribunals of exception, and by the permanence of armed conflicts so heavily influenced by economic interests and emotional attitudes.

These wars should not belong to the reality of a world involved in a veritable social evolution and inspired by hopeful expectations.

To these factors, one should add the sociological one caused by the compulsion of collectivism, a word here used in its loose sense. This pressure finds its more significant expression in the more cogent aspects of the youth movements, as much as in the social thinking of the revolutionary Church.

These factors act, as a matter of fact, in different social groups, but they integrate themselves in order to convey to the world the message that our system of values must be changed.

If we want to consider now how Man's attitude is changing in relation to Nature, and if we want to study the process by which his former one may be abandoned, we must briefly analyse the evolution of scientific thought.

Two tendencies have guided scientific thought from the middle of the last century, up to the breaking point which occurred in the twenties. One of them considered science as an intellectual adventure, in which the aesthetic essence was its own "raison d'être". This pure intellectual approach might, or might not bring concrete results for the benefit of Man, but its end was not primordially the fulfilment of Man's material needs.

In opposition, the second trend, which reflected Bacon's philosophy, admitted science essentially as a lever of action which would give Man absolute control over Nature.

Two world-wars led to a situation where one observes the gradual disappearance of those who, guided by the first tendency, exercised their scientific activity oblivious of any particular use of its results, no matter what potential utilization they could have.

This tendency is reinforced by the increase in the cost of science, which brings into the picture the need for immediate benefits which can scarcely come from abstract science, and the use of econometric analysis so frequently hermetic and often unrealistic.

The Baconian attitude pervades nowadays all scientific activities and is now anchored in the minds of millions in the world. And this was as it should be, because it has brought to mankind not only progress, comfort, and affluency, even happiness, alas too haphazardly, but at the same time, it has given to Man a sense of superiority that upgrades its ego.

The forces leading to a reconsideration of our position in relation to nature are diverse.

The most significant of these forces is taking shape as a result of Man's interaction with Nature. Man is destroying his natural environment, and creating an entirely antihuman one, which will be, at not so long a range, unfit to support his life. This is the consequence of technical and natural phenomena such as massive urbanization with the rupture of many social and biological equilibria — for instance the loss of "forestries", so dear to the souls of men, from common folk to poets, but also so important for the cycle of oxygen — and the misuse of natural resources of which one of the best examples is the indiscriminated spraying of DDT.

What one is observing now is the issue of the long process which began when Man ceased to be a hunting creature to become an agricultural one. It has gained impetus during the colonial era, and achieved its peak with our modern technological times.

In this destruction of the environment, one finds in general ignorance, overconfidence in the powers of science, greed, and an urge for immediate success.

An analogy may illustrate the change of attitude Man has been subject to. One may say that, up to now—and I believe this is at the bottom of Baconian thought—Man has had towards Nature the attitude of a gambler playing a "zero sum game", as defined by von Neuman, a game in which a player's gain is someone else's loss. By fairplay or fraud, Man has always won. He begins to perceive now that for his own sake, he must play with Nature and his environment, and even with his microcosmos, a "non zero sum game", in which opposing players gain or loose together, thus being forced into partnership.

Reality, political events, and a new trend of thought has thus steered Man to a new position in relation to Nature and his own environment. It dawns that for his benefit, he has to change his conduct towards Nature in order that the words once used by Isaiah come true:

Instead of the thorns shall come up the cypress,
instead of the briar shall come up the myrtle.[3]

Does our recognition of what is happening mean a more or less radical change of our unrestricted acceptance of the admitted interpretation of

Bacon's philosophy, or does it just mean an adaptation of the baconian disposition towards an evolving situation?

The frequent utilization of the expression "irrational use of natural resources" in international congresses and in reports of national and international organizations, as much as the importance given in large numbers of countries to the question of the conservation of Nature, shows an awareness of the problem which overshadows the idea of a simple adaptation of the baconian disposition to a present plight.

Any definition of Man's environment will show the complexity of the second criterium presented. The environment may be defined as "the sum of natural resources and those created by Man, as well as the socio-economical structures in which he lives. It exists in a dynamic state of balance on which act both the non-human bio-mass, and Man himself".[4] Thus, the environment evolves.

The fact is that most of the features that characterize Man's life, are the outcome of his relationship with his environment. As a matter of fact, to live is to react to the various changes of the ambient which surrounds the living being. It is like that, that their behaviour is established. However, environment has not been Man's preoccupation, up to very recently. Suddenly, it becomes apparent that it cannot be neglected. One may say that part, at least, of the anguish and dissatisfaction prevalent in modern society reflects the diffuse sensation that environment has not merited our respect, and has not received its proper place in the process of social evolution. As was pointed out by Dubos: "Man is an element of the environment in its whole; he cannot achieve his mental health and conserve it, if the circumstances fail to establish the 'health of the environment'. This expression designates the physical and biological system in which Man lives. It implies not only the survival of the system, but also its aptitude to evolve in such a way as to allow Man to do the same. The future is as important as the being."[5]

The criterion for choice of priorities based on the interaction between Man and his environment encompasses all fields of science. Priorities in this domain follow three broad lines, comprehending those which have a global dimension—such as overall air pollution, ocean contamination and the cycle of oxygen, for instance—regional ones of national or multi-national character—of which a good example is the destruction of life in certain rivers, as a consequence of industrial pollution—and human ones —of physical nature: noise, carbon monoxide pollution, and psychobiological ones, as for instance mental stress in certain types of popular housing, or produced as a consequence of deprivation of elementary conditions of life in slums.

The span of old scientific disciplines and new ones, many of which have a multidisciplinary character, needed to deal with this question, ranges from the domain of natural science to that of the social ones. As a matter of fact, one cannot conceive the study of the interaction between Man and his environment without stressing the importance of such an integration.

However, another point should also be stressed. It is the need to introduce the study of ecology for the non-specialist, i.e. to increase the content of the teaching of ecology at University level, which has been emphasized in Recommendation N° 10 of the International Conference of the Biosphere, held at Unesco in September 1968.[5] It should however be considered that this teaching should go down another step, and that the introduction of science-teaching at the primary level—a highly supported move nowadays—should be done through the elementary teaching of ecology encompassing the fundamentals of natural sciences, and of the conservation of Nature and its resources.

Only the increase of understanding of the importance of protection of environment, can produce an overall action for its defence. General information and education are the essential ingredients to achieve this needed understanding. This is why long-term programs, concerned with education at all levels, should be endorsed. Only through education can general information be obtained.

On the other hand, to cope with the problems already present, short-time priorities have to be established. They must be related to the urgency with which some of the challenges have to be overmastered. Some of these challenges may be fought with knowledge that already exists. Others, however, and probably the majority, need the undertaking of more intensive and extensive research and development, in order to be met. The difficulties of these tasks should not obscure their need.

Science and development

The comparative study of the scientific development, in developed countries and in less-developed ones, would lead us to consider how the social and economic differences existing between them, may influence the criteria less-developed countries must choose in order to establish their science policies. The first question one is tempted to ask is whether the criteria to be used by poor nations are the same as those which brought the developed countries to their present stage of evolution.

The question is a complex one, and will give margin to some comments: it seems clear that in the short-term approach, the answer is a clear-cut one. The differences between the developed countries and the less-developed ones are of such an order that the strategy the last ones must apply is at present quite different from that which is being applied by developed countries.

But the real problem is to decide, on the long-term approach, if the developing nations should engage in the same course, step by step, that the developed ones have followed in their evolution. For less-developed countries, the urgency of reaching the most adequate science policy is such that they have to overpass some of these steps. The selection of these steps is, nevertheless, the heart of the matter.

This is the reason why a close analysis of the scientific evolution of the developed countries becomes so important for the underdeveloped nations. It is clear that no science system from a country can be carbon-copied by another, but some are easier to be assimilated than others, and thus serve as models.

One may admit that the development of science in rich countries has been more or less an harmonious evolution encompassing all fields of research and development, even if some of them have received a bigger impulse. This has not been the case, and probably will never be, for developing nations. Where scientific and technological development exists in these countries, it is mostly due to the need to answer the challenges brought about by the natural and social environment. In consequence, some sectors have had a much greater development than others, and as a result, these specific domains have outgrown largely the others and have become isolated from them.

This is particularly the case, on one hand, for medical research, and on the other, for certain fields in countries rich in certain natural resources, such as oil, in which particular lines of research and development have been strongly furthered.

Two examples, taken from Brazil, may be illustrative. One, in the medical domain, and the other, in the sphere of economic challenges. The first was the establishement of the "Instituto Oswaldo Cruz", as a consequence of the eradication of yellow fever from our littoral. The second, the establishment of the "Instituto Biológico de São Paulo", as a consequence of the danger for the whole economy of the country—based at the time exclusively on the export of coffee—by the threat to our coffee crops presented in the early twenties by a predacious parasite, a coleoptere classified as "Hypotenemus hampei". Both institutions have given important contributions to the national science. One simple example justifies all the expenditures undertaken at the Instituto Oswaldo Cruz. It is the discovery of the American trypanosomiasis, which gave impetus to the study of parasitology and pathology, furthered the development of tropical medicine, increased the autochtonous knowledge of the fight against parasite vectors, and even enhanced medical practice in the interior.

What becomes quite clear is that science policy and scientific priorities for developing countries cannot obey a uniform rule. For various reasons, the Advisory Committee for the Application of Science and Technology of the United Nations[6] has tried to establish a classification of developing countries, with the objective of determining what type of different measures should be implemented in nations at different stages of development. The scientific and technological development of poor countries has, however, to follow some general rules. Some of its problems have to be solved at once. The most prominent ones are food and energy, to which one should add particular medical challenges—as schistosomiasis—in certain regions. However, if a long-range and simultaneous effort is not planned and pursued, all efforts will be of no durable kind. This long-term effort includes science and education, and basic research, directed to a certain number of goals.

This long-term plan, and its fulfilment, must take into consideration special conditions, inherent to each national case, as the existence of a particular problem, the human resources available, and the challenges which have to be fought in each case.

There can be no doubt that the short-term programs which are being complemented or studied on the international scene—and aim in general at the "transfer of technology"—absorb almost exclusively the attention of national and international planners and politicians.

Taking a candid view of the present situation of the world, it seems that it should be so. Industrialization, as a consequence of technology, and as its principal scope, should provide for riches that would, in a further step, create the autochtonous technology and the scientific structure which every country must possess to be really independent, while increasing at the same time the wealth of every inhabitant of the world.

This idea was strongly presented at the United Nations Conference for the Application of Science and Technology to Development, held in Geneva in 1963. It has practically led to the oblivion of long-term policies, which are obligatory components of the scientific policy of developing countries, and should be included in any international agreement.

One has to state, as strongly as possible, that in this assertion there is no disdain for the short-term approach. The blatant success of the work done in India, West-Pakistan, the Philippines, Mexico and Turkey, in crop production, undertaken as a joint effort by the Rockefeller Foundation, the Ford Foundation, and the respective national Governments, is a contribution for the future that justifies all our hopes. In this effort, the use of irrigation, fertilizers, and the sowing of new-bred mutants, have passed from the stage of successful pilot-projects to an extraordinary harvest. Even if it is a unique example, it shows, nevertheless, the importance of the direct, short-term approach, which in this particular case, may be considered as a breakthrough. At the same time, this success substantiates the point of view which defends the long-term approach. It shows that development can only be reached by means of modern techniques, which should not be the privilege of generous assisting foreign experts, but mastered by the indigenous specialists.

Some of the most important of these advanced techniques which have to be introduced as fast as possible in developing nations, in an overall perspective, are those related to the utilization of computer techniques. Basically important in almost every field of research and development, their contribution in the processing of retrieval and dissemination of data—one of the most serious handicaps to developing countries in their way to progress—is such that great efforts should converge to achieve this objective. A resolution proposed by the Government of Rumania to the 23rd (1968) General Assembly of the United Nations,[7] will be a mark-stone in calling the attention to this formidable lever for development.

The mastery of new techniques, however, implies a knowledge which can only be obtained through research. This is a new argument in favour of the coupling of short-term planning to long-term programs.

The example of the so-called "green revolution" aforementioned, indicates how research useful for developing countries should be implemented. The basic research done in such a well-succeeded venture, has been undertaken at international institutes, some of them outside the area of application of the knowledge, but all of them placed in the developing countries (for instance, Mexico and the Philippines).

The establishment of long-term policies is not an easy task. It needs understanding, courage and almost always intensive capital investment. The policy includes the whole educational system, the establishment of scientific structures, the imposition of institutional changes, as well as the gearing of the national information network for this objective.

Furthermore, a long-term policy of non-immediate results is badly accepted in general by the Governments of less developed countries who wish to establish their prestige by showing the completion of initiatives which are of promising rates of interest.

It is also against the interest of the general trends of economic expansion of the developed countries. It has, however, for developing countries, the same importance as the policy of adjusting human population growth to fit their economic development.

Another reflection should be made. The close connection between the social evolution and the interaction between Man and his environment shows that the ecology of any country—its "national" ecology, to give to this word a larger meaning—must influence research and scientific education. This is particularly true for less-developed countries. The need to understand their national and social environment was made very clear at the Geneva Conference. At the debates held at that occasion, a statement was made over and over again. It repeated that there can be no transfer of technology without "adaptation". Adaptation, however, in the sense it was used, signifies the full knowledge of the natural and social conditions of the nations where technology is to be transferred. This can only be acquired through locally done research, a research complementary to the one undertaken in rich countries.

Even if the need for the development of autochtonous knowledge has not been supported as strongly since the Geneva Conference, either by bilateral, or multilateral agreements, the necessity of reconnoitering the local conditions of developing countries, points again to the importance of long-term programs.

But another argument should be added. It grows from experience. As a matter of fact, it is quite clear, from the observation of what is going on in particular regions of the world, that as a result of the absence of the long-term components of scientific policy, the world is entering—if it is not already fully immersed in it, in an era of "technological colonialism", an expression used without political inferences—which must be avoided for the benefit of peace.

The intention behind the emphasis given to the fostering of research in less-developed countries, does not imply that their scientific community will contribute at once, or in years to come, necessarily, to progress by inventing new technological procedures. Some technological improvements have nevertheless already been achieved in developing countries. However, they are rare, and as such precious exceptions. What the emphasis given implies is that without the autochtonous element, it will be very difficult, if not impossible, to establish a real technological development, in less-developed countries, as the users of technological achievements cannot utilize them in a rational way, understand all their social implications, and protect the natural resources against irrational use, and conserve them whenever conservation is needed, justified and possible. This concept is expressed definitely by René Maheu when he says that: "Development can only be achieved when science ceases to be an imported magic to become the customs of its people."

Thus, transfer of technology, not accompanied by the upgrading of the national scientific educational level, and the introduction of modern techniques for scientific research, will only create despair, frustration and inefficiency.

Summing up, one could say that the strategy of implementing science in less-developed countries, should follow, in general terms, the rules that have insured the progress of the rich nations. However, in the establishment of science policy for the underdeveloped countries, one has to take into consideration the particular characteristics of their ecological, demographic and economic conditions.

At the same time, developing countries have to face immediate challenges, which will bring, as a result, that some streaks of research will outgrow the overall scientific development of the country.

This should not obscure the fact that the harmonious evolution of any country depends on the establishment of a solid basis of knowledge and of scientific structures. Thus, short-term efforts, which may bring the building-up of significant developments in specific isolated fields, must be complemented by the long-term approach of science impletion, which requires the fostering of science education and basic research.

The need for research in developing countries cannot be overstressed, even if one considers the financial difficulties which have to be overcome. Research, including basic research, is one of the foremost levers for the social and economic development of less-developed countries.

The outpassed idea, mentioned before, that basic research is to be conducted only in developed countries, brings as a result an increase of the gap existing between developed and developing countries, and results for these in the impossibility to cope with scientific and technological problems they are faced with. Even the measure, already discussed in international circles, proposing that part of the budget and investments for research in developed countries should be devoted to research of interest for underdeveloped ones, is but a partial solution to the problem. A substantial part of this research must always be undertaken "in loco". One may admit that only in a very first stage of their development, "transfer of technology", from developed countries to underdeveloped ones, should be considered as the sole possibility in the strategy of development. But this critical period must be a short and transitory one, in order not to hinder the evolution of developing countries and perpetuate a much undesirable situation.

In trying to absorb the most fitting models from developed nations to establish science policies for developing countries, even if confining it to the sole perspective of economic development, one should recall the wisdon of the Sages. A Chinese proverb teaches us that:

Give a man a fish,
He will eat a meal.
Teach him how to fish,
He will eat forever.

And in the Book of Proverbs[8] one finds the following:

By wisdom a house is built, and by
Understanding it is established;
But it is by knowledge that it is filled
With precious and pleasant riches.

Some words should be said on ecological problems. In this context, the situation of less-developed countries is certainly more serious than that existing in rich nations. The need for a rapid exploitation of natural resources, the lack of understanding of the importance of preservation, the desire for unreasonable profits, are conducting these countries to a point of no-return.

Forests are chopped down, rivers are being dried up, and deserts are taking the place of luxuriant green plains. This shows the need to reinforce in developing countries research and scientific education in the domain of ecology. The formation of multidisciplinary groups able to cope with such problems should be one of the primordial preoccupations of their national scientific planners.

Another aspect should also be mentioned. It is the effect on native populations of abruptly introduced technology. In some cases a reaction, which in terms of biology could be called a rejection, makes its appearance; in others, the over-optimistic acceptance of modern gadgetry—always very superficially—produces a disruption of all pre-existing social equilibria. This does not mean in any way that we should abandon the benefits of technology for primitive communities. But to avoid the predatory character it may have in destroying the characteristic social life of these collectivities, something that has happened many times, a close collaboration between the social sciences and the natural ones is more than necessary.

Only with this integration will the application of science and technology —or its creation—produce real benefits. As a matter of fact, only the better knowledge of the social background of any nation will allow for the preservation, during the process of technological development, of the most significant and important elements of its native culture indispensable to secure its real independence.

Conclusions

As stated before, this paper had not meant to establish a list of priorities. Some general remarks, however, may be appropriate, using as a basis the comments aforementioned.

A common element of the last two criteria presented is the study of Man and his environment. But the study of Man begins with the knowledge of molecular biology, and leads to the field of brain research, both fields of science which belong, in an academic point of view, to basic science. It is clear that in the perspective of basic science, many other disciplines present a great interest, or a renewed one. However, as most of them are connected almost exclusively with the progress of knowledge or are too-well established, they are not mentioned.

Human fertility needs a special reference. The incognita which still exist about this problem are a source of constant anxiety in a world where the demographic explosion becomes a menace.

In the same order of importance, we have to place the study of human adaptation. Even if one may expect that the studies of spacial medicine will increase our knowledge of the problem, we are still far from knowing how our homeostatic system reacts over a long-term perspective to the small and continuous changes which are brought by the modification of the environment.

This environment demands a major emphasis on the study of the multi-disciplinary science which is ecology. Reinforcement or renewal of research in certain of its areas is needed today. It requires the revigorating apportion of techniques of other sciences, such as, for instance, those developed in solid state physics, or in nuclear studies. The list of priorities would depend, here again, on each particular case. Certain disciplines have begun to be fostered in a more rigorous way in recent years. Others must be still stimulated. Great extension must be given to the field of Man's psycho-physiology in relation to his environment. The difficulties involved in equating proper type of research in this field are so great that one feels a certain hesitation to give to this field the necessary impact. This hesitation must be overcome. It thus seems that efforts in the field of animal behaviour must be strongly encouraged.

Truthfully, one sees that the list of priorities in science is long and almost unlimited, when one analyses the changing social conditions in such a diverse wide world as ours.

The dilemma one faces is to decide whether one should embark in an enterprise of short results, or choose a more moderate pathway, where reflection and long-term achievements are the principal characteristics. The first may bring immediate interest. The second, the establishment of a solid basis for the future. However, the manner in which to blend, and in what proportion, is the crux planners have to face. Let it be emphasized, however, that general science education—one of the fields in which pedagogy has made its greatest leaps in modern times—is a fundamental basis for the rational use of science by Mankind. Not for power but for the real human benefit and progress.

Scientific humanism will be the outgrowth of the general science education. It will make Man able to understand his life, to use the inventions his ingenuity has created, and to harmonize his behaviour with the environment he lives in. It will enable him to manipulate the machinery of modern civilization, without losing the sense of beauty and harmony. It will give him culture as an integrative adaptation to the changing environment in which he lives, a culture which can be "the culture for each man", of which spoke André Malraux.

Notes

[1] Monod, J., Leçon Inaugurale au Collège de France, 1967.

[2] Foucault, M., *Les mots et les choses,* Gallimard, 1967, p. 353.

[3] *Book of Isaiah* 2–51.

[4] Chagas, C., L'Homme et son Milieu, Conference for the Non-Governmental Organizations, Unesco House, 1969.

[5] Dubos, R., Intergovernmental Conference of experts on the scientific basis for rational use and conservation of the resources of the Biosphere, Unesco House, 1968.

[6] Document E/4178, United Nations Economic and Social Council.

[7] Resolution no. 2458, Rumania, United Nations General Assembly (23rd), 1968.

[8] *Book of Proverbs* xxv.

THE TEACHING OF KNOWLEDGE
AND THE IMPARTING OF VALUES

The Importance of Biological Ways of Thought

By Conrad H. Waddington

Institute of Animal Genetics, Edinburgh, Scotland

It is clear from the summaries that have been circulated among the participants to this symposium that many people at this meeting will be addressing themselves to the problems with which the world in its present state confronts us, and to which we are called upon to make answers based on our ideas of values and purposes. I propose, therefore, in the short time available, to confine myself to the rather philosophical issue: have we any right to assert that values do have a place in a world of facts? It is notorious that most of the influential official philosophies of the present day deny that ethical statements have any definable meaning, or that values can be grounded on anything more substantial than mere emotional responses. I think that the initiative of the Nobel Foundation in organising this meeting will be fully justified if we can find a consensus here that values do actually have a place in a world of facts, and it is to this question that I shall address myself.

I shall do so from the point of view of biology. It will be easier to express my argument if I begin by giving a short account of some ideas that have arisen within my own special field of biology, which is embryology. In studying the processes of embryonic development, as indeed in all other branches of science, one must follow simultaneously two rather opposed courses. On the one hand, one must try to be analytical and to discern the simplest entities whose properties and interactions can account for the processes under investigation; on the other hand, one must try to comprehend more and more thoroughly the full richness of the phenomena in which one is interested. The first line thought has led so far to the wonderfully simple and powerful facts and theories referred to as molecular biology. The second requires that we should not forget, in fact that we should try to comprehend further, the complex organs and functions of the adult body to which the embryological developmental processes give rise. This is especially important because it is these complex global properties which are critical for the most general process in the biological world, namely evolution. The forces of natural selection do not impinge directly on to the genes with which molecular biology is concerned. The question for natural selection is: does the lion catch the antelope and eat it, or does the antelope escape? It is quite a second order question whether the lion is successful because it contains some particular form of an enzyme, or whether it has got unusually effective muscles for jumping, or because its nervous co-ordination is specially efficient.

It is in such complex organs that the embryologist—like natural selection —must interest himself. Clearly, they are built up by the interactions of large numbers of individual elementary components, of which much the most important are genes. An organ, then, is something which appears in a multi-dimensional phase space. Further, the embryologist is interested in the organ not only as it exists in semi-invariant form throughout the adult life of the animal, but still more in the processes by which it comes into being as the animal develops out of the egg. He is, therefore, concerned with a pathway of change, which can be thought of as the line in phase space which describes the time-trajectory along which the developmental processes will proceed.

Now, it is an observed empirical fact that such developmental time-trajectories exhibit a property which can be compared to stability. That is to say, if by some experimental intervention we change the conditions of a developing system, e.g. by cutting a piece off an embryo or otherwise altering it, there is usually a very strong tendency for the disturbed processes to change in such a way that they eventually come back to a further point along the trajectory they had originally been following. We see this in many sorts of phenomena, in regeneration and regulation of defects. If a developing system is in conditions in which it can develop at all, it usually shows a strong tendency to develop into its normal end-result, more or less independently of what insults it may have suffered on the way there. The time-trajectory in phase space is therefore surrounded by a region, like a cylinder, which represents all that range of altered conditions which can be compensated for. Another visual model one can make is to picture the time-trajectory as a stream running down the bottom of the valley; if the water is diverted from its normal course up one hillside, it will find its way down again and join the stream bed at some later point.

The concept of stabilised time-trajectories of this kind arises very naturally in biology. Rather surprisingly, it seems to have been little developed in the physical sciences, although there are aspects of those, for instance in Chemical Engineering, which involve just the same kind of logical structures. In biology the word "chreod", derived from two Greek words meaning "necessary path" has been introduced as a short and convenient name for such stabilised developmental pathways.

Now a chreod could be described in quite another language. Instead of saying that a system is following a chreod, one could say that the system exhibits a tendency to reach a defined goal or endpoint. Man can, of course, easily design such systems. The principles of their design are now usually referred to by the fashionable term Cybernetics. They involve the invention and building of suitable self-correcting control mechanisms involving feedback. Good examples are the automatic pilots that will fly a plane along a preset flight path, or the target-tracking anti-aircraft gunsight, which is designed to track an aircraft and shoot a shell to the position where the aircraft will be by the time the shell gets there.

The relevance of ideas like this to the subject we are discussing becomes clearer if one uses still another type of language to describe them. One could say that systems which tend to attain a definite goal exhibit an unconscious purpose. The behaviours of an automatic pilot, of a target-tracking gunsight, or of an embryo, exhibit all the characteristics of an activity guided by a purpose, except, of course, that the systems are not conscious, and cannot possess anything with the character of a conscious human intention. Their purposes must be unconscious purposes, but that does not prevent them having all the other characteristics of purpose.

This would not, perhaps, be a very important conclusion if we continued to believe that there is an absolute distinction between the world of facts and the world of human purposes. The philosophy of the last few centuries has been dominated by the twin dogmas: Hume's disjunction between "is" and "ought"; and the Cartesian dualism which asserts a total separation between matter and mind. As Monod pointed out yesterday, Hume and Descartes were concerned to refute an Aristotelian or animistic ontology, and to clear the way for Newtonian science relying on material causality. But that was three centuries ago. The biological investigations that have been made since then into the mechanisms of perception, by which alone we come in contact with the world, show the matter in rather a different light.

Consider vision, which is our most important mode of perception. What actually happens? We find ourselves undergoing an experience, in which we can see, and recognise, a particular thing or fact. We learn that light waves emitted from the object are focussed by the lens of the eye to form an image on the retina. But how are the properties of this image correlated with those of the object from which the light waves were emitted? We now know that the eyeball is continually jiggling about, so that the retina is in continuous motion and the image is continually wobbling about from one cell to another. Again, in front of the retina, in the path of the rays coming through the lens, there are retinal arteries which must interrupt the image; and the retina is a two-dimensional surface, and yet we normally see things in three dimensions; finally, every time we see some well recognised object, such as the face of a friend, we see it in the somewhat different light and from a different angle of vision than we ever did before. Yet, in spite of all these apparent impediments to the formation of a clearcut retinal image comparable to a photograph in a camera, we show a great ability to recognise definite objects, particularly if they are well-known within our visual experience.

Perhaps the best way of expressing this situation is to say that the visual entities to which we give names are, in fact, chreodic systems. They are self-stabilising structures within a multi-dimensional space of variations. Each system consists of a "centre of attraction", which controls a certain volume of the variation-space around it. Any visual experience which falls into the area controlled by a given centre of attraction is attracted into the centre. If we see something which is reasonably like the face of our friend John, then we say "yes, that's John's face", even if we have never seen it under these lighting conditions or from that angle before.

Now, as was said above, the concept of a self-stabilising system is very closely akin to that of an unconscious purpose. We must, therefore, come to the conclusion that something with the same logical structure as an unconscious purpose is involved in the very process of perception.

The early scientific world was dominated by the physical sciences, and based its philosophy on the supposition that man comes simply face to face with a world of hard external facts, in that he can make a clear distinction between the subjective and the objective; and it asserted that the latter is the only topic for scientific discussion. This has led us to the present physico-technological world, in which so many people fear that they will find themselves, their whole person, reduced to a numbered entry in a computer memory store. I think the biological sciences would argue that the situation is quite different. We start by having experiences, and in the attempt to analyse these into components which can usefully be sorted out and manipulated, processes similar to unconscious purposes (chreodic processes) play an essential part. We cannot recognise anything in perception without some participation of our own mental system of attractive centres controlling areas of variation. There can be no total separation of the subjective and objective. For such a philosophy, which holds that in the last resort they can be nothing which is just a "thing", there would be little temptation to try to reduce human beings to the level of things.

It is against this background that we have to approach the subject of human values and conscious purposes. Man carries out many sequences of behaviour that are chreodic in the sense that they incorporate an unconscious purpose. If you run downstairs to answer a telephone, your conscious purpose may be to answer a question you know will be put to you; but your actions involve an enormously elaborate set of muscular movements, adjustments of your centre of gravity, and length of stride, and so on. These are all embedded in a self-stabilising chreod, which can probably cope with slight stumbles and get you to the bottom of the stairs without falling. This is a typical unconscious purpose; but in man such purposes can become fully conscious, and in this instance would in fact do so if you had recently sprained your ankle, and had to think very carefully about how to walk without putting undue strain on it.

Now one can use the word "value" in a general sense, when it would be equivalent to "the goal of a purpose". More usually, however, and in the context in which we are speaking here, we use the word to mean an *ethical* value, or a value in a closely related field such as aesthetics. The values are then the goals of a particular class of human purposes. Moreover, we usually use the word to refer to a rather broadly defined goal, which may be relevant to a large number of more particular and restricted purposes. Some of these purposes would be conscious ones, but a broadly defined value, such as "truth", may be relevant to many actions in which we do not explicitly and consciously number it amongst the goals. This makes "value" a more comprehensive notion to discuss than "purpose" in connection with the human system of ethics.

What then is the particular character of that class of purposes or goals which we subsume under the name of ethical values, and how do they arise? It is clear that there are many conscious human purposes, such as winning a game of chess, or getting the best value for money when buying a new motor car, which do not involve anything we should call an *ethical* value. What is the distinction? I have argued[1] that the particular character of ethical values is defined by their developmental involvement with the processes by which the human individual becomes a functioning part of a new type of evolutionary process, based on the cultural, or socio-genetic, transmission of information from one generation to the next, which is the major distinction which separates man from the other animals. The developing human individual becomes an "ethical animal" by the operation of the same processes as those by which he becomes a member of a species with a socio-genetically transmitted system of evolution. I am not certain whether the association of these two processes, of making-ethical and making-cultural, are logically necessarily combined; what I am arguing is that in fact they happen to be combined in this world as we know it.

To the biologist, the most important characteristic of the human species— so important indeed that it could be used to define what is human as against what is animal—is that man has developed this second system of transmitting information from one generation to the next. All animals, including man, transmit information through the DNA in their gametes. Man in addition transmits information in the form of conceptual thoughts encoded into language, either verbal or written. There are, of course, anticipatory adumbrations of such cultural transmission to be discovered amongst animals—bees, birds, the higher vertebrates that nurture and tutor their young, —but it is only the human species which has developed its capacity to formulate abstract concepts, and arbitrary symbols into which they are encoded, sufficiently to have at its disposal an effectively new system of herediti and therefore of evolution. There is no reason to believe, in fact there is every reason to doubt, that the evolutionary changes which, since the period of paleolithic hunters, have produced man of today, capable of flying faster and higher than any bird, of living in a greater range of terrestrial and marine environments than any single species of animal or fish, and capable also of experiences of the kind we might symbolise in the names of Shakespeare, Bach and Rembrandt, has depended to any important extent on changes in the DNA transmitted through his genes—although, of course, many such changes have probably occurred during this time. Man has not escaped from the pressures of biological evolutionary processes dependent on natural selection of genes, but he has added to these a new dimension of evolution based on cultural transmission, which is incomparably more rapid in its operation, and which dominates the whole area of his positive advances.

The achievement of a reasonably efficient social mechanism for transmitting information is man's greatest evolutionary triumph. That is not to say that the mechanism is easily acquired or maximally efficient. For it to work at all, it is necessary that each individual human being should be brought to realise that certain sounds, or certain black squiggles on paper, are to be understood as *symbols,* which convey meanings. Much of the process by which the individual is made capable of taking part in the socio-genetic transmission system is carried out in the first few months after birth. It has been argued recently by some linguists, e.g. Chomsky, that the present-day human beings have already at birth, some inborn linguistic abilities. Genes determining such characteristics of the nervous system would have little selective advantage, and little chance to spread through the population, until such time as lanquage actually became used. It seems most probable that in the initial stages of the development of language the whole training of the individual in its use must have taken place after birth. There is clearly an enormous selective advantage in being able to use language efficiently, and the selection for the ability to learn language would be expected to lead, by the process that I have named genetic assimilation, to the fixation of such abilities in the genotype. It is in this way that one can understand how the inate abilities referred to by Chomsky might have arisen. They would be a secondary refinement of what had initially been a wholly phenotypic adaptive process.

The training of the newly born human individual to realise that certain sounds and sights are symbols occurs in conjunction with another lesson it must learn at this time, namely, to behave as a member of a social group. The newly born human baby must be an almost pure solipsist, scarcely able to distinguish self from not self, and with no awareness that there are other people to whose lives and wishes it must accomodate its own. Into this individualistic, solipsistic paradise there burst simultaneously socially accepted symbols (language) and socially accepted norms of behaviour. Essentially the baby learns to become a member of the socially transmitting community by hearing its parents or others saying "no". This is the most important lesson it will ever learn, but it is also easy to understand that it must be one of the most traumatic. The lessons come from outside what must seem to be an all inclusive I-centred solipsistic universe. It is probably for this reason that the rules governing these aspects of social conduct which are transmitted to the child in its very first weeks of life are so often given a transcendental or supernatural authority. It is these values which acquire the peculiar character which we label as "ethical" and which we feel tempted to grant a status beyond the reach of rational criticism. And it is because they are associated with these all important social rules that certain sounds are accepted as words symbolising meanings.

The process of "making cultural" and "making ethical", crudely speaking "works". Man can succeed in evolving by cultural means. But it is easy to see that the processes might be much more efficient than they are. They tend to leave everyone attaching more authority to ethical values than is their due. We all have some hankering after absolute Good, much more than we have after any other absolute. I have discussed this at some length in my book *The Ethical Animal* and I shall not pursue the matter further here. I will only say that it seems to me that it is in the imperfections and exaggerations of these culturalising and ethicalising processes that we should seek the explanation of the evil side of man's character. Koestler has argued that man suffers from an inbuilt anatomical defect in his nervous system, which produces his destructive and aggressive characteristics. I would not deny that there may conceivably be some inbuilt neural defect of this kind; but if there is, I think it would have arisen in much the same way as the neural bases for linguistic ability about which Chomsky speaks, i.e. by selection for what was originally wholly a developmental reaction to external circumstances. The basis for the "dark side" of man lies in the imperfections of the new evolutionary mechanism he has developed; and it is a second order question whether or not some genetic predisposition in this direction has by now been built into his genotype.

The argument so far has run through two stages: that something akin to an unconscious purpose is built into the very act of perception by which we distinguish items in our experience and is therefore an inescapable part of the world of fact; and that the process by which the developing human individual acquires the ability to take part in socio-genetic transition of information also endow him with a set of conscious purposes of the particular character we recognise as ethical. We now need to approach the question, what types of ethical values would this point of view lead us to choose. Monod argued that the choice of an ethical system is like the choice of a set of axioms on which to found mathematics. Without necessarily fully agreeing I will, for the moment, adopt this point of view. And I would point out that, although in mathematics we are free to choose whether to build up our geometry on Euclidian or a variety of non-Euclidian axioms, when we need to deal with the world of objects of the size of our own bodies, we find that it is the Euclidian axioms which are by far the most appropriate. They are so appropriate, indeed, that we almost certainly have some genetic predisposition to their adoption built into our genotypes, eg. the capacity of the eye to recognise a straight line.

I should like to argue that something of the same kind is very probably true of ethical axioms. If we wish to develop an ethical system which we can apply to human life as we know it, there are probably some ethical axioms which we are almost forced to incorporate. They would be the common ground which we find between all the major ethical systems of different religions and groups of mankind—such values as truth, respect for self, respect for others, and respect for something larger and more embracing than one's immediate experience (God? Mankind? The whole creative universe?). I suspect that for these too the human race has by now acquired some built in genetic predisposition. If he has the "engineering fault" in his nervous system referred to by Koestler, it seems equally plausible to suggest that he has a similarly built in predisposition towards certain ethical values which have the same degree of general relevance to human society as do the Euclidian axioms of geometry to the material world. The point to my mind is not so much the degree to which these two types of reaction to the socialising-ethicalising process have been as yet genetically assimilated; what is important is that this process has this dual-aspect, of light and dark, of positive and negative.

The best summary of this point of view is the story of the fall of man in the Garden of Eden. It was by eating of the fruits of the tree of Knowledge (cultural transmission of information) in the context of sexual reproduction (which must include the rearing of a family) that Adam and Eve came to the knowledge of Good and Evil (values and anti-values).

Note

1 Waddington, C. H., *The Ethical Animal,* 1960.

Social and Psychological Change, Human Needs in Developing Countries of Africa

By T. Adeoye Lambo

University of Ibadan, Nigeria

First of all, I should like to express my deep appreciation to the Organizing Committee and the Nobel Foundation for asking me to participate in the Nobel Symposium. I believe this symposium will not only play a vital role in promoting and further activating our intellectual and academic disciplines but will also reinforce the ideals and goals that are common to us, thereby deepening our international understanding. A Symposium on Alfred Nobel's ideals in the light of changing values could certainly generate an acceptance and a sense of belonging to a world community dedicated and committed to certain social values and having a purpose and allegiance greater than national achievement or aspiration.

It is my honour and privilege to speak for the African continent. I am here not only in my personal capacity, but also as a representative of many societies on the African continent undergoing transitional stress. In spite of our diversities, violent political and other institutional changes, instability of value system, and symptoms of extreme state of flux, the peoples of Africa have a lot in common with other societies differing greatly with respect to both culture and conditions of life; certainly we share the same basic human aspirations: to banish ignorance, poverty and hunger and to relieve distress and exalt human dignity. This would seem to fall in line with Pauling's doctrine of minimization of suffering.

Africa is the second largest continent on the globe and claims one quarter of the world's land surface. It has the highest concentration of underdeveloped and rapidly developing societies. This huge but largely undeveloped continent claims well over 50 of the 125 political units on the globe; it has a rate of progress (political, social, economic) unparalleled in history and shows a remarkable and almost bewilderingly complex diversity of ethnic grouping, culture and potential resources. But its living standards are appallingly low.

In many of their societies, recent economic, political and social changes have influenced considerably the pattern of life, including many of the basic traditional ideologies, and family structure and function. These changes in many cases are leaving permanent reverberations in the value systems of the cultures of Africa. In this phenomenal task of telescoping centuries of social and economic progress of advanced countries to achieve a near-miracle of transformation from subsistence to market economy, from traditional to new social and political norms, the needs (especially social and psychological welfare) of the individual are inadequately met, poorly planned and of low priority. This is in contrast to the sizable investments of limited resources into prestige schemes because of their symbolic value.

It is in the light of these attributes of Africa and my own deep involvement in Africa's contemporary problems of change and vigorous adaptation, for both scientific and human reasons, that I have chosen "Social and Psychological Change, Human Needs in Africa" as my topic for this lecture before this most distinguished audience.

The struggle for social change in developing countries can legitimately be regarded as an extension of a world-wide struggle to create new social norms, to extend human rights and to create measures that would improve the conditions of human life, and ultimately to promote the total well-being of mankind. This inter-national dimension is crucial for the continued viability of developing nations. This convergence of interest should provide the necessary motivation for co-operative international endeavours in this and other areas.

The problems of social change are shared by both the developing and the developed countries, though some of the problems are more pronounced in developing countries, where the demands for social reform, political independence, and new economic structure are producing a pattern of change that is too rapid and disruptive at some points, too slow at others. Many highly developed nations, for example, contain islands or groups within them that are socially and economically disadvantaged; racial, ethnic or cultural minorities that are not fully integrated into the opportunity systems and the political life of the country; and the internal conflicts that inhibit social growth, integration and full and effective participation.

As a citizen of Africa and of the world I feel a particularly strong moral obligation to be concerned with these problems because of the special role which many of the developing nations could play in world affairs,[1] if only they are able to survive, establish their independent identity and generate the impetus for constructive social change—change in the direction of economic development and social justice and of stable political institutions that are legitimately national and optimally democratic. I know that many developed nations have shown a lack of sensitivity to and understanding of the struggle for certain desired and desirable social changes in the developing world. Here, I would like to refer, in passing, to the ethical and moral implications of determining the priorities in development for the emerging nations through technical and other forms of assistance which can and has indeed misfired on many occasions because value preferences are normally implicit in some "technical assistance" programmes and in the "games of Nations" generally—here I borrow Miles Copeland's terminology.[2]

I must apologise for speaking in personal terms but this is necessary not only to make my point clearly but also to demonstrate how difficult it is to work in the area of social and psychological change, or in other areas pregnant with value considerations, as a purely disinterested observer, merely looking at whatever presents itself. I suspect that it is easy to delude ourselves about the disinterested nature of our research when our assumptions reflect the dominant value preferences within our society.

In terms of substantive issues, this paper will focus on certain selected areas, namely, socio-psychological implications of rapid urbanization, industrialization, population movements, adjustment and other adaptational changes of African peoples to Western culture and, lastly, symptoms of adaptational failure in various parts of Africa, especially psycho-social problems arising out of unmet needs. From the point of view of my own work in Africa, the questions on my mind have always been: what can be done to minimize transitional stress, render less harmful and less traumatic the impact of social change, make people accept new standards, new norms— social, economic, political—in the difficult phases of transition from tribal and traditional family controls to modern urban and industrial life and relations? Is it possible to make interaction between traditional norms and economic and social growth lead to mutually reinforcing trends rather than to irrepressible conflict? And, lastly, what changes in attitudes and values of young people would be conducive to the desired institutional changes in our societies in Africa? I should like to emphasize that the spectrum is so diverse and wide that no attempt at detailed treatment will be made in the time given to me for this lecture.

Socio-psychological implications of population-change and movements

It is relevant here to point to the fact that most African countries today have been found to have a high rate of population growth with changing age structure. Variables such as fertility, mortality, sex—and age-composition have been undergoing changes, with notable repercussions in the socio-economic sphere. Studies based on the dynamics between population trends and structure, economic factors and social conditions in the developing countries in relation, for example, to the rates of social morbidity, such as crime and delinquency, are very few. Such studies are essential to elucidate the influence and significance of certain prevailing demographic, economic, and social factors. We are still substantially ignorant of Africa's major potentialities.

It has been reliably estimated that between 35 % to 40 % of the populations of the new African nations are under the age of 15 years. Because of their anticipated fertility rates, they will, by 1975, according to U.N. 'medium' projections, have still larger proportions of their total population under 15 years of age. In view of the fact that there is now a comparatively greater number of people in the lower age-group, the increasing rate of crime and delinquency in certain areas of the population of the developing countries would seem to be due to the increase in the general population at risk.

More important and directly relevant to the subject of this lecture is the fact that such a large proportion of young persons in the population requires that a greater part of the limited resources of these developing countries be allocated to "social" investment rather than to purely economic investment. The presence of such a large proportion of young persons creates many social and psychological problems, namely, the intergenerational gaps between the young and the old and their attendant psychological problems.

Social advances create new demands and many of the ageing and highly tradition-oriented African people lack the necessary physical and emotional resources to adopt a new set of roles and accept transformation of values. There are new concepts of leadership, of power and prestige. There are new social, educational and economic demands, demands for job opportunities, coupled with the readiness of the young to activate change quickly. Unfortunately, the educational systems inherited by many of these emerging nations lack the sensitivity and the thrust to activate a new socio-political ideology for national needs. Therefore, one of the pressing needs of the developing countries is the adaptation of the educational system to national needs. Africa does not only need to emphasize the need for science and technology but the educational system should also encourage the growth of art, poetry, music and other creative talents.

In their present state of economic development—a phase which is fairly technologically static, but during which changes are anticipated in attitudes and institutions necessary for later technological advance—and with the pressure of over-population in some areas, many African countries cannot meet the growing needs of their people. Consequently, many young people are frustrated and bewildered; others turn migrant, seeking opportunities to meet these needs; in many cases, the families stay behind and usually this is the beginning of the disruption and erosion of family ties. The problem of unemployed youth is a growing one in Africa although it is not an uncommon feature of developing countries. Thus the greatest wastage today in Africa lies in the area of human resource. In some countries with intensified social and educational programmes, such as in Southern Nigeria, the imbalance between the pace of social and educational development and the rate of economic growth and opportunities has been acute.

Mass shifts of population from the rural to urban areas continue unabated in Africa and denundation of the rural regions now seems fairly inevitable. Extensive industrial projects (e.g. Volta Dam hydro-electric project in Ghana, the Kainji Dam in Nigeria, the Kariba Dam on the Zambesi, Factories, etc.) attract migrant workers from wide areas around, some temporary during construction and others who will become permanent employees. Camps are usually set up around or near the projects, often in areas where there are few or no opportunities for recreation and young adult workers, with money to spend and no family restrictions, turn to alcohol, drugs, and other "pastimes". Young people all over Africa are on the move to sell their labour and to look for better opportunities.

Instead of vigorous and imaginative plans for guided rural transformation, the rural areas are characterized by imperceptibly slow growth and lack of incentives; general values, attitudes and motivations are directed towards the urban areas. There is less concern for the orderly growth, for the provision of much-needed infrastructure—water, electricity, roads, welfare and social services, educational institutions—at a rate necessary to stem mass movements and drifts from the rural areas. Gordon (1966) in his plan for rural development in Nigeria observes, "The question must be asked why Government and organized society generally in West Africa, view rural poverty, malnutrition and ill-health, with such equanimity or indifference, ..." If we consider rural transformation to be a desirable goal and if some of the elaborate programmes designed to stimulate, for example, agricultural development in some of these countries are considered necessary for the achievement of this goal, more information is required on the current profile of the prevailing social phenomena. It is also necessary to identify what impels, motivates, causes and stimulates the desired change. Greater analytical treatment of the situation, rather than the traditionally descriptive approach, is needed to understand and feel the forces at work.

In many African urban areas, especially the newly-evolved, stable social structures are lacking and, because of this, urbanism has been incriminated as one of the main causes of increased rates of crime, delinquency, and breakdown of law and order. This notion is not strictly true. The main error resides in the fact that comparison with tribal social life is often (and unconsciously) made when analysing certain features of urban social life. In doing this, there is always the primary assumption that urban phenomena are usually destructive and full of problems. This assumption is false. However, an individual who comes from the rural environment to an urban area may discover that his behaviour pattern is not appropriate and might have to alter his custom and adopt new habits so as to participate in urban institutions and structures.

One of the most important findings of our recent work, however, is that social disorganization of the primary institutions is more prevalent in urban areas than in the tribal culture. It is the dissolution, fragmentation, and lack of functional capacity of the primary social institutions (i.e. family) in the towns which form the core of many social problems, such as employment instability, political and social disturbance, and educational maladjustment. We now have at least some reasonably unanimous evidence incriminating the impact of rapid social change and scientists working in other countries (Odegaard, 1932,[3] 1945,[4] 1961,[5] Jaco, 1957[6]) have produced overwhelming evidence to show that migration to a metropolitan area or main city of a country may have a more adverse effect on mental health than migration elsewhere. Lambo (1962)[7] coined the term "malignant anxiety" as overt emotional and psychological reactions to rapid socio-cultural change experienced by individuals psychologically ill-equipped and who were partially or wholly divorced from their primary or corporate groups.

There are many ecological and other features of the urban setting that are contributary to social disorganization. With regard to the family life, the structure and functions of the urban setting are not always desirable, especially for the newcomers with economic problems. In many African metropolitan areas, zoning was created by the colonial powers, leading to creation of segregated areas and the creation of "neutral zones". In the post-colonial era, with rapid social, political and technological change, involving rapid industrialization, concomitant development of many satellite communities has taken place on the periphery of large towns (e.g. squatters in Kinshasa); others have remained and expanded since the colonial times (native "communes" in Dakar and in the middle of Kinshasa), and these communities have provided "laboratories" for special studies of all features of social disintegration.

In the light of our recent observations, some of the special psycho-social features of a peri-urban setting studied showed lack of support for coping with typical stresses, disrupted communication, lack of empathy, diffuse and vague identification with social groups because of the amorphous social structure of the family and the group in urban areas. Under these conditions of institutional change and transition, such areas as childrearing and development have also undergone profound change. For example, in many urban homes, especially of the newly arrived, mental and emotional factors in the development of the child are not given full play. There is no consistency of relationships, there is an impaired balance of acting out, mastery and love; evidence of other defects in many aspects of child-rearing related to emotional security, optimal mental development and expression of drives is often present. Stimulation and opportunity for sensory, motor and integrative experience in the environment are considerably reduced.

Here, I should like to refer briefly to the findings of our earlier work (Leighton, Lambo et al. 1963)[8] which showed that change *per se* did not necessarily provoke disastrous psychological reactions but that the determining factor which provoked adverse reactions was the violent impact which caused disorganization or disintegration within the community and, more potently, within the family groups. Using the indices of crime, delinquency, alcoholism, sociopathy and strives, high prevalence was associated with areas of socio-cultural disintegration, in contrast to integrated communities which showed lowest rates. Socio-cultural disintegration was characterized in these communities by breakdown of affective communication, economic pressure, dis-socialization, insecurity, conflicts of value system, confusion of social roles, problems of identification with the group, to mention only a few. It is important to note that lowest prevalence of these 'symptoms' of adaptational failure was found in areas—rural or urban—in which change has occurred in such a manner as to permit, through the process of social symbiosis, the replacement or fusion of certain traditional patterns with new ones that are equally stable and functionally meaningful. Adaptation has also been found to be successful and individuals found to be free from a sense of social isolation, social insecurity and anxiety in situations where transferred traditional institutions and cultural patterns have been effectively utilized to promote effective inner cohesion.

Adjustment and adaptational changes of African peoples to the impact of Western culture

The three phenomena—population increase, changing age structure of the population, and population movements, especially from rural to urban areas —have been incriminated as being at the root of most current psychosocial problems in Africa.There are innumerable areas in which adaptation— partial or full—has occurred. The legal system and judicial practices, individual as opposed to collective ownership of property, personal as opposed to collective responsibility for liability, new political and economic system, new social structures and concepts, the new status of women in all spheres of activity and the gradual disappearance of the extended family, are glaring examples of features of modern African society.

One of the most striking features of the traditional cultures of Africa is their flexibility, adaptability and other built-in factors for maintaining a high degree of socio-cultural homoestasis in the face of many major and rapid changes. Most of these cultures seem to have a high threshold of tolerance for rate and impact of change and, measured by the rate of integration of western ways of life and values, these cultures would seem to be highly responsive to new opportunities, new demands and new experiences and this may be partially due to the high need for social achievement inherent selectivity in the traditional African cultures. In some instances, traditional organizations have been reinforced by modern techniques—proper accounting of money and written records of proceedings at meeting (Lloyd, 1959).[9]

This inherent property of thriving in the midst of difficulties, of showing capacity for positive and constructive growth under stress, of ability to promote spontaneous resolution of conflict, and of mimicking other cultures has been termed by me "psychological rebound phenomenon". The same characteristic is manifestly displayed in the basic psychological structure of the African peoples. The overpowering vitality of these cultures is reflected by the African emphasis on life and not only life *here and now* but life transcendental—the basis of ancestor worship.

This phenomenon has proved to be the determining factor for maintaining an overall good mental health within the population in spite of the continual social disruption and instability of the social institutions which are constantly under stress. This is clearly shown in the way individuals have absorbed new secular types of religions and the cultures have evolved others which are manifestly syncretic in their structure, and in the minimal psychological impact of a disruptive kind which the introduction of western educational system has had. The remarkable ability of certain Africans to assume and mimic western values and behaviour with precision in their day-to-day lives and the readiness with which these values can be shed under stress shows this attribute of the cultures clearly. These psychological attitudes and behaviour proved to be one of the greatest obstacles to the development of creative, imaginative and independent ideas in the immediate period of the post-colonial era.

On the other hand, the vigour and the vitality as well as the durability of the traditional institutions are responsible for their persistence and for causing perennial conflicts and continuities between existing systems of values and new social, political, and economic institutions. They are also responsible for the slow evolution of national identity and overall political idiology and for the negligible changes in value and beliefs in those sensitive areas on which the cultures have laid down precise "prescriptions" and guidelines, (e.g. tribal politics, intergroup relations), which tend to impede the development of stable and shared social values and the evolution of national purpose and allegiance greater than tribal or sectional interest.

Educational efforts would have to be directed at identifying the most constructive ways in which tribal identity can be functionally integrated and can strengthen national institutions, and the ways in which international participation can advance the national cause. The development of a stable political system, durable social values, presupposes some conception of nationhood and ideological commitment to the state.

Before drawing this lecture to a close, I will attempt to formulate the overall strategy for promoting greater well-being, i.e. freedom from insecurity and fear, in emerging societies of Africa. The crucial question is; what techniqes of change can be developed and used in the attempt to build new patterns, new values, that would minimize friction and the use of violence? There is no grand and all-inclusive design to take care of all contingencies.

The individual's integration into the larger group, his acceptance of his assigned new role, may depend on how the larger group (system) facilitates the performance of his various other roles, and the satisfaction of his social and psychological needs. He should have the opportunities to take part in social planning and social change, to be creative, to take initiative and to be rewarded for doing so. We must not overlook the fact that one of the fundamental human needs is for security and dignity. Today, fear is the most dominant psychological obstacle in the effort to relate and integrate many diverse groups, interests and attitudes in Africa. Here I refer to M. J. Field's outstanding work in Ghana, *The Search for Security*. This fear (and suspicion) constitutes a threat to human relations, to positive and creative growth of institutions, so vast as to dwarf any other.

It may be necessary in order to allay anxiety and promote security to regard the entire "social system" as made up of separate, independent subsystems each with its own characteristics and functions. Each system may have its unique form of organization and inter-relationships. Each has its own history and heritage. But while these sub-systems have these unique characteristics, they are also related to and dependent on each other in a number of important ways. The crucial function of integration will be brought about by the people themselves—people who have the capacity and the motivation to effect change in themselves and in the institutional structure. I am sure this is a struggle of which we would like to be a part and to which we would want to contribute in the best way we can and that is the reason why we are all here.

The African societies are in state of social and psychological flux. They are ambivalent (deep resentment and suspicion, co-existing with a paradoxical sense of paternity) in their relationships both within and without the groups but, in my view, the prognosis augurs well for the future as we begin to see some evidence of acceptance of national awareness, national loyalties, and national role. The sense of psychological optimism and omnipotence of thought that characterized the early phase of political independence almost a decade ago (and which equated political independence with economic and social freedom and property) suddenly gave way to a sense of severe frustration, despair, apathy and pessimism leading to internal strives and crisis. This is now being replaced by a sense of realism, with emphasis on co-ordinated planning and on transforming man and his values and, lastly, on making the evolving institutions goal-seeking.

Africa, towards the end of this century, should begin to evolve stable and serious leadership, new socio-political values and beliefs and new ideology that will pay extremely high dicidents. If this prediction is realized, then the psychological effects of the conflicts and continuities between existing systems of values and evolving social, political and economic structures, would be desirable and promotive.

Notes

1 Worsley, P., *The Third World,* London, 1965.
2 Copeland, M., *The Games of Nations,* Weidenfeld & Nicolson, London.
3 Odegaard, O., *Acta Psychiat. Neurol.,* Supplement 4, 1, 1932.
4 Odegaard, O., *Acta Psychiat. Neurol., 20,* 274, 1945.
5 Odegaard, O., In: Lambo, T. A., ed. *Proceedings of the First Pan African Psychiatric Conference,* Abeokuta, Nigeria, 1961.
6 Jaco, E. G., Social Factors in Mental Disorders in Texas, *Soc. Prob. 4,* 322, 1957.
7 Lambo, T. A., *J. Ment. Sci.,* 1962.
8 Leighton, A., Lambo, T. A. *et al., Psychiatric Disorder Among the Yoruba.* New York, Cornell Medical Press, 1963.
9 Lloyd, P. C., "The Yoruba Towns Today", *Sociological Review,* vii, 1959.

Reason, Prejudice and Intuition

By Jerome S. Bruner

Center for Cognitive Studies, Harvard University, Cambridge, Mass., U.S.A.

It was the fashion and the pose of 19th century Science to draw a sharp line between fact and value on the one hand and empiricism and "pure thought" on the other. Fact was the coin of Science, empiricism was the method by which it was minted. To treat matters of less than fact and to do so speculatively was, of course, perfectly respectable—so long as he who did so had no illusions whatsoever about the relevance of what he was doing for science. For it had no relevance. How better to recapture that attitude than to quote one note of Humboldt, commenting in 1881 on J. R. Mayer's brilliant effort to show the logical necessity of the mechanical equivalent of heat:

Lately, the followers of metaphysical speculations have tried to stamp the Law of the Conservation of Energy as an *a priori* valid one and they are celebrating J. R. Mayer as a hero in the field of pure thought. What these people consider as the zenith of Mayer's contribution, namely, the metaphysically formulated would-be proofs for the *a priori* necessity of this last, will be considered the weakest point of his argument in the eyes of anyone who is used to the severe scientific method of the natural scientist. This must have been the grounds for his work having remained unknown in the circles of natural scientists. (*Wissenschaftliche Abhandlung,* Leipzig, 1882, vol. 1, p. 68.)

Times have changed and, indeed, the theoretical physicist may even have become top dog in "the circles of natural scientists". The revolutions of Mach, of Einstein, of Bohr have, at least for the insider, changed radically the need for a "cordon sanitaire" between things derived from thought and things derived from observation. But what persists is the sharp line indeed the deep moat that exists in our minds, between matters of knowing and matters of valuing. And so, in Stockholm in 1969, we can appropriately hold a learned symposium on the subject "The Place of Value in a World of Facts" (or, as it might equally well have been put, "The Place of Fact in a World of Values"). And each of us senses in a troubled way that by virtue of the separation we have gone astray. Let me examine this question, first technically as a student of human information processing, and then culturally as an intellectual engaged in the values of his times.

Let me say first that virtually everything we have found out about the nervous system in the last quarter century, in the fine and in the gross, speaks against any conception of "neutrality" either in the way we obtain information or put it together for the guidance of action. It was Lord Adrian who, at the Laurentian Symposium in the early 50's, put the matter well when he remarked that each time nerve impulses entered a synoptic nucleus enroute from a sense organ to the brain, they underwent editing. This is not the occasion to pass in detailed review the editorial policies of the human nervous system, but since in their collectivity they constitute its immanent prejudicial routines, we must pause for a quick sampling of the bias of neural activity.

To begin with, the sense organs at the very periphery all seem to be governed by sharpening-up routines. Contours of stimulation are sharpened in the retina, we know from Granit's[1] pioneering work, and the touch sense is particularly remarkable in being transformed from neural perturbation in form of a graded deformation of the skin and its receptors to a sharp representation of boundary.[2] We are biased in spatial senses to sharp contours and objects. There is also ample evidence in various sense departments that stimulation by no means consists simply of arousal of sense organs from outside, with selectivity occurring by processes that operate on the centralward route. There are also centrifugal impulses from the central nervous system to the sense organs and quite peripheral synapses that turn the sense organ gain up and down selectivity as required by internal state —as illustrated in a variety of studies e.g. Lindsley (1958),[3] Galambos (1956),[4] Hernandez-Péon (1956)[5] and others. At still another level, there is provision for giving priority to those forms of stimulation that diverge from stored neural models of the organism's usual environment, and the activating system of the reticular foundation mediates highly selective orienting reactions when something new or different is encountered.[6, 7] Along the same line, it is now necessary to consider, in the operation of feedback, not only the role of stimulation from outside, exafference as von Holst and Mittelstaedt[8] has called it, but also the corollary discharge that carries information of intention, reafference. For the latter form of nervous discharge not only provides forewarning and lead time to the sensory and motor systems that makes it easy to distinguish between shaking a stick ourselves and being shaken by one, but also provides a criterion for judging whether the shaking is going as intended and/or expected. In short, the *requirements of action* play an important role in governing neural selectivity as well, and we know from the pioneering studies such as those of Held[9] that acquisition of useful knowledge of the environment cannot be achieved unless there is intended action into the context of which stimulation from the senses can be put. It is the discrepancy between intention and attainment—the difference between "Istwert" and "Sollwert"—that provides the data for correction. Add to these prejudicial mechanisms another that inheres in the rather limited capacity of the nervous system to process information—the fact that it can handle at any given moment about 7 ± 2 independent events and that the length of the moment in question is somewhat less than a few seconds for material to get recorded for accessible long term storage or be lost and become inaccessible thereafter. The mode of coping with this highly limiting property of the nervous system is to chunk information into models, to make swift inference from incomplete data lest the whole lot get lost, and to stay set for those sources of information that either guide the enterprise that is in progress or give a hint that the venue is about to change.

Finally, it is by now quite plain that the nature of the models in terms of which information is ordered and stored is highly preadapted and reflects a long history of primate evolution. And while it is true that language and culture provide man an enormous flexibility for reordering and regrouping his knowledge of the environment, here again there are strong predispositions to see things in terms of invariant causal relationships, to structure events out of ongoing processes, to use the forms of grammatical syntax in such a way that, as many since Humboldt[10] have pointed out, we read our symbolic forms into nature—or, rather, can only easily experience those aspects of nature that conform to them (for example, as *topic* & *comment* as in predication). Language is "second signal system" that frees us from stimulus control. So that surely the conclusion must be that in the nature of things, man, like other animals is highly prejudiced in his acquisition of knowledge, is specialized in imposing highly selective forms on a world of stimulation, and has a nervous system massively dedicated to carrying out his intentions and furthering his values. Surely, it cannot be the human nervous system that gives warrant to sharp distinctions between fact and preference, between reason and intuition, between rational and irrational. In the nervous system, intention precedes information gain. Let me turn now to another clue.

The great Dutch physicist, Kramers, is quoted by Tisza as follows:

In the world of human thought generally and in physical science particularly, the most fruitful concepts are those to which it is impossible to attach a well-defined meaning.

It would be hard to deny the point. There is some deep sense in which certain rich ideas compel a clarification and elaboration that is astonishing in its effectiveness. The history of science and the history of philosophy almost depend on such ambiguities for their shaping. Perhaps it is in the process whereby we generate powerful and dispassionate consequences from ideas-in-flux that we can find the means by which men develop a separation between fact and the context of reason on the one hand and value and the context of preference on the other. I rather suspect that there is some little understood technology of thought that separates the two domains and that will concern us eventually. In the main, the process consists, as we all know, of finding techniques for increasing the independence of that which is known or to be known from the knower. It involves creating a powerful fiction concerning an external world with deep regularities and a series of techniques that make the task of transmitting knowledge about this hypothesized world manageable. Criteria of proof, consistency, sufficiency of evidence, indeed of clarity itself become increasingly free of the individual inquirer and in certain respects become conventionalized and simplified in a fashion to make room for the journey-man as well as the genius in science—although the two play quite different roles. The great American philosopher C. S. Pierce wrote a famous paper in the logic of science just about a century ago with the beguiling title, "How to make our ideas clear". Its power, like that of much public science, was precisely to bring science-making within the reach of the intelligent journey-man whose way could be paved by the important advice that his propositions must be reducible to an "if ... then" form if they are to be amenable to test. Meanwhile, the genius could go on generating the concepts to which, in Kramer's phrase, "it is impossible to attach a well-defined meaning".

The striking thing about science as a program of thought and observation is that, given at the outset the prejudicial nature of human thought and information processing, science should have been so fantastically successful in isolating one feature of knowing from the prejudicial content of the whole. By its very transmissible nature it could become a socially organized craft. It took a novelist, Herman Wouk, to get at the essence of military organization, putting into the mouth of a character in *The Caine Mutiny* the plaint, "The Navy is a system devised by geniuses for execution by idiots." So too with science: it too can be executed with decorum by men of tunnel vision provided there are also those who can see to the hilltops dimly.

But what gives science its broader impact, its eventual dominance, is not simply that it constructs the model of a world that is invariant across different knowers and observers, but rather that this model is predictive of whatever it is that it chooses to study—call it reality, for that seems to be the common term. This is the metaphysical puzzle, and however it is resolved, it is quite plain that since prediction leads to control, science soon carries over into the design and control of our environment, so that man becomes the first organism to shape the habitat in which he is to live and to alter his own capacities by developing amplifiers and prosthetic devices for his senses, his muscles, his reflective and ratiocinative activities. (Newton's image was the voyage of discovery that eventually found the islands of truth.) At this point in ontogenetic history, evolution becomes Lamarchian and reversible (though it has cultural ratchets) rather than Darwinian and virtually irreversible.

One of the most perplexing things about the growth of science, given its slow emergence from the rich confusion of human prejudice, is that it could pose eventually as neutral, as valuefree, as transcending human prejudice. The claim, of course, was based on the ground that science was a description of reality—Newton's *hypothesis non fingo* or Humboldt's extraordinary assumption that one needed only empirical observation to "recognize" the Law of the Conservation of Energy. Today, we would be far more likely to accept the thesis that *any* construction of the universe, including that of science, is selective, is premised on certain axioms and perforce must leave out of account certain crucial features of experience in the interest of discovering invariant properties of others. Science is one way of knowing, and a highly special achievement it is. But, in no sense does it annul the other powerful processes of ordering experience, indeed may make no contact with them at all. Niels Bohr, true to the principle of complementarity, told me of his difficulty in applying the principle of fairness to his children: "You cannot know someone at the same time in the light of love and in the light of justice," And so it is between various ways of knowing. There is an irreducibility from a psychological point of view that makes the claim of reductionism not so much vain as absurd. But I do not wish therefore to leap to the conclusion that fact and value are isolated and inimical and constitute a hopeless gap. Yet before turning to this matter directly, there is one last matter to consider.

It is, of course, the issue of technology and *its* neutrality from values. For just as science made its claim to neutrality with respect to values, so too did the technologist, riding the coattails of the new Objectivism. Technology, went the claim, is neutral in the sense that it can be used for any ends, in behalf of any values, and is subject to revision of objectives on call. Today, there is widespread doubt as to whether this is indeed anywhere near the truth, for what is most characteristic of technology is that its operation always requires an institutional restructuring of the society that uses it—cadres, corporate enterprises (private or public), even new social classes. And these in turn develop a dynamism and an ethic of their own that are far from neutral. One also wonders then, as the young of today quite justifiably do, whether science itself may have inherent in it this same initially invisible consequence about the proper conduct of life, the appropriate organization of society, and an adequate deployment of pre-judice and passion.

In any case, the consequence of science and technology, as far as the beliefs of many people are concerned, can be roughly summed up in the following terms. Science increasingly holds up for praise a criterion of truth and of significance that transcends individual preference and passion. If truth then is objective, impersonal, and universal, then it must somehow be in opposition to what is subjective, personal, and particular. So that the oppositional contrast to objective science must be personal relevance.

With respect to technology, it originally held out the promise that where before we were subject to fate, now we bring the environment under our own control. But who is the "we" in this statement? For it now may be the case that to use the fruits of technology, we must organize the society in a fashion that demands a higher level of human and social organization than we are prepared to accept. Or if this is not the case, then it is true that the basic *human* issue in technology is not so much the tools as the sociological decisions we make to use them. We dare not use tools any longer simply because they are there, for that has turned out to be a too dangerous mortgage to buy. So, in the main, science appears to have had the effect on many people that it leads them to feel their personal experience is more remote than ever from the universal truths about the objective world. And technology, rather than fulfilling its promise to replace fate with human control, has managed to make many people feel more impotent as cogs in the social machine than ever before. One becomes the more concerned about this turn of events since it appears to involve an alienation of the young at a point in their lives when they should feel a lift at the prospect of taking control of the society.

What can one say about the future of reason, belief and intuition where science and values are concerned? I should like to argue that the present ferment is truly revolutionary and not another example of a Luddite reaction against technical innovation based on a selfish desire to hold one's own or even to hold one's own position at the center of some psychological universe. And here I must go back to the beginning of our discussion and our delineation of the prejudicial context of the nervous system. It was the American psychologist Edward Tolman who made the remark a generation ago that "behaviour reeks with purpose". I have been struck anew these last several years in my studies of the development of sensorimotor competence in human infancy that intention precedes instrumental achievement. Even before the infant in the opening months of life can use his hands under visual guidance, appropriate objects visually presented at appropriate distances evoke coordinated anti-gravitational activity in the trunk and shoulders and a working of the mouth—the eventual destination of objects first grasped. It is an organizing intention that gives initial shape to subsequently organized skill. Again, this is quite consistent with the selective bids of the nervous system.

Let me suggest that the revolution through which we are now living has something of the same order about it. The tension that exists today grows precisely from the fact that the means and the methods we have devised seem increasingly to be determining our purpose, rather than our purposes determining the choice of means to their attainment. We are questioning in a new way such old ideals as science for its own sake. This is not to say that the forming values of science—e.g. the habit of truth—are at issue but rather to inquire whether in social fact science is or ever could be exclusively or principally conducted for its own sake. Given, say, the importance of the world population crisis, is there not some built-in priority that is given to reproductive biology? Don Price in his excellent book, *The Scientific Estate* quite rightly notes that science fought for centuries to rid itself of purpose, including direct social purpose, yet it may well be that the great invention we are now in process of making is precisely how to reintroduce social purpose into the scientific enterprise in a way that does not distort the ideals of truth and open inquiry. It no longer suffices to claim today, and I believe *should* no longer suffice to claim, that laissez-faire science is what best serves human purposes. Given the present organization of science, the notion of laissez-faire is irrelevant in any case. For modern science is no longer organized as a laissez-faire venture and we will cripple our efforts if we seek such ideals.

But a supply of scientific knowledge does not, as the history of technology shows, automatically create a demand for its conversion to technology. It seems to depend on certain, usually implicit values in the society, and it often appears that these values are so implicit as to be unconscious. Was it inevitable that the private motor car was introduced with so little prior concern for the way it would change the conception of the human habitat? Must we always be surprised by technology?

It seems to me that here lies part of the answer to the puzzle of how we may relate matters of fact and matters of value. For plainly, we are now entering an age where the analysis and implementation of purpose is growing increasingly more powerful and more subtle. The disciplines I have in mind are modelling and simulation—often with the aid of modern computing devices that can take account of many more variables than ever before dreamed of. And here I must return to Kramer's remark about the powerful, indefinable ideas. I know that human intentions in their variety are just of that order. Just as the process of refining such ideas in one way has made science powerful, so it may well be that the art of making our purpose clear may depend on an effort to render our values and intentions in terms of the acts we wish to perform. Yes, one will readily admit that something must also be left to blind man's buff. But there is a long way between blind man's buff and Russian roulette.

I am very well aware of the puny physique of the modern discipline that can be called "policy sciences". But I plead that we avoid the error of consigning efforts at modelling and simulation to the reason of gadgetry or science fiction. It is quite true that the use of these techniques is limited to well formed questions, but again I would urge that we attempt to find out whether such ill formed maxims as "It's better to give than to receive" are composed in some interesting way of more elementary propositions put together in an entering grammar of values. I would certainly make much of the policy sciences in early education.

All of this in turn works its way back to the issue of science proper and its relation to values. The cry is for relevance, human relevance *in* science. But need this be such a mysterious matter and need it be a rallying cry in the contrasting form human relevance *or* science? We know that much of science consists of following "fruitful" leads of a kind that have the sweet smell of powerful generality about them. We also know by now that all prizes cannot be taken by frontal assault. But we also know that generating interest and offering facilities in certain general areas of inquiry pays off in new, fundamental ideas. I believe that increasingly we are able to sense through wise assessment where such general encouragement is needed —even today, it would be likely that the general phenomena of organic growth need to be better understood, that reproductive biology is both urgently in need of pursuit and of the greatest practical significance, etc. Monod at this symposium has justified the study of biology as crucial to survival with dignity.

Recall a point that modern anthropologists like Washburn, Dart, Howells and others are fond of making. It is that it does not take long in terms of human history to *devise* a tool that soon becomes widespread. What takes time is learning the different contexts into which the tool can be fitted. The digging stick went virtually unchanged for thousands of years as did the simpler biface stone hand tools of the Paleolithic. But they were changing in the range of applications to which they were put. So it is with science. I doubt we will rest any longer behind the initial slogan of science for its own sake. It is for man's sake, for the furthering of human purpose. We began by remarking that knowledge generally is organized for the furtherance of intention. I do not believe that science is an exception to this deep general rule. Disinterestedness is the means of science. The human interest is its end. Given the existence of intention, sharply defined as it can be or should be, science at very least provides the means whereby we minimize chagrin in our efforts to achieve those objectives. *What* those objectives "shall" be will be clarified enormously when we discover first what is possible. This is where we are now. The issue of what we "want" or "prefer" is, I think, minor by comparison.

Notes

[1] Granit, R., *Receptors and Sensory Perception.* New Haven: Yale University Press, 1955.

[2] Békésy, G. von, *Sensory Inhibition.* Princeton: Princeton University Press, 1967.

[3] Lindsley, D. B., The reticular system and perceptual discrimination. In H. H. Jasper, et al. (Eds.), *Reticular Formation of the Brain.* Boston: Little, Brown and Company, 1958.

[4] Galambos, R., Suppression of auditory nerve activity by stimulation of efferent fibers to cochlea. *J. Neurophysiol.,* 1956, *19,* 424–431.

[5] Hernandez-Péon, R., Scherrer, R. H., and Jouvet, M., Modification of electrical activity in the cochlear nucleus during "attention" in unanesthetized cats. *Science,* 1956, *123,* 331–332.

[6] Sharpless, G., and Jasper, H., Habituation of the arousal reaction. *Brain,* 1956, *79,* 655–680.

[7] Sokolov, Y., *Perception and the Conditioned Reflex.* Translated by S. W. Waydenfeld. New York: Macmillan, 1963.

[8] von Holst, E., and Mittelstaedt, H., Das Reafferenzprinzip. *Naturwissenschaften,* 1950, *37,* 464–476.

[9] Held, R., Plasticity in sensory-motor systems. *Scientific American,* 1965, *213* (5), 84–94.

[10] Humboldt, W. von, *Über die Verschiedenheit des menschlichen Sprachbaues.* Berlin, 1836. (Facsimile edition, Bonn, 1960.)

Art and Self-Transcendence

By E. H. Gombrich

The Warburg Institute, London, England

A humanist invited to address an audience largely composed of scientists may well be forgiven if he feels a little apologetic. The study of art certainly offers ground for apologies. Its systematic or philosophical branch called "aesthetics" has now been in existence for more than two centuries, but I, for one, share the scepticism about these endeavours which Father Vincent Turner S. J. summed up in an essay called "The Desolation of Aesthetics".[1] As historians we may feel a little more respectable, but even here our specific conclusions about styles and attributions are rarely testable and sometimes no better than anybody's guess. But on second thoughts I do not feel apologetic about the presence of a student of art in a conference concerned with values. Even though aesthetics may not have got far in pontificating about the Beautiful, the Sublime or the Expressive, even though the critics have shown their notorious fallibility in the face of masters past and present, the historian of art can at least tell you what artists thought about value and he, in his turn, may reflect about these thoughts.

Here we must first take cognisance of the Platonic tradition which paradoxically dominated Western philosophies of art—paradoxically because Plato, as we know, had banished the artist from the ideal Republic as a mere conjuror whose skill could never reach the intelligible world of ideas, which is also the world of values. And yet it was the faith in the existence of such a world which inspired the artist with an idea of transcendent perfection against which alone they wanted their art to be judged.

Dante whom these notions reached in their Aristotelian transformation tells us, before he described the ascent to the Paradiso, that the intention of art is often frustrated by lack of responsiveness in matter.[2] The idea cannot be fully realised in the medium. The artist's hand, he says elsewhere, is never perfect, it will always tremble and thus fall short of reproducing the idea.[3] This, of course, is particularly true when the artist's aim is to describe or portray the perfection of beauty, where the highest flight will always fall short of reality and every artist must resign himself to giving up the pursuit of perfection.[4]

History tells how this philosophical conviction spread among the studios of the artists in the Renaissance[5] and became the academic doctrine which

was formulated in its authentic Platonic form by Winckelmann's friend An-
ton Raphael Mengs in his *Reflections on Beauty* in 1762.

> Since perfection does not belong to mankind but only to God and since
> nothing can be conceived by man except what can be apprehended by the
> senses, the Almighty has impressed on man a visible idea of perfection and
> this is what we call Beauty ... We might compare it with the idea of the geo-
> metrical point. Such a point being infinitely small is incomprehensible, but since
> we feel the need of forming a sensible notion of the point, we call a dot a point.
> I should like to suggest that perfection is like such a mathematical point.
> It comprises in itself all the most perfect qualities, and these cannot be found
> in any material object, for whatever is matter is imperfect. Thus we have to
> imagine a kind of perfection adapted to human understanding, and it is this
> image we call beauty, which is visible perfection in the way a dot is a visible
> point. True perfection is only in God, but beauty therefore reflects a divine
> reality.[6]

In our history books the fight against this academic doctrine is generally
represented as a fight for liberation against an outmoded classicism. But
I think we miss much of the real drama if we fail to understand the
psychological trauma that resulted when this metaphysical prop was no
longer holding up the artist's self-respect. The discovery that ideals of beauty
varied according to time and place suggested that all norms in art were
subjective and that the idea of an immutable world of perfection had been
as much a dream in art as it was in religion. The only value left to the
artist was fidelity to his own self. It is the creed so nobly expressed in
a letter by Courbet in 1854:

> I hope to make an unprecedented miracle come true in my life, I hope to
> live all my life by my art, without departing by an inch from my principles,
> without ever having lied for a single moment to my conscience and without
> having covered even a stretch of canvas as large as my hand with paint to
> please anyone whoever it may be to have it sold.[7]

You will notice that Courbet, who said he could not paint an angel
because he had never seen one, believed as passionately in realising a
value as any academic artist. But the loss of a metaphysics had made it a
more difficult creed, and if proof of this assertion were wanted I could
refer you to many of the leading twentieth century artists, artists such as
Kandinsky, Klee or Mondrian who tried to revert to some version of Platon-
ising mysticims by which to sanction or sanctify their artistic mission.[8]

I am afraid few of these efforts are even intellectually respectable and
I would be the last to recommend them to you. But I wonder if we may
need this kind of metaphysics to justify a more than subjective theory of
art, one that explains and accepts the demand for self-transcendence and
some notion of perfection.

I should like here to refer you to two papers by my friend Sir Karl Popper in which he stresses the emergence of problems in nature and in history as the emergence of what he calls a "third world which is neither the world of things or facts nor the world of subjective feelings.[9] For problems allow of solutions, some better, some worse, some perhaps perfect.

Take an elementary artistic problem that may go back to the dawn of history: the decoration of a pot with an evenly spaced row of marks. Whether or not we postulate a subjective 'decorative urge' that drives the craftsman on, he must still submit himself to the objective realities of the situation and work out the number and the intervals of marks till they fit. A richer pattern, covering a wider area would demand correspondingly more attention to the limiting factors involved. However, this attention is likely to be rewarded by the discovery of fresh relationships emerging unplanned between the decorative elements, and these might be exploited and adjusted in their turn. On this model it is easy to see how the craftsman's experience can crystallize in simple rules of procedure which can become embodied in the tradition, enabling the next generation to take certain problems in their stride and advance to the solution of fresh ones which are always likely to emerge.

I am quite aware of the fact that the type of problem I have chosen is too simple by half. It belongs at best to the problems of the craftsman rather than to that of the artist. What counts for the artist, it may be argued, is not the acquisition of skill but the expression of the self. The theory of "abstract expressionism" concentrated indeed on the artist's mark as a graphological trace of his spontaneous and unique gesture which thus became a means of "self discovery". But as a historian I would reply that the problems and values of art—including even those of abstract expressionism —have emerged from the problems and values of the craft. It is a fact of history that most of the great artists of the Western tradition have felt involved with the solution of problems rather than with the expression of their personality.

Let me quote at least one more witness to illustrate what this feeling looks like from the inside, as it were.

Writing to his brother about the consolations and dangers of drink, van Gogh speaks of his demanding work:

the mental effort of balancing the six essential colours, red, blue, yellow, orange, violet, green. This is work and cool calculation, when one's mind is utterly stretched like that of an actor on the stage in a difficult part, when one has to think of a thousand different things at a time within half-an-hour.

After that, van Gogh admits, he must relax and drink and smoke, but I'd like to see a drunkard before his canvas, or on the stage ... Dont think that I would ever artificially work myself into a feverish state. Rather remember that I am engrossed in a complicated calculus, which leads to the quick production of one rapidly painted canvas after the other, which have, however, been calculated at length *beforehand*. And so, if they tell you that it is done too quickly, you can reply that they have looked too quickly.[10]

What is this calculus, this balancing act of which van Gogh speaks with such conviction as his mental work? It is precisely the desolation of aesthetics that we cannot formulate it with the same precision as we can formulate the problems of science or the rules of a game. Even if we had the artist here to explain his aim of fitting colours of shapes into some complex configuration of contrasts or consonances, there would be nothing but your sense of courtesy to prevent you from saying "so what?—We can see that it is hard to do and to get it all as you want it, but is it worth it, is it a value, is it art?"

Remember that in asking this question you would only ask what young artists have so often asked their teachers when they rejected one problem in favour of another that seemed to them more worth pursuing. And yet I think we would be wrong to conclude from this that the values pursued by van Gogh or any other master were therefore totally subjective and illusory.

The problem he had set himself was not only his personal whim. It had emerged in the context of art, he had learned about it in his contacts with fellow artists whom he admired or rejected, whom he wished to emulate or even to surpass. If anyone, van Gogh happens to be an example of this aspect of self-transcendence, of this feeling that artists are engaged or ought to be engaged in a common pursuit.

Though art differs very much from science, what he and we mean by art still has this in common with the scientific quest for truth that it is felt to be cumulative. No problem is ever solved without new ones emerging.[11] It is true that in this process values appear to change, beauty may be felt to be less important than tension, or feeling less artistic than cold purity. The tremendous Rembrandt in the National Gallery here—which alone makes it worth coming to Stockholm—embodies different values from the gem of a Watteau in the same Gallery.

In recent times this undeniable fact that different styles and periods have pursued different problems and values, has led to impatient questions about the relevance of past values. Why should we bother to concern ourselves with an art that embodies values different from our own? Rumour has it that here in Sweden the demand has even been raised that the teaching of art history should be confined to the art of the last hundred years, because this alone could conceivably be relevant to our own age.

You will not be surprised to hear me say that this parrot cry of relevance seems to me total nonsense. If there is one thing about which, in my view, the teachers in faculties of the humanities should not feel apologetic it is about their interest in a variety of values and value systems. The ego-centric provincialism of people who so lack the capacity for self-trans-cendence that they can only listen to what touches their own individual problems threatens us with such intellectual impoverishment that we must resist at all costs.

The first thing we have to learn is that people have different values and pursue different problems. Perhaps we can only learn about values at all in considering this range and diversity. In all civilizations men have set themselves problems of skill and daring that demand outstanding qualities for their solution. The mastery of games and of feats of prowess show men submitting to some kind of value and we can all admire these achievements even if we do not want to join in the game. True, there is the story of the Chinese Mandarin who wondered at the exertions of foreign diplomats in their daily games of tennis: "Even if, for some obscure reasons, these balls had to be tossed around, could not this strenuous chore be left to the servants?"

Our modern Mandarins who look at the arts of the past with similar incomprehension are less excusable. For art has come to embody even higher values than has the game of tennis: in games it is skill which counts, and the skill is measurable through the institutions of matches and tourna-ments. He is master who has come on top. No doubt there is an element of this standard in art. There certainly was a time when mastery in building, carving, bronze casting or painting was mainly seen in terms of such skill. Only that this skill was at that time rarely pursued for its own sake. It was harnessed to other values, the values of religion, of power or of love.[12] The art with which a temple or palace was adorned with rich, intricate and precious decoration, the marvels of goldsmithwork with which the wealthy bridegroom may have wooed his bride, all this showed art in the service of ulterior aims which did not preclude the commission for such important displays of skill going to the most consummate master of the craft.

Maybe it was precisely in this context that the concept of art began to transcend the concept of mere skill. You remember Dante stressing the gap that must of necessity separate the poet's craft from the description of heavenly perfection. This feeling which is no doubt of religious origin has become enshrined in the tradition of art where it has emancipated from religion. Once this tradition had emerged, art could no longer be seen like games as a contest of skills. Indeed it is the paradox of this tradition that the virtuoso is almost seen as the negation of the artist. For the virtuoso who knows all the rules and all the tricks has failed to see that his contest is not with other artists, past or present, but with the Platonic idea of perfection which always demands higher and higher exertions in the pursuit of the problem. It is the humility and dedication demanded by this outlook which has made the great artist the successor, in popular estimation, of the Saint, even where his life and personality may have been far from saintly.

The religion of aestheticism, the religion of Oscar Wilde, of Bernard Shaw's Dubedat in *The Doctor's Dilemma,* or of Hermann Hesse's *Glasperlenspiel* does not appeal to me very much. It lacks that awareness of distance that his religion gave to Dante. The value that has emerged in the Western tradition of art is precisely that feeling of an infinite pursuit that precludes the self-satisfaction of the aesthete.

I once happened to meet a member of a famous string quartet and asked "how long they had played together". "Never yet", he replied, "but we have tried for twentynine years."

The performing artist has, as his standard, the masterpieces he wishes to realise and which, in the nature of things, cannot emerge absolutely flawless, because he is only human and his hand, like that of Dante's craftsman, always trembles. But his attitude towards the masterpiece is mirrored, on a higher level, by the creative artist's feeling of the existence of values which will always transcend his skill. He senses the challenge of the problems which his tradition and his task present to him. He feels and rightly feels, that his own powers alone would never suffice to bring the shapes, sounds and meanings into such perfect harmony, and that it is never the self, but something outside himself, call it luck, inspiration or divine grace that helps to bring about that miracle of the poem, the painting, the symphony he could not have willed.

Before you dismiss this feeling as metaphysical sentimentalism, let me remind you of the theme of this conference, the place of value in the world of facts. Most of the participants of this meeting have rightly decided to confront the pressing problems of the world of facts which they have come here to discuss. But even the greatest optimist would not be disposed to deny that many of these problems are not capable of solution. You need only look into the papers to read of intractable conflicts of interest and of that dreadful power of mass emotions which must indeed make the hand of the reformer tremble. The problems in the realm of art, in the world of values of which I have spoken may also be recalcitrant, but there is no intrinsic reason here why the solution should always elude the artist bent on ordering a large but limited number of elements which may and do fall into place and come right, as do the tones in one of the great fugues by Bach.[13] Such an artist, as I have said, works within a medium that is preshaped by tradition. He has before him the benefit of countless experiments in creating orders of a similar kind and value. Moreover, in setting out to create another such ordered and meaningful arrangement of tones, he will discover new and unintended relationships during the process of creation, which his watchful mind can exploit and follow up, till the richness and complexity of the work transcends in fact any configuration that could be planned from scratch.

In this respect the pressures and bonuses of a continuous period of evolution in art may indeed have something in common with those evolutionary processes which culminated in the complex beauty of a shell or a spider's web.[14] In the past such works of nature were considered by theologians to prove the existence of a conscious creator in what was called "the argument from design".

Strangely enough our age which has rejected this argument has yet fallen for a conception of creativity in art which sees only the individual creator and his state of mind. It forgets that even Bach, great as he was, could not have invented that marvellous medium that is the Western system of music—or if it does not forget it, it tends to regret such traditionalism and to imply that every artist should invent his own system. Even where the creative agent is not believed to be the conscious self it is somehow personalised as the spirit of the age, the class situation or the unconscious.[15] But taken by themselves none of these explanations is ever sufficient to account for the coming into being of such meaningful complex orders as a fugue by Bach.

I believe that this failure has not been without effect on prevalent conceptions about the meaning of art to the individual. The emphasis on objective problem solutions which I have presented has as its corollary the idea that we can strive to understand a work of art. Such understanding may never be exhaustive, but it will always demand a thorough familiarity with the traditions and the problems within which the work took shape. Not that this understanding, this grasp of the problem which the work attempts to solve, is the same as approval. We may understand the problem but reject the values it embodies, for we remain free agents and have a right to say that even a masterpiece that rests on a long tradition strikes us as evil rather than good. There is such a thing as refined cruelty, and there may also be refined depravity embodied in art. But both the effort freely undertaken in search of understanding, and the freedom to submit or to reject, have suffered neglect through the emphasis on subjective response which is conceived to be largely automatic. In its vulgarised form it demands nothing more of the work of art than that it should "switch us on" or "send us", like a drug. Small wonder that we have seen the emergence of a new term, the term of "escapism", to censure those who seek refuge from the world of facts in the opiates of art.

I do not want to deny that there can be some moral force in this disapproval. But I should like to argue that there is a greater moral force in the belief that in freely submitting to a great work of art and exploring its infinite richness we can discover the reality of self-transcending values.

I realise of course that this conception of art has an old-fashioned ring. The Victorian cult of uplift which offered art as a non-committal substitute for religion has understandably repelled many genuine lovers of art. Thus the young find it hard to share the feeling of awe with which former generations responded to the classic masterpieces of poetry, painting or music because they held out the promise and the solace of a realm where values had been realised.

Ladies and Gentlemen,

the title of this symposium, "The Place of Value in a World of Facts" is of course taken from a book by the great pioneer of Gestalt Psychology, the late Wolfgang Koehler. I had the privilege of attending Koehler's lectures in Berlin in 1932, shortly before the catastrophe which threatened to extinguish the sense of all values from Western Civilization. I hope it is still remembered how courageously Koehler opposed this disaster. In the first months of Nazi rule, while he still held his chair in Berlin, he dared to write a newspaper article against the purges of the Universities. When I was fortunate to meet him again in Princeton, shortly before his death, conversation fell on this episode, and he told how after the publication of this protest he and his friends spent the night waiting for the fatal knock on the door which fortunately did not come. They were playing chamber music all night long. I cannot think of a better illustration of the place of value in a world of fact.

Notes

[1] Todd, J. M. (ed.), *The Arts, Artists and Thinkers. An Inquiry into the Place of the Arts in Human Life,* London, 1958.

[2] Paradiso I. 127–129.

[3] Paradiso XIII. 76–78.

[4] Paradiso XXX. 33.

[5] Panofsky, E., Idea. Ein Beitrag zur Begriffsgeschichte der älteren Kunsttheorie. *Studien der Bibliothek Warburg* Ed. F. Saxl, Hamburg, 1924.

[6] Mengs, A. R., *Gedanken über die Schönheit und den Geschmack in der Malerei.* Zürich 1762. (Slightly paraphrased in the interest of readability.)

[7] Courthion, P., *Courbet raconté par lui-même* II, Geneva, 1950, pp. 78/79.

[8] Ringbom, S., Art in the Epoch of the Great Spiritual. Occult Elements in the Early Theory of Abstract Painting, *Journal of the Warburg and Courtould Institutes,* 1966. Vol. 29.

[9] Popper, K. R., Epistemology without a knowing Subject. *Logic, Methodology and Philosophy of Science.* Vol. III. Ed. by van Rottselaar and Stahl, Amsterdam, 1968.

Popper, K. R., On the Theory of the Objective Mind. *Akten des Internazionalen Kongresses für Philosophie I.* Vienna, 1968.

[10] Gogh-Bonger, van, J., (ed.) *Verzamelde Brieven* III (Vincent van Gogh) Amsterdam, 1953. Letter 507, summer 1888.

[11] Popper, K. R., Of Clouds and Clocks. An Approach to the Problem of Rationality and the Freedom of Man. *The Arthur Holly Compton Memorial Lecture,* Washington University, St. Louis, 1966.

Gombrich, E. H., *The Story of Art,* London, 1950. (With examples of the emergence of fresh artistic problems.)

[12] Gombrich, E. H., The Use of Art for the Study of Symbols, *The American Psychologist* XX, 1965. Reprinted in J. Hogg (ed.) *Psychology and the Visual Arts,* Harmondsworth, Middlesex, 1969.

[13] Tovey, D. F., *The Integrity of Music,* Lecture I. London, 1941.

[14] Gombrich, E. H., Visual Discovery through Art, *Arts Magazine,* November 1965. Reprinted in J. Hogg (ed.) *Psychology and the Visual Arts,* Harmondsworth, Middlesex, 1969.

[15] Gombrich, E. H., Freud's Aesthetics, *Encounter,* January 1966. (In this paper I have tried to show that Freud's theory of art was not predominantly expressionist.)

Tillyard, E. M. W. and Lewis, C. S., *The Personal Heresy,* Oxford, 1939. (The second author's contribution presents a forceful case against current ideas of art as self-expression.)

Freedom and Necessity in Poetry

By W. H. Auden

England/U.S.A.

What I have to say is really only a gloss on two lines by Goethe:

In der Beschränkung zeigt sich erst der Meister
Und Das Gesetz nur kann uns Freiheit geben

Most of what I know about the nature of poetry or, at least, about the kind of poetry I am interested in writing or reading, I learned long before the notion of writing poems ever occurred to me. Between the ages of six and twelve I spent a great many hours of my waking hours constructing a private sacred world, the principal elements of which were two: a limestone landscape based on the Pennine Moors in the North of England, and an industry, leadmining. It was, unlike a poem, a pure private world of which I was the only human inhabitant: I had no wish to share it with others, nor could I have done so. However I needed the help of others in procuring me the raw materials for its construction. Others, principally my parents, had to provide me with maps, guide-books, text-books on geology and mining machinery, and when occasion offered, take me down real mines. Since it was a purely private world, theoretically, I suppose, I should have been free to imagine anything I liked, but in practice, I found it was not so. I felt instinctly, without knowing why, that I was bound to obey certain rules. I could choose, for example, between two kinds of windingengines, but they had to be real ones I could find in my books; I was not free to invent one. I could choose whether a mine should be drained by a pump or an adit, but magical means were forbidden.

Then, one day, there came a crisis, I was planning my Platonic Idea of the Perfect Concentrating Mill, and I had to choose between two types of a machine for separating the slimes, called a buddle. One type I felt to be the more 'beautiful' or 'sacred', but the other one was, I knew from my reading, the more efficient. I suddenly and clearly felt that I was faced with what I can only call a moral choice: I knew it was my duty to resist my aesthetic preference and choose the more efficient.

What, then, did I learn from this somewhat odd activity? Firstly, that the construction of any secondary world is gratuitous, not a utile, act, something one does, not because one must, but because it is fun. One is free to write a poem or to refuse to write one. However, any secondary world we may imaginatively construct necessarily draws its raw materials from the Primary World in which we all live. One cannot, like God, create *ex nihilo*. How much and how many facts one takes can vary very greatly. There are some poems, the songs of Campion, for example, which take almost nothing but the English language, so that, if one tries to translate them into another language, nothing is left of value. There are others, poems, The Divine Comedy, for instance, which include a very great deal from the Primary World, its history, its landscape, its theology, its astronomy etc.

Any individual poet, however, is not completely free to choose what raw materials he will use, he can only use those which stir his imagination, those which he finds enchanting or numinous, and this is a matter outside his will to choose or change. A psychologist might, no doubt, be able to explain why, in my childhood, limestone and leadmining so enchanted me; I only know that, in fact, they did.

Lastly, any secondary world is, like the Primary World, a world governed by laws. These may be very different from the laws of the Primary World, and may vary from one secondary world to another, but for each there are laws. Though a poet has a very wide range of choice in deciding what these laws shall be, his freedom is not unbounded, but must be suited to the contents, just as, while there are many kinds of rules for various card-games, all of them have to fit the fact of a pack of four suits of thirteen cards each ranging from the King to the Ace. To return to my buddle problem. Though, at the time, I knew I must, against my inclinations, choose the more efficient, it was only later that I came to understand clearly why. Even in an imaginary world a machine cannot escape the law of machinery, namely, that efficiency of function takes precedence over beauty of appearance.

So, in the case of poetry, all poems must submit to the laws of the language in which they are written, which is not the poets private property. A poet cannot invent his own words or attribute his private meaning to them; he has to use words, however rare, the meaning of which can be found in some lexicon or other. Again, though he may sometimes depart from normal syntax, he can only do this with great care, or what he writes will become unintelligable.

If I try to define in one sentence what a poet does when he writes a poem, I would say this: he attempts to transform a crowd of recollected occasions of experience into a community by incorporating it in a verbal society. I must, therefore, define what I mean by the terms crowd, society and community. A crowd is composed of $N<I$ members whose only rela-

tion is arithmetical: they can only be counted. A crowd loves neither itself nor anything other than itself; it exists neither by choice or necessity but by chance. Of a crowd it may be said, either that it is not real but only apparent, or that it should not be. A physicist, for example, assumes that disorderly occurrences in Nature are apparent, not real, and seeks to discover the laws behind the appearance. A poet, on the other hand, knows that he starts from a real crowd of experiences, which it is his duty to transform.

A society is comprised of a definite or an optimum number of members, united in a specific manner into a whole with a characteristic mode of behaviour which is different from the modes of behaviour of its component members in isolation. A society cannot come into being until its component members are present and properly related: add or substract a member, change their relations, and the society either ceases to exist or is transformed into another society. A society is a system which loves itself, and to this self-love, the self-love of its members is totally subordinate. Of a society it may be said that it is more or less successful in maintaining its existence.

A community is composed of N members united, to use a definition of St Augustine's, by a common love of something other than themselves. God, music, stamp collecting, or what-have-you. Like a crowd and unlike a society, its character is not changed by the addition or subtraction of a member. In a community all members are free and equal. If, out of a group of ten persons, eight prefer beef to mutton and two prefer mutton to beef, there is not a single community with two dissident members, but two communities, a large one and a small one. To achieve actual existence, a community has to embody itself in a society or societies which can express the love which is its raison d'être. A community of music-lovers, for example, cannot just sit around loving music like anything, but must form itself into societies like choirs, orchestras, string quartets, etc. and make music. Of a community it may be said that its love is more or less good. In inorganic nature, communities do not exist, only societies which are sub-members of the total system of nature, enjoying their self-occurrence. They can exist among men, and, I think, among some animals, but they do not necessarily exist there.

Poems are verbal societies, but it is important to remember that we use words for two quite different purposes, as a communication code between individuals to request and supply information necessary to our functioning and existence, and as Personal Speech. Many animals have communication codes, and in a social animal, like the bee, this code may be extremely complex, but so far as we know, no animal is capable of Speech proper.

Our use of language as a communication code is best illustrated by those phrase-books for tourists visiting foreign countries. Such a phrase as: "Can you tell me the way to the railroad station?" When I address this question to a stranger in the street, I do so because it is information I must have if I am to catch my train. I have no personal interest in the one I ask, nor he, when he answers, any personal interest in me. We might as well be other people.

But we are also capable of Speech. In speech, one unique person addresses one or more other unique persons voluntarily: he could remain silent if he chose. We speak as persons because we desire to disclose ourselves to each other and to share our experiences, not because we need to share them, but because we enjoy sharing them. To understand the nature of speech, we must begin, not with statements in the third person, like *the cat is one the mat,* but with Proper Names, the first and second personal pronouns, words of summons and command, response and obedience. Poetry is personal speech in its purest form. The subject matter of poetry is, as I said earlier, a crowd of recollected occasions of personal feelings and ideas. The nature of the final order of a poem is the outcome of a dialectical struggle between these occasions and the particular verbal society of system into which the poet is attempting to embody them. As a society, the verbal system is actively coercive upon the occasions it is attempting to embody; what it cannot embody truthfully it excludes. As a potential community the occasions are passively resistant to all claims of the system to embody them which they do not recognize as just; they decline all unjust persuasions. A successful poem is, as the psalmist says: "A city that is at unity with itself". In my own case, and I suspect that this is the case with most poets, at any given time, I have two concerns on my mind. On the one hand, certain experiences which seem to me of value; on the other certain problems of language and reflection, style, diction, metre, etc. which interest me. Consequently, I am engaged on a double search: the experiences are looking for their needed form, and the form is looking for the suitable experiences. It is only when these find each other, that I am able to begin writing a poem. The form cannot be selected arbitrarily nor can one say that any given form is absolutely necessary. The nature of any given language limits choice. For instance, in Greek, hexameters and pentameters are a 'normal' metre; in English, though they can be written, they sound eccentric. Similarly, though alexandrines and decasyllabics can be written both in French and English, it is not a pure matter of chance, that alexandrines are the staple metre of French verse, and decasyllabics of English.

Poetry is concerned with human beings as unique persons. What men do from necessity or by second nature cannot be the subject of poetry, for poetry is gratuitous utterance. As Paul Valery said: "In poetry everything that must be said cannot be said well." It is essentially a spoken, not a written word. One can never grasp a poem one is reading unless one hears the actual sound of the words. In so far as one can speak of poetry as conveying knowledge, it is the kind of knowledge implied by the Biblical phrase: "Then Adam knew Eve his wife"; knowing is inseparable from being known. To say that poetry is ultimately concerned with only human persons does not, of course, mean that it is always overtly about them. We are always intimately related to non-human natures and, unless we try to understand and relate to what we are not, we shall never understand what we are. As Emerson wrote:

> Man is an analogist and studies relations in all objects. He is placed in the centre of beings and a ray of relation passes from every being to him. And neither can man be understood without these objects, nor these objects without man. ... Because of this radical correspondance between visible things and human thoughts, in poetry all spiritual facts are represented by natural symbols.

Again, to say that a poem is a personal utterance does not mean that it is an act of self-expression. The experiences a poet endeavours to embody in a poem are experiences of a reality common to all men: they are only *his* in that this reality is perceived from a perspective which nobody but he can occupy. What by providence he has been the first to perceive, it is his duty to share with others.

The job of poetry, of all the arts, then, is to manifest the personal and the chosen: the manifestation of the impersonal and the necessity is the job of the sciences. Even there, the word necessity is ambigous: it might be better to say the unchanging or unhistorical which changes according to unchanging laws. Physics, for example, has dicovered the velocity of light, but no physicist can say that the velocity of light must be what in fact it is, that it could not have been different. Like art, pure science is a gratutious and personal activity, and I am convinced that the stimulus to scientific enquiry is the same as that of artistic fabrication, namely a sense of wonder. As Nietsche said:

> Art says: 'Life is worth living': Science says: 'Life is worth knowing'.

Scientific knowledge, however, is not reciprocal like artistic knowledge: what the scientist knows cannot know him. Hence the language of science and the language of poetry are at opposite poles. As Wittgenstein has said:

> It is not the name of a person, nor 'here' of a place, and 'this' is not a name. But they are connected with names. Names are explained by means of them. It is characteristic of physics not to use these words.

In fact the natural sciences could not realize their true nature until an impersonal universal language had been invented, from which every vestige of poetry has been eliminated, namely Algebra, of which Whitehead wrote:

Algebra reverses the relative importance of the factors in ordinary language. It is essentially a written language, and it endeavours to exemplify in its written structure the patterns which it is its purpose to convey. The pattern of the marks on paper is a particular instance of the pattern to be conveyed to thought. The algebraic method is the best approach to the expression of necessity by reason of its reduction of accident to the ghost-like character of the real variable.

One rather curious link between the Arts and the Sciences is the fact that political theories, based like Plato's, on analogies to artistic fabrication, or based like those of Leontiev, the Marxist, on analogies to science, both inevitably produce in practice political tyranny.

A poem, or any work of art, is but one secondary world out of an infinite number of possible secondary worlds. Therefore, the poet is free to choose whatever thoughts and words suit this particular poem, and to treat all that don't suit it as if they did not exist. Secondly he aims at producing a verbal object which is complete in itself and will endure without change.

A political state that was really like a good poem would be a nightmare of horror. The population would be fixed by law at a figure: any super-fluous or recalfitrant persons would have to be exterminated, and those permitted to exist would be forbidden ever to change their job.

Political analogies from science overlook the fact that science is based on experiment. The scientist forms a hypothesis and then tests it by an experiment, the objects of which are assumed to have no will of their own, or, at least to be incapable of changing their minds. If the experiment falls to confirm his hypothesis, then he must abandon it.

I think Rosenstock-Huessy is substantially right when he says:

The scientific method cannot lead mankind because it is based on experiment, and every experiment postpones the present moment until one knows the result. We always come to each other and even to ourselves too late so soon as we wish to know in advance what to do.

Needless to say, I do not believe that The Arts for the arts, can lead mankind, either.

But politics has to do historiconscious with persons who have wills of their own and opinions which they can change. Suppose that as a politician I make the hypothesis that a rational or 'scientific' agriculture would be a collectivised agriculture. I collectivise it: the peasants are rebellious and food production drops. Does this disprove my hypothesis? Not necessarily.

I can always argue that the apparent failure of my experiment is due to the malice or stupidity of the peasants, and that, if I continue with it long enough, they will change their minds and come to realize that I am right. This means tyrany because in politics there is always a distinction, unknown to science, between truth and justice.

The existence of human beings is dual: as biological organisms made of matter, we are subject to the laws of physics and biology: as conscious persons who create our own history, we are free to decide what that history shall be. A true notion of what is just can only be arrived at by a collaboration between science and art. Without science, we could have no notion of equality: without art no notion of liberty. Justice means recognizing that two apparently contradictory statements are both true, namely, Hard Cases make bad Law, and One law for the ox and the ass is oppression.

Let me conclude these remarks into a poem which is concerned into both Art and Science, as *Ode to Terminus,* the Roman God of boundaries.

Ode to Terminus

The High Priests of telescopes and cyclotrons
keep making pronouncements about happenings
    on scales too gigantic or dwarfish
    to be noted by our native senses,

discoveries which, couched in the elegant
euphemisms of algebra, look innocent,
    harmless enough but, when translated
    into the vulgar anthropomorphic

tongue, will give no cause for hilarity
to gardeners or house-wives: if galaxies
    bolt like panicking mobs, if mesons
    riot like fish in a feeding-frenzy,

it sounds too like Political History
to boost civil morale, too symbolic of
    the crimes and strikes and demonstrations
    we are supposed to gloat on at breakfast.

How trite, though, our fears beside the miracle
that we're here to shiver, that a Thingummy
    so addicted to lethal violence
    should have somehow secreted a placid

tump with exactly the right ingredients
to start and to cocker Life, that heavenly
    freak for whose manage we shall have to
    give account at the Judgement, our Middle-

Earth, where Sun-Father to all appearances
moves by day from orient to occident,
    and his light is felt as a friendly
    presence, not a photonic bombardment,

where all visible do have a definite
outlines they stick to, and are undoubtedly
    at rest or in motion, where lovers
    recognize each other by their surface,

where to all species except the talkative
have been allotted the niche and diet that
    become them. This, whatever micro-
    biology may think, is the world we
really live in and that saves our sanity,
who know all too well how the most erudite
    mind behaves in the dark without a
    surround it is called on to interpret,

how, discarding rhythm, punctuation, metaphor,
it sinks into a drivelling monologue,
    too literal to see joke or
    distinguish a penis from a pencil.

Venus and Mars are powers too natural
to temper out outlandish extravagance:
    You alone, Terminus, the Mentor,
    can teach us how to alter our gestures.

God of walls, doors and reticence, nemesis
overtakes the sacrilegious technocrat,
    but blessed is the City that thanks you
    for giving us games and grammar and metres.

By whose grace, also, every gathering
of two or three in confident amity
    repeats the pentecostal marvel,
    as each in each finds his right translator.

In this world our colossal immodesty
has plundered and poisened, it is possible
    You still might save us, who by now have
    learned this: that scientists, to be truthful,

must remind us to take all they say as a
tall story, that abhorred in the Heav'ns are all
    self-proclaimed poets who, to wow an
    audience, utter some resonant life.

The Valuation of Values

By Frede Castberg

University of Oslo, Oslo, Norway

The famous Professor Hans Kelsen, who has during the course of some 60 years given highly valuable—although violently contested—contributions to the philosophy of law, has said that "the validity of a value is the validity of a norm".[1] It may be doubtful if this is so in every field of human valuations. But I think it is a correct statement as far as moral and legal, i.e. all deontological values are concerned.

This paper intends to discuss such values as form the basis of political systems of valuations, also called political ideologies, that is systematized ideas about how society ought to be organized, good and evil distributed among its members.

My intention is to give a short survey of some of the historically most important political ideologies from the last two centuries as seen in their historical context. But I will especially try to undertake a confrontation of those ideologies, to analyze their fundamental valuations and try to clarify the contrasts as well as the similarities in their ideological elements.

I am not concerned with the conflict of values which constantly troubles lawyers in their appreciation within a definite, so-called "positive" legal system. Certainly in this field too, difficult questions arise concerning priority of aims and between conflicting ideas of justice. But these conflicts have to be solved on the basis of the definite legal system concerned and the valuations which are peculiar to it. On the contrary, we are here confronted with political ideologies, that is to say that we are confronted with such systems of valuation as are not based on any social establishment. The political ideology is generally formed in opposition to all other value systems in the same field,—*also* to that of actual, positive law.

Our starting point will be the distinction between pronouncements of a factual character on the one hand, and valuations on the other. However, we will first regard the ideologies we present, as being themselves historical facts. This means that we treat these value systems from what we could call the "external" point of view. Our point of view so far will be that of the history of political and philosophical ideas. It is only in some short final reflections that we will touch the valuation problem from an "internal" point of view. We will then be faced with the following problem:

Is it possible to say anything reasonable about which are the objectively *right* elements of valuation in that field of mutually conflicting ideologies which our historical survey has shown us?

Historical survey

1. In the *Declaration of the Rights of Man and Citizen,* adopted by the French National Assembly in 1789, are formulated some of the most important principles—at that time called principles of "Natural Law"— which are still the ideological basis of the constitutional systems, at least in the Western world. The Declaration of 1789 proclaims the sovereignty of the people, the principle of legality and the inviolable Human Rights. The principle of legality had for a very long time been recognized in the Anglo-Saxon world in the formula: "Government of Law, not of Men." Against oppressive governments the right to resistance was recognized not only by the French revolution, but by the American revolution as well.

2. One feature of this ideology was bound above all to give rise to violent opposition in many European countries. That was the proclamation of inviolable and imprescriptible Human Rights, based on Natural Law, even protected by the simultaneously recognized right to revolt. The historical school in German legal philosophy as well as English traditionalists and utilitarians attacked in violent words such futile and dangerous abstractions. The great German lawyer, Fr.v. Savigny spoke of the "stupid, pretentious and totally hollow idea" of a legislation of this kind. In England Edmund Burke was the most brilliant and influential spokesman for conservatism, tradition and stability. And Jeremy Bentham declared that the doctrine of Natural Law would have a tendency "to impel a man, by the force of conscience, to rise up in arms against any law whatever that he happens not to like. What sort of government is it that can consist with such a disposition" he asked.[2]

3. I think it is correct so say that the dominating feature of utilitarian philosophy, especially as presented by John Stuart Mill is a firm belief in intellectual liberty. However, freedom of speech is recognized by John St. Mill, not as an innate Human Right but as a means to promote the well-being of society. The same utilitarian approach to freedom of speech is also characteristic of the reasoning in those numerous decisions of the United States Supreme Court which right up to the present day have protected freedom of speech against oppressive and intolerant legislative or administrative actions.

Hand in hand with the utilitarian movement for intellectual freedom also went the policy of "free enterprise" or "laissez faire" in the relation between state and private activity in economic life. This was the ideology of the "capitalist class" in the widest sense of this word. No interference in private economic life, even when the working class seemed to sink into increasingly miserable conditions of life.

4. It is not surprising that in this situation should crop up not only prudent and peaceful movements of social reform, but also in a violent, clearly revolutionary ideology such as Marxism.

If we should try to summarize in a few words the dominant features of Marxism as it was elaborated by Marx and Engels in the Communist Manifest of 1848 and in their writings during the following decades, it may be correct to take as starting point the class-war theory: The history of mankind in the Marxist view has to be seen as a war between the economic classes of society at any time. Law and morals are "superstructures" of economic relation. The State is nothing but a means for the ruling class to suppress the others. The determinism which governs development in human life leads inevitably in industrialized society to an ever increasing gulf between the situation of the ruling, capitalist class and that of the underpaid workers. This will finally provoke the great catastrophe in the form of a proletarian revolution, the victory of the working class and the establishing of the proletarian dictatorship. The final result will be the classless and stateless society.—In spite of the reduction of law and morals to "superstructures" of class-domination, it is obvious that the Marxist ideology has very definite ideas of "justice", as far as the distribution of the income from production is concerned. The economic theory of the Marxist-ideology pretends that all economic value is created by labour. The right distribution of the output of production should therefore be: to everyone according to his work. But when the final aim has been realized and the classes and the state are abolished, the principle of distribution should be: to everyone according to his needs.

The historical materialism of Marxism is a kind of philosophical determination with qualifications of its own. It does not only imply the conviction that everything happens with causal necessity, but according to this theory it is seen possible to foresee the coming development. The proletarian revolution and dictatorship is bound to take place. Nevertheless, it is regarded as a duty of the working class to help to realize these events. And although the bourgeois class, according to the same theory, acts under the same law of necessity and in harmony with their own class-determined morals, their resistance against the working class is met with a feeling which can hardly be described otherwise than as moral indignation.[3]

5. It is an interesting phenomenon that the first political regime which in this century was established in sharp opposition to the Marxist Communism, obtained its victory through the ruthless leadership of a man himself originating in revolutionary socialism. Benito Mussolini turned away from Marxism and adopted a warlike nationalism when he fought for Italy's entry into the First World War in 1915.

The glorification of war, the protest not only against "Bolshevism" but also against individualism and internationalism—all these things are characteristics of Italian Fascism.

In 1922 Mussolini proclaimed: "We have created our myth. The myth is a belief, a passion. It is not necessary that it (the myth) is a reality. It is in fact a reality because it is inspiration, hope, belief and courage. Our myth is the Nation, our belief is the greatness of the Nation."[4]

The Italian Fascism has also a front against the old laissez-faire doctrine. In one of his speeches on the Fascist "corporate State" in 1935 Mussolini declares: "Today we are burying economic liberalism."

6. Through many years the Fascist regime had the character of a personal dictatorship. The same is of course to an even greater degree a dominating feature of the National Socialist regime in Germany. Here the principle of "Führung und Gefolgschaft", that is the absolute authority of the Führer and the unconditional obedience of the people, is the declared ideal very early in the National Socialist movement. The Führer incarnates the true will of the people. As Adolf Hitler himself declared in the German Reichstag after the bloody repression of the opposition within and outside the party in June–July 1934, he could act as "oberster Gerichtsherr des deutschen Volkes"—he was above all judges and courts in Germany. The ideology was based on a mythical cult of "the blood and the earth", that is to say a glorification of the Germanic race. The other sinister feature of this race doctrine was the violent antisemitism, with its wellknown disastrous consequences during the Second World War. National Socialism also followed up the inheritance of German military history, from the idealized picture of the great warrior Frederic the Second right up to the Preussian militarist ideology as the international world learnt to know it, not least through General v. Bernhardi and many other writers before the First World War.

7. The horrors of the Second World War have certainly had the most far-reaching consequences on people's thinking and feelings all over the world. One of these consequences is a general reaction against the ideologies of dictatorship and of racial discrimination. Surprising as it may seem, all the peoples gathered in the United Nations have accepted the principles of

democracy, the rule of law and the inviolable Human Rights. The supra-positive principles recognizing the fundamental Human Rights have led the German tribunals after the war to look upon the Nazi cruelties in wartime as punishable crimes in spite of their having been authorized, even ordered, by the highest Nazi authorities on the basis of the then established rules of positive "law". Characteristic of our postwar evaluations is also a general feeling of responsibility for developing peoples which has led to national and international initiatives of assistance.

8. But one thing is ideological principles and political ideals. Quite another is the real political and social life which the new generation is now con-fronted with. It seems that the whole "establishment" with its economic exploitation and so-called manipulation, as it can present itself in many countries today, makes numerous groups of young people desperate. New ideological prophets have turned up with new revolutionary slogans on their coat of arms.

I shall not here venture to say anything about what importance we have to attribute to these signs of unrest, within and outside the universities, not least among the youth, all these protests, all these cries for power for new groups in society.

The ideologies in their causal connection

1. No doubt, writings of the philosophers and other authors have played an essential role in the development of the systems of political, ideological doctrines. It is sufficient to mention names like Rousseau and Locke in connection with what is sometimes called "the ideas of 1789", Burke, v. Savigny and de Maistre for the ideological counteraction against those ideas. Bentham and the father and son Mill for the utilitarian philosophy and political liberalism.

The relationship between Hegel's philosophy of history and the historical materialism of Marxism has often been demonstrated or discussed. Even more conspicuous is the influence of Georges Sorel's *Réflections sur la violence,* on Mussolini's Fascist ideology—what il Duce has himself ex-pressly underlined.[5] It is easy to see this kinship if we study Sorel's ideas of the myths, which—even though they may be illusory—he regards as the great driving force of history. The belief in the coming revolutionary gen-eral strike is in Sorel's view such a myth, which will inspire the working class to courage and honour.[6]

Both Fascism and National Socialism are also stamped by Friedrich Nietzsche's philosophy: Life has to be dangerous, war is glorious, humility and modesty are contemptuous qualities. There are also reminiscences of the Nietzschian idea of "superman" in the National Socialist racial theories, of which however, the anthropological pretentions were based on racial propagandists like Houston Chamberlain and others.

The new democratic and humanitarian principles of our time can draw from a host of authors in many different fields of literature. Even what we recently have seen of tendencies to revolt against the fundamental structure of the post-war society have their ideological prophets. One of them is, of course, Professor Marcuse with his preaching of "repressive tolerance" for the benefit of progress as well as his strong criticism directed against the established, capitalist society.

2. Nevertheless, it is also obvious that the victory of any political ideology in political and social life necessarily also has its background in economic and other purely material circumstances and in important historical events. There is no doubt that there is a close connection between the triumph of the revolutionary ideas of liberty and equality in France in 1789 and the foregoing growth of the French third estate in wealth and power. The reaction following the revolutionary events in France must be regarded not least as a counteraction and movement of protest against the bloody events during the revolutionary period. Utilitarianism and economic liberalism follow the industrial revolution, just as Communism is the understandable reply to injustice and suffering, striking proletarians in the wake of economic "laissez-faire". And could Fascism and Nazism have had their victory in Italy and Germany without a basis in an economically depressed and mentally frustrated "petite bourgeoisie"?

In our present time the principles of political democracy, racial equality and social solidarity are recognized in most parts of the world, although often in a lip service only. But would the broad recognition of these ideas have been possible without the events of the Second World War and the allied victory? And in the fight for full recognition of racial equality the disinherited races themselves have used their new force and influence in full.

Analysis of the ideologies

I have tried to show some fundamental features of certain political ideologies of eminent historical importance. And I have drawn attention to some elements in their literary as well as social, especially economic, background.

One might ask: Are these ideological doctrines more than a varnish over the interests of classes, groups and even single personalities and over individuals' and groups' feelings and love of power? I think the answer must be that although such factors may be the underlying, sometimes unconscious, motives for a great lot of ideological spokesman, the ideologies are there. And their real influence in thought and action in political and social life have been, I think, indisputable.

I shall try to examine the ideologies here mentioned, to find out the elements in their valuations, to compare these elements, to see their similarities as well as their contrasts and to explore their relation to each other. And of course, their valuations of political and social aims and means always imply at the same time negative valuations of the attitude adopted by other ideologies to the same problems.

1. One feature is of course common to all political ideologies, and that is the viewpoint: *aim-means*. The very essence of a political ideology is that it has in mind some future organization of human society, i.e. future laws, institutions, actions. The ideology will therefore necessarily recommend means to realize these aims. And these means are then considered rational and effective in view of the realization of the aims.

When the political ideology, which we here have called "the ideas of 1789", included the principle of legality, it was certainly not least because this principle, if carried through in the State, was thought to realize the security and the predictability on which all cultural life depends.

In the utilitarian doctrine freedom of speech was recommendable as the indispensable means of social progress. The ideology of economic "laissez-faire" regarded free enterprise as the sure means of promoting general prosperity in society. To the Marxists, the dictatorship of the proletariat was thought to be the effective means to realize, under certain conditions, the wellbeing and the happiness of the working people.

All these assumptions are based on convictions concerning purely *factual* relations. The adherence to the principle of legality or "rule of law" supposes that the realization of this principle will in fact create the desired conditions for culture and progress. All propaganda for free enterprise is based on the supposition that this system is in fact the most effective means for the economic wellbeing of society as a whole.

Neither is there any doubt that the National Socialist propaganda for racial discrimination was based on convictions concerning some asserted "facts" as to the special qualities of the Germanic race (vigour, courage, faithfulness etc.) and the very different and unpopular qualities of other races and of the Jewish race in particular—all these "facts" put forward with incredible sureness and arrogance by the so-called scientific race experts of the ideology. On the other hand, the increased knowledge of facts in this field seems now to have destroyed the very basis of the ideologies of racial supremacies and racial disqualifications.

But it is unquestionable that very often, what the ideologies assert to be facts, is more the result of feelings of hatred or sympathy than the outcome of an objective study of factual phenomena. Propositions which present themselves as concerned with facts only, may in reality express valuations.[7]

2. Besides these ideological elements of aims-means-considerations and factual assumptions, we also find in all ideologies in modern time the idea that the final aim should be the wellbeing of society—some society of one or the other category. Very different ideas are covered by such expressions as social utility, welfare or social wellbeing and progress. In orthodox, classical revolutionary Marxism the group whose wellbeing should be the nearest aim, seems to have been the working class. It is quite otherwise of course in the National Socialist ideology. In the interesting draft of a new German "Peoples Law Book" ("Volksgesetzbuch") from 1942 which was elaborated by the distinguished German Professor Justus Wilhelm Hedemann, the very first article reads: "The highest Law is the welfare of the German people."[8]

On the other hand, the ideology which intends to bind the world together today, expressed in the Charter of the United Nations and in the Declaration and Covenants of Human Rights, obviously has in mind mankind as a whole.

In many of the ideologies we have been confronted with, it is easy to discover a more or less marked "ideal of personality", that is: a conviction as to the short of individuals which are wanted in the society concerned. The Fascist and the National Socialist ideologies had in common the picture they had formed of man as he ought to be: Hard and courageous, dependent upon himself—totally different from what the National Socialists called "das sicherheitsbedürftlige liberale Bürgertum". The glorified qualities were at the same time just those which the authoritarian ideologies regarded as belonging to their own people's national and racial character. But it was also this idealized national character which State and party should realize through education and propaganda.—Certainly, these were ideals of personality in sharp contrast to the ideals of Christianity and to the humanitarian ideas in our time.

3. Besides the viewpoint: aim-means in the ideological reasonings, another element is not less important: the protest against what is regarded as social injustice.

The ideology of freedom and equality of the 18th century's revolutionary movement was directed against the *unjust* privileges of the "ancien régime", just as Marxism stigmatized the capitalist profits and demanded *justice* in the form of income as the pay for work. The National Socialists protested for their part—at least in the beginning of their movement—against the unjust, so-called "rent slavery". And they protested against what they regarded as manifest injustice inflicted upon Germany by the Treaty of Versailles.

Neither can anyone deny the strong feeling of injustice which underlies the demands in our time to abolish every form of racial discrimination.—

In my opinion, it is unquestionable that the demand for justice cannot be regarded as being only a special form of the demand for social utility. Justice and social utility may perhaps in most cases coincide and lead to the same result. But this is not always so.

There may be many situations where a generally accepted aim would be well promoted by measures which however must be regarded as obviously unjust.

The economic welfare of the great masses may, for instance, be well served by the sacrifice of the economic interests and rights of a small group or a single person. But the respect for traditional ideas of justice may stand as a hindrance.—Terror may be an effective means to maintain social order in any agitated society. But if directed against innocent people it will be regarded as unjust.—The large incomes based on fortunes in capitalist society may be useful as a means of increasing production. But the Marxists are certainly not the only ones to regard such incomes and the ensuing differences of living standard as unjust.

A fascinating and dramatic illustration of the conflict between views of social utility and passion for individual justice was given to the whole world during the Dreyfus affair in France during the last years of the 19th century. On the one hand the fanatic defence of the prestige of the army, the Catholic church and the pretended national interests of the country. On the other hand, the conviction that justice towards a single individual must prevail on all considerations concerning the prestige, order or other interests.

Principles with objective validity

In what I have said until now, the viewpoint has been, so to speak, from outside. My intention has been to present the different ideological systems in their historical context, to analyse their contents and to find out their similarities as well as their opposition to each other. I have tried to avoid not only personal valuations, but also any attitude to the very question of the possibility of making valuating statements of objective validity.

I use this last expression in the meaning of a validity which is more than a subjective, interior, psychological experience.

The short presentation I have given of some few, important ideologies has drawn attention to the well-known fact that human appreciations of right and wrong in political life very often stand in opposition to each other in a way which seems to make any search for objective validity hopeless. Not only are the ideas of aims and means, of facts and ideals and of the meaning of justice very often fundamentally different. But even when many values are recognized in principle by all parties, these values are, as a general rule, incommensurable quantities. No scientific exploration of social life can answer the question as to which value shall have priority in the conflict between for instance economic efficiency against social justice, social security against freedom of speech or between the right of personal liberty against the right of society to protest itself against crime.

In the year 1911 the late, great Swedish philosopher, Axel Hägerström, delivered his inauguration lecture at the University of Lund with the title: "About the truth of moral ideas." His standpoint was that moral ideas ("representations", Swedish "föreställningar") are expressions of feelings and never can be true or false. His "realist" philosophy has, as is well-known, created a whole philosophical school in Sweden. He has, partly in an indirect way, to a great extent influenced thinking also in the other Scandinavian countries. This was, I think, one aspect of a general revolt against all metaphysical elements in social sciences, legal reasoning and scientific moral philosophy.

This is not the place to take up a full discussion of this philosophy. I will only say that I, for one, agree with the realist attitude of the "Upsala philosphy" in one point: I agree that neither moral nor legal statements can be true or false. But I persist in thinking that they can be correct or incorrect, objectively valid or not valid. A statement, for instance, concerning what is the correct applications of a legal rule is not the expression of a hypothesis about the probable, future decision of courts. It may be correct and thus a valid expression of what is law, even if the courts will not take the same stand. There is nothing illogical in believing in objectively right or wrong statements on positive law, even if there is no possibility of "verification" of such statements in the scientific sense of the word. Now, from a logical point of view, there is no difference between the content of a proposition on positive law, meaning: this is valid law in this or that country, and a proposition on law as it ought to be—"natural law" or proposition "de lege ferenda" or whatever you care to call it.

In my opinion it is misleading to characterize every statement of valid principles of law or morals as "metaphysical". There is, after all, a difference between a statememt of religious belief on the one hand and a statement of valid law or moral or principle de lege ferenda on the other. It does not seem reasonable to use the same word for so different things only because we are in both fields faced with statements which can not be verified.

Our conviction of valid principles of natural law is based on reason. Such conviction is, however, not without a basis in factual valuations in social life. In spite of the host of contesting ideologies in human history, there seem to be many valuations at any time which are in fact accepted by a great number of human societies. To illustrate this, mention may be made of "the general principles of law recognized by civilised nations", which Article 38 in the Statutes of the International Court of Justice has made a recognized source of law. And "the laws of humanity and the exigencies of public conscience" are expressly referred to in the preamble of the Hague Convention on Land Warfare of 1907.

If I should try to formulate some specially important principles, which in my opinion can be regarded as having general validity in our world of today, I have no doubt in placing the right of property and the binding effect of contracts high on the list. The restrictions of property rights and of freedom of contracts of course vary considerably according to the differences of the prevailing economic systems. But the very principle of property and contractual rights must be—and seems in fact to be—recognized everywhere.—Negative rights against the state such as freedom from torture and freedom from slavery also belong to human rights, independently of their recognition in legal documents. In any advanced society in our time freedom of speech and democratic government belong to the same category.

The principle of justice, as a claim based on reason, is not a sheer expression of feeling, as asserted by some or without any content as asserted by others. Although the application of the principle of justice depends on the chosen criteria, justice has to be applied in human society, as already shown by Aristotle. Its practical importance in political life in our time is obvious. It is sufficient to mention again the violent revolt against racial discrimination—a typical cry for "justice".

The principle of justice will always have new application in the light of new and more refined psychological observations and in consequence of the growth of humanitarian understanding. Fundamental norms with objective validity have not a definite content given once and for all.

The conviction that some fundamental values and principles have an objective validity must of course be characterized as a statement of a postulate. So far it has no other and stronger basis than the personal interior experience to which the realist philosophy will attach no validity at all.

But, after all, there is a difference of principle between the stand that any statement of valuation is nothing but a personal feeling, and the conviction that some of one's fundamental valuations are objectively right and valid.

Notes

[1] Kelsen, H., Die Geltung eines Wertes ist die Geltung einer Norm. *Österreichische Zeitschrift für Öffentliches Recht*, 1965, p. 3.
[2] Lloyd, D., *Jurisprudence*, London. 2nd ed., 1965. See excerpt of Bentham, p. 127.
[3] Tingsten, H., *Den svenska socialdemokratiens idéutveckling*, I, 1941, pp. 94–96.
[4] Mussolini, B., *Der Geist des Faschismus*. Ein Quellenwerk, herausgegeben und erläutert von Horst Wagenführ. München 1940, p. 86.
[5] See the Collection, ed. by Horst Wagenführ, p. 90.
[6] Sorel, G., *Réflections sur la violence*, p. 179 and pp. 206–49.
[7] Myrdal, G., *Objektivitetsproblemet i samhällsforskningen*, 1970.
[8] "Oberstes Gesetz ist das Wohl des deutsches Volkes."

Biases in Social Research

By Gunnar Myrdal

Institute for International Economic Studies, Stockholm, Sweden

1

"Perhaps the greatest tragedy of the human experience is that our under-standing of man and his behavior has not kept pace with our knowledge of how to control nature"—I quote this sigh from the end of Harrison Brown's paper on *Resource Needs and Demands*. This sentence expresses a truth that is so obvious to everybody that it has become a commonplace.

In the final instance, this is a complaint, first, that the social sciences have not kept pace with the natural sciences and, second, that what knowledge about society that has been acquired, has met greater difficulties to become applied as social engineering.

To start with the problem of application first, the contrast is striking. Whether it is a question of new products, new processes to produce a pro-duct, advances in medical technology, or improvements in military weaponry, an invention—often made possible by basic research—is almost sure to become rapidly applied.

The evaluation of an invention in terms of immediate costs and effects by private enterprise or by the state is simple and, in a sense, objective and almost automatic. Competition between private enterprises and between states assures application. And this has created a situation which has made thoughtful natural scientists and technologists fear that uncontrolled advance in natural sciences and in their technological application is leading to disaster.

Even assuming that we social scientists had been able to develop a system of rational social engineering by which the state and the intergovernmental communities should be able to control and direct that application of natural science and technology in the common interest, it would be a long and cumbersome road towards having that engineering applied. This would imply a political process, which naturally falls outside the natural scientist's field of study, as does the process by which the decisions are now being made.

As they themselves are not social scientists, the only thing they can do is to complain about the absence of effective social engineering which would redirect and control the dangerous *laissez faire* in the application of the research results in natural sciences, which they see evolving.

There would be very much to add in order to clarify the inhibitions and obstacles meeting the application of that rational and radical social engineering, which the frightened natural scientists are asking for but I will have to leave that out in this context.

But let me proceed to the even more fundamental problem of why the social sciences themselves are so obviously lagging in comparison with the rapid, and acceleratedly rapid, advance of natural sciences.

One part of the answer is that social reality is very much more difficult to observe and analyse.

We never reach down to constants. If we economists, for instance, establish by observation the income or price elasticity for, say, sugar, it is valid only for a particular sample of a social group in a single community at a particular date—not to mention that the concept of elasticity itself loses what I call adequacy to reality, and thereby analytical usefulness, in underdeveloped countries that have no markets where demand plays against supply, or very imperfect ones.

In the final instance, the objects of our research in the social sciences are always living, conditions, institutions and human attitudes. These phenomena regularly combine changeability and rigidity in an unstable and to a large part inscrutable pattern—this is the reason why we never reach down to constants. The relevant institutions and attitudes are exceedingly difficult to define, to observe, and to analyse.

I should add here that when some of us attempt to emulate the methods of natural scientists working with simpler problems, this has regularly led to a dangerous superficiality in approach. An analysis which is paraded as particularly "strict" and "rigorous" is regularly, when scrutinized, found to be lacking in both logical consistency and adequacy to reality. In particular, it has made social study even more defenseless than ordinarily against biases.

2

Let me now after this preamble come to the main thesis of this brief paper: the prevalence of biases in social research. Biases are ordinarily not cognizant to the researchers, either individually or collectively. The problem is seldom discussed. I can even say that it is systematically shunned.

It should be the object of two social science disciplines, that belong to the least developed ones: the sociology of social sciences and of scientists, and the logic of social sciences. Keeping up naivity about what he is doing as a researcher and about the influences under which he is laboring, and at the same time remaining unaware of, and uninterested in, the methods of logic to protect the integrity of his research, the ordinary social scientist believes that his analysis and inferences are simply founded upon his observations of facts. He is what the philosophers call a positivist, which is fraught with danger for a social scientist while it is only limiting for a natural scientist.

Now we all know that when we look back at any earlier era, we regularly find that not only popular discussion but also the work of the social scientists were biased in the sense that their approach was influenced by dominating national or group interests in the society they were part of. However, like contemporary social scientists today, they were firmly convinced that their analysis and inferences were founded simply upon their observations of facts.

Let me choose an example that stands in the focus of interest at this symposium: the conditions in the underdeveloped countries. There was, right up to the Second World War and the liberation of the colonies, that went as an avalanche over the globe, a distinct theory about the peoples in these colonies, that can be recognized in scholarly studies as well as in popular thinking.

The peoples in the colonies were assumed to be differently constituted from people of white European stock. They lacked interest in improving their lot. This theory was given learned expression by the economists in the so-called backward sloping supply curve.

It was underpinned by observations of their different cultural traditions, attitudes and institutions. The hot and damp climate in the tropic and sub-tropical zones, where the colonies were located, was also given an important role. At the basis, though often carefully concealed, was the racial inferiority doctrine.

This theoretical approach led to a false conception of that particular part of reality: the colonial peoples and their living conditions. It can now in hindsight be seen to have been opportunistic and apologetic. It relieved the countries which ruled the colonies and the rich countries generally from responsibility for their poverty and their lack of development. Let me stop there for a moment and assert more generally that the tendency in social research, that results in biases, is regularly opportunistic.

With the liberation of the colonies—and the assertion of greater independence of a number of other countries, particularly in Latin America, which were even earlier formally, but not really, independent—we have seen a tremendous increase in research, and economists have ridden the crest of the wave. This was, incidentally, not a spontaneous development of social science, but quite obviously a reflection of the large political changes: the liberation of subject peoples, the craving for development of their articulate spokesmen—and the cold war that gave importance in the developed countries to what happened in these new countries.

3

And so appears an entirely new approach to their problems. It is, however, regularly equally biased, though in a new direction.

The racial inferiority doctrine has disappeared, which is an undivided advance, since it has no scientific basis.

But the climatic explanations have also disappeared. One can read all the plans and hundreds of books and articles on underdevelopment, development and planning for development without meeting the word climate. That is not an advance, since climate does play a role, usually though not always as an obstacle to development.

More important is the virtually complete avoidance of awkward facts in the sphere of institutions and attitudes, which stand as obstacles and inhibitions for development. The fact, for instance, of corruption and its recent increase in almost all underdeveloped countries is seldom touched upon, even in writings focused on administration and administrative reform. The adverse consequences for productivity of very low living levels—people being incapacitated by bad health and simply lack of food—are also forgotten in the development models.

Behind this new approach is, first, the uncritical application of concepts, models, and theories which have fairly successfully been used in the developed countries. In developed countries attitudes and institutions are adjusted to let through the development impulses unhampered, or they will rapidly become adjusted to do so. And levels of living even of the masses are so high—partly because of social security measures—that a marginal change will not alter productivity.

Behind the new approach is also what I call "diplomacy in research". These two sources of biases are unidirected and support each other.

Optimistic biases are even reflected in the new terminology. Underdeveloped countries are, as you know, now commonly referred to as "developing" countries. This is of course begging the question—by a loaded terminology—whether a country is really developing or whether it is likely or even possible that it will come to develop, questions that can be answered only *after* study.

This fussy terminology may seem unimportant by itself. But it is important as an indication of the deeper biases in present scientific approach.

4

The postwar approach in research and policy is as opportunistic as was once, not long ago, the colonial theory.

If this new approach were correct, that is, if we could abstract from climate and, still more, the whole system of awkward facts in the field of attitudes and institutions and the productivity effects of levels of living when those are very low, our responsibility in the rich countries for the welfare and progress of underdeveloped countries would be less costly to meet. The need for aid from developed countries would be smaller.

These opportunistic biases are spread over the whole field of research. It is, for instance, a fact that international trade between countries on widely different levels of productivity and income works for increasing inequality, if we do not control the forces in the market. It is also a fact that the widening income gap between developed and underdeveloped countries has become a political issue of rising importance.

But the theory of international trade we have inherited taught, instead, that international trade worked for equalization of incomes and, in particular, wages. And in recent years the econometricians have devoted much labour to showing how, under very specific and unrealistic assumptions, international trade could have this fortunate influence.

5

In the political field this bent of mind and this direction of research is parallelled by the almost complete failure of the Second UNCTAD Conference last year to wring any concessions from the developed countries, even to abstain from commercial policies obviously descriminating against underdeveloped countries.

In regard to aid from developed to underdeveloped countries the professional staffs of governments and intergovernmental organizations are grossly falsifying the statistics. Ordinary business transactions, sometimes of an exploitative nature, are reckoned as aid. Even the aid accounted for in public budgets can only partly be considered as genuine aid, for the United States probably much less than half.

These false statistics are widely quoted not only in the press and in the political discussion but are used in their work by professional economists and experts.

Looking at the political deeds, aid, even padded in this biased way, has been stagnating during the sixties, which was supposed to be the Development Decade. It has actually fallen if we deflate the figures with appropriate indices for the rise of prices, as we should do but usually do not. Compared with the rise in wealth and income in the developed countries the decrease in aid becomes even more conspicuous.

6

On this point I should stress, that this vulnerability of social science research for influences of opportunistic biases has no close correspondence in the natural sciences.

In the natural sciences you may complain about the direction of your research upon problems that is not to the highest degree furthering human welfare or, indeed, may be damaging and dangerous. But in the actual pursuit of a specific problem I see little entrance for systematic biases. So this is another difference between natural and social sciences, emanating from the fundamental differences I referred to above in the first section.

Let me add, however, that there is no reason to expect that a natural scientist, if he would turn to reflect on society, should be more immune against biases. His expertise would permit him, for instance, to point out that the technology now available should make it possible to feed double as large a population at the end of this century. But about the economic, social and political processes needed to realize that possibility, he would be no more an expert than any ordinary citizen.

His influence may even be to cause a misjudgement of the problems of these processes. The present technocratic euphoria in Washington and elsewhere related to the new "wonder grains" is a typical example of the optimistic biases due to a logical shortcut of the economic, social and political processes that might prevent that particular technological advance from having instead disastrous results for the populations at large in the underdeveloped countries.

7

I can only hint at the means to overcome biases in social research.

It would, first, be of importance that social scientists became more sophisticated about the way they are apt to be influenced by the opportune interests prevailing in the society within which they live and carry out their work. That is what I referred to as the sociology of science and scientists.

Second, they should better know the logic of social research. There can be no such thing as disinterested research. Valuations enter into social research not only when drawing policy conclusions but already when searching for facts and when establishing the relationship between facts. To have a view of society assumes a viewpoint. There are no answers, except to questions. Any viewpoint on, and any questions about, society contain valuations.

This is still seldom understood. The social sciences emerged some two hundred years ago from the metaphysical, and more precisely teleological, philosophies of natural law and utilitarianism. In these philosophies objective values were supposed to exist, i.e., to be facts and to be ascertainable.

By becoming less clear about this philosophical foundation of objective values or even evading them to the point of landing into naive positivism, the social scientists have not solved the problem about the role of valuations in determining their research. They have regularly followed a tradition where they solve complicated problems with one equation missing. This is what opens the door for uncontrolled biases.

The way to overcome this difficulty is to select and make explicit specific value premises, tested for their feasibility, relevance and significance. Bringing the valuations—which are always there, even though mostly hidden—out into the open, dissolves the indeterminateness that otherwise makes biases possible.

From what I said about the massive biases which are at present distorting the views on underdeveloped countries and the relations of developed countries with them, it will be clear that I cannot pretend that I am expressing a common view of social scientists.

As moreover you cannot expect me to give more than a hint in this brief address of very complicated interrelationships, you will excuse me for overcoming the shyness of advertizing my own writings. In a little book published by Pantheon Books, New York, *Objectivity in Social Research,* I try to give a brief and easily accessible treatment of the main methodological problem involved. In another book, to come out with the same publisher, *The Challenge of World Poverty,* I have pursued in some detail a demonstration of the massive biases in social science research in regard to underdeveloped countries, the field of study which today I selected to illustrate my thesis since it stood so much in the focus of this symposium.

THE NEW REPUBLIC—SCIENTIST, HUMANIST AND GOVERNMENT

Creativity and Social Change

By Ivan Málek

Czechoslovak Academy of Sciences, Praha, Czechoslovakia

Two notions which accompany man during all his life are discussed, namely *creativity* as the basic faculty of man and *social change* which he causes permanently by his creativity. Consequently new conditions for the further development of the creativity are constantly created. The power of the human development lies just in the mutual dialectical interaction of these factors, the former representing a *human constant* (in the dynamic and open sense), the latter a necessary *social motion,* in which and through which this human constant can develop and apply itself.

I shall try to show how, to what extent, with what possibilities and under what prerogatives these two factors influence and determine the present stage of the development, which is sometimes characterized as the beginning of the scientific-technical revolution. I shall also try to analyze what needs to be done to improve the interaction between the two factors for the better future for man.

I. *Creativity as the basic human faculty, its development in human society*

It follows from this introduction that the *leading hypothesis* on which I base all my arguments is that *man is basically a creative being,* and that the creativity distinguishes him in the fylogenetic sense from all other species. Creativity is the basic content of life and joy of man. We can speak about *human life* and *human fulfilment* only when the creativity of man is realized.

I believe, it is not necessary to define *in detail,* what I mean by creativity. It is the faculty which always, in some way, results in transformation of the existing reality, be it natural, material or spiritual, and in introducing new elements given by personal specificity and thus in creating a new reality, a new starting point for new transformations. This process of a continuous creation draws upon not only individual experiences but also upon the activities of small and large—today almost universal—societies. However, this historical experience (individual, family, national, all-human) is only a tool and substance of a new reality. Thus creativity is a faculty and joy not only of the individual but also of the collective, just as man is not only an isolated personality, but a member and creator of a wider social collective as well.

The origin of this creativity has a deep phylogenetical basis. The need for man to survive in nature has evolved into a need, both physical and spiritual, to create new things and to adapt his living environments. In the beginning this *need* materialized in the creation of various new physical realities and means which enabled man to survive in the struggle with nature. Gradually it became independent partly due to the successes accomplished and grew into a *joy of creation*. At the same time was developed the *pleasure of learning the environment* and finally man himself. Man, on the basis of this cognition evolved a desire to probe into and find new connections and to apply the cognition as an obvious part of daily life. At the start—and surely for a long time—this process of cognition was carried out by trial and error and the experiences gained were not those of a single life time only, but were accumulated in human memory. For its maintenance, religious and ethical rules were created. This strenghtened the awareness of a social community, in which individual contributions of personal creativeness were self-evident. However, at the same time it blunted the awareness of creativity as a basic feature of each and every human being.

Therefore the development and application of creativity did not proceed easily. It was, and still is, full of contradictions. For example, things which man invented for himself and to enrich his life, turned against him. In the main, however, it can be said that during ages the process of developing creativity and its application has become more rapid. In the early stages it was for the mass of the people limited to the solution of the *daily problems* of man and their collectives. Later on however it associated more pregnant individuals for the solution of more complex and long-term problems. The ability of abstraction became a foundation of every such "experiment" and developed into greater depth and became a basis and instrument not only for more exact solutions, but also for their systematization (e.g. the development of calculation), mutual understanding and strengthening of personal and social experience and practice (e.g. the development of language and writing).

However, the consequences of this accelerating process were again full of contradictions. On the one hand they initiated social and political changes (revolutions) that liberated wider circles of people from limited and suffocated conditions of creativity and this opened a possibility for participating more freely and on their own decision in the social process. On the other hand this process evolved into what we call the industrial-technical revolution. But this also had, and has, its own deep contradictions from the point of view of the development of individual creativity. It created for instance a greater abundance of goods, improved mental and physical human conditions and it condemned wider circles of people to a direct, inescapable tie with the creations, machines and systems, which tended to determine increasingly the lives of people. The basic, day-to-day activity of man, the aim of which was to attain a higher living standard, have been in most cases isolated from his creativity. Creativity in its most pregnant form began to be more restricted to a social elite, such as scientists, artists and organisers or following from the holding power in which case it had a very different character. For the majority of people creativity were confined to the leisure time and private hobbies. Mankind came to a threshold which some call the affluent society, which usually means that man is relieved from the daily lack of goods, but at the same time the need of man for a creative life was forgotten. In the countries that have reached the threshold of affluency, means are put into motion, by considerations other than primary regard of the human needs. This trend of development is augmented also by the fact that the majority of people in communities which have not yet reached the frontiers of these possibilities, regard them as final ideal.

This development has only to a small degree man's interests in the focus. It is opposed to the fact that creativity, defined as the ability to create new values, joy and the necessary talent from the human needs, is the basic, *general* faculty of man. Its advocates try to prove by various arguments (also pseudo-scientific), that such an ability and need is only exceptional, limited to a small part of the population. From this point of view human happiness is only achieved by fulfilment of basic (and always more costly) *material* needs. This is why society should concentrate its efforts to selecting those rare talents, enwrap them in all possible care and freedom. Through them society should ensure the need of a socially creative elite, whereas that "non-creative" mass needs only "panem et circenses".

This conception proves to be wrong as soon as new conditions of production and social changes put new forces into motion. These forces are already in the process of formation in some places, elsewhere for the time being arise only spontaneously. These conditions are frequently not understood in their deepest essence and only in a few cases their consequences are fully realized.

Is creativity restricted to a minority of the people, an elite?

Before I start arguing in detail I have to prove that the starting hypothesis, that *creativity* is a basic, essential and general faculty of man is significant and justified. If we accept this, then it is obviously necessary to analyse the needs for creativity so that it could manifest itself as a basic element of social conditions. This will enable us to confront past and present social changes with this human faculty and to determine whether the changes are really in the human interest and, if not, where and why they have failed.

I believe that there is no better proof for creativity as a human norm and non-creativity as a pathological state, than in human ontogenesis. What a rich spectrum of creativity and constant appearance of new situations which meet a human being from the period when he is not able to walk. How eagerly he looks forward to and takes the opportunity to develop the natural need of creativity! The majority of contradictions and clashes which the child has with its parents and teachers stems from the fact that it has this urge but is restricted. Perhaps psychologists and pedagogues will agree with me that in this respect there is no basic difference between different children, with the possible exception of those mentally retarded. However, in the mêlée of the adult world including school, to which the child is exposed, the possibility and opportunity of creativity are constantly being reduced especially by the civilisation and technical development of society. The child meets more and more a prefabricated world, which is not the world of his creativity, but an adult world, where creativity has been extinguished to a large extent by the life-style and development. Instead of being able to create new realities the child is being led and also stimulated by uses of the basic methodological instruments such as language, writing and calculating to take over and reproduce ready-made clichés. The majority of children are gradually being led into conditions created by the industrial and technical society. It is deprived of its basic need and even of its awareness and selfconfidence. If we really want to know the extent of the creative capabilities of children, we probably have to assess them in the earliest, pre-school period, at the time when restricting influences have not yet overcome that need.

Creativity, self-confidence, self-esteem and self-assurance

We have shown that the present way of life, starting by the introduction of young people to the production process and ending by the incorporation of a majority of people in the industrial production does not enable them to apply and develop their creativeness in their own occupation. As a consequence the awareness of creativity gradually disappears and this basic human faculty at the most finds its applications during leisure time and in hobbies. That is why we encounter an inner restlessness, which follows from a yet unquenched thirst for creativity, with those whose social belonging has not yet deprived them of the awareness of this need. In my view that is one of the sources of a growing social restlessness of youth and of their critical resistance to the established state of society and establishments in general. Even if their opposition is rather spontaneous and even if they are not able to find solutions it is very dramatic and intense just because it expresses the dynamics of a suppressed creativeness.

Hereby this need is connected with what we may call self-confidence, self-assurance and self-esteem. Only little attention has been payed to this complex faculty until now, although in my view, it is one of the key motivation elements, the development or suppression of which decides not only the degree and quality of the application of capabilities of each individual in society, but also his ability to become a constructive or destructive member of narrow or broad human collectives. It is an inseparable part of what we may call a human personality. Starting at the tenderest age its development is determined by the social status of each individual and by the means of education and social environment. Its foundations are being laid at the earliest age when the child in its elementary development creates the awareness of its ego, when it looks for and constructs the separation of its ego from the world of people and things. They are being strengthened and weakened during the whole educational period. A directive and strict education towards discipline, little regard to the growing personality, small possibilities in a creative activity, little stimulating recognition of the results of work and behaviour and the emphasis on all shortcomings and failures, all this will hamper the development of this human faculty. Man cannot exist in a society without this protective and motivational complex of qualities, because everything in him, especially in the critical periods of development resists his being only a passive component of human collectives, he tries to find replacements for a sound self-esteem and self-confidence, whose value is small and frequently negative. Here is cerntainly another source of various manifestations of young people at the time of their adolescence, which can lead them on a wrong path forever.

What appears to us as inexplicable explosions of non-constructive or destructive behaviour, is frequently nothing more than a desperate effort to show off personality.

This effort frequently issues as a lasting opposition to the society and can lead to a revolt on different levels and values. In other cases this need for self-assurance and growth of personality is by constant restriction being suppressed, stifled and killed. Human beings arise who are submissive, passive, easy to manipulate, but who at the same time may be full of complexes manifesting themselves by the inability of a genuine, deep friendship. They are not necessarily social rebellions but always unfulfilled and dissatisfied executors of orders, who are constantly alert and in a defensive posture. They certainly fit into an industrial society like a component of a complex of machines, because they do not believe in another possibility of their application. At the same time they are a source of unrest and dissatisfaction, which, however, cannot issue into a new deed. It is obvious that such characters can enjoy the gifts of an affluent society but are not adapted to the development of society, when the contributions of science and technology will free man from that self-dependance, and will require active creative applications in all the spheres of human activity.

I believe that a large contradiction will emerge because the present educational process with all the above mentioned consequences, form the character of people for many decades to come.

What are the conditions required for the sound development of creativity?

From what has been said above about the ontogenesis and phylogenesis of creativity it appears that there are certain vital conditions that must be fulfilled if it is to arise, develop and find its application.

To begin with the development of the human young: Primarily what he requires from the beginning is a *sufficient degree of individual freedom,* from the tenderest infancy to school age and the age of adolescence. It should be of such a nature that it does not hamper the initiative, but at the same time is guided by the interests developed and the stimulative relations to the environment so that it does not grope about but is capable of concentration both of his own free will and under the impact of good examples.

This of course is possible only in a *society enjoying a sufficient degree of freedom,* for otherwise the freedom will be accepted as an illusion, and is bound to lead to disappointment and resignation. It is only a free society in terms of both internal and external relationships that can guarantee the highest possible degree of equality and the opportunities for everyone.

What is further needed is a *full measure of activity,* not only creativity of the reproducing type but above all, of the enterprising, constructive kind and in addition an activity occupying not only the hands but calling for intellectual activities as well, which create new links with things and people in the environment. An activity of this kind must constantly be kept in harmony with the needs and possibilities given by age and its aims must be accessible and such that they can be reached. The path to these aims should be a new one so that it is being experienced as a constant adventure. Such a rich and multiple activity used to be ensured to a full extent by life during natural conditions by direct creating activities on the great part of people. However, this activity tends to decrease, or even disappear in highly civilized societies where it is replaced by "prefabricated" things which manipulates the child and gives him no chance to interfere. In my view this is also a deficiency of the television and the radio if these are not used as tools, means and stimuli to develop individual activities. The loss of this natural education, the importance of which has been appreciated by all educationists—for example our own Comenius but also the wellknown biologist Purkyne who devoted a special chapter to it —must be compensated for in a purposeful way at all present levels of education. It cannot be ensured by the kind of education children are given today.

However, these activities cannot be confined to manipulating objects, symbols and to sequences of thinking but must concern the child's movements including physical education of a kind which is adjusted to age but at the same time does not lag behind the development of the child's own potentialities while it serves to develop its capabilities by constantly attempting to surpass the results achieved.

The existing education as well as the manner adopted in educational processes does not adequately take into account the significance of movement, of physical and mental changes and transformations. Neither does it recognize obstacles that are necessary to give the child a chance to overcome them. And yet it is only the constant achievement of new results a pleasure of overcoming, that gives satisfaction and that gives rise to those factors of great social significance which we call self-confidence, self-esteem and self-assurance. Only people with a sufficiently sound education are able and ready to embark upon new adventures of cognition, and at the same time to know how to harmonize their own conduct with the needs of the community.

To achieve this sound educational development it is necessary to ensure that the education, the development of individual creativity, shall be performed in constant contact with the group of associates as well as in competition with them. In this way a sufficiently critical measuring rod of one's own conduct and of one's own successes and failures may be developed.

A further requirement is that the entire atmosphere of the educational environment in the family, in school and among the mates should be such that the budding creativity and self-confidence are not nipped in the bud by the chill of lack of understanding, or broken by the resistance of misunderstanding, by criticism or castigation or ill-considered punishments. When it is found necessary to limit the freedom of individual movement and expression in terms of discipline and organized activities as part of the school system this should be an island in the ocean of movement and creative activity, and not the reverse.

In establishing conditions for the development of creativity it is of importance to ensure that ontogenesis is able to repeat to a considerable extent the phylogenetic development, though naturally with an accelerating trend. Nowadays children develop more quickly and are being affected by a steadily growing flow of information.

This can serve to secure a firm foundation for the development of creativity which is going to enrich the continuity of the historical experience by its own resources. However, it is at the same time necessary to observe and foster constantly the changes which the child or a young person of today finds himself experiencing, and by taking account of this need to make the room for the development of this creativity.

And later on when the human young has reached the years of adolescence and independenec it is essential to show particular discretion in opening the space for giving scope to their ideals and for satisfying their needs for adventures. It is this period that tends to be one of the freezing points for the development of creativity and self-confidence attached to it.

What about the creativity of the adults? As long as the entire educational process has not been nipped in the bud leaving in its place a barren land of mere vegetating existence, a set of certain conditions are needed also in this case to enable creativity to preserve its fervour and social value.

It is essential for man to see his prospects, not so much for safeguarding the material means as for ascertaining himself in the society. He too wishes to have the uncertainty of adventure built into the security of everyday life, and sometimes he prefers the uncertainties of life in order to be able to embark upon the uncertainty of that adventure. If deprived of this possibility he may try to find the thrill of life in gambling, game, betting and the like.

However, in the case of adult yet another factor is needed to supplement the satisfaction they find in their work. I mean time for personal concentration and contemplation. Children and young people do not seem to lack this in most cases. The present-day life affords only few opportunities for this. Therefore, it is essential for the working system and regime to give thought not to leisure time that will be killed in one way or another, but to leisure that makes concentration possible and prepares the ground for it. And yet so few grown-up people know how to appreciate leisure time. Even its utilization for the various hobbies associated with creation of small things is a reflection of this creativity. Even if leisure time has not coalesced with the main stream of the social assertion it has nevertheless its own social value, since it serves to enrich not only the individual himself but also, through him, the society and human relations.

Even in the case of adults it is necessary to overcome crises of self-confidence, particularly in view of the contemporary rapid development of knowledge and its utilization in life. The person who does not feel the need (and pleasure) of constant education very soon finds himself at the limits of his possibilities and of effective assertion in society. Here, too, it is true that a man must not become engulfed in the group only, but must see in it his own share, the imprint of his own thinking, his capabilities and experience. That is why it is so difficult to apply and preserve creativity in the mechanics of an assembly-line production: Hence the acute danger of enslavement through which man is tied to the machine unless, by using it, he produces new values bearing the stamp of his own activity.

And it is exactly in these directions that the development of human creativity has been profoundly affected by the social changes which are beginning to emerge around us and the direction and impact of which we have been trying to ascertain, assess and have sufficiently prepared to face them.

Before leaving this chapter on creativity as the *basic and decisive* human quality, let me quote:

Teilhard du Chardin: "Process of humanisation: the better realisation of man's intrinsic possibilities has barely begun." "Few human beings realise more than a tiny fraction of their capacities or enjoy any but a meager degree of possible satisfaction and self-fulfilment."[1]
Lewis Mumford: "The main business of man was his own selftransformation, group by group, region by region, culture by culture. This self-transformation not merely rescued man from permanent fixation on his original animal condition, but freed his best developed organ, his brain, for other tasks than those ensuring physical survival."—"Mans own nature has been constantly fed and formed by the complex activities and interchange and self-transformations. "—"Because of the extremely complex structure of man's brain uncertainty, unpredictability, counter-adaptability and creativity are constitutional functions, embedded in man's neural structure."—Creativity: "readiness to meet unexpected dialogues".—"Order and creativity are complementary."[2]

II. *Social changes*

Robert Oppenheimer: "Our World is a new world, in which the unity of knowledge, the nature of human communities, the order of society, the order of ideas, the very notions of society and culture have changed and will not return to what they have been in the past. New is the change of quality."[3]
Bertrand Russell: "Liberation of creativeness, I was convinced, should be the principle of reform."[4]

In the first part of our deliberations we proceeded from the hypothesis that creativity was the fundamental human quality identical with what is often termed "self-realisation". We have briefly outlined the way in which its possibility of asserting itself had developed along with the evolution of the society and stated what conditions are required by ontogenesis.

In the ensuing part of our reflections we will turn to the other level, the social one, in which this self-realisation is to take place. Here we proceed from the assumption that in our society the process of transformation has been accelerating which may make a substantial way for a process in which ever wider sections of the society could assert creativity. In so doing we should remind ourselves of the starting point of the present deliberations, namely the assumption that creativity is the source of transformations in society, and that these in turn may create a suitable precondition for the development of human creativity. Therefore, individual creativity and social change are two phenomena which together form a dialectical unity.

That is why it will be our endeavour in the following to consider the nature of these changes, the direction they are taking, the basic driving factors underlying them and the aims they have set themselves, while confronting these facts with the requirements of the development of creativity, i.e. with the process of humanization of man.

Confidence in the ability of the present development of mankind to bring a better future for man is widespread and generally accepted, even to such an extent that many people, irrespective of the system in which they happen to live, tend to believe that this better future can be achieved without sharp struggles and grave contradictions.

*The confidence, however, has many various sources
and assumes various forms*

In many rich capitalist countries where the features of the industrial society are fully developed and established, the notion prevails that these countries have found adequate sources of economic growth to ensure increasing material welfare and that the basic social changes have essentially materialised. No revolutionary changes but only a continuous development towards this "affluent society" are going to be necessary, since the social system affords sufficient scope for carrying out the scientific and technical revolution which is expected to continue to bring ever new possibilities for ever widening sections of the population. At the same time it is believed that the increasing possibilities will eliminate the danger of further social transformations of the type called for by Communists. Some people even go so far as to find confidence in the system under which this growth of affluence has been taking place to such an extent that they try to evoke the conviction that even the development of present-day socialist countries is bound to take this course, i.e. after having passed the stage of their social transformations they too, will—in carrying out the scientific and technical revolution—assume a form approximating the structure of "affluent society".

However, parallel to this conviction, there has been growing awareness, particularly among young people, the scientific intelligentsia and among some economists, that the affluent society publicized and created in this way does not manage to satisfy man's internal needs. Others seem to arrive at the conclusion that the affluence attained is not a sign of a sound state of society and that, on the contrary, the system itself by which this result is being achieved is not only uneconomical, but that it tends to make society deviate from its true ends, that it brings about its own inherent ruin entailing a new kind of enslavement of man. Admittedly this kind of criticism, particularly among young people, frequently has no corollary in an awareness of what other solutions may be possible, thus leading to a nihilistic anarchist attitude rejecting everything that exists. At the same time, however, it indicates that explosive material signalling the possibility of new changes has been accumulated.

In the socialist countries changes have been effected in the basis of production the main purpose of which has been to liberate man from material dependence and material exploitation and to bring about a situation in which each individual might realise himself in accordance with his best qualities. The awareness of these aims and the actual changes carried out have been a source of a great moral movement, and have convinced many that the main and decisive transformations by the socialist revolutions will be followed by other nations as well.

However, the socialist countries have until now been using up most of their potential by creating a basis of production without which no such level of material means could be achieved and which, at the beginning of the socialist transformations has not been sufficiently developed in most of these countries. At the same time there was, and in many cases there still is, a rather wide-spread notion that the changes made in the possession of the means of production have *by and in themselves* given sufficient impact on the development of the productive forces to make it possible to catch up with the most developed capitalist countries with respect to their material prosperity. This is even combined with the notion that the peaceful co-existence between the socialist and the capitalist countries is associated primarily with economic competition, and will be brought about within these social structures.

It was not until later (even in spite of the analyses made at the 23rd Congress of the Communist Party of the Soviet Union which pointed out the inevitable ascendancy of qualitative transformations) that an increasing number of people came to realise that the social changes already effected were not sufficient to ensure further economic development. To the extent in which economic successes associated with the initial stages of simple industrialization had begun to exhaust themselves there has been a growing awareness of the fact that even the present-day socialist system is in need of further qualitative changes if it is to exploit the potentialities it has created by socialization. People came to realise that it was the decisive aspects of a socialist society, consisting mainly of the liberation of man, had not yet been possible of attainment. It was man's self-fulfilment that would constitute the main source of further development of a socialist society and enable it to make a decisive contribution to the social transformations that were to bring new prosperity to mankind. That is why even the necessary changes in the application of those factors that should put in motion any further development of the productive forces, and which are connected with the concept of the scientific and technical revolution, must necessarily be combined with significant changes in the human relations that are directly at variance with the above-mentioned ideals of a socialist society.[5] Though it is now being realised that in reforming and reconstituting the corresponding economic system it is possible to draw upon some of the experiences and the economic successes of the capitalist countries, it has also become clear that the task of confronting society is a much more complex one. What is actually needed is an entirely new system of economic stimuli which would correspond in the best possible way with the relations of production brought about by socialisation and would at the same time be free from those consequences exploiting man in a new way. Thus it has become clear that a series of additional changes is what the socialist countries are confronted with, that "Peaceful co-existence" with the capitalist countries is a much more complex assignment and process than it had been imagined by some, and that the actual implementation of the ideas which had given rise to the socialist countries has only just begun.

This optimism concerning mankind's future development is sure to have been fostered by the liberation of the absolute majority of the former colonial countreis from colonial influence. At the same time this transformation has brought up a tremendous number of problems, concerning economic development and systems, the further development of independence, the problems of hunger and natality, or the system of education and further cultural contribution of these countries to the world treasury. These are problems which must necessarily be solved before success in any other social changes in the other, already developed parts of the world can even be envisaged.

From the point of view of our recollections it will no doubt be of importance to see what course—together with the solution of the basic material problems—is going to be taken by the process of asserting and developing the natural creativity of people in these countries. The fact is that they are entering on the present era of industrial and scientific development possessed of an entirely different historical equipment. They are deficient in what has constituted the thousand-year old historical foundation of European society. On the other hands, they possess many positive features resulting from their direct contact with nature and from the application of the natural creativeness which has not as a rule passed through the polishing and refining influence resulting from labour dependence and the enslavement by the system of machinery. There are good reasons to believe that in these countries more of the natural need and joy to create something has been preserved untouched. The question is whether the present developmental process in these countries will succeed in exploiting the foundation of human creativity or whether it is going to repeat the development of present-day industrial society.

The third source of confidence in the future is the present rapid development of science. Wider sections of the population are becoming increasingly aware that most of the positive features that have been opening up for the development of the existing society are, directly or indirectly, the consequences of scientific discoveries and their application in technology. This is also the reason why a growing measure of support is being accorded to science in the advanced countries. All aspects of science have been growing at an exponential rate. Alongside with the development and promotion of natural sciences an ever increasing parallel support is being given to the development of social sciences as well. The hope is being repeatedly expressed that it is this development of science that is a safeguard for a better future, whether material or cultural. At the same time, however, there has been the warning memento consisting in the well-known fact that a large part of those funds which are decisive from the point of view of production costs are being used on armaments. Thus along with hopes, new fears are besetting man. The scientists themselves are becoming increasingly aware of their social responsibility vis-à-vis this dilemma. They are becoming aware that in spite of their growing influence upon society and its management in each individual country they are nevertheless unable to assert this responsibility devolving upon them on their own, that the question whether the results of their work will be utilised is going to be finally and conclusively answered by the circles that wield political power. They are, therefore, more determined than ever before to enter into a dialogue with politicians and society.

III. *Between hope and frustration*

There seems to be a prevailing confidence in the world today that transformations are under way, which can be expected to lead to a better life.

At the same time however, the question of what a better life really means is very contradictory and most commonly it seems to be associated with a materialistic prosperity only. The notion that this better life should bring about a real liberation of man, i.e. giving full scope to his creativity, generally crops up only in individual reactions, and has not as a rule been a decisive part of the systems responsible for the transformations. Moreover, in deep subconsciousness this process is steadily outweighed by the fears of war, all the more so as a very substantial proportion of the values created is destroyed or debased as being a part of the machinery earmarked for war. Thus man, tossed around between hope and frustration, more and more frequently resorts to a primitive and elementary life philosophy which is more or less vegetative in its character. Even this attitude is in itself part of the accruing social transformations and part of an awareness that they are unavoidable and indispensable. In this awareness of social change and in its evaluation several interesting aspects can be detected:

(*a*) Those social changes that are under way are regarded as historical necessities and inevitable regular phenomena. The advancing reality devolving from the development of the productive forces is mainly due to the rapid development of science and by its applications. This historical necessity has been termed scientific and technical revolution /in contradistinction to the former *industrial* revolution/. It is assumed that it will not only lead to a fast increase in human prosperity but that it will at the same time call for significant changes in human relationships if it is to develop and to be fully realised. On the other hand, the automation of the manufacturing processes together with the wide application of computer techniques are expected to create the prerequisites for man's gradual liberation from labour that is not intellectually exacting and for the increase of man's leisure time. On the other hand, this will demand a far greater attention to both man's environment and his daily regime, for it is only such conditions that are going to enable us to study these as an objective regular phenomenon and to lend them such features as are most advantageous for the development of man's capacities. Naturally, this entire process is necessarily going to affect the existing systems of society organization in all its parameters. That is why emphasis must be put on developing social sciences as well and, within their framework, the science of Man and his living environment. The degree of readiness on the part of existing social systems to carry out these indispensable transformations must be assessed. In doing so the danger is being realised and emphasized that the changes now under way might remain restricted to the sphere of materialistic "affluence" which would necessarily result in a further and harder enslavement of each individual.

(*b*) Another approach consists in the description and assessment of the existing realities, particularly of the ways in which they are applied in the present types of social order, the capitalist and the socialist ones, as well as of the ways in which these realities are reflected in the conditions of the developing countries. At the same time this stimulus is associated with the desire to render a service to this development, or potentially to influence future development with a view of removing the possibilities and the basic underlying causes of devastating conflicts. It is pointed out that the time is close when the bondage of the nations will be abolished, and conditions created for the peoples to enable them to make their own contributions, thus enriching not only their own countries but also humanity as a whole. That in the socialist countries the possiblities of exploitation of man on the basis of private ownership of the production means has been eliminated, and in the rest of the developed world—the capitalist countries—this exploitation will change its character of *direct* exploitation. In addition, changes in production processes and in their system have been transforming the attitude and consciousness of the working class. It is from this that some progressive people in capitalist countries firmly believe in the possibility of convergence of the development of the socialist and the capitalist systems. This in turn may lead to eliminating the risk for conflicts but also to a better utilization of the experience gained from the development of the productive forces up to the present time. Others tend to reject this view as being too simple and essentially wrong, pointing out the interests of the ruling classes and the struggle deriving from them, but are ready to admit merely economic and cultural peaceful competition between the two systems. It may be possible to have a better scientific understanding of the conditions and prerequisites of the development within these systems and to provide the individuals of a society with a better foundation for appreciating their own actual conditions and for developing social relationships better suited for their self-realization, thus speeding up the way to a better life for man on earth in general.

These differing views are also responsible for the shaping of divergent opinions on the necessity, the forms, and the character of a world-wide social revolution, which as some believe, should disrupt this system of common changes already under way.

(*c*) The third view of social changes is one of postulates. It is being acknowledged that mankind finds itself at the crossroads of its existence: On the one hand, there are growing possibilities for an unprecedented development of man and his life, of making him truly free to realise his humanity and to enjoy security in life and, on the other hand, it is asserted that his activities tend towards accumulating the charge of a chronic or an acute catastrophe that will—by degrees or in one sharp explosion—bring him to the verge of self-annihilation. It is considered that in this respect scientists bear and extraordinary responsibility in society not only as creators of values and of phenomena causing dilemmas, but also as those who are expected, and able, to see the consequences of the development in progress. Some people, especially the young, are affected by this dilemma in such a shattering way that they refuse to take part in those activities which they regard as being primarily responsible for this contradiction. Some of them even go so far as to turn away from science as being the main reason for the problems, and are unable to see the more specific causes of these phenomena inherent in the system of social organisation. The scientists themselves are becoming increasingly aware of their responsibility and are endeavouring by means of a collective effort to pass from the narrow viewpoints of their own specialised fields to the wider connections of social conditioning with a view to explore and establish the fundamental features of social changes, and by their joint efforts to assist in their application.

(*d*) The fourth view tends to concentrate on notions concerning the *aims* which the transformations are supposed to fulfil. There is a widely held view that, thanks to the development of science and to the possibilities it creates for people's common welfare, and thanks to the extensive experience and knowledge regarding the development of human society, the time has come when it is indeed *possible* to realise the highest ideals of human society, and that it is to these ends that all efforts, whether in the scientific or political and cultural spheres, should be directed. There seems to be more prevailing belief that under the present conditions it is not any longer a Utopia to set oneself these goals, and that, on the contrary, it is essential to corroborate this belief with definite actions and measures, both in the individual countries and in the international relations. In this connection the possibilities are being discussed of creating functional prerequisites for a higher level of organization of mankind by putting into effect the respective aspects of these ideals.[6]

I believe that all the above-mentioned views are valid in their own way. They express the existence, the necessity as well as the possibility of transformations, and demonstrate that the historically inevitable course of events tends to indicate that we should try to ensure that the changes are directed towards the achievement of those eternal ends and dreams of mankind, repeated so many times by the greatest of its representatives throughout the long period of its development. Those who are not mere participants in these changes but who devote a great deal of thought to them, bear the responsibility for not allowing any chance to be lost, for endeavouring to direct the gigantic wave of changes in this particular way, for knowing how to define society's aims and how to win ever wider sections of the population for them, for being capable of releasing people from their new subjection to things and to rigid systems and finally for being in a position to make use of the fresh findings and possibilities afforded by science and technology for establishing systems that will lead to a gradual liberation of man and of his capabilities and ensure a real prosperity, not the false one towards which regrettably, they are so often driven today.

IV. *Toward the full development of human creativity*

It is necessary to try to outline the essential features of the systems that we are convinced can result in this gradual liberation.

In the first part of my paper I have tried to show that creativity is the decisive quality in which a free man asserts his humanity. That is why I think it is important to measure every demand for a social organization and every single feature and transformation of it by the extent to which it is capable to serve the development of human creativity in particular. I have referred to creativity as an individual quality but also pointed out that it is only in society that it can find its complete fulfilment. Even if it is our conviction that creativity emanates from a natural need of every individual, it is generally its joint result and fulfilment of a need in society that is its measuring and stimulating factor. The aim of the society cannot therefore be that kind of liberation which does not impede or disturb the possibilities of the rise, development and application of creativity, but a liberation which stimulates directly—by its common ends and values—the delight of creativity, and thus tends to enhance the individual feeling by its social value. It is probably herein that the findings and characteristics expressed by the attributes of "homo ludens", "homo faber" and "man—a political being" are seen to combine. If any of these aspects of creativity is adversely affected by the social system, the system becomes an unsound one, no longer possessing the strength of a developing organism; it ceases to be an open system capable of development, and bearing and carrying out within itself the sources of its own transformation. At the same time this disturbing influence need not necessarily be caused by direct repudiation or suppression, but also be setting subsidiary, false ideals and ends which in large sections of the population may satisfy only one of the natural features concentrated and fulfilled in creativity, and *de facto* subtlely leading people away from that basic need, the need to get to know creativity as well as the delight in it as such. I believe that many features under which the "affluent society" is envisaged by many people mean nothing if not this character of false ends, needs and ideas is eliminated. Let me repeat that any such suppression of the fundamental human needs—even the one achieved by the false aims—is bound to become a source of a social movement which will be all the more enduring, the further the given system leads people away from the need to assert the creativity.

I am not trying to analyze all the substitutes that are being offered to men because they were generally known as early as ancient history, "panem et circenses". I believe that the economic strength, as well as weakness, of the capitalist system lies in the fact that while it keeps the economy in motion by creating and imposing these imaginary needs it also tends to lead man away from his human goals.

What then are the requirements for changes in an organization and in society that can be exptected to permit the highest measure of assertion of human creativity?

I will try to summarize what I regard as the basic requirements in the light of the proceding reflections without claiming that they are in any way exhaustive or systematic.

If creativity is the basis for humanity then it may be generally stated that what is called for are conditions which enable the greatest possible number of individuals to evolve, develop and assert their own personality, i.e. to reach a situation in which man has created a complex system of values both personal and oriented towards the society. These values should be of such a nature that man feels fully integrated, fulfilled, self-confident, and bears an attitude of trust and esteem towards others. He must not feel the necessity of resorting to self-defence reactions vis-à-vis the society.

I have tried to prove that creativity while possessing the individual aspect is at same time endowed with a social one.

Thus any demands for social organisation as well as for changes in the social system must possess features safeguarding the individual requirements as well as those designed to create the indispensable social atmosphere in which these individual needs may be realised.

I will treat them separately starting with those concerning respective individuals, and passing on to the assumed social ones even though it is clear that they are both indissolubly linked.

Individual requirements are those related upbringing, education, and the possibilities of social self-assertion, of making oneself socially useful. While speaking of upbringing I would like to stress what I consider the basic prerequisite—which is also projected into education and social usefulness, namely the need not to disturb in any way the development of that complex of qualities which I have called sound self-confidence and self-assurance. It is this complex alone that will ensure both the assertion of creativity and its harmony with the society. The formation of this complex is affected by the family, by the possibility of activity and work together with people around us, team work in a group and by the whole of education. In all these respects the individual needs to encounter confidence and other stimulating influences which should be as little restricting as possible. In fact, the above-mentioned complex of self-confidence is derived from this common confidence which the child and the adult encounter all along in their own development. Even when it leads to discipline it must find its way to grow into a conscious discipline which does not make itself felt as a restriction but as a free decision. This is the basic feature that must also be part of the process of incorporation into social institutions.

I fear that nowadays most of the basic influences are in a critical or an aggravating condition rather than in one that would be in harmony with the needs of a developing creativity. The family as the basic institution which in the decisive initial stages of human life should provide the environment of security, confidence and collective warmth has been disintegrating rapidly and no substitute form can be found.

Therefore, it is now necessary to give a purposeful thought to the family as an institution and consider whether the function of the family remains intact. If it does not we have to decide to what extent, from what age of the child and by what type of institution it can be replaced. If it does remain intact at least to a partial extent, then it is essential to cleanse it of both the deposits of the past and of the disintegrating features of the present, and by *purposeful* efforts on the part of the society safeguard these functions of the family ranging from education for parenthood, for bringing up children, to material security (in the best sense of the word) and to create at the same time all preconditions for making the best of its life as a group.

Personally I am convinced that for the initial stages of man's development, particularly in terms of the most valuable common significant aspects of personality which are going to find their expression in the development of creativity, the family is irreplaceable even today. Even the slightest disturbance of the family's inner elements is bound to be reflected just in these most important and most valuable aspects of the children. On one hand, its desintegration is due to the fact that it enables certain elements of the past to survive (family property, ownership, etc.) but, on the other hand, it is not given what it needs and its social significance is underestimated.

Thus one tends to forget that the family does not endure by its foundation but by a systematic and purposeful development of its qualities, which must be well and clearly defined and fostered as a priority by the joint efforts of the family members and the society. And it is the education of children to creativity, and thus to social self-assertion, that constitutes the basic element.

Nor does the second decisive factor—the possibility of an active approach to the environment (nature and society) find itself in a better predicament. Starting with the preschool period and throughout the entire period of school education conditions are decidedly unfavourable. With the growing urbanization and the civilizing development of the environment the development of creativity and the possibilities of the "natural polytechnical education" tend to decrease. It is substituted by a "prefabricated world" provided at second hand by for instance television and radio, a world with which one can do nothing. The child has no chance to verify its own powers and capabilities. Few conscious measures for the sake of development of human personality are being taken.

It is here that the process of urbanization, one of the basic elements of the society in developed industrial countries, has also become one of the basic factors in the direction of the development of creativity. It will probably be necessary to undertake a more detailed analysis of the extent to which this change is decisive and determining, and further what kind of reserve resources can be discovered in creativity to make up for the loss of those talents which have endowed with natural powers of perception and with the capacity to create, to transform things. Though the process of urbanization affects the entire structure of society, transforming the relationship between men and thus also their self-realization in the social process, I do believe that its impact on children and youth is the most significant, and that it is this impact from which we must proceed.

There is no doubt therefore that it is now time to contemplate this aspect of human development with a tenacity of purpose, and that we should reserve sufficient scope, possibilities and free activity to allow the child in its ontogenesis to pass through the phylogenesis of human work, and to acquire the basic philosophical categories not by means of words but by means of activity from the most tender age.

While in the case of the previously mentioned factors one can witness a deterioration of conditions for the development of creativity, in the case of education I would prefer to call it a critical stagnation of the system which had been created in its essence by Comenius and other pedagogues as a revolutionary system more than three hundred years ago, i.e. before the threshold of the Industrial Revolution. Nowadays while a multitude of items of knowledge are pouring in, man's role in the structure of society has changed, but educational efforts have remained the same.

What is it that I regard as their shortcomings and deficiencies? The rigidity of the system, its static nature so alien to the child's dynamics, the fact that pupils are largely treated as *objects* of the educational effort, including those cases where they emerge as pronounced subjects, as small personalities, that it affords very few possibilities for the pupil's own, and always to a certain extent individually specific, self-realization, that at a time when children are already capable of independent reasoning and of acquiring the basic methods of cognition, the system tends to fill them with isolated items of knowledge, thus ruining and repressing the delight felt in the cognition process.

Therefore, the main task for education is still considered to be to pour over into the pupils a certain amount of knowledge, which tends to become obsolete far more rapidly than ever before, instead of trying to develop *all the capabilities* lying dormant and more or less undeveloped *in every child*. Teachers seem to forget that with children the process of the development of capabilities is accelerating, and that it is dangerous to lag behind this development.

It is true that we have witnessed many reforming efforts. However, these have been concerned for the most part only with the teaching of individual fields and mostly with their enlargement and the utilization of new techniques and not with a critical analysis and a transformation of the educational system as a whole. Thus the reforms have essentially remained at the present level and have been lagging behind the requirements of modern education.

That is also why they have not been able to build a good foundation for what it is being felt as the need of a life-long process of education. The fact is that they have not given most children and young people any opportunity to expanse the *delights* of finding out about things as a basis for creation.

The educational influence of the group, so significant for the development of creativity that can be applied and usefully employed in present-day society, has declined partly because of children living in a "prefabricated world" which, even in the present form of school instruction, tends to drive children into individual contacts with items of information. There is no systematic and purposeful effort to establish a good atmosphere in which the widest possible sections of children and youth could participate in joint efforts and where creative individuality would combine with the pleasure that comes from collective co-operation in solving common problems and achieving common goals. Unless given the possibilities of getting to know these things children's character will evolve into narrowly egoistic ones they will lead essentially lonely and empty lives, unable to apply joyfully the powers of their own creative personality to the activities of wider circles, and thus also uncapable of learning the joy of creative fellowship of the kind required by the existing development in so many fields.

It would not be difficult to project the influence of these or similar facts into the adult age. However, here it is the phenomena of the social order that come more into the forefront, i.e. phenomena in which individual creativity is to find fulfilment and to undergo further development. Yet it is my belief that from the point of view of man's future the decisive measures to be taken should start with children and youth without any delay and irrespective of social systems. This is not to say that they will ever escape being influenced by the social structure, but considerations of these measures can be undertaken with a far greater degree of freedom and independence of the social system in question than subsequently the realisation itself of creativity in life.

What then are the demands imposed upon society, its organizations and its changes by the necessity to return creativity to man?

I am not going to undertake a detailed analysis but I will try to enumerate the basic qualities which should be present in that social structure which would best know how to develop that dormant, today mostly suppressed and oppressed wealth of creativity. The actual systems can find in these general features the criteria for their progressiveness as well as their own future.

If by creativity we mean the desire and need to create new things then it naturally follows from this premise that even the society in which it is to find its fulfilment must be an open dynamic system. An open system is not retarded by the habitual schemes and established powers but is self-critically seeking and opening up all the items of its existence to the flow of the new movement. Such a system must not only have an independent perspective but also yield enough inner strength that will fill that openness with motion. The tendency must be change and each partial change must be a basis for new changes. It is in this that the dialectical connection between creativity and the open character of the system consists. Without the open character of the system, without its basic requirement for change, every creativity is bound to meet with rigidity, and to exhaust and shape its energy to set the rigid spots in motion, and there will be no space left for new ideas and a positive contribution. Without creativity, and without the need to install the new openness the system would not possess a sufficient amount of content and of dynamics.

Apart from the individual creativity any society that has not yet overcome the contradictory forms impeding the movement forward is seen to accumulate the social force of creative opposition. These are, for instance, the forces of social antagonisms that had set afoot social revolutions. As a rule the individual and social creative forces come closer together in the process, and we are therefore not surprised to find that it is the most active creative individuals in society who establish links with the socially most effective and most important forces. This is also why the leading intellectual strata in the periods of struggles for social liberation came close to the working class which had actually been, and still is, the dynamic force of progress.

Another feature which is closely bound up with the first may be called the democratic character of the system. What I mean by this is the widest possible opportunity for participation as actively as possible in the social events and undertakings of the society. This presupposes that measures must be taken to ensure fully the feed-back flows of information in society which are subsequently followed by a constant stream of active self-realization in all the various structures of society. Everyone should have the possibility to know the basic directions of the further development of his own society, its real condition and the degree as well as the form in which the movement of that development is taking place so as to be able to verify on his own in a critical way the degree and the direction of its fulfilment.

Moreover, facilities must be created to enable him to communicate his critical and stimulating opinions in such a way that there should be the least possible difference in the *actual* level of information in the various forms of the structure. At the same time the individual must feel that his participation is being regarded as important, that it is being appreciated and that conditions are being created to make it possible. Therefore all ways of manipulation of men must be eliminated. By manipulation I mean the way of treating people when people are object of influences exerted by such means which are not accepted by them whole-heartedly. This kind of manipulation is effected not only by political instruments but also by economic, ideological, educational and cultural ones, and cannot assert itself effectively except where a perfect system of information and a low level of those being manipulated prevails.

Another factor, ostensibly an irreplaceable one, is social democracy. This I take to be a situation when every member of a society has equal possibilities of such a participation given by the very essence of its organization. This constitutes the basis of social creativity. I am convinced that any inequality with regard to the ownership of the means of production is incompatible with this. That is why I consider as a fundamental matter of principle the abolition of their private ownership which tends to create entirely different classes, namely of those who are able to participate fully, and of those who are dependent on them with regard to this participation in one way or another. It is also in this that I see the inaccuracy and fallacy of concepts regarding the convergence of systems in examining the differences in the ownership of the means of production. Though some external operative elements, especially the economic ones, seem to come closer together, though the level of material welfare rises considerably, regardless of these differences, that difference in structure which is decisive for affording the possibility of participation still persists. Those holding the view that this difference between the systems tends to become less important, object by saying that even in those systems where private ownership of the means of production has been abolished, the possibility of this participation has not been safeguarded. They are right in saying so but they do not realize that efforts to remedy this temporary shortcoming, will not be opposed by that body of forces who tend to back and reinforce one another, and who control the means of manipulation by which they can easily maintain conditions advantageous to themselves.

This is also the reason why I regard the changes towards socialism carried out in the World in the recent decades, in spite of all their present shortcomings, as key changes from the point of view of the world's humanisation.

This brings us to another question: What kind of demands should be put to the governing structures? They should certainly be of such a nature that they do not hamper the realisation of the open dynamic system. They should therefore not be instruments of preserving the *status quo* but of its constant shift forward, so that they may act as factors of change for every step. The task of the political parties in our own system (particularly of the Communist-Party which having carried out social transformation has accepted the responsibility of leading its people to self-realisation) can be no other than to see to it that the endeavour aiming at ever greater humanisation should be systematically promoted and that it should aim at achieving the participation of all. Thus its activities are primarily focussed on preparing the road and making available the means to effect changes leading in the direction of this progress. It must identify its efforts with the needs of self-realization of all inhabitants, who thus will see their own world on this road, affording them as much as possible in the way of their desires and the needs of personal effort and self-fulfilment, the more will be.

In the world of science this naturally implies that the governing structure will be all the more successful the more it will adopt working methods of contemporary science from which it will take over just this method of constantly seeking the most successful resources and ways of solution which it will subsequently make valid with the assistance of all. This means that the structure will need a very diversified system of science permeating the entire society as a mycelium, close to and accepted by all, well sponsored but at the same time not restricted or constrained in its adventurous quests of the new. Thus a situation should arise favouring constant transformations and one of a creative need for changes felt by ever widening sections of the population.

All this may well appear as a Utopia, it may look as merely reasoned abstraction and construction created by thought alone. Nevertheless, I am convinced that many of the above features are being put into effect, notwithstanding all the entirely contradictory tendencies to one extent or another, in this or that degree of perfection or imperfection. However, it is the task for science, particularly for political sciences to contribute *with the aid of all the other sciences, both social and natural,* by a conscious scientific deed towards giving a concrete shape to the system of management and towards the fulfilment of the society, which would at the same time be a contribution to a more purposeful implementation of the basic principles. Here the criterion ought to be the measure in which that requirement of development and realization of human creativity is being fulfilled—for it is only along these lines that dynamics and a steady condition of society can be sought and attained.

It is from the requirements gradually laid down in the course of our reflections that the role of the intellectuals today, whether artists, scientists or others, seems to follow quite clearly. In present-day society the intellectuals constitute a section of a particular social group which is helping to seek and discover new roads forward, and to win even larger sections of the population to pursue these roads. There is another aspect that seems to follow from this with equal clearness. It is important to devote attention to the younger generations of society. These should be given greater and earlier opportunities for self-fulfilment by the measure of the experience gained by them. Here the obvious presupposition is that they shall also have more opportunity of preparing for the participation. The level of information communicated to them should be particularly perfect both with regard to the body of knowledge and with regard to the possibility of its bilateral development without of course constraining their natural dynamic view calling for transformations. Thus they may become, in the same way as science itself, a significant factor operating in the direction of changes and against rigidity. There is no doubt that a substantial part of the nation-wide unrest among young people reflects the need of their self-realization and of seeking new ways towards achieving this.

Up to now I have confined my arguments to individual countries. Someone might demand that the whole problem be viewed from the all-world standpoint. I do believe, however, that both in the analysis and in the realisation of our aims in the individual countries we are still the earliest stages and are thus unable to outline the wider world system. As a matter of fact, we have been witnessing big contradictions not only between the individual existing systems but inside them as well, including those we had believed should have no room for such contradictions. It is becoming obvious that internationalism notwithstanding its common aims has not yet acquired sufficiently elaborated concepts and principles which might enable it to outline joint solutions. On the other hand, however, I feel most strongly that any particular solution offered should be a constant object of international scientific study, of an impartial scientific analysis of the situation, and of the aims and means.

From this point of view the realization of a certain type of system in individual countries should be viewed as an experimental solution, and it should be clear from what hypothesis it proceeds, and in what ways the individual items are being tested in the experiment.

The question to ask here is: Are we now ready for this kind of joint world effort, do we possess the necessary tools?

I am afraid we don't—at least not to a sufficient degree. Yet even so it is with the aid of science that the ground is being prepared on an international scale for joint solutions of some of the most urgent problems facing mankind like education, hunger and life environment.

Within science itself and in its international co-operation intense changes have been occurring lately which are clearly in the line of those requirements that we have proposed as the basic needs for development.

It is perhaps possible to say that notwithstanding all the contradictions and critical situations devolving from the present divided world there have been certain elements that may be regarded as the first hesitant steps towards an all-world joint solution of those basic problems of the humanisation of man, i.e. the development and fulfilment of all his creative capacities and pleasures. Of course, there are also all-world dangers following from the application of civilizing.

Notes

[1] Walker Ch. R., *Technology, Industry and Man; The Age of Acceleration,* New York 1968.

[2] Mumford, L., *The Myth of the Mandarine Techniques and Human Development,* New York 1966.

[3] Oppenheimer, R., *The Open Mind* 1955.

[4] Russell, B., *Autobiography, The Middle Years.*

[5] Richta, R. *et al., Civilisation at the Cross-Roads,* Praha 1966.

[6] Málek I., World Order and the Responsibility of Scientists ... *Daedalus* 95: 644–665, Boston 1966.

Facts, Values and the Future

By Torgny T. Segerstedt

University of Uppsala, Uppsala, Sweden

Man has always been forced to adjust himself to a changing reality. In order to do so he must try to predict coming events and if possible to influence the structure of the future. A lot of man's irrational behaviour, as magic and soothsaying, is an expression of his will to predict and influence the future. Science and research can also be regarded as an effort of man to adapt himself to physical and social reality. In contradistinction from magic, scientific behaviour is rational, that is you base your predictions on systematic observations and theories which can be verified or falsified.

The central question is the nature of future. Is future (a) something which already, in some sense, is there as a reality and which we are approaching but never can influence or (b) is future something which is continually being created by our own actions or (c) is future something which partly exists and partly is created? It is evident that the place of value in a world of facts depends on how you define future: valuation and choice have only meaning in alternative (b) and (c). But it seems also to have consequences for our possibility to predict (or perhaps the meaning of prediction) if we believe (a), (b) or (c) to be true.

For that reason it is important that we try to define the concept of future. I think that in futurology more attention ought to be given to that concept. It may be fruitful to talk about different strata in the structure of future.

1. The basic stratum is the stratum described by established laws of nature. We know for certain that the sun will rise next morning, that water will boil at the same temperature next year as today, that electric currents will behave in the same manner as before, that there will be a total eclipse of the sun the 11th of August 1999, and so on.

2. The second level or stratum is formed by human decisions in the past. The decision 10 years ago to exploit the Swedish rivers will influence life for generations. The same is true of decisions with regard to our educational or our agricultural policy. The best example is perhaps what happens to our countryside. There are very few natural areas and we fail to realize that much of what we see is the result of man's activities over the centuries, in his search for food.[1]

3. The third stratum consists of our decisions of to-day and their foresee-able consequences. If we really could control all the results of our actions of to-day and predict their consequences, the importance of stratum (2) will gradually diminish.

With regard to stratum (1) our possibility of making predictions is de-pendent of our knowledge of the laws of nature. But it is stratum (2) and (3) which are giving us the problem of forcasting or predicting. When we are discussing our possibility of predicting the future we often say that we have traces or signs of the past, but that there is no sense in saying that there are signs or traces of the future. Is that really a correct statement? In *Analysis* of 1966 there is an interesting discussion of that problem be-tween R. G. Swinburne of the University of Hull and Quintin Gibson of the Australian National University.

We certainly have signs and traces of the past. Such signs are buildings, monuments, inscriptions and documents. But it is a matter of discussion if such signs could be described as causes of the present. It is a difficult epistemological question to determine or define historic causality. Can we in any sense talk about signs or traces of future events? I think we can say that the buds of the trees, the roots in the soil, pregnant animals are traces or signs of future events. They can be described as elements of the future, but they are not causes (or not the only causes) of future. We could perhaps do the following statement: All conditions being equal, these trees will, because of the buds be green next spring. On the other hand it is possible for us, if we have sufficient knowledge, to manipulate the buds or the roots and change future. It is evident, as Arvill pointed out, that man's basic needs has changed his environment. Consequently we can say that,

(a) Man can create his future natural and social environment or reality.

(b) When man manipulates the roots, seeds or animals he in a sense com-municates with the future; he sends messages about his present hopes and demands and how he hopes to get them realized and satisfied in the future.

(c) There is a feedback on his present situation. His expectations or predictions of our future events influence his present decisions. There are two elements determining his decisions and actions; the knowledge of his present situation and the knowledge of the future. His knowledge of the present and future is determined by his scientific progress and endeavour, that is, by knowledge about true relations between phenomena.

The problem with regard to our prediction of future and our adjustment to future life is the difficulty of coordinating and surveying our rapidly increasing knowledge. The increasing bulk of knowledge is getting more and more divided into compartements, that is specialized and for that reason difficult to control. Each specialist may be able to forsee the consequences of his applied knowledge, but he can not forsee the consequences of a total application of scientific knowledge and the relation of his applied science and other applications of knowledge.

That may be said to be the reason why we have got all these problems with regard to man and his environment, for example the problem of population explosion, air and water pollution, and many other difficult problems. Arvill says that man, in order to survive must "control his numbers; he has the capacity to do so. He has sufficient knowledge and means now, not merely to avoid debasing his environment but also to enhance and enjoy it more fully. He must assert his will to do so, and replace a generally *laissez faire* attitude toward his environment by positive, substantial and sustained interventions to manage all his resources."[1] But in order to assert his will in this way he must have a comprehensive knowledge and a set of values according to which he can give priorities to certain fields of knowledge. And there must be some kind of interplay between our system of values and our system of knowledge.

Our first problem is to find some kind of starting point for our systematic knowledge. As our concern is the future of society and man in society, I believe it to be useful to start from some basic ideas about society. According to my view it is evident that in all human groups and consequently in society there are three functions which have to be fulfilled. Those three functions are (a) reproduction, (b) socialization, that is education and learning, and (c) production of goods and necessities.

Grouped around these functions there are always some kind of specific human groups. From a systematic point of view you can say that in agrarian societies all three functions are carried out in the same group, that is in the family. In industrialized societies the functions are realized in three specific groups as the family, the educational group (school or university) and in working groups (factories, offices, etc.). If we have a three-group society we usually have a fourth function, the leisure time function. The leisure time function is important, but may nevertheless be characterized as derived.

My plan is that we ought to put all expected break-throughs in research in relation to these functions. For example: What do discoveries in biology mean for family life, for education and for our work life? How does new knowledge in electronics influence education, communication and our work? What is the implication of modern medicine with regard to our family life, the length of our lives etc.? How does new ways of producing goods influence our environment and what does that mean for our biological life, our genetics, for example? All these questions could be much more specific, but they can only be answered if scholars from different fields of research cooperate.

By asking questions of that kind it is possible to construct alternative models. If we have two models, A and B, we can say that if we give priority to biological research we will realize model A, if we give priority to physics we will realize model B. Both are facts, but if we choose A or B depends on some kind of value; we prefer either A or B. On the other hand we must understand that no single scholar or nation can decide about priorities. When discussing priorities we must always be integrated in an international system of scholars and research. For that reason our discussion of value ought to be international and we must try to reach some kind of common international value standard. It is of course a problem if we really can agree about some basic values.

But even if we are fully aware of the relativity of valuations we could perhaps say that society must survive and if society is going to survive the three basic functions must be carried out. If society is going to survive new members must be born, they must be introduced into the social environment and they must produce food, drink, shelter and cloths. If we agree about these values and their more sophisticated derivations we can also agree that if model B does mean that one of the basic functions can not reach its aims, then model B must be abandoned. These are just outlines of a value system which must be the foundation of scientific policy and of giving priorities.

I would however like to suggest a reservation: It is primarily applied research which should be confronted with our common standard of values. I think it is best if basic research could go on without such a confrontation. I admit that this is not an easily solved problem as basic research is getting more and more expensive. On the other hand experience has taught us that free research may give unexpected but positive and beneficial results.

When giving priority to a specific kind of research we have choosen our future. For that reason it is important that at the same time as we are constructing alternative models of our future we determine indicators or criteria which can function as a kind of landmarks and tell us if we are moving in the right direction or not. Up to now we have decided a lot of actions, social reforms, for example, without pointing out criteria how to determine if we really are successfully approaching our goal. I believe it to be an important task of social science to construct indicators or criteria which can tell us if we are moving in the right direction with regard to facts and values.

Note

[1] Arvill, V. R., *Man and Environment*, London, 1967, p. 27.

Scientists in Politics

By Linus Pauling

Stanford University, Stanford, Calif., U.S.A.

The greatly increased understanding of the nature of the world and the tremendous technological developments to which it has led during recent decades have forced scientists to become involved in politics. I believe that this involvement must become ever greater in the future, and that it will lead to a changed world organisation such as to provide the opportunity for the most satisfying lives for all people, and to minimize the amount of human suffering.

The most striking example of the changes produced by scientific discoveries is the change in the power of destruction that has been placed in the hands of the leaders of the great nations through the development of nuclear weapons, after the discovery of nuclear fission. I have estimated that the world's stockpiles of nuclear explosives now amount to 600,000 megatons; that is, about 100,000 times the amount of high explosive used during the whole of the Second World War. If we use the ratio of deaths to tonnage of high explosive achieved in the bombing attacks of the Second World War, 0.4 persons killed per ton of high explosive, the existing nuclear explosives are calculated to be enough to kill 240,000,000,000 people, which is 70 times the number of people on earth. The power of death and destruction by the existing nuclear explosives is so great that in official discussions of the effects of nuclear war (in relation, for example, to the construction of fallout shelters and blast shelters) it is customary to assume a nuclear attack with only about one thousandth or one hundredth of the existing nuclear explosives.

It is clearly irrational to think of waging war with weapons that could destroy our civilization and wipe out the human race. The problem of eliminating war and replacing it by a system of world law is so difficult, however, in a world characterized by injustice and dominated by nationalism, that little progress has as yet been made toward that goal. The politicians and national leaders have not yet called upon the scientists for help in analyzing the extremely complex problems that must be solved if war is to be abolished and replaced by world law based upon an accepted ethical principle, and in searching for acceptable and practical solutions to these problems.

In the meantime the world continues in a limbo, with the threatening cloud of possible overwhelming death and destruction overhead. The great nuclear nations refrain from war with one another, but they use their military might against smaller nations: the United States on a great scale in the evil war in Vietnam, and the Soviet Union on a small scale in Hungary and Czechoslovakia; and, together with France, Germany, Great Britain, and Sweden, they increase the horror of wars between small or underdeveloped nations, in Africa and Asia, especially, by selling jet fighters and bombers, rockets, tanks, and other instruments of modern warfare to these nations at the rate of billions of dollars worth each year. To stop this traffic would be an important act.

The steps that have been taken toward the abolition of war and the control of nuclear weapons have involved political action by scientists. The international agreement forbidding the testing of nuclear weapons in the atmosphere was formulated by Great Britain, the Soviet Union, and the United States, was signed by most of the nations in the world, and became effective on 10 October, 1963. The political contribution of scientists to the achievement of this treaty was of two kinds. First, it was scientists who recognized that the radioactive materials released in the atmosphere by the bomb tests would cause great somatic and genetic damage to people all over the world, continuing for many generations in the future, and who issued statements about this damage and public appeals for a bomb-test treaty that, in the course of time, exerted significant political pressure on the governments. Second, the difficult technical problems involved in the formulation of the treaty were discussed informally in several Pugwash conferences by scientists from many countries, and an understanding of the facts was reached that permitted a politically acceptable treaty to be written.

Individual scientists have, of course, also made great political contributions by government service, both as members of government agencies and as advisors to the heads of nations. These contributions are, for the most part, not made public, and I shall not attempt to discuss them, but shall leave this matter to the next speaker, my old friend Glenn Seaborg, whose work in the service of the United States government exemplifies outstandingly the contribution to the world's welfare that can be made by a scientist who chooses this way of aiding humanity. The goal of a better world cannot be achieved without a much larger number of dedicated scientists in important government posts, to which they can bring their special knowledge and understanding.

There is also the possibility that scientists could play an important part in politics by occupying leading posts in the legislative and executive branches of governments. This aspect of scientists in politics is now the least significant, in most countries. There is no scientist in the Congress of the United States, although many questions that are debated in the two Houses of Congress are related to science, and might be significantly illuminated by their discussion by several scientists serving as Representatives or Senators.

Those rather few scientists who have been candidates have been defeated by the lawyers or business men or professional politicians who opposed them, or, in the very rare cases when they have been elected, have served only a single term. I fear that the training of a scientist, the inculcation of the sort of morality that lies at the basis of all science, respect for the truth, unfits him to serve in the Congress. This point is illustrated by the recent debate about the system of antiballistic missiles that was requested by the Administration. At a time when the Vietnam war and other Pentagon expenditures, totalling 80 billion dollars per year, are interfering with programs of social and educational progress and are causing a rapid rise in the cost of living, it was proposed to exacerbate the difficulties by constructing a small system of antiballistic missiles, at a cost of 10 billion dollars or more, as the first of a number of new strategic weapons systems that would cost 100 billion dollars or more over the next 10 years. Many outstanding scientists testified that the proposed system of missiles was not needed for the protection of the nation, and that this sort of acceleration of the arms race might well lead to ultimate catastrophe by upsetting the existing balance of destructive power between the U.S. and the U.S.S.R. These scientists included all four science advisors of Presidents Eisenhower, Kennedy, and Johnson (James R. Killian, George B. Kistiakowsky, Jerome B. Wiesner, and Donald F. Hornig), as well as Herbert F. York, former Director of Research and Engineering in the Pentagon, and Hans Bethe, the outstanding theoretical physicist whose opinion on nuclear weapons and missiles is usually given greater respect than that of any other person. The Administration was not able to muster any significant counter-arguments. Many Senators were convinced by the arguments, and announced that they would oppose the ABM system. It was clear that the Senate was nearly equally divided. When the vote was taken, in August, 1969, it was 50 to 50; the fight to stop the construction of the ABM system was lost by one vote. The New York Times, on 22 August, 1969, reported that the crucial vote, by Senator Henry L. Bellmon of Oklahoma, was not cast by him on the basis of the merit or lack of merit of the ABM proposal, a matter of tremendous concern to the whole world, but was instead sold by him to the Nixon administration; his price was the ouster of a political enemy, a 33-year-old Treasury Department lawyer, from his post.

I cannot contend that there are no venal scientists. But I do contend that there are few so venal as Senator Bellmon, or as Senator Thomas J. Dodd of Connecticut, who was censured by the Senate for having appropriated for his own use the sum of $125,000 from a political fund, but who still serves in the Senate. Scientists do not go into politics because they are unwilling to follow such evil practices, are unwilling to resort to the dissimulation, double-dealing, and chicanery involved in the life of many successful politicians.

We may ask why, despite the strong rational arguments against the ABM proposal, President Nixon and his advisors should have supported it so strongly. I have no doubt about the answer. President Nixon was placating the military-industrial complex, the Pentagon and the defense contractors, by giving them another 10 billion dollars taken from the people as a whole.

It is the military-industrial complex that is the greatest bar to progress toward a better world, and it is the military-industrial complex that scientists, students, and other people working for the betterment of the human condition must fight.

The power of the military-industrial complex in one country, the United States, can be measured by its present annual budget, 80 billion dollars. Of this sum 45 billion dollars is used for military procurement—the purchase of weapons and other goods—and 89 percent of the contracts, totalling 40 billion dollars per year, are given to contractors without competitive bidding. The profits to the contractors under this system amount to about 10 billion dollars—described by the Milwaukee Journal as "an alarming record of gross inefficiency, if not downright plunder; ... just plain graft ... the catalog of blunder and abuse is a national disgrace." Senator Proxmire has estimated that a proper system of management and procurement by the Pentagon would save 15 billion dollars per year without reducing Pentagon effectiveness.

President Nixon is indebted to big business. He is paying the debt by billions of dollars of excess profits on military contracts, including some billions from the ABM system, which his administration pushed through the Senate by unscrupulous means.

How can the forces of militarism be overcome? How can a system of world law be developed to take the place of war in the settling of disputes between nations and to permit (in the words of J. Tinbergen) a true global economy to be organized to maximize world welfare, undisturbed by national frontiers or national policies detrimental to the rest of the world?

Most people live under an accepted legal system, which is based on a moral principle, described as justice. The systems of law represent the effort to apply a basic ethical principle to the disputes that arise between people or groups of people. But the nations of the world do not accept law in settling their disputes with one another; they reject morality, and rely on war, on military might, which permits the continuation of great injustices, the satisfaction of national, corporate, and personal selfishness.

I believe that the existence of stockpiles of nuclear weapons that could destroy the world forces us to extend the system of law and morality to include all human activities. In the words of the Oslo Statement, unanimously adopted on 7 May 1961 by the participants in the Conference Against the Spread of Nuclear Weapons: "Restriction of loyalty to within national boundaries is obsolete, and loyalty to the whole of mankind is now a necessity. Individuals must bear personal responsibility for acts contrary to the interests of mankind."[1]

The theme of this symposium is "The place of value in a world of facts". The world of facts, which includes the theories that correlate these facts, is the world of science. Value is equivalent to morality, to ethics. I believe that it is possible to formulate a fundamental principle of morality, independent of revelation, superstition, dogma, and creed, and acceptable by all human beings, in a scientific, rational way, by analyzing the facts presented to us by the evidence of our senses.

The evidence of my senses tells me that I am a man, like other men. When I cut myself I am hurt, I suffer, I cry out. I see that when some other person cuts himself he cries out. I conclude from his behavior that he is suffering in the same way that I was. None of my observations leads me to believe that there is something special about me that sets me apart from other human beings, in any fundamental way; instead, I am led to believe that I am a man, like other men. I want to be free of suffering to the greatest extent possible. I want to live a happy and useful life, a satisfying life. I want other people to help me to be happy, to help to keep my suffering to a minimum. It is accordingly my duty to help them to be happy, to strive to prevent suffering for other people. By this argument I am led to a fundamental ethical principle: that decisions among alternative courses of action should be made in such ways as to minimize the predicted amounts of human suffering. This principle is, of course, not new. There are essentially equivalent principles in all the major religions and in the ethical systems of almost all philosophers, among whom I may mention especially John Stuart Mill and Henry Sidgwick.

Suffering and happiness are, of course, closely related. I might take as the basic ethical principle that decisions should be made in such a way as to maximize human happiness, human welfare. I feel, however, that there is so much suffering in the world, much of it unnecessary and avoidable, that it is better to place the emphasis on minimizing suffering.

To minimize suffering we must provide every person not only with adequate food and shelter, but also with education to the extent that he can benefit by it, with the opportunity to develop himself to the fullest extent, to exercise his creativity, to express his personality. Freedom of choice in personal actions is essential; also the preservation of different cultures, which enrich the world, and the preservation of the world's natural wonders, the redwood forests, the mountains, the lakes, which should not be sacrificed to the advancing technology.

I have contended that the principle of the minimization of human suffering is a scientific principle, with a logical, scientific basis. I do not disagree with Professor Jacques Monod, who said that ethics must be based on axioms, just as geometry is based on axioms. Professor Waddington then pointed out that, although different geometries may be developed on the basis of different axioms, all people agree that in the practical world we can accept Euclidean geometry and its axioms. I feel that, although we have theoretical freedom allowing various ethical systems to be formulated, the choice of a reasonable and practical ethical system is highly restricted by our knowledge about the nature of the physical and biological world, and that the only acceptable ethical systems are those that are essentially equivalent to that based upon the principle of the minimization of human suffering.

This principle, or an equivalent one, has for a long time been used and is now used to a considerable extent by individual human beings, but not by business corporations or by national governments. In business the principle of maximizing profits takes precedence over the principle of minimizing human suffering. In the actions of governments patriotism takes precedence over morality; governments strive to do harm to people of other countries with apparently greater zeal than to do good for the people of their own countries.

One of the tasks to which scientists and other people interested in the place of value, of morality, in a world of facts might apply themselves is to search out the causes of human suffering in the world today. Militarism is one of the major causes of human suffering. In addition to the suffering caused by the death and injury of millions of people in the wars that are now going on, there is a tremendous amount of suffering that results from the waste of a large part of the world's resources in war and militarism, resources that in a peaceful world could be used for the benefit of the people of the world. Militarism now costs the world over 250 billion dollars per year. This amount of wealth, wasted on war and militarism each year, is greater than the total annual personal income of two thirds of the people of the world.

In addition to the misuse of a large portion for militarism, the very unequal distribution of the rest of the world's wealth is one of the greatest causes of human suffering. It is sometimes contended that the flagrant waste of wealth by the extremely rich, the jet set, oil multimillionaires and others, is of little significance, because their number is so small. This statement is shown to be false by the following facts, which I have gathered from the handbooks of economic statistics. I think that, because of the possibility of keeping part of the income of the rich secret, the maldistribution of wealth is actually more extreme than is indicated by these numbers.

In the United States, for example, five percent of the national income is allotted to (or seized by) one third of one percent of the people, and another five percent is the total income of 20 percent, the poor people. Thus, there is a factor of 60 between the average reported incomes of the very rich and the poor. The factor is still greater in many countries: as great as 600 in Peru, for example, where, in addition, the miserably poor constitute over 90 percent of the people. In the world as a whole, two thirds of the people, the miserably poor, numbering 2,300 million, have a total income equal to only 10 percent of the world's income. An equal total income, 10 percent of the world's total, is enjoyed by a miniscule group, the unconscionably rich, who number only one tenth of one percent of the people of the world. The ratio of the average income of the world's rich and the poor is thus about 700.

We may ask what the effect would be in alleviating human suffering if a moderate redistribution of the world's wealth were to be achieved. Let us consider only a transfer of a part of the income of the unconscionably rich 0.1 percent of the population, leaving them still affluent, to the miserably poor two thirds of the world's people. The rich people would remain happy, to the extent that happiness is determined by having a rather large amount of money, and the misery of two thirds of the world's people would be very considerably alleviated through the doubling of their income.

An additional great amelioration of the misery of the poor could be achieved by the allocation to them of the resources now wasted on war and militarism, and still more, in the course of time, by increases in production through the use of modern technology. I assume, of course, that there will be a halt in the shockingly great rate of population increase, and that the populations of most countries will soon begin to fall toward the levels that will permit each person to live a full and satisfying life.

The practical problem of achieving such a change in the distribution of the world's wealth is a great one. Scientists and scholars should begin now to analyze this complex problem, and to formulate a practical schedule of progress toward the goal of a world worthy of man's dignity, intelligence, and sense of justice.

The proposal that I make is that the transfer of an increasing share of the world's wealth be made from the unconscionably rich to the miserably poor. The sum that seems to me to be reasonable is 200 billion dollars per year, about eight percent of the world's total income. If, over the course of a transition period of perhaps a score of years, the income of the now very rich people, numbering about three million, were to be correspondingly reduced, they would not, I think, be caused to suffer very much. They would still be affluent, with incomes of $100,000 per year per family, after the 200 billion dollar decrease. Just a few days ago a political commentator reported his estimate that one woman, married less than a year ago, had already cost her wealthy husband 20 million dollars, including five million dollars for jewels and several hundred thousand dollars for clothes. I do not think that the deprivation and lack of fulfillment that would result from inability to accomplish such conspicuous waste would constitute a significant amount of suffering.

On the other hand, the allocation of an additional 10 percent of the world's income to them would greatly diminish the suffering of the poor people of the world, especially the people of the developing nations, but including also the poor in the United States and other technologically advanced countries.

There are many problems involved in such an effort to decrease the amount of human suffering by a modest redistribution of the world's wealth. One problem is that of achieving such a change in a population without disrupting its culture. Economists seem to agree that reasonable progress of a developing nation could be made if its annual income could increase steadily at the rate of about 10 percent per year. This increase for all the poor nations would involve only a percent or two of the world's income.

Academician Millionshchikov has reported that the scientific approach to the problem has made it possible for some of the central Asian countries to develop rapidly, and that an important part in this development was the result of making higher education, in universities and technical schools, available to the people. I am sure that improvement in education is essential, in order that every human being be enabled to lead a good life.

Another problem to be solved is that of how to get the wealthy people, who are also powerful, to give up part of their wealth. I shall not solve this problem today, but shall content myself with posing it.

I believe that it is necessary to attack the problem of the great amount of unnecessary human suffering in the world. I believe that it is only scientists who can analyze this problem in a sufficiently thorough way, and formulate the procedures by which it may be solved. My own simple analysis shows that if even a modest redistribution of the world's wealth could be achieved there could result a great decrease in human suffering. But how is this goal to be achieved, what actions should scientists take? I am sure that, in addition to analyzing the problem and formulating possible ways of reaching the goal of a better world, scientists will have to take various political actions: as individuals, to educate the people, by explaining the problem and the proposals, as science advisors, to educate the leaders of governments, as participants in international conferences, to achieve world-wide understanding of the issues and as informed political-action groups, to apply pressure on the governments and voters.

I am hopeful for the future. I believe that nuclear war can be avoided, and that, in the course of time, the institution of war can be abolished. I hope that the present unjust distribution of the world's wealth can be rectified, in the course of time, by peaceful methods, through the process of evolution of the existing political and economic systems. We can now see the advantages and disadvantages of the existing systems, of Capitalism and Communism; surely we are wise enough to recognize the possible improvements.

I am encouraged by the revolt of the young people against the world which their elders have made, against its evil and injustice. I hope that they do not forget, as they grow older, but that instead they will join with the following generation in carrying out the changes that are needed to achieve a world of justice and morality, in which all human beings cooperate to keep the amount of human suffering to a minimum.

Note

[1] The statement is given in an appendix of the book *No More War!*, by Linus Pauling, Dodd, Mead and Co., New York, revised edition, 1962.

Science, Technology and the Citizen

By Glenn Seaborg

Chairman U.S. Atomic Energy Commission, U.S.A.

Let me begin with a warning—and end on a note of hope. Simply stated the warning is this: Over the next few decades—before the end of this century—mankind will have to face and resolve challenges that may well determine the shape of its life for centuries to come, if not its very survival. There is no doubt that many of these challenges are a result of the rapid growth and cumulative effect of science and technology. There is also no doubt that they are bringing into direct confrontation what many men have tried to separate—fact and value. One aspect of this is that science and morality have been brought face to face. But what I believe will result from this confrontation, albeit after the period of anxiety and agony we seem to have entered, will ultimately be a united force to raise men to a new level of rationality and humanity.

What we are witnessing today in all the tension and turmoil of our times is perhaps the physical birth of "mankind"—a "mankind" we have only re-cognized in the ideal but which we have never had to deal with so directly—as a world community, as nations or as individual citizens, all the moral laws, all the religious teachings, all the poetic and philosophical writings that have exhorted us to recognize the brotherhood of man, that have urged us to understand and respect nature, to act justly and humanely toward our fellowman—all these are being made physical imperatives by the power of "neutral", "amoral" science.

What I have been asked to speak on today—Science, Technology and the Citizen—is a subject that goes right to the heart of this matter of human survival and progress because in a sense it is now the rate at which men can increase, assimilate and wisely apply knowledge that will determine our success or failure. If it seemed true before, today it is almost an absolute truth that "Human history becomes more and more a race between educa-tion and catastrophe". We can see this vividly in the major challenges before us—in our efforts to avoid nuclear annihilation, in our dealing with environ-mental problems, in our efforts to control and feed the world's population, our struggle to plan our urban growth, to better organize our complex transportation and communications systems and to carry out all this within political, economic and social systems that would respect human rights and recognize the importance of human dignity.

Furthermore, we can see that these challenges are rapidly becoming common to men everywhere. They are not contained by national boundaries nor are they unique to any particular political ideology. Today a growing number of leading citizens throughout the world—men and women in the arts and sciences, in education and industry—have recognized these new facts of life and are joining forces for the purpose of alerting their fellow citizens and their political leaders to these problems and the urgency that must be attached to dealing with them. One international group that has taken upon itself the task of sounding the alarm over these problems, and of trying to search out solutions to them upon which political will can be exerted, is the Club of Rome. This "Club" is an informal organization whose members, representing various scientific and intellectual disciplines as well as various nations, have been drawn together by their common concern for the future of this planet and its inhabitants. While I do not wish to dwell on the activities of this particular group, let me just touch on a few of the ideas that have stimulated them, as they are typical of much of the thinking of today's concerned citizens everywhere.

A central idea upon which most of this thinking revolves is the fear that the dynamic civilization we have created may be producing change faster than we can understand it, adapt to it, or control it. Such change is producing ever-widening gaps which in turn are creating conflicts and crises ever more difficult to deal with. These gaps are already threatening human society. They will grow as the tempo of change quickens. And unless we recognize their causes and deal with them rationally they will become chasms that will engulf us completely.

Examining this concept more closely, what are some of the specific gaps and growing crises that could carry us towards this abyss?

We have a planet of limited physical resources being threatened by the prospect of a larger human population than it can sustain.

We have this population, as a whole, growing not only faster than its ability to provide basic sustenance—food, water and shelter—but fostering a higher standard of living leading to greater expectation, with a lag in fulfillment and hence resulting in greater frustration and open conflict.

We have within this growing population some segments that struggle to subsist, while others produce and consume so abundantly that their greatest threat is pollution caused by their own waste.

We have most segments of this same growing population differing to a great degree in their understanding of common problems and in their ability to deal with them—divided further by differences in race, religions and cultural backgrounds and historically reinforced political ideologies.

Furthermore, we have these differences maintained by economic barriers that have their roots in concepts rapidly becoming anachronistic in a world where a reasonably satisfying, if not abundant, life could be achieved for the largest part of the population.

And above all this, we have much of the world political leadership able to maintain its power primarily by preying on those ideas that divide men; unable and perhaps unwilling to create the climate of mutual trust and co-operation, the necessary agreement and self-sacrifice, to start their nations and the world on a new course of peace and progress.

But perhaps the greatest tragedy of our time is that all of this is happening during a period when mankind's body of knowledge, its emerging power and control through science and technology, could reverse this course toward crisis and chaos. Scientifically and technologically we have at hand or can gain the means to control population growth, to continue and even advance "the Green Revolution" taking place in agriculture, to abate pollution and conserve natural resources, to plan and build new urban centers, more and better housing, transportation systems and medical and educational facilities. All this is not beyond the capability of modern man, and the realization of this disparity between our potential and the current state of affairs is a source of great frustration to many people throughout the world.

I take hope in the fact, however, as I've indicated before, that an increasing number of the world's citizens and its leaders in many walks of life are becoming cognizant of these problems and of the existence of their potential solutions. In my own country I am encouraged by the growing recognition of the need for national goals and by President Nixon's recent establishment of a National Goals Research Staff to help determine toward what ends our country's efforts and resources should be directed. I believe that the President's creation of an Environmental Quality Council is highly significant. I also attach great importance in my country to the thinking and writing being done over the relationship of science and technology to current conditions by such groups as the Committee on Science and Public Policy of the National Academy of Sciences, and those committees of the Congress that have so avidly explored the close relationship between technology and society.

The great questions before us as citizens of the world—and they are questions that must be answered by those of us at conferences such as these and by thinking, concerned people throughout the world—are:

How do we move from awareness and alarm to agreement and action?

How do we create and crystallize a universal urgency over such life-and-death matters for mankind when so much of that mankind remains educationally and spiritually fragmented?

How do we achieve global goals, a global commitment and a global course of action toward the solution of global problems in a world where the first priorities of so many must remain tied to their daily existence, where insecurity—real or imagined—shackles so much human creativity?

I do not mean to imply that the answers to such all encompassing questions will be, or should be, forthcoming from any one meeting or number of meetings such as this symposium. I do believe, however, that such international meetings can establish the international "frame of mind" necessary to explore these questions in a positive way. They may help to clarify those issues that divide men, to crystallize world opinion where there is agreement, and to establish a concerted intellectual leadership which can influence and work with the national and international political leadership necessary to turn ideas into plans and programs that will win public support. Perhaps the most important steps that can be taken by those who recognize the true nature of these problems and the urgent need for their solution is to convince top political leaders of this urgency and enlist their aid in effecting solutions; any measures short of this will probably not be successful.

In what I have said to this point you may readily see exposed the attitude and outlook of a scientist. As such I am inclined to delineate problems in a logical and systematic manner, to attack them with confidence and a positive outlook. This approach naturally carries over into my life as a private citizen and as a public official. But I would be the first to admit that there are powerful forces in the world today at work against such an attitude. What are some of these forces? How might we combat them? Let me devote some time to these questions.

For one thing, our system of modern communications, effective as it is as an instrument of public education, is producing a dangerous side-effect. I believe too many people, bombarded daily by the mass media's pessimistic and disheartening emphasis on such subjects as pollution, poverty, the problems of controlling an exploding population and explosive political and military power, are falling victim to negativism and despair. Filled with a mixture of shocking facts and gloomy forecasts, they are too readily accepting the belief that we cannot or will not turn the tide of our mounting problems. They see only disaster ahead. In his book *So Human An Animal* René Dubos refers to this doomsday feeling as "the new pessimism" and says of it: "As the year 2000 approaches, an epidemic of sinister prediction is spreading all over the world, as happened among Christians during the period proceding the year 1000." Later, when speaking of the "new optimism" he states: "Despite the foreboding of the tenth century, the world did not come to an end in the year 1000 . . ." He goes on to point out that "The new optimism finds its sustenance in the belief that science, technology, and social organization can be made to serve the fundamental needs and urges of mankind, instead of being allowed to distort human life".

My agreement with Dr. Dubos' last statement, I believe, classifies me as a "new optimist," and to be such today entails a certain responsibility which is often difficult to bear. I find it both frightening and pathetic that when I give a talk or write a statement that reflects some optimism and hope for the future so many people respond so gratefully, almost as drowning men grasping at straws. I believe we must fight such despair and emphasize that today's problems, as big and as pressing as they are, are not insurmountable. Physically we are better equipped than at any time in human history to resolve those problems and realize many of man's age-old dreams. And our awareness of our problems and our knowledge of the urgency with which we must deal with them are also positive factors that are going to work in our favor despite the current pessimism they create.

In addition to overcoming the paralysis of negativism and despair today, we must combat the general surge of antitechnological feelings taking place by establishing a more balanced and reasonable view of technology. The current outcry against technology has its roots to a great extent in the environmental problems that are receiving so much public attention today, particularly in the United States. Because our productivity has moved far ahead of our current ability or past desire to handle the waste products associated with it, the discomforts and dangers of the latter are overbalancing the comforts and advantages of the former. The natural, or at least simplistic, reaction to this is to "turn off" technology, to return to earlier days and simpler ways. Even if this were possible—and we know it is not—I do not think, after a little reflection, that most of the people sharing this view would want to go back in time. I am inclined to agree with the spirit of the old French proverb "Ah, for the good old days—when we were so unhappy".

One of the problems we face in dealing properly with our technology today is that many of us have conditioned ourselves to a certain attitude about it. Our attention in recent years has been focused on all that is harmful, crass and ugly in our world, and seeking a scapegoat we point to technology. In order to avoid blaming ourselves for our excesses, our shortsightedness and any other human failing we point the finger of quilt at "the machine", "the system", "the establishment". In this particular exercise of self-redemption we conveniently overlook the many benefits of the technology of the past, but more importantly, what it might accomplish for us in the future were we to direct it wisely.

Technology can be directed creatively so as to bring human society into close harmony with its natural environment. It can be made to create more wealth with less waste—both waste products and waste of human and natural resources. It can be made to create beauty where we have let it spawn ugliness. It can be made to bring man both greater security and more individual freedom. What it does, however, will be accomplished only when we stop blaming it for our shortcomings, reassert our mastery over it and agree on what we want it to do.

We must also be willing to pay for advancing those scientific and technological developments that we find necessary to meet our agreed-upon goals. Particularly in the pursuit of a healthier environment there are large costs involved that, directly or indirectly, must be shared by society as a whole. With population growths and a rise in the standard of living we must upgrade those technologies that will abate air and water pollution and control and manage solid waste. These are matters of international concern even though environmental pollution currently poses a greater threat to the more industrialized areas of the world. In this regard, I am pleased to see that the United Nations has voted to convene a Conference on the Human Environment in 1972.

During the coming years much will have to be done in the way of "technological assessment"—in wise planning for the development of man's new tools and for their application toward the most human goals with a minimum of harmful impact on the natural environment. All in all, we must not be *against* technology—we must be *for better* technology.

Somewhat akin to the rise of the anti-technological attitude, but perhaps potentially more dangerous, has been an increase in anti-rationalism. Many people, seeing so much in the world that seems irrational, are doubting man's capacity to progress through reason. Their feelings were summed up perhaps by a statement made by Dr. Michel Crozier, a sociologist from France, one of the 90 "intellectuals" from 20 countries who attended a conference in the United States last December. Dr. Crozier warned us to "Beware of the temptation—difficult to resist—of the arrogance of rationality" and stated that it was "a kind of folly" to assume that "a rational view of the world based on the inevitability of scientific progress can cope with a fragmented, culturally diverse society full of complex emotional problems".

In response to Dr. Crozier's warning about "the arrogance of rationality", I recognize his concern and that of many other people who see in today's strong, emotional and diverse reactions to our problems the lack of effectiveness in appealing to reason. But I would hate to see some of man's current irrational behavior become an excuse for his acting and reacting on the basis of hate, fear, hysteria and ignorance.

In thinking along these lines I recall reading some time ago the remarks of an American statesman which gave me some concern and cause to ponder over how our attitudes towards reason can affect the course of history. The thought that bothered me was this: "Rational men tend to assume that all other men are rational. This is not only a false but a dangerous assumption." What concerns me here is basically the same thinking as Dr. Crozier had expressed and the direction in which it might lead us. If we do not at some point—and, admittedly, on faith—trust in the power of reason and act accordingly, we will either end up living under the worst kind of organized tyranny or in a physical and spiritual jungle.

And in some of the attempts to place the blame for our current plights on science and technology or "the system" or "the establishment" we find people going beyond an attitude of anti-rationalism to a posture that must be described as anti-intellectualism. This attitude is somehow tied to the ridiculous notion that the intellect and the emotions are divorced entities, that the thinking man cannot be a man of deep feeling and sensitivity. I believe that quite the opposite is true. Those who develop their minds, who understand the scientific disciplines, who think most deeply and broadly about man and nature, about the physical forces and the beauty of this earth and the universe—those individuals can achieve a far greater degree of sensitivity and emotional awareness than anyone who rejects the power of his mind. We need today more than ever men and women who can combine great intellectual power with a new depth of feeling and awareness. We particularly must convince our student generation that such a combination is both possible and necessary to human survival today.

In summarizing my position thus far, I say we must counteract these three negative forces—despair, distrust of technology and anti-intellectualism—by reemphasizing the potential of man, the contributions and potential benefits of science and technology and the supreme importance of knowledge and intellectual development allied with human sensitivity.

If there has been much pessimism and negativism expressed these days it has certainly not been evidenced by inactivity or withdrawal. Quite the opposite is true. Our technological society has created a greater arena of involvement. And while this should be a prerequisite to the solution of our problems it is also a complicating factor. Reactions to environmental and social problems and to the growth and impersonalization of government and social organizations, aided by the fantastic increase in human communication, have caused a new explosion of citizen participation in recent years. At the same time as the need for more efficiency in handling society's affairs becomes greater so apparently has the citizen's need or feeling for more participation in, and control of, his own destiny. Many problems are growing because of moves toward decentralization and participation in an era calling for greater cooperation and coordination. Citizen groups concerned with numerous causes have increased in size, number and activity. They bring pressure on all levels of government. They confront industry, education, and sometimes one another, on a variety of issues. The major, overall issue which arises from their activities and agitation is the question of the role of the citizen—the layman.

In a world of increasing specialization, technical complexity and the large-scale, rapid change that takes place beyond the understanding and control of the underinformed though concerned individual, can we win the race between education and catastrophe? Can we create through education the kind of citizenry, and can they in turn supply the political leadership, that will recognize and deal effectively with the problems of our age? Can we achieve the wisdom necessary to agree on and set national and international goals for mankind, to set priorities, plan and carry out peacefully the necessary social and institutional changes, to allot the necessary resources even if they demand sacrifices—can we do all this to achieve the kind of world that now seems necessary to assure human survival?

I know there are those who on hearing these references to planning, to establishing goals and agreeing on values, will immediately challenge me with questions of whose goals and values we will follow. These are always valid questions when planning is discussed in a democratic society. They are even more important to raise when one is speaking of the future of a mankind that is still composed of peoples of various cultures, of different background, languages, temperaments and ways of life. But we must begin to put these things in perspective with the vital things that all human beings everywhere on the globe share in common and which are being affected by technological change—among them the air we breathe, the water vital to our life, the health of man-made systems we now share across political and natural boundaries and barriers. There are common values and long-range goals for mankind as a whole, the pursuit of which does not lead to a homogenized mankind or technological tyranny. In fact, there are global goals today, such as world peace, control of population and the elimination of hunger, that if not given the utmost priority could eventually produce conditions in this world that would reduce discussions of cultural values to almost metaphysical arguments. I believe it can also be shown that a rational world based on the wise and constructive application of science and technology can be one in which human diversity and freedom are enlarged.

Until recently most people have been convinced that the world must choose between a tyranny of total planning or the unknown that evolves from the interplay of free, competing forces. Today science and technology make a different set of courses not only possible but necessary. In the past we have exploited both man and nature. Today it is becoming possible to exploit knowledge—and in a way and to an extent that will allow us to establish new and healthier relationships between man and man and man and nature.

I contend that knowledge—particularly as advanced by today's science and technology—is our newest and by far our greatest form of capital. And I believe that the universal recognition of this fact is in itself a value that can radically change our world for the better.

To be speculative for a moment about this use of knowledge as capital, let me give you an example of how scientific progress and technological innovation might give us the opportunity to solve what is becoming a major environmental problem in many areas of the world—the management of waste. In the matter of dealing with our growing amount of waste either by disposal—which produces no economic return—or by partial recycle—which most likely involves some economic penalty—let us think in terms of an era when we can literally close the cycle of resource to man and back to resource. At the moment this ability to create something from basic elements, use it as a product or service, and economically reduce it back to its basic element for future use (with no adverse effect on nature) seems somewhat like fantasy. Yet, in a paper[1] prepared recently by two scientists with the U.S. Atomic Energy Commission, the prospect of man's being able to do this is offered as a possibility for the future—one that may become a reality within the next few decades. The paper to which I am referring, to be published under the title "The Fusion Torch—Closing the Cycle from Use to Reuse", presents two concepts for the application of the ultra-high temperature plasmas now available in fusion experiments and eventually in controlled fusion reactors. The first concept involves the use of the plasma as a fusion torch "to reduce *any* material to its basic elements for separation". The second concept makes use of the fusion torch "to transform the energy in the ultra-high temperature plasma into a radiation field, to permit process heating to be done *in the body* of a fluid".

These concepts, when brought to fruition through the development of controlled fusion, would give man a degree of control over matter he has never had before. They would allow him, on a large-scale and economic basis, to desalt water, process urban sewage, perform plasma chemistry, produce electricity through fuel cells and recycle essentially all solid waste. These processes would be based on the use of energy derived from a virtually unlimited fuel source, the heavy hydrogen in sea water, on a power system of very high thermal efficiency, and which, because it involves fusion rather than fission, produces a non-radioactive "ash"—helium—a valuable by-product that will be in short supply by the year 2000.

The remarkable potential of the fusion torch will, of course, depend on the success attained in the achievement of controlled thermonuclear fusion. At present new progress has been cited by U.S. and U.S.S.R. scientists in this field, our Soviet colleagues having made particularly great strides recently. No doubt much work lies ahead, but if a concept such as the fusion torch can give us some day an essentially pollution-free world in which natural resources are so wisely conserved, this goal is worth enormous effort.

But having presented this one picture of science as what some might call "a source of salvation", let me be perfectly frank. While I believe that we should encourage and pursue strongly our programs for large-scale technological advances, I do not believe we should put all our faith in big scientific breakthroughs or the "technological fix" to solve our problems. We must work in all ways and on all levels to put science and technology to the service of man. Ultimately I think we will see that the science that accomplishes the most for human progress over the coming decades will not be the product of a few revolutionary discoveries or startling innovations but the fullest rationalization of the knowledge, tools and systems we already have at hand supplemented each day by small but important new discoveries and advances.

Perhaps one cause of some people's adverse reaction today toward rationality is that the abundance of information available and the complexity of situations often overwhelm us. One just cannot absorb and understand all that is going on in the world. It is difficult enough to keep up with one's own speciality, to maintain order in one's own daily life. Feeling that way leads many citizens to withdraw from participation and accept the words and directions of the experts. Many others tend to go to another extreme and, on the basis of what is often very superficial and sometimes false information, become their own experts—very vocal and active ones in many cases. This poses a great problem for both the specialist and the layman today. But it is one that can and must be overcome. We must find better ways to understand, coordinate and put to use man's enormous and growing store of knowledge.

What are some of the ideas and tools at our command to help us in this aspect of the race between education and catastrophe? For one thing, we have, and are developing further, new ways to organize and communicate information. I think that over the coming decades we are going to see enormous strides in the application of the computer and that it will become a central part of the lives of all of us. Today we are still going through the stage where, while we may marvel at many of the things the computer can do, many of us still fear it, resent it and are only too happy when we can catch it in error. But in a world of many more people, far more complicated than it is today, we are going to be vitally dependent on the computer, and learn soon that its benefits will far outweigh its drawbacks and that it will grant us greater freedom, not become a tool of restriction and repression.

One particular way in which the computer will serve to do this is by allowing us to create projections of possible futures or models of complex systems. These processes might be considered as an aid to—or perhaps a synthetic form of—wisdom. They give us a greater ability to look into the future in terms of what might happen should we act or not act in certain ways. Thus they allow us a wider range of choice, more freedom to select values, as well as a clearer picture of certain responsibilities. For example, if we can "see" the pattern of urban growth in a country and forecast many of the attendant problems we can plan to avoid them. We can project alternatives, evaluate them and offer people a choice. We can break the pattern of the cancer-like growth that is symptomatic of so much of today's civilization.[2]

Another example of environmental planning made possible by the computer is that of building a model of a river system to study what effect human growth and activity might have on it. Studying such a model, into which numerous interacting variables can be fed, gives us the overall knowledge we need to manage such a natural resource, to control its pollution, to determine how much industry, power and other use a waterway can sustain and remain ecologically healthy. In the future we will have to depend on the computer to give us this kind of information and correlate the studies of all the experts—rather than depend on limited individual knowledge or often unreliable speculation. Too much of today's wisdom is merely eloquent hindsight and is not going to help us in the future as much as a better correlation and projection of forces at work.

The fact that we have not had enough correlation of knowledge in the past and have been getting our errors called to our attention through such feedback as pollution, increased crime, violence and social unrest and other signs of great stress is a major reason for public loss of faith in science. The benefits of scientific progress are quickly forgotten, or at least overshadowed, by the immediate problems it seems to have created. What we have in evidence is a sort of "What-have-you-done-for-me-lately" attitude. As a result, "control" of science and technology (an extreme form of the required planning function) has become an issue of our time. Nuclear power, computers, electronic surveillance, significant advances in biology and genetics, all these represent real or imagined potential threats to the public as well as potential benefits. In addition to the growth of many interdisciplinary councils, committees and advisory groups—which can be beneficial in making science work for the greater good of society—we can expect to see the rise of many "watchdog" types of government and citizen groups to protect us from what they believe are the excesses of science.

I think that what most critics overlook in evaluating science and technology is society's—the public's—own past role in the problems created. Any benefits and advances if used excessively, with poor judgment, with misunderstanding of their influence or of the need to balance them with other influences, can become a horror. Take the medical advances that have prevented epidemics and prolonged life, and if you do not balance them with birth control you face a new disaster. Take modern mechanized agriculture that, while producing more food, causes a flow of rural workers into cities, and if you do not balance it with greater education and newer opportunities for those displaced workers you face another explosive situation. Take any of the processes that add to civilization—modern water and sanitary systems, more efficient industrial production, larger power plants—and if you do not control and plan for their side-effects as well as their products and services you are in trouble.

Only in recent years has it fallen to the scientist and engineer to be responsible for both sides of the coin—to innovate and to worry about the ultimate effects of his innovation. This is a responsibility the citizen is going to think he can pass off such a responsibility by passing restrictive legislation to "control" science. In the future we face even more complex scientifically initiated issues in such things as biological and genetic controls, personality and mental changes through drugs, the uses of space and the seabeds, the extended use of computers and automation, and many other advances, some of which we may not anticipate at the moment.

Clearly a new kind of relationship between scientist and layman is now vitally needed—one involving deeper thought and understanding on the part of both parties. I think that Don K. Price, Dean of the John F. Kennedy School of Government at Harvard University, phrased it most effectively when he stated:

we are now at a point where we need to rethink the fundamental relationship of knowledge to power, of science to politics, in our society. We can no longer put together Jeffersonian optimism about the liberating effect of science with Jacksonian optimism about the universal competence of the average citizen, and make the combination work in an era of relativity, existentialism, and the prophesies of a psychedelic paradise.

As I just indicated, in an effort to rethink this relationship many people have reacted by suggesting that science be controlled by restrictions on scientific investigation. This, I believe, is a dangerous approach, particularly when it interferes with basic research. Naturally, there are always going to be some restrictions on basic science through the priorities exercised in funding its research projects. But to try to forecast the inevitable human application of a field of research and judge its future value to mankind is very unwise. It is all but impossible to anticipate the contributions of basic research to various technologies. Sometimes what may seem to be totally irrelevant material turns out to hold the key bit of information to understanding a complex system or making it work. This point was emphasized in a study completed last year in the United States by the Illinois Institute of Technology Research Institute for the National Science Foundation. This study— "Technology in Retrospect and Critical Events in Science" (TRACE)— explored the contributions of basic research, classified as "non-mission research", to five technological innovations of worldwide significance: the electron microscope, oral contraceptives, the video tape recorder, magnetic ferrites and matrix isolation. Among other things, the TRACE studies showed that about 70 percent of the ultimate development of these innovations was the result of "non-mission" research. Some of this research was conducted decades earlier and the investigators naturally had no insight into the eventual applications of their work. Even without such studies as TRACE it should be obvious to all of us that science and technology today form such a whole and organic entity that we cannot cut off or starve any part of them without serious and sometimes unpredictable repercussions somewhere within the system.

This inability to anticipate the final human application of science is less true in applied research where we can predict to some extent the future value of our work. And we can exercise the greatest control in developmental work on specific technologies. Even here we find sometimes that a particular development can have additional beneficial applications we may not have conceived originally, or that potentially it has both great destructive or constructive applications. The latter point, I believe, holds the greatest significance for scientist and citizen. I think it forces us to a new level of maturity. Again, it puts mankind to the test. The real issue before us is not control of science—but control of ourselves. Can we grow? Can we increase both the extent of our knowledge and our capacity to understand it and use it constructively? Can we evolve in social creativity as well as in the technological creativity we have shown over the decades and centuries? Can we become feeling, thinking creatures whose empathy and rationality can encompass a global mankind and a global environment? These are the basic questions with which we are all struggling today—here at this symposium and around the world as expressed in the thoughts and actions of men everywhere.

As part of this questioning has been the continuing of a debate that has taken place throughout the ages on the nature of man. There are those who see man as inherently aggressive. There are those who see in today's violence and man's inhumanity to man the true man. And there are those who disagree with these ideas and see in the positive contribution of today's civilizations a humanity capable of great care and concern for its members. Some feel even more hope for the future because of the values being stressed by the new generation. I am inclined to side with those who believe that the evolution of a higher man is both possible and essential, and I would agree with the statement that Dr. Joshua Lederberg has written for this symposium: "The most important ethical inference from the fact of human evolution is that we are still perfectible. It is one of the least debatable of human purposes that our posterity should be wiser than we are . . ."

When I began my remarks I stated I would end on a note of hope. That note can only be a personal one but I think that many of you, though expressing it differently, share these feelings: I believe we are witnessing the rise, not the fall, of man. Through my own contacts and dealings with people all around the world—in science, government, education and many other walks of life—I have come to feel that much more is being done that is constructive and for the good of mankind than most people imagine. Perhaps the current emphasis on the problems and evils that abound in the world will serve to drive us to new attainments and therefore will act as a positive force. I hope so.

We must not let the acute awareness of today's problems have a demoralizing and debilitating effect on us. We must not let the search for solutions to these problems divide us when we should be united. We must work against such trends because never before has a unity of will and purpose been as necessary to our survival as it is today.

How will we achieve such a unity? Will it grow from the knowledge and the reason that I have spoken of? Not entirely. But I believe they have shed light on a third element which when combined with those two can bring us closer to Eden. That element and its effect on man was expressed so effectively by the Jesuit scientist-philosopher Teilhard de Chardin that I would like to conclude with his words: "Someday, after mastering the winds, the waves, the tides and gravity, we shall harness for God the energies of Love, and then, for the second time in the history of the world, man will discover fire."

Notes

[1] The Fusion Torch—Closing the Cycle from Use to Reuse by Bernhard J. Eastlund and William C. Gough, Div. of Research, U.S. Atomic Energy Commission. Wash—1132, U.S. Government Printing Office.
[2] See Paper by C. A. Doxiadis at this Symposium.

Rebellion in a Vacuum[1]

By Arthur Koestler

London, England

Hoping to discover at long last what the verb "to educate" means, I turned the other day to the Concise Oxford and was amused to find this definition: "Give intellectual and moral training to". And further down, to drive the nail home: "Train (person) ... train (animals)". I would not be surprised to see, when the next rioting season starts, a bonfire of C.O.D.'s; and that definition, with its Pavlovian echoes, certainly deserves no better. But I am doubtful whether much would be gained by replacing the offensive term "training" by "guidance". That sounds nice and smarmy, but it begs the question. Guiding by whatever discreet methods always implies asserting one's mental powers over another person's mind—in the present context, a younger person's. And the ethics of this procedure, which not so long ago we took for granted, is becoming more and more problematical.

My own preference is for defining the purpose of education as "catalysing the mind". To influence is to intrude; a catalyst, on the other hand, is defined as an agent that triggers or speeds up a chemical reaction, without being involved in the product. If I may utter a truism, the ideal educator acts as a catalyst, not as a conditioning influence. Conditioning or, to use Skinner's term, social engineering, through the control of behaviour is an excellent method for training Samurais, but applied on the campus it has two opposite dangers. It may lead to a kind of experimental neurosis in the subjects, expressed by a violent rejection of any control or influence by authority. On the other hand, it can be too successful, and create the phenomena of conformism, with a broad spectrum ranging from a society of placid yes-men manipulated by the mass media or controlled by the Thoughts of Chairman Mao.

The alternative to conditioning is catalysing the mind's development. I can best explain what is meant by quoting a passage from a book I wrote some years ago on creativity in science and art.

To enable the student to derive pleasure from the art of scientific discovery, as from other forms of art, he should be made to re-live, to some extent, the creative process. In other words, he must be induced, with proper aid and guidance, to make some of the fundamental discoveries of science by himself, to experience in his own mind some of those flashes of insight which have lightened its path. This means that the history of science ought to be made an essential part of the curriculum, that science should be represented in its evolutionary context—not as a Minerva born fully armed. It further means that the paradoxes, the "blocked problems" which confronted Archimedes, Copernicus, Galileo, Newton, Harvey, Darwin, should be reconstructed in their historical setting and presented in the form of riddles—with appropriate hints—to eager young minds. The most productive form of learning is problem-solving. The traditional method of confronting the student, not with the problem but with the finished solution, means to deprive him of all excitement, to shut off the creative impulse, to reduce the adventure of mankind to a dusty heap of theorems.

Art is a form of communication which aims at eliciting a re-creative echo. Education should be regarded as an art, and use the appropriate techniques to call forth that echo—the "recreation". The novice, who has gone through some of the main stages in the evolution of the species during his embryonic development, and through the evolution from savage to civilised society by the time he reaches adolescence, should then be made to continue his curriculum by recapitulating some of the decisive episodes, impasses, and turning points on the road to the conquest of knowledge. Much in our textbooks and methods of teaching reflects a static, pre-evolutionary concept of the world. For man cannot inherit the past; he has to re-create it.[2]

This is what I meant by education as a catalytic process. But now comes the rub. Assuming we agree that the ideal method of teaching science is to enable the student to rediscover Newton's Laws of Motion more or less by himself—can the same method be applied to the teaching of ethics, of moral values? The first answer that comes to mind is that ethics is not a discipline in the normal curriculum, except if you specialise in philosophy or theology. But that is a rash answer, because implicitly, if not explicitly, we impart ethical principles and value-judgments in whatever we teach or write on whatever subject. The greatest superstition of our time is the belief in the ethical neutrality of science. Even the slogan of ethical neutrality itself implies a programme and a credo.

No writer or teacher or artist can escape the responsibility of influencing others, whether he intends to or not, whether he is conscious of it or not. And this influence is not confined to his explicit message; it is the more powerful and the more insidious because much of it is transmitted implicitly, as a hidden persuader, and the recipient absorbs it unawares. Surely physics is an ethically neutral science? Yet Einstein rejected the trend in modern physics to replace causality by statistics with his famous dictum: "I refuse to believe that God plays dice with the world." He was more honest than other physicists in admitting his metaphysical bias; and it is precisely this metaphysical bias, implied in a scientific hypothesis, which exerts its unconscious influence on others. The Roman Church was ill advised when she opposed Galileo and Darwin, and from a rational point of view was lagging behind the times: but intuitively she was ahead of the times in realising the impact which the new cosmology and the theory of evolution was to have on man's image of himself and his place in the universe.

Wolfgang Köhler, one of the greatest psychologists of our time, searched all his life for "the place of value in a world of facts"—the title of the book in which he summed up his personal philosophy. But there is no need to search for such a place because the values are diffused through all the strata of the various sciences, as the invisible bubbles of air are diffused in the waters of a lake, and we are the fish who breath them in all the time through the gills of intuition. Our educational establishment, from the departments of physics through biology and genetics, up to the behavioural and social sciences, willy-nilly imparts to the students a *Weltanschauung*, a system of values wrapped up in a package of facts. But the choice and shape of the package is determined by its invisible content; or to change the metaphor, our implicit values provide the non-Euclidian curvature, the subtle distortions of the world of facts.

Now when I use the term "our educational establishment", you may object that there is no such thing. Every country, every university and every faculty therein has of course its individual character, its personal face—or facelessness. Nevertheless, taking diversity for granted, and exceptions for granted, there exist certain common denominators which determine the cultural climate and the metaphysical bias imparted to hopeful students practically everywhere in the non-totalitarian sector of the world, from California to the East Coast, from London to Berlin, Bombay and Tokyo. That climate is impossible to define without oversimplification, so I shall oversimplify deliberately and say that it is dominated by three R's.

The first R stands for Reductionism. Its philosophy may be epitomized by a quotation from a recent book in which man is defined, in all seriousness, as "nothing but a complex biochemical mechanism, powered by a combustion system which energises computers with prodigious storage facilities for retaining encoded information". This is certainly an extreme formulation, but it conveys the essence of that philosophy.

It is of course perfectly legitimate to draw analogies between the central nervous system and a telephone exchange, or a computer, or a holograph. The reductionist heresy is contained in the words "nothing but". If you replace in the sentence I have just quoted the words "nothing but" by "to some extent" or "from a certain angle" or "on a certain level of his many-levelled structure", then everything is all right. The reductionist proclaims his part-truth to be the whole truth, a certain specific aspect of a phenomenon to be the whole phenomenon. To the behaviourist, the activities of man are *nothing but* a chain of conditioned responses, to the more rigid variety of Freudian, artistic creation is nothing but a substitute for goal-inhibited sexuality, to the mechanically oriented biologist the phenomena of consciousness are nothing but electro-chemical reactions. And the ultimate reductionist heresy is to consider the whole as nothing but the sum of its parts—a hangover from the crude atomistic concepts of nineteenth century physics, which the physicist himself has abandoned long ago.

The second of the three R's is what I have called elsewhere the philosophy of Ratomorphism. At the turn of the century, Lloyd Morgan's famous canon warned biologists against the fallacy of projecting human thoughts and feelings into animals; since then, the pendulum has moved in the opposite direction, so that today, instead of an anthropomorphic view of the rat, we have a ratomorphic view of man. According to this view, our skyscrapers are nothing but huge Skinner boxes in which, instead of pressing a pedal to obtain a food-pellet, we emit operant responses which are more complicated, but governed by the same laws as the behaviour of the rat. Again, if you erase the "nothing but", there is an ugly grain of truth in this. But if the life of man is becoming a rat-race, it is because he has become impregnated with a ratomorphic philosophy. One is reminded of that old quip: "Psychoanalysis is the disease which it pretends to cure". Keep telling a man that he is nothing but an oversized rat, and he will start growing whiskers and bite your finger.

Some fifty years ago, in the heyday of the conditioned reflex, the paradigm of human behaviour was Pavlov's dog salivating in its restraining harness on the laboratory table. After that came the rat in the box. And after the rat came the geese. In his recent book, *On Aggression,* Konrad Lorenz advances the theory that affection between social animals is phylogenetically derived from aggression. The bond which holds the partners together (regardless whether it has a sexual component or not) is "neither more nor less than the conversion of aggression into its opposite". Whether one agrees or disagrees with this theory is irrelevant; the reason why I mention it is that Lorenz' arguments are almost exclusively based on his observations of the so-called triumph ceremony of the greylag goose, which, in his own words, prompted him to write his book. Once more we are offered a *Weltanschauung* derived from an exceedingly specialized type of observations, a part-truth which claims to be the whole truth. To quote the Austrian psychiatrist, Viktor Frankl: "The trouble is not that scientists are specializing, but rather that specialists are generalizing".

A last example for the second "R." About a year ago, a popular book on anthropology was heading the bestseller lists in Europe and America: *The Naked Ape—A Zoologist's Study of the Human Animal* by Dr. Desmond Morris. It opens with the statement that man is a hairless ape "self-named *homo sapiens*. I am a zoologist and the naked ape is an animal. He is therefore fair game for my pen". To what extremes this zoomorphic approach may lead is illustrated by the following quotation:

The insides of houses or flats can be decorated and filled with ornaments, bric-a-brac and personal belongings in profusion. This is usually explained as being done to make the place 'look nice'. In fact, it is the exact equivalent to another territorial species depositing its personal scent on a landmark near its den. When you put a name on a door, or hang a painting on a wall, you are, in dog or wolf terms, for example, simply cocking your leg on them and leaving your personal mark there.

To avoid misunderstandings, let me emphasize once more that it is both legitimate and necessary for scientific research to investigate conditioned reflexes in dogs, operant responses in rats, and the ritual dances of geese— so long as they are not forced upon us as paradigms for man's condition. But this is precisely what has been happening for the best part of our middle-aged century.

My third R is Randomness. Biological evolution is considered to be nothing but random mutations preserved by natural selection; mental evolution nothing but random tries preserved by reinforcement. To quote from a textbook by a leading evolutionist: "It does seem that the problem of evolution is essentially solved ... It turns out to be basically materialistic, with no sign of purpose ... Man is the result of a purposeless and materialistic process ..."[3] To paraphrase Einstein, a non-existent God plays blind dice with the universe. Even physical causality, the solid rock on which that universe was built, has been replaced by the driftsands of statistics. We all seem to be in the condition which the physicist calls "Brownian movement" —the erratic zigzag motions of a particle of smoke buffeted about by the molecules of the surrounding air.

Some schools of modern art, too, have adopted the cult of randomness. Action-painters throw at random fistfuls of paint at the canvas; a French sculptor achieved international fame by bashing old motor cars with a demolition machine into random shapes; others assemble bits of scrap iron into abstract compositions, or bits of fluff and tinsel into collages; some composers of electronic music use randomising machines for their effects. One fashionable novelist boasts of cutting up his typescript with a pair of scissors, and sticking it together again in random fashion.

These schools of contemporary art seem to derive their inspiration from the prevalent bias in the sciences of life—a kind of secondary infection. Randomness, we are told, is the basic fact of life. We live in a world crammed full with hard facts, and there is no place in it for purpose, values or meaning. To look for values and meaning is considered as absurd as it would be for an astronomer to search with his telescope for Dante's heavenly paradise. And it would be equally absurd to search with a microscope for that ghost in the machine, the conscious mind, with its ghostly attributes of free choice and moral responsibility.

Let us remind ourselves once more that the essence of teaching is not in the facts and data which it conveys, but in the interpretations that it transmits in explicit or implied ways. In terms of modern communication theory, the bulk of the information consists of interpretations. That is the core of the package; the data provide only the wrappings. But the recurrent, embittered controversies in the history of science prove over and over again that the same data can be interpreted in different ways and reshuffled into different patterns. I have just quoted a distinguished biologist of the orthodox neo-Darwinian school. Let me now quote another eminent biologist, C. H. Waddington, who, based on exactly the same available data, arrives at the opposite view: "To suppose that the evolution of the wonderfully adapted biological mechanisms has depended only on a selection out of a haphazard set of variations, each produced by blind chance, is like suggesting that if we went on throwing bricks into heaps, we should eventually be able to choose ourselves the most desirable house."[4]

One could go on quoting such diametrically opposed conclusions drawn by different scientists from the same body of data. For example, one could hardly expect neurophysiologists to belittle the importance of brain mechanisms in mental life, and many of them do indeed hold that mental life is nothing but brain mechanism. And yet Sherrington was an unashamed dualist; he wrote: "That our being should consist of *two* fundamental elements offers, I suppose, no greater inherent improbability than that it should rest on one only". And the great Canadian brain surgeon, Wilder Penfield, said at an interdisciplinary symposium on "Control of the Mind" at which we both participated: "To declare that these two things (brain and mind) are one does not make them so, but it does block the progress of research."

I quote this, not because I am a Cartesian dualist—which I am not— but to emphasize that the neurophysiologist's precise data can be interpreted in diverse ways. In other words, it is not true that the data which science provides must automatically lead to the conclusion that life is meaningless, nothing but Brownian motion imparted by the random drift of cosmic weather. We should rather say that the *Zeitgeist* has a tendency to draw biased philosophical conclusions from the data, a tendency towards the devaluation of values and the elimination of meaning from the world around us and the world inside us. The result is an existential vacuum.

At this point I would like to quote again Viktor Frankl, founder of what has become known as the Third Viennese School of Psychiatry. He postulates that besides Freud's Pleasure Principle and Adler's Will to Power, there exists a "Will to Meaning" as an equally fundamental human drive:

> It is an inherent tendency in man to reach out for meanings to fulfil and for values to actualise. In contrast to animals, man is not told by his instincts what he must do. And in contrast to man in former times, he is no longer told by his traditions and values what he ought to do. Thousands and thousands of young students are exposed to an indoctrination along the lines of a reductionist concept of life which denies the existence of values. The result is a world-wide phenomenon, more and more patients are crowding our clinics with the complaint of an inner emptiness, the sense of a total and ultimate meaninglessness of life.[5]

He calls this type of neurosis "noogenic", as distinct from sexual and other types of neuroses, and he claims that about twenty per cent of all cases at the Vienna Psychiatric Clinic (of which he is the head) are of noogenic origin. He further claims that this figure is doubled among student patients of Central European origin; and that it soars to eighty per cent among students in the United States.

I should mention that I know next to nothing about the therapeutic methods of this school—it is called Logotherapy—and that I have no means of judging its efficacity. But there exists a considerable literature on the subject, and I brought it up because the philosophy behind it seems to me relevant to our theme. However that may be, the term "existential vacuum", caused by the frustration of the will to meaning, seems to be a fitting description of the world-wide mood of infectious restlessness, particularly among the young and among intellectuals.

It may be of some interest to compare this mood with that of the Pink Decade, the 1930's, when the Western world was convulsed by economic depression, unemployment and hunger marches, and the so-called Great Socialist Experiment initiated by the Russian Revolution seemed to be the only hopeful ideal to a great mass of youthful idealists, including the present speaker. In *The God That Failed,* I wrote about that period:

> Devotion to pure Utopia and rebellion against a polluted society are the two poles which provide the tension of all militant creeds. To ask which of the two makes the current flow—attraction by the ideal or repulsion by the social environment—is to ask the old question whether the hen was first, or the egg.

Compare this with the present mood. Today the repellent forces are more powerful than ever, but the attraction of the ideal is missing, since what we thought to be Utopia turned out to be a cynical fraud. The egg is there, but no hen to hatch it. Rebellion is freewheeling in a vacuum.

Another comparison comes to mind—another historic situation, in which the traditional values of a culture were being destroyed, without new values taking their place. I mean the fatal impact of the European conquerors on the native civilisations of American Indians and Pacific Islanders. In our case, the shattering impact was not caused by the greed, rapacity and missionary zeal of foreign invaders. The invasion has come from within, in the guise of an ideology which claims to be scientific and is in fact a new version of nihilism in its denial of values, purpose and meaning. But the results in both cases are comparable: like the natives who were left without traditions and beliefs in a spiritual vacuum, we, too, seem to wander about in a bemused trance.

It is of course true that similar negative moods can be found in past periods of our history, variously described as *mal de siècle* romantic despair, Russian nihilism, apocalyptic expectations. And there have been Ranters, Messianic sects and Tarantula dancers, all of whom have their striking contemporary parallels. But the present has a unique and unprecedented urgency because the rate of change is now moving along an ever steeper exponential curve, and history is accelerating like the molecules in a liquid coming to the boil. There is no need to evoke the population explosion, urban explosion and explosion of explosive power; we live in their midst, in the eye of the hurricane.

This brings me back to my starting point. The ideal of the educator as a catalysing agent is for the time being unattainable. Exceptions always granted, he has been a conditioning influence, and the conditions he created amount to an explosive vacuum.

I do not believe that the crisis in education can be solved by the educators. They are themselves products of that *Zeitgeist* which brought on the crisis. All our laudable efforts to reform the universities can at best produce palliatives and symptom-therapy. I think that in a confused way the rebellious students are aware of this, and that this is why they are so helpless when asked for constructive proposals, and why no proposed reforms can satisfy their ravenous appetites. They are, simply, hungry for meaning, which their teachers cannot provide. They feel that all their teachers can do is to produce rabbits out of empty hats. Up to a point the rebels have succeeded in imparting this awareness to society at large, and that, regardless of the grotesque methods employed, seems to me a wholesome achievement.

Notes

[1] This paper was prepared for a symposium entitled "The University and the Ethics of Change" at Queen's University, Kingston, Canada, November, 1968.
[2] *The Act of Creation* (London and New York 1964), pp. 265 f.
[3] Simpson, G. G., *The Meaning of Evolution*. New Haven, Conn., 1949.
[4] In *The Listener*. London 13.11.1952.
[5] In *Beyond Reductionism—The Alpbach Symposium,* ed. A. Koestler and J. R. Smythies, London 1969.

Alternatives to Violence: The Need for a New Way of Thinking about International Relations

By Otto Klineberg

University of Paris, France

A discussion of alternatives to violence at this particular moment in our history is important, but in some ways discouraging. We are living in a period characterized by a great deal of violence; many writers have referred to the prevalence of a "culture" or "sub-culture" of violence. We are witnessing a tremendous increase of concern with the problem, including the publication of a substantial number of books dealing with the nature of violence or aggression. The literature is rich also in suggestions of ways in which violence may be reduced, and international cooperation and understanding facilitated. The prevalence of violence sometimes blinds us to the many alternatives that have been followed in the past and that might be more fully developed in the future. There are many historical examples of the successes obtained through non-violent resistance; through cooperative enterprises at the inter-group or international level; through mediation and conciliation which have replaced violent confrontation; through the discovery of "superordinate goals" in which groups depend upon one another for success; through contact and information about others which reduce fear and prejudice; through the improvement of living conditions which reduce frustration, and as a consequence reduce aggression as well.

All of these alternatives are important, and can be effective, at least under certain conditions. They are all limited, however, by the human factor, by the willingness or unwillingness of people and their leaders to look for such alternatives, to try them out. There are those who believe that a change in the economic system, the substitution of a "competitive" capitalist by a presumably "democratic" socialist system, would reduce international violence, but so far there has been no indication of a reduction in the use—and sale—of armaments when such economic and social changes have occurred. Vietnam is paralleled by Czechoslovakia. Something more, or different, is evidently needed.

Albert Einstein, in a letter written in 1946 expressed the issue clearly.

In his words, "The unleashed power of the atom has changed everything except our ways of thinking . . . We shall require a substantially new manner of thinking if mankind is to survive". The search for alternatives to violence has too often been hampered and handicapped precisely because the "manner of thinking" followed the old, outmoded and outdated channels. To take a specific example, a number of social scientists (Charles Osgood, Jerome Frank, Amitai Etzioni) have with considerable cogency argued that the cycle of hostility between nations can be broken if one side undertakes unilateral actions (which may be symbolic or substantial) reflecting its desire for a reduction in tensions; this in turn would generate "a series of reciprocal gestures of good feeling" (Etzioni 1969).[1] Etzioni believes that the late President Kennedy undertook such unilateral action in 1963 by stopping all nuclear tests in the atmosphere; this "psychological gesture" was reciprocated by the Soviet Union, and for a time considerable *détente* between the two super-powers was achieved. Only for a time, however. The prevailing nationalistic attitudes and values were too powerful to permit a rational, psychologically sound program to be carried to its logical conclusion. What was lacking was a "new manner of thinking".

Can anything be done to help bring this about? Can anything be taught —through the mass media, in schools and universities—to establish a climate of opinion conducive to a peaceful approach to international relations?

To raise the question, "Can world peace be taught?" is almost to invite a negative answer. In a field in which passion predominates, how can we expect knowledge or reason to be effective? Even in connection with attitudes that are less emotional, one social scientist (Katz, 1947)[2] refers to "psychological barriers to communication", and two others (Hyman and Sheatsley, 1947)[3] indicate "why information campaigns fail". No one can deny that the supplying of information through the mass media will often have very limited influence; most of us "tune in" on material which we find palatable, and "tune out" the rest. What has been called "selective inattention" frequently makes it impossible for information to reach us if we are not already predisposed to accept it.

The situation is somewhat different, however, in the case of what has unkindly been called a "captive audience", whose members cannot easily turn the dial to a different program or move to another lecture hall. Our students constitute such a captive audience, even though they have recently shown certain signs of restlessness in their captivity. They, too, are of course able to "select" what they hear or remember and may even distort what they do hear, but on the whole they are more accessible to what we have to offer and less likely to avoid it completely. Some years ago (Rose, 1947)[4] a sociologist evaluated the effects of university courses dealing with intergroup relations (or "race") and found that in the majority of cases the changes that occurred were in the expected direction. Research is continuing actively in the attempt to clarify the factors involved in the well-known phrase of Lasswell: "who says what, to whom, under what conditions, and with what effect". The results give no basis for complete pessimism with regard to the influence of information. With regard to the mass media as well as to courses in school or university, a number of investigations testify to the fact that they do exert an influence, but they also indicate the need to temper our optimism with caution and self-criticism. The fact remains that the attempt to change attitudes in this manner has never been tested on a large scale nor with an adequate application of the full resources available.

What can be taught? In what follows I have chosen a few examples which seem to me to be both relevant and important, and in connection with which there appears to be enough scientific consensus to permit us to speak with some assurance. I make no claim to have covered all, or even nearly all, the topics which satisfy these conditions.

I turn first to the question of the inevitability of war, and its relation to the allegedly instinctive character of human aggressiveness. Several public opinion studies indicate that the view is widely held that human nature being what it is, war will never be eliminated. Such a position may have tremendous practical implications, in view of what has been called the "self-fulfilling prophecy" (Merton 1949)[5] or the "principle of expectancy" (Allport 1950).[6] If we expect an event to occur, and if that event is one on which human actions can exert an influence (as distinct from expecting rain tomorrow, for example), then expectation can make that event more probable, since it will inhibit or reduce any attempt to avoid it. On that basis, the belief in the inevitability of war may help to make war inevitable.

A number of recent publications which have received a wide popular acclaim have *seemed* (I underline the word *seemed*) to support this belief. I refer to Konrad Lorenz's book, *On Aggression,* Audrey's *African Genesis* and *The Territorial Imperative,* and Desmond Morris' *The Naked Ape.* Though differing widely in other respects, all three of these writers have placed the accent on man as a biological animal, and on man's behavior as due mainly to his biological inheritance. In a review of books by the first two of these writers, Kenneth Boulding expresses the view that their great popular success is due to the fact that they are seen as justifying aggression by describing its biological roots, as giving man the right to say "I am aggressive because I can't help myself". Control of aggression is thus seen as fruitless since aggression—including war—is inevitable.

I believe that these writers underplay the role of social and cultural factors in human behavior, and overemphasize the behavioral continuity with other animal species. Of course man is biological, but he is also social; he is biosocial. At the same time, Lorenz does indicate that aggression can be sublimated—in sport, in scientific competition, and in many other ways. Those who have inferred that Lorenz regards any particular form of violence, such as war, as inevitable, have therefore done him an injustice. The whole argument between those who give aggression a biological basis, and those who place the accent on learning, is in many ways meaningless, a "non-problem". Even if aggression has biological roots, it can be expressed in so many different ways; its manifestations encouraged or limited; directed against other human beings or re-directed and sublimated; used when it "works" or reduced or discarded when it is unsuccessful.

Instruction in this area might include a better understanding of the biology of aggression, its nature and its limits, the various ways—direct and indirect—in which it may be expressed, the possibilities of sublimation, the effects of society and culture on the encouragement or reduction of aggression and the role of learning in determining the extent of aggressive behavior. With specific reference to war, it should be helpful to identify the many different ways in which wars have arisen in the past (through economic, territorial, religious and other causes); to stress the existence of societies without war, as well as those which were warlike at one time but are so no longer; to insist that war is not inevitable.

A second major topic, the subject of a vast literature, but one in connection with which a great deal of popular mythological thinking prevails, is that of race. The term itself has been widely misused and abused, applied not only (and correctly) to groups that differ genetically and physically, but also (incorrectly) to those differing in language, religion or nationality. More important, the concept of race, however used, has been widely associated with the notion of a genetic hierarchy, of superior and inferior "races", with the implication that the former have the right to dominate and exploit the latter. Such an attitude inspired the thought and actions of those peoples engaged in colonialism and imperialistic expansion, although it was frequently rationalized as "the white man's burden" of the British, or the "mission civilisatrice" of the French. It still serves as the basis for the national policy of South Africa and Rhodesia, as well as for "racism" of varying degrees of virulence elsewhere. Its most extreme form, leading to the physical extinction of millions of people, was of course characteristic of Nazi Germany. It is safe to say that "racism" has so far caused much more destruction than the atomic bomb.

The general position of biological and social scientists who have studied this topic can in my judgment best be described as one of extreme scepticism; their verdict is that a genetic "racial" hierarchy has not been adequately demonstrated, that it has never been scientifically proved. (I am not stating that we can conclude with confidence and certainty that there are no inborn psychological differences between races; I am convinced, however, of the tremendous importance of social and cultural factors in producing differences which have sometimes been regarded as hereditary; I feel safe in concluding that no adequate scientific evidence as to the existence of such innate differences has ever been offered.) A number of years ago Gunnar Myrdal indicated that he knew of no important issue in which there was a greater discrepancy between the position of scientists and that of the general public, and he called for an "educational offensive" to reduce the gap. He was thinking primarily of the problem of race in the United States, but the concept of racial superiority and inferiority is not limited geographically. In some areas of the world, notably the southern part of Africa, it appears to contain the seeds of war.

The "educational offensive" for which Myrdal called has in part been undertaken, particularly by Unesco, which in a series of publications and statements has attempted to place the issue of race in its proper scientific perspective. It is obvious, however, that a tremendous task for educators remains to be done. Inter-group conflict, whether based on race or other ethnic distinctions, may have abated somewhat in certain parts of the world, but it has certainly been exacerbated in others. It is attached to religion in northern Ireland, to language in Belgium and Canada, to national origin in parts of Southeast Asia, to race—or the idea of race—in many places. It is widespread, virulent and contagious.

Schools and universities, as well as the mass media, have a task to perform here which is tremendous in its implications. The available material is rich, and has never been adequately exploited. Possibilities for inclusion are, for example, an understanding of the biology and genetics of race, as well as of the arbitrariness of racial classifications and of the criteria applied; the demonstration that genetic similarities between human groups are far greater than the differences; the fact that antagonisms between ethnic groups are not inevitable, and that when they do occur they may take many different forms, of which racial conflict is only one among others; the history of changes in attitudes, the present acceptance of groups which at one time suffered discrimination (for example, the Protestants in France, the Quakers in England, the Irish in the United States); the lack of any demonstrated relationship between race and intelligence or personality; the fact that all existing nations are genetic mixtures; the irrationality of our prejudices and the fact that they may be directed against unknown and even imaginary groups; the "costs" of prejudice and discrimination, which cause conflicts within a society, and impede the effective utilization of available talents and capacities.

We turn now to a third major area. Reference was made above to the fact that the behavior of groups is shaped not by their racial origins but by their education, history and culture. The fact remains that groups do differ, and the question arises as to whether an awareness and understanding of such differences may contribute to better international relations. This has been one of the major preoccupations of Unesco, which at various times and in various ways has undertaken to facilitate the acquisition of an accurate knowledge of others. It has frequently been argued that if peoples become acquainted with one another, through contact or the mass media, hostility will necessarily give way to friendship. On the other hand it has been pointed out that even a great deal of information regarding the Nazis, for example, would not have resulted in a favorable attitude toward the Germany of that period. It was indicated earlier that information can have a favorable effect, but not always, nor under all conditions, and that educators had the special responsibility to discover the conditions under which contact and information exert a positive influence. It seems reasonable to conclude, however, that it is safer to base our relations with other peoples on knowledge rather than on ignorance. A number of years ago Allport suggested that we may have gone too far in stressing the differences among peoples, and he called rather for an "encyclopedia of human similarities". It is better in my judgment to become aware of both the similarities and the differences.

As far as content is concerned, the material is of course abundant; the problem is to make a choice out of what has been produced and published. On the whole, universities have not entirely neglected this area, and courses in history and anthropology in particular have in part performed the task required of them. Again it must be asked, however, whether a great deal more should not, or could not, be undertaken. At the present time, teaching about national cultures is included in the training of many diplomats, of special envoys engaged in activities such as the Peace Corps or technical cooperation missions, of military men sent abroad, of businessmen with international interests, and many others. The question arises as to whether many people, including students, have enough opportunity to acquire comparable information.

Within the broad area of similarities and differences among ethnic groups there appear to be a number of aspects which should receive special attention. These might include, first, an understanding of customary behavior, ranging from the apparently trivial (such as table manners) to the clearly important (values, goals, etc.). Secondly, there is needed a wider perspective on the making of nation-states, and the complicated historical process involved in national integration. Impatience and even condemnation, for example, with regard to the conflicts within the new African states, might be tempered by information concerning the difficulties faced in achieving unity in such "advanced" countries as Germany, Italy or France. Thirdly, more emphasis should be placed on the interdependence of national cultures, the borrowings that have taken place since the beginning of history. Linton has written amusingly and convincingly about the varied elements that enter into the life of a "100% American". French history might be presented not only to show what France has contributed to civilization, but also what the rest of the world has contributed to France. Finally, although this list is by no means complete, there should be a reduction of insularity in the teaching of history and politics. The all-too-frequent concentration of attention on "our" nation usually means neglect of what has happened elsewhere.

There is another aspect of this problem which appears to me to be highly significant, and which is primarily psychological in nature. I refer to what has been called "ethnocentric perception", and which indicates the almost universal tendency to see and judge external events from a nationalistic or ethnocentric bias. It is this ethnocentric perception which makes it difficult, and sometimes impossible, to understand the point of view of those with whom our nation is in conflict. There are, of course, exceptions—Americans opposed to the Vietnam war, Russians who have criticized the Soviet move into Czechoslovakia, Germans and Italians who condemned Fascist aggression—but they *are* exceptions. The more usual reaction is: *we* are right, therefore *they* must be wrong.

I have described this tendency as psychological, but it is also related to the way in which history is usually written. A content analysis of the same conflicts or wars as described in history text-books used in the various countries involved has revealed that this tendency is indeed widespread. We (whoever *we* may be) were peace-loving; *they* were the aggressors; we fought bravely and honorably; they were cruel and irresponsible. With regard to contemporary events, it is only necessary to compare the two descriptions of the same event as presented by the North Vietnamese and the Americans or South Vietnamese, or by the Arabs and the Israelis. Historically, the accounts of the American Revolution or the War of 1812 in British or American text-books, or of the War of 1870 in those used in French or German schools respectively, often appear to be describing different occurrences altogether.

In many cases exactly the same behavior is right when *we* do it, and wrong when *they* do. *We* intervene in another country to support the legitimate government, *they* in order to suppress the oppressed people who seek change. We feed the hungry as a consequence of our humanitarian impulses, they in order to win political allegiance. This mechanism (akin to the Freudian concept of rationalization) may lead us literally to *see* the same phenomenon as changing its character according to its source and to label it differently. I am firm, you are obstinate; I am economical, you are stingy; my child is independent, yours is disobedient. At the national level, our soldiers fight with great bravery, theirs like fanatics; our large stock of armaments is solely for defense, theirs is clearly a preparation for attack. This list could be continued almost indefinitely.

It has been argued that the quality most urgently needed in connection with international understanding is that of empathy, the capacity to put ourselves in the other's shoes, to look at the world through his eyes. This does not necessarily mean that we will accept his view, but it should at least make us aware that there are alternatives to our own particular manner of looking at the world—and possibly and occasionally, reasonable alternatives.

This whole topic is related to one which has long attracted the attention of psychologists, namely, the nature, origin and influence of national stereotypes—the images or "pictures in our minds" regarding our own and other national groups. The tendency to generalize, to attribute characteristics to *the* Americans, *the* Germans, *the* Italians, etc., is so widespread that two Netherlands psychologists (Duijker and Frijda)[7] have gone so far as to regard it as universal and inevitable. Some years ago (Buchanan and Cantril)[8] Unesco conducted a study among adults in a number of different countries, and found that respondents everywhere were prepared to attach labels to nations; the results differed in detail, but in all cases one's own nation was regarded as the most peace-loving of all! A more recent study of children in nine different countries (Lambert and Klineberg)[9] discovered that everywhere this tendency to stereotype developed at a relatively early age.

National stereotypes have a complex origin. They appear in the expressions in common use in many languages, in the stories and anecdotes that contain an ethnic reference, in the representations of ethnic groups in the mass media, and they are of course related to the prevailing economic and political situation. In connection with this last point, it has been argued (by Raymond Aron, for example) that stereotypes are not the causes but the consequence of international relations; when the political situation is favorable and friendly, the stereotypes will be positive, and in the opposite situation, negative. It seems more likely that the relation is a circular one, and that once the stereotypes have developed, for whatever reason, they will affect our perceptions and consequently our behavior with regard to others. Psychological research indicates that there may be actual distortion in what one sees or reports concerning other ethnic groups as a reaction to the prevailing stereotype. In a study conducted in Montreal, Canada, by Wallace Lambert of McGill University, which was presented to students as an experiment on judging character and intelligence from the sound of the voice, it was demonstrated that those who spoke in French (Canadian) were usually judged to be inferior to those who spoke English, even though, unknown to the students, it was the same bilingual speakers who were heard in both languages. This occurred even when the student judges were themselves French-Canadians. When the speaker spoke in a "Parisian" French accent he was not judged or "heard" to be inferior. One can certainly argue that the stereotype arose as a consequence of the inferior social and economic status of the average French-Canadian, but its existence, for whatever reason, did affect the perceptions of the judges, and presumably their attitudes and actions as well.

The stereotypes are usually assumed to be true, either in whole or in part, on the theory that if everybody (or nearly everybody) believes that the Irish are pugnacious or the Jews mercenary, there must be some basis for such a judgment. Here, too, there is a considerable amount of relevant sociological and psychological research, from which the conclusion may be drawn that some stereotypes may contain a certain amount of truth, but that others may develop without any demonstrable basis in reality. One investigator (Lapiere) who studied the stereotypes concerning Armenians in Fresno County, California, reported that they were all clearly false. This means that any sentence referring to the psychological characteristics of *the* Scots, *the* Americans, or *the* Brazilians, must be regarded with suspicion unless and until more solid data are available.

Stereotypes change in the course of time, and a knowledge of such changes may help to introduce an essential scepticism in their application today. The Germans were not considered aggressive a hundred years ago; they were so considered as a consequence of the two World Wars (Hans Kohn). The stereotype of the Hungarian changed markedly throughout the history of Europe (Den Hollander). The Irish are today considered excessively combative and pugnacious, but—also about one hundred years ago—the German philosopher Feuerbach regarded them as particularly calm and stolid. His theory was that "Der Mensch ist was er isst" (man is what he eats) and that the potato diet of the Irish induced a sluggish and unaggressive disposition!

In introducing any or all of the topics I have proposed, the mass media, schools and universities are faced with one major problem which is extremely difficult, and in some cases impossible, to resolve. Many of the issues discussed here touch directly the emotional complex of nationalism, national identity, national loyalties. We are living in a period characterized not only by the recent emergence of many new nation states, but also by the continuing rivalries and even hostilities among older nations, together with an increasing tendency toward the development of passionate loyalties to sub-groups characterized by differences in race, language or religion. Have we any reason to hope that nations will at this moment in our history devote themselves to the encouragement of the international viewpoint symbolized, but as yet far from realized, by the United Nations? Can we teach attitudes that question the validity of national or ethnocentric perception and judgment, and that involve an empathic response to the positions held by other, even "hostile" nationstates? Would we be allowed to do so?

Something can, however, be done. Since we are all of us, at least in principle, opposed to war, there should be no great difficulty in presenting material relating to the nature of aggressiveness and the non-inevitability of war. Since most of the governments of existing nations, with the exception of South Africa and Rhodesia are, at least in principle, against race prejudice and discrimination we can, in the spirit of the Universal Declaration of Human Rights, marshall the scientific evidence relevant to this issue. With regard to nationalistic attitudes, many of us would like to be able to point out their anachronistic and potentially lethal character, particularly in their extreme form. How far we can go along these lines depends on the situation within each country, but it is clear that even in this field a great deal can be done. Teaching along these lines has already begun in many places; history textbooks are being rewritten, in part under the auspices of Unesco; the interdependence of peoples is becoming clearer; knowledge of the culture of others is receiving greater emphasis than ever before. All of this has so far, however, touched too few individuals and too few institutions. We are challenged to do much more. It is time that we face that challenge.

The "educational offensive" which is here advocated should be combined with attention to the other "alternatives" to which reference was made above, but with a critical appreciation of their limitations as well as of their potential value. Much has been said and written, for example, about the contribution to understanding that comes from contact between nations, through travel, study abroad, participation in international meetings and conferences, and so forth. The effects of such programs, though they are strongly recommended by many and are probably useful on the whole, have never been adequately evaluated. They improve international attitudes in some situations, but not always; we need to know why. Considerable faith has also been expressed in the value of aid extended to developing countries, so that their standard of living may be raised to an adequate level. Such programs have so far received only a fraction of the attention and resources which they require in order to be effective. The fact must be faced that the increase in the technological gap, in spite of the aid that has been given, results in "relative frustration", since there is even grater distance than before between "their" level of comfort and "ours"; this may actually increase international tensions in spite of programs designed to reduce them.

Most of what has been presented here implies that violence can best be reduced or replaced by changing "the minds of men". It is maintained that public opinion, public attitudes, have a tremendous role to play. We have so far not been serious enough about helping to determine the nature of that role, and the factors that move it toward violence or understanding respectively. We need a public opinion freed from its slavery to chauvinism, prepared to follow leaders who stand for cooperation, ready to seek alternatives to violence. We need a new way of thinking, and a major educational program to bring it about.

One final word. The attitudes and behavior of students throughout the world have filled some of us adults with dismay, some with admiration, and some with both. It is probable that many if not most of us have been shocked by the resort to violence although we must recognize the fact that the violence has not all been on one side. We have reason to be encouraged, however, by the concern expressed about what has happened and is happening in our world; by the *prise de conscience* about world affairs. There is cause for satisfaction also that much of the student "confrontation" is related to the elimination of racism, of war and war-related activities, of excessive nationalism and chauvinism. In addition, the students have been asking for "relevance" in our teaching. Perhaps the students, together with like-minded people of all ages, can lead us to that "new manner of thinking" that we so sorely need.

Notes

[1] Etzioni, A., Kennedy's Russian experiment. *Psychology Today,* 1969, 3, 42–45, 62–63.

[2] Katz, D., Psychological barriers to communication. *Ann. Amer. Acad. Polit. Soc. Sci.* 1947, *250,* 17–25.

[3] Hyman, H. and Sheatsley, P. B., Some reasons why information compaigns fail. *Publ. Opin. Quart.,* 1947, *11,* 412–423.

[4] Rose, A., *Studies in reduction of prejudice.* Chicago: Am. Council on Race Rels., 1947.

[5] Merton, R. K., *Social theory and social structure.* New York: Free Press, 1949,

6 Allport, G. W., The role of expectancy. In H. Cantril (ed.) *Tensions that cause wars*. Urbana, Ill., Univ. of Illinois Press, 1950.

7 Duijker, H. C. J. and Frijda, N. H., *National character and national stereotypes*. Amsterdam, Nort-Holland Publ. Co., 1960.

8 Buchanan, W. and Cantril, H., *How nations see each other*. Urbana, Univ. of Illinois Press, 1953.

9 Lambert, W. E. and Klineberg, O., *Children's views of foreign peoples*. New York, Appleton-Century-Crofts, 1967.

FREE OR DIRECTED RESEARCH—
A CHOICE FOR THE INDIVIDUAL AND
FOR SOCIETY

Science Policy—Changing Concepts

By Alexander King

Director-General for Scientific Affairs, OECD, Paris, France

By a science policy is meant a deliberate and coherent basis for national decisions influencing the size, emphasis, institutional structure and creativity of scientific research and its application. Probably no country has yet achieved such a situation, but many are striving towards it. The very concept of a policy for science, conjures up ideas of planning and regimentation which appear, at least at first sight, to be trends which run counter to the nature of creative research, academic freedom etc. But this, as we shall see, is not necessarily the case. Policies for science are however necessitated by the present extent and high cost of research programmes throughout the world, its obvious relevance to a whole range of contemporary problems and the fact that most of its financing comes directly or indirectly from governments.

The initial phase of science policy

Three phases in the development of science policy can be distinguished. The pre-history as it were, extends until the beginning of the Second World War. Governments have long sought specialist advice on particular problems and in some cases, such as the creation of the Royal Society of London by King Charles II in the middle of the seventeenth century, even sought to institutionalise the scientific advisory function. The founding fathers of the United States gave great importance to the possibilities of science in opening up their new continent and exploiting its natural resources. By the beginning of the present century many governments had created national observatories, standards laboratories, geological surveys and other specific scientific facilities. All these efforts were sporadic and not always well sustained; seldom were they conceived in a policy framework. Some countries, it is true, did evolve measures for the development of their national scientific resources, which however general, could be regarded as constituting a policy. The National Research Council of Canada for example deliberately set about the building up of science in the Canadian universities through the award of fellowships and only, when the scientific community had become sufficiently strong did they proceed to the creation of national laboratories, necessary in a country so vast and so little populated.

The first World War, in which technology for the first time made a real impression on the military arts, saw a considerable upsurge of national scientific effort, which gave rise in many countries to government research agencies such as the medical and agricultural research councils in Great Britain and its Department of Scientific and Industrial Research or the independent but government supported National Research Council in Washington.

The second phase

The Second World War, which was fought and won on a basis of technology, quickly showed, at least amongst the Western allies that the existing institutions for scientific research were far too weak and too limited in their scope to sustain the technological efforts required. The ad hoc organisations created to take over in the emergency, and especially the American Office for Scientific Research and Development gave brilliant proof that the knowledge and inspiration of academic scientists could be vastly effective when faced with vital technological problems. Not only did this lead to major technological achievements such as the harnessing of nuclear energy, the building of rockets which later made possible space research and the complexities of radar, but also the development of penicillin, DDT and the anti-malarial drugs and the surprisingly successful application of the scientific method to military systems through operations research.

At the end of the war, governments and the people generally convinced of the dominant influence of science for defence, realised its enormous potential for the development of the economy and for human welfare. Science had become an important ingredient even of foreign policy, not only through the bomb but by the national prestige which its achievements generated. Science budgets increased rapidly and the last twenty years have seen an unprecedented increase in the amount of research undertaken, its level of sophistication and in the proliferation of its institutions.

The economic impact of science has received particular attention. Investigations in the United States and elsewhere have indicated that both research and education are important ingredients of economic growth. Dennison for example claims that 60 per cent of the growth of the Gross National Product of the United States since the beginning of the century cannot be ascribed directly to the traditional inputs of capital and labour and that the greater part of growth appears to derive from quality improvements—for example in the skill of labour (including that of management) and the increased quality of capital utilisation due to new products, materials and processes made possible by scientific discovery. The explosive expansion of scientific activity, the full impact of which has not yet been felt, has necessitated the creation of national science policies. Not only is there a recognition by governments and industry of the importance of science for national well-being, but its own nature and structure have changed. Not only is there a large increase in the extent of research carried out, but also in its cost per unit, due to increased sophistication of instrumentation. At the same time, the boundaries between fundamental and applied research have become more diffuse and new interdisciplinary subjects of the greatest importance, both to our basic understanding of the universe and of ourselves and to technological development have arisen at the interfaces between the classical groupings. In applied research, the complex problems facing scientific attack require a multi-disciplinary effort and it has not yet proved easy to work out methods of co-operation between the natural sciences and engineering on the one hand and the economic and behavioural sciences on the other—especially within the rigid structures of many European universities.

In spite of the great increase in research budgets, the burgeoning of science itself holds out great possibilities for further research, much greater than the resources available. This is especially true for the smaller, highly industrialised countries whose knowledge of and competence in all fields of scientific development is not so much different from that of the giants, the U.S.A. and the U.S.S.R., but which possess but a mere fraction of the resources to pursue research and to apply it.

Governments therefore began to find themselves in a dilemma some ten years ago, when claims for support of research programmes began greatly to exceed the possible resources, and pressure groups of scientists advanced arguments for support of their own fields, only a proportion of which could be provided despite the high quality of the proposals. The problem was to increase the total volume of resources and to secure a wise and fair allocation of resources in terms of promise and of national needs. In most countries therefore national science policy bodies began to emerge and to advise on these matters. These generally consist of scientists and economists and are often presided over or report to a minister for science or in some instances the prime minister. Their activities extend well beyond resource allocation and include responsibility for the coverage and balance of the national research effort, the compilation of statistics of research and development, understanding of the conditions which favour research creativity, the articulation of research and education, the relationship of science with industry, the place of scientific research in the process of technological innovation, scientific aspects of aid to the developing countries and a whole variety of other topics. A wide spectrum of institutional patterns has arisen, some countries for example having created a minister for technology in addition to his colleague for science.

The rate at which science policy structures have been evolved can be measured by the participation at the three meetings of science ministers, convened by OECD. At the first meeting, held in 1963, less than a third of the Member countries were represented by science ministers; most of the others were ministers of education, indicating that even at that recent date science was still institutionally regarded as an element of cultural policy. By the time the second ministerial meeting was held in 1965, most countries had a minister specifically designated for science, while at the third meeting, held early in 1968, science ministers were in a number of cases accompanied by their economic colleague.

It has proved extremely difficult to create a rationale for the allocation of limited resources to the seemingly limitless demands of the research community, pure and applied. Ministers, with the best of scientific advice find it difficult to determine whether, for example, high energy physics or molecular biology offer greater immediate promise and should have greater emphasis; different departments of government are in competition for research resources, changing national policies concerning large-spending developments for defence, nuclear energy or space can influence brutally, the continuity of research in less expensive and less sensitive fields.

In a few countries the attempt was made to allocate centrally a comprehensive national science budget between the various governmental departments and agencies possessing research needs. This formal cake-cutting process has however not worked out too well. After all, within a particular sector such as health or agriculture the amount to be spent on research, while determined to some extent by the nature of particular problems and the promise of new knowledge to solve them, is nevertheless in competition with other departmental expenditures on administration and services as well as capital demands for example for new hospitals. The research element is thus determined by political rather than by scientific decision which makes allocation from a single national research budget somewhat artificial.

Although this problem has not yet any rational solution, development of national science policies with the advice of the scientists themselves has placed the distribution of research resources on a basis of informed common sense. The participation of scientists in these decisions has also ensured that the establishment of priorities and the programming of research, made inevitable by the circumstances described above has not interfered seriously with the detailed activities of research scientists at the fundamental level, nor has it attempted to influence the free choice of academic workers to follow the lines of their own inspiration. The major possibility of distortion in some countries has come from the offers of contracts from government agencies and industrial firms to university research leaders to undertake particular research projects, within their own fields, but not necessarily in directions they would have otherwise chosen. The scientists are of course free to reject such overtures but the resources they provide make accept-ance very tempting and if excessive can lead to a distortion of free research.

The third phase

Science is now beginning to face up to a whole series of problems of policy importance, many of which have hardly been touched or have not seemed to be of primary importance until now. A high proportion of these relate to the impact of science on other aspects of national policy and of the evolution of society. There has been for some years a clear recognition that science policy has two aspects namely, *policies for science* itself, the allocation and management of its resources and the maintenance of its creativity and secondly, *policies through science,* i.e. the influence of new knowledge on the whole range of public policy from health, welfare and prosperity through to defence and foreign policy. This was well expressed by the report issued in 1963 of a group of independent scientists and economists to OECD, entitled "Science and the Policy of Governments". "It (science policy) too often connotes only a policy limited to the needs of science per se and excludes the effects of science and technology on the full spectrum of national policies ... Maximum exploitation of scientific opportunities requires programmes that combine concern for the growth of science itself and provision for the rapid, deliberate application of its fruits to human welfare." While research institutions for the application of science to particular sectors of economic and social activity have long existed, the problems of the total use of science for society have seldom been considered comprehensively by governments and the last ten years of science policy (phase II) have largely concentrated on policies for science rather than policies through science, although the economic impact of technology has received increasing attention. Emphasis is now changing rapidly towards the broad consideration of science as a major influence on the development of society and this is already necessitating basic rethinking of its rôle.

Some of the contributing reasons for this change are as follows:

(a) While science and technology contribute to economic growth, there is not an automatic and direct relationship as was at one time, somewhat naively assumed. The whole process of innovation has to be considered. The question is therefore posed as to what types of science contribute to growth and how their contribution can be assured and optimised. There is at the same time a need to look at the place of fundamental research more systematically, its importance for growth, yes; but also its rôle in education and its intrinsic value as a factor of contemporary culture.

(*b*) The nature of science is changing rapidly; not only is the interface between basic and applied research becoming more diffuse to an extent that new institutional approaches are requested, but the importance of interface subjects between the traditional sciences have become significant both in their own right for the extension of knowledge and for important technological advances. Furthermore the nature of many of the problems to which new research can and does contribute requires multidisciplinary attack and particularly, simultaneous consideration of technological, economic and social elements. This need is difficult to meet especially in Europe within rigid structures in university and government and seldom encouraged by forward looking and dynamic policies.

(*c*) Research and development expenditures, which have risen so steeply in recent years are now levelling off in most countries (Germany and Japan are present exceptions). This necessitates a closer look at priorities and a reassessment of national goals and how new knowledge can help in their achievement.

(*d*) Recognition as already stated that decision as to the extent and nature of science programmes for particular sectors, such as health or environmental conservation, are normally political decisions in competition with other sectoral requirements and not necessarily matters for central allocation.

(*f*) The public image of science has changed. Its mystique has largely evaporated and its negative manifestations through the bomb, biological and chemical warfare, destruction of the environment and social uncertainties and individual alienation which the unwise application of technology has so often brought are now prominent in the public mind. The formerly desirable objective of national affluence, to which science and its discoveries have so clearly contributed is also demonstrating its ugly face, with symptoms of social disorder, university troubles, pollutions of all kinds and the monstrosity of urban development. In addition there is an increasing unease that science and its methods are creating a technocratic elite, bent on soulless planning, destroying or ignoring cherished values and almost completely lacking contact with the individual citizen. These symptoms cannot be dismissed and science itself will have to make great efforts to re-establish its position of objectivity. Its "good" products are sought and welcomed, its "evil" aspects are blamed on the scientist. Yet science itself is not Dr. Faustus of our age; the conflict of good and evil, sharpened and highlighted by new knowledge is within each one of us and within our societies and our political systems.

(*g*) Growing appreciation of the gap between the rich and poor countries, of the fact that research mainly serves to make the rich richer, and that the interacting problems of world food and population are susceptible to scientific attack is persuading many people and especially the young, that the priorities of science are ill chosen.

(*h*) The growing dissatisfaction with economic growth as an end in itself, the rising tide of conservationism, and the bad conscience of advanced societies concerning the slowly developing countries. These pressures of opinion will no doubt influence governments towards a deep reassessment of national goals and force both national science policy authorities and the scientific community to reconsider the rôle which science should play in the last decades of this century. This entails a re-examination of the place of basic research, of the functions of higher education and of the emphasis of technological development. It will further emphasise the need to consider these matters in a broad socio-economico-technological sense.

The systems approach to science policy

The third phase of the development of science policy therefore abandons to a large extent the hitherto assumed concept of science as an autonomous system, producing knowledge for its own sake and incidentally although importantly making possible all sorts of applications through the quite separate process of technological development. It stresses rather science as an important sub-system in the national system and hence emphasises the possibilities of national development *through* science. The question arises immediately as to whether a national science policy can be developed effectively and coherently in the absence of or in insufficient contact with equally coherent policies or at least strategies for education, for economics and for social development. Government responsibilities have become so enlarged and deal with matters so complex while at the same time contemporary science is too pervasive of national policy as a whole for its policy to be left exclusively in the hands of the scientists. The economist by himself, the sociologist, the administrator or the politician is likewise impotent to solve in isolation most of the problems of the world today.

The impact of science in public affairs can perhaps be expressed best in terms of interacting systems. The total national activity or system is conveniently, although in a somewhat arbitrary and over-simplified manner divided into a number of sub-systems or sectors such as those of defence, education, health, industry, agriculture, social welfare, foreign policy etc., for each of which exists some degree of conscious policy associated with more or less clearly formulated national goals. All of these activities overlap to some extent with the others although the interfaces between them and the zones of overlap are not too well delineated. In fact the machinery of government, designed for operation in a less complicated world of slow change obscures the overlaps and makes difficult the solution of problems and the administration of services concerned with these unexplored no-man's lands. The scientific effort of a country represents one such sub-system most of whose area overlaps with the other systems in a three dimensional model. There is indeed at the centre of the science sub-system an area which does not cover areas of the other national sub-systems, although it possesses an important and diffuse interface with the subs-system of education. This is the area of fundamental research, that part of the science sub-system which represents its reproductive mechanism and essential for the maintenance and constant revitalisation of the whole. This is the area for which a science policy in the simpler sense (policy for science) is possible, although even here, the proportion of total resources available is governed by diffusion across the interface from education (research manpower availability) and its optimum size depends on many factors other than the maximum good of science itself. There are for example many feedback mechanisms from the various zones of interlap. The areas of intersection with other subsections such as agriculture or health cannot be governed by policies determined by science alone, but represent *zones of penetration* of new knowledge and of scientific method per se into the total fabric of society.

Problems of contemporary society

Hitherto the main areas of scientific application of concern to governments have been those of defence, agriculture and health, together with a concern for the background support of industrial development. There will certainly remain important preoccupations, but in addition a whole series of new problems are arising and are becoming increasingly pressing, which governments alone can attack. Many of these are problems of the deteriorating environment; others arise from the quick and too little foreseen mushrooming of urban development; some are essentially social problems, while that of ensuring the relevance of the education system is perhaps basic to all. In general, these are problems of our contemporary civilisation and most marked in the most highly industrialised societies. They are mainly derived, directly or indirectly, from the growth of technology either as a result of the phenomenal economic growth which it has produced or else are undesirable and often unforeseen side-effects of technological development—in other words manifestations of affluence and effluence. Collectively they represent a major threat to the stable continuity of our societies and possibly to their very existence.

It may be necessary to enumerate some of these problems in more detail. They include firstly all the *problems of the environment* including that of the accumulation of increasing proportions of carbon dioxide in the air with the probability of dangerous thermal effects in the future. Then there is the problem of water, not only in relation to pollution, but conceived as a major national resource and necessary for industrial, agricultural, domestic and amenity purposes. Availability of water can be a major limitation on human development and already its multiple use and its closed-circuit employment are becoming important. Other pollution problems of air and the oceans, thermal and noise pollution are increasingly pressing. They may not prove too intractable, but their solution will require much careful research and measurement, negotiation between governments and industry and international harmonisation of legislation. Removal of sulphur from the air, for example, will represent an added charge to industry which will be difficult to enforce, except on an international scale so as to avoid loss of competitive advantage to the firms of a particular country proceeding unilateraly.

A second series of problems relates to *urban growth,* the cluttering of cities with the automobile, suburban sprawl, increasing transportation difficulties, the mounting problem of the removal of solid waste, and in general the increasing discomfort and sense of frustration of city dwellers. Allied to this are the problems of transportation in general, both surface and in the air, the soaring death rate from road accidents with high economic as well as human costs.

These and other matters produce a rising rate of social disequilibrium —high rates of crime, delinquency and drugtaking, large numbers of people who just do not see the point of working for a living and reject the values of contemporary society, an increasing resistance to control and planning in which the individual has little say and the threatened invasion of individual privacy by the government operated data banks, a general sense of alienation and isolation, all of which are disruptive trends.

There is also the *educational complex* of problems, a realisation that young people are being trained for life in a world that is evaporating rather than the future into which they will emerge. Innovation in the educational system is an imperative but the resistance is enormous. The university situation is a particular case with a large and increasing proportion of the 18–24 age group retained in an artificial and quasi-adolescent status within establishments which are inherently academic in their objectives and aiming in general to provide for the relatively small proportion of those who have a devotion to scholarship or well defined professional objective. This would seem to be a situation of frustration to the many and essentially unstable, quite apart from its vulnerability to political exploitation.

Finally there are the problems of *poverty and underdevelopment;* in industrialised societies these are manifest in ghetto and race difficulties, but by far the major danger lies in the poverty gap between the industrialised nations and the third world, with the associated world problems of food and population.

These matters are, of course, in their totality far beyond the range of science and technology, but both in cause and in attempted solutions, science has a big part to play, not only through technical elements, accessible to research attack, but also by application of the scientific method in formulating and delineating the problems, perceiving and evaluating the importance of their interaction and in the development of technological, social and integrative forecasting as well as of dynamic socio-economic planning methods. This applies also to the parallel crop of problems concerned with defence and security, which are beyond the scope of this paper.

These problems areas have three features in common. Firstly they are of a global character and appear to arise at a certain stage of development irrespective of the political or economic system. Secondly they are multivariant in their nature and, in particular, contain technological, economic and social elements, thus demanding a multidisciplinary attack for their solution. Finally they are interconnected, and proposed solutions to one problem may give rise to unexpected side effects elsewhere. There is need therefore for comprehensive diagnosis of the cause of the disease rather than the removal of a few obvious symptoms.

Challenge for science policy

If science is to become a major and deliberately employed instrument of national development it will have to be used to contribute positively to the attainment of the goals of society and not merely to evolve passively, produce new knowledge and only incidentally to solve problems created by its own misuse. In order to do this, science or rather the scientific method will have to help in the formulation of national goals. This does not mean that science and scientists should determine what there should be, that is essentially a political matter for governments and the individual voter, but in making clear the real nature of the possibilities and by describing the elements which might combine to make possible a series of possible and alternative futures, globally and in a sector to sector sense. Lacking a clear statement of goals, research can only contribute fractionally and intermittently and often with the appearance of damaging side effects.

Such a concept requires changing attitudes on the part of scientists, in particular towards the application of new knowledge. This is not simply asking for the stress to change from fundamental to applied research in the hardware sense; it means more deeply a concentration of the best intellectual effort to the solution of society's problems, a scientific delineation of the various areas of difficulty, a study of the mutual interactions between them, a clear formulation of the likely issues. All this is inherent in the systems approach to science policy mentioned above and is necessary if we are to diagnose the disease, understand its causes and mechanisms and not merely to attack and demolish a few of its more obvious symptoms.

There are many structural and other consequences of this approach. Above all the multidisciplinary attack on problems already stressed has deep implications for the educational system and for the structure of universities, particularly those in Europe. It requires also a growth and maturity in the social sciences and an intimate articulation between these and the physical and biological sciences. It needs also new techniques of management, both within science itself, in technological development and in government activity. The old, vertical structures of university faculties and of government departments can hardly respond to the multi-variant problems of tomorrow. A further extension of this is the need to develop dynamic techniques of integrative forecasting, of evaluation of trends and of participative planning.

On the national level this integrative approach will be very difficult to achieve. It is doubtful whether the functions of the type of science minister which have become traditional during the last decade are appropriate. It may be that what is needed is a senior minister, preferably a deputy to the prime minister, responsible for longer term problems, a minister without departmental responsibility but with concern for long term strategies for economics, science, technology, education and social policy and supported by a high grade staff for forecasting evaluation and problems of interaction. The rationale behind this suggestion is that problems which were formerly of long term significance and whose solution could be delayed in favour of more pressing matters within the normal political process have now become matters of medium term significance due to the accelerating pace of change and hence require earlier attention, lest their neglect develop a series of not too distant crises.

Science policy and the scientific community

While the developments described in this paper are presented mainly in relation to governmental responsibility, it is clear that the scientists, industry and the public at large must have a large say in their consideration. Scientists are of course well represented in most national science policy bodies and government research councils and have quickly appreciated the nature of the problems; judgement by peers is generally accepted for the award of fellowships and research grants. On the other hand the scientific community, in contrast to individual scientists, has in recent years had rather little influence on government decision making in most countries. Certainly pressure groups, enthusiastic for their own specialisation have succeeded both nationally and internationally in obtaining support for expensive and often highly significant projects especially in fields such as high-energy physics and radar astronomy. Science's own world organisation, the International Council of Scientific Unions has proved effective in organising specific research projects of global coverage such as the international geophysical year but has too feeble a financial support to develop its full potentiality.

Some of the problems raised in this paper demand a more systematic and coherent approach by the scientific community, to reassess their position in contemporary society, their responsibilities as well as their privileges, their attitudes towards governments and towards the use made of their own results. It must be admitted that on the whole the academies have not responded quickly or well to the challenge of the new conditions. The United States Academy of Sciences is however one of the most obvious exceptions in the manner in which it has developed its activities and thinking during the last few years evolving a collective statesmanship in science and able to provide to the American administration a second opinion to that of the government's own advisors with whom, however, it retains harmonious relations. This concept of collective statesmanship is perhaps the main desideratum for the scientific community in relation to its future role. Industry also has an important part to play and important contributions to make. Probably the most technologically advanced firms with their flexible structures, acceptance of forecasting and their adoption of methods and structures for the management of complex technological systems, have more to contribute to governments on planning, forecasting and modern management than any other section of the community.

International considerations of the future role of science and technology in influencing the development of society and towards the solution of world problems such as those of food and population are beyond the scope of this paper. The problems of the third world are of dominant importance for the future, but if the industrialised nations with their still considerable capacity for growth are unable to solve the problems of the highly industrialised societies, their capacity to tackle the wider issues will not be great.

In conclusion it should be reiterated that there is a need for reappraisal of national and international approach to science policy, a better delineation of the problems of contemporary industrialised societies, for a more deliberate and comprehensive attack on these problems by multidisciplinary scientific means and a reassessment by the scientific community on its role in the new society and its potential influence on development. For these reasons the present discussions are particularly to be welcomed.

Visible and Invisible Innovation—
The change of Human Consciousness toward
a Multi-channel Society

By Yujiro Hayashi

Tokyo Institute of Technology, Tokyo, Japan

Human society, whichever form it may take, or in whichever stage of growth it may be, is without exception related to the environment surrounding human beings. But looking at society only as human beings and the environment surrounding them is too static. If expressed dynamically, society consists of human desire and its corresponding environmental function. Mankind, in its long history, has always acted on its environment for the satisfaction of its own desires, and as a result the environment has taken on a certain function. With the newly acquired function, human beings developed new desires, and again changed the function of the environment. This relative correspondence between desires and functions has continued until today in a cause and effect relationship. Consequently, there has always been something of a discrepancy between desires and functions and this discrepancy has become the motivating factor of social change. However, at the same time this discrepancy may cause frustration leading to social tensions.

Turning to modern society, we notice a conspicuous dualism. For example, in Japan, we have what is called the "Showa Genroku" (Showa Tranquil and Prosperous Period). Japan seems quite peaceful, but at the same time, violent disturbances, such as the university riots and disruptions, can be shown to be other than accidental. What does this mean? To put it otherwise, present-day societies obviously have two faces. This phenomenon exists not only in Japan, but all over the world, and is becoming a noticeable characteristic particularly in industrialized countries. I would like to call the dualism noted previously "the futuralization of society".

The dualism may be explained as follows. Human desires can be roughly divided into non-individualistic desires and individualistic desires. Social functions may then be devided into two corresponding categories, which I will call fundamental function and elastic function.

Non-individualistic desire . . . . . Fundamental function
Individualistic desire . . . . . Elastic function

Using this model, a condition like the "Showa Genroku" in Japan can be thought of as resulting from a corresponding relationship such as that between non-individualistic desire and fundamental function. This may indicate that this relationship works well, while it seems that the relationship between individualistic desire and elastic function does not get on so well. That is, in many cases the gears don't mesh, and as a result, this appears on the surface as a phenomenon of social frustration. Whether we can solve this social tension or not depends on how we can manage this kind of correspondence. In other words, by expanding the elastic function in our society, it should be possible to relieve social tensions in the future.

However, why has the increase in importance of individualistic desire become so pronounced recently? I would like to draw the attention to technological innovations. Much has been said about it, but I think that people without noticing it, have overlooked their part in changing the human value system. The horizontal and vertical effect of technological innovations is well known from the work by Erich Jantsch on technological forecasting.[1] I would like to point out the importance of the horizontal effect of post-war innovations, i.e., their social influence.

J. D. Bernal viewed the relationship between science and society historically, placing the "Age of Private Science" between the seventeenth and nineteenth centuries, or around the industrial revolution, the "Age of Industrial Science" between the 1920's and 1930's, and the "Age of Governmental Science" from and including World War II onwards. By pointing out that the next phase will be the "Age of World Science" he emphasized the necessity of close international cooperation for scientific studies. Without waiting for his pronouncement, we can say that the remarkable result of technological innovation during the post-war period was the great impact on the masses. This influence invited a repercussion effect on a world-wide scale. As a result, new value systems were originated one after another. I will call this the "accumulation effect of innovations".

It is obvious that there are two types of future society which may be predicted, namely the future as an *extrapolation* and the future as an *accumulation*. The former is perhaps a continuous future while the latter would be discontinuous. It seems to me that until now, the methodology of forecasting has been based mostly on extrapolation. Most methods describing the future society which are based on say a level of income would fall in this category. I don't doubt the importance of these methods and even in the future they will be quite effective and appropriate, but it seems to me that we have been too indifferent to the development of an accumulation-type future. With regard to the accumulation effect of technological innovations, let us examine how this effect is revealed in an international situation.

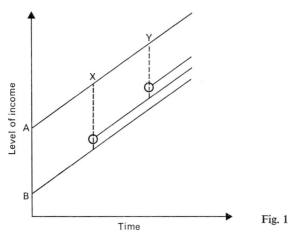

Fig. 1

Let's take Country A and Country B. Suppose Country A has a much higher level of income than Country B, i.e., A is an advanced nation and B a developing one. Although their pace of development may differ, their levels of income are continuously rising, hence they are both furthering their development. At a given time, technological innovation X is made in Country A, and at another given time, another technological innovation Y is made in the same country. In this case, both X and Y are technological innovations generated from within the society of Country A. I will call this "endogenous technological innovation", which means that the technological innovations occured naturally in Country A according to social needs. However, these technological innovations are not confined only to Country A, since they will also influence the neighbouring Country B. When the technological innovation X is made, it definitely influences Country B, despite the fact that Country B (from Country A's point of view) seems to have scarcely any social needs for receiving the technological innovation. The same can be said about innovation Y.

In other words, to Country B, X and Y are "exogenous technological innovations". Therefore, unless these are transmitted from Country A, it might as well be said that at the time, there was no need in Country B, which could motivate their generation. However, whether or not the need exists prior to the time of introduction, once the innovations enter the society, a new value system based on the innovations must be created in Country B. This relationship may be illustrated by the diagram below.

Therefore, the new value system in Country B based on innovations X and Y should obviously be understood as a discontinuous change. Country B's new value system might seem extremely irregular from the vantage point of Country A's value system, but this is because it is viewed from the value system of Country A. If it is viewed from the standpoint of Country B's new value system, it may not seem so irregular.

It has been stated many times that unless we are very careful in our aid to developing countries the aid might easily be wasted. Let us take a typical example: In a certain country, people keep a TV set and a refrigerator in a small hovel, while others who walk barefoot drive cars.

These are often quoted as being funny and lopsided conditions of living. Perhaps from the point of view of the value system of the advanced donor countries, such life patterns seem very irregular, but from the people's viewpoint, it is not strange at all but simply a matter of course.

The same can be said about Japan. Many Japanese who have lived for a long period abroad feel that post-war Japanese life is very unbalanced, and they point out how odd it is that Japanese people possess many durable consumer goods and enjoy their vacation by driving a car, yet living in a single 3×3 meter room. However, those living in Japan don't feel that this is strange or unbalanced at all. In short, this is only a difference of the two value systems, and to draw a definite or clear-cut conclusion is not easy.

Those who insist that this life pattern is irregular usually also point out that prices will increase and the balance of international payments will go into a deficit. Certainly, with respect to the actual situation in developing countries, this point is not wrong. However, the reason for it may be that these countries are imitating the economic policies of the advanced countries. In other words, this condition has emerged because the developing countries have had no social structure appropriate to their value systems. If they were to evolve and put into practice a different social structure to fit their value system, then their prices would not rise even if they continued this type of life pattern and they would not have a deficit in their balance of international payments.

It is difficult to tell how such a structure could be formed, and it is not easy to find a typical case. However, it may be claimed that an analogous social structure does exist in the evolution of the Japanese post-war economy. The post-war Japanese life pattern has certainly been very irregular from the point of view of many other countries. However, Japan has so far survived without any serious economic depression. This is because Japan did not only imitate other advanced countries, but synthesized its own unique social structure, and boldly put it into practice such as in the indirect financing system. From this point of view, it may seem ironic that technological innovations could have such a world-wide influence. We may now put down the following brief conclusions:

1. Technological innovations have certainly united the world markets. From thereon, as stated by Drucker, they have brought about a new epoch with a change "from international economy to a world economy".

2. As a result, universal demand for certain items of merchandise has . arisen. One may say that borders have ceased to exist as a result of technological innovations.

3. Nevertheless, this has created everywhere new value systems which vary according to the stages of economic development.

4. Accordingly the value systems need appropriate social structures.

The unification of the world would necessitate more and more pluralistic social structures. Up to now, we have unconsciously accepted the idea that the world would be unified by technological innovations and thus, that social structures would also become unified, but I must oppose to this belief as a contradiction to real conditions.

The same kind of thing may manifest itself in every society because whenever a technological innovation occurs, a difference in value systems arises between those who were born and raised before the innovation and those who were born after it. Seen in a historical perspective, this kind of difference existed even before the age of rapid technological development. During the post-war period, technological innovations were made at a very high rate. This permitted a co-existence of various accumulation effects of discontinuous value systems.

Let's discuss a hypothetical family unit in Japan which consists of an old man who has lived more than 80 years, his son, his grandson, and his greatgrandson. When the old man was a boy, trains did not exist. At that time, there was no other way to go from Edo (now Tokyo) to Kyoto than by palanquin along the road. This took about one month. When the boy got old enough to be aware of it, the first locomotive was put into operation, and it then took only about two days to get to Osaka from Tokyo. For him, this was a very fast vehicle compared with the palanquin which had been used prior to that time. When he was in middle age, express trains were running between Tokyo and Osaka taking only one night. Of course this was a very fast vehicle for him. Then, when he got old, the New Tokaido Line was opened up and it took only three hours to travel the same distance.

For the old man, this was an unbelievably fast vehicle. But his son, the grandfather of the youngest boy, never experienced traveling by palanquin. When he was born, the locomotives were already running, although it took two days from Tokyo to Osaka. For him, express trains and the New Tokaido Line were very fast, but he would surely feel that travelling by palanquin would be too slow.

Now when the old man's grandson reached the age where he became aware of things, express trains had already linked Tokyo and Osaka in an overnight run. Although for him, the New Tokaido Line is fast, he thinks that the ordinary train taking an entire day and night, and the palanquin are extremely slow.

By the time the youngest boy was born, the New Tokaido Line was already in operation between Tokyo and Osaka, taking only three hours, which does not seem surprising to him. Needless to say the conveyance which his father and grandfather talked about were exceedingly slow. For him it is foolish even to talk about them.

In this hypothetical family, there coexist four different evaluation systems concerning the speed of vehicles. Among them, there is a discontinuity which cannot be filled. It is not a question of "right" or "wrong", because after all, it is the evaluation systems that are fundamentally different. Therefore, discussing the speed of vehicles among the different systems is irrelevant. The following scheme tries to explain the relationship between the system ("family members").

A	B	C	D	From Tokyo to Osaka
↑	↑	↑	○	The new Tokaido Line (three hours)
↑	↑	○	↓	Traveling by express train (about half a day)
↑	○	↓	↓	Traveling by train (one day and one night)
○	↓	↓	↓	Traveling by palanquin (about one month)

Evaluations

↑   Fast
↓   Slow

Symbols

A = Great-grandfather
B = Grandfather
C = Father
D = Son

○ = Time position of A, B, C, and D resp.

This is what I call invisible innovation. In other words, visible innovations may cause invisible innovation. The sequence may be explained as follows:

Human desire → visible innovation → change of environmental functions → invisible innovation → new desire → visible innovation → . . .

Consequently, we must forecast "how social change will take place by technological innovations" instead of forecasting "which technological innovation shall take place in the future society". For this purpose technical relation tables may be useful.

Now I would like to present an interesting case from Japanese TV broadcasting. There were two groups, one at the age of about 20 years and another at about 40 years. The interviewer first asked the group members "Are you satisfied in the present society?" Everyone in the first group answered "No" and about 80% in the other group answered "Yes." Then the interviewer asked "why?" Everyone in the "young" group answered that "I don't know", and about 50% of the "middle-age" group answered that "present society has improved considerably over the past society".

What does this mean? I think that the outcome of this interview illustrates the difference of the value systems between two generations. Older generations tend to conserve the values shaped during the pre-war period. The value system of the younger generation is more elastic than that of the older generation.

The generation of the 20-year-old group has always been living with technological innovations. For them the conditions of the environment has changed continuously, so a standard of values has not been possible to establish. Even if a certain system of values were established today, it would be substituted by a new system tomorrow. Consequently, it is not correct to say that the younger generation has another, or too many value systems and therefore they must answer "I don't know".

The diversification of certain value systems or the coexistence of different values is probably the most basic characteristic of modern society. If it is caused by technological innovations the tendency should be even stronger in the future.

It does not matter how strong this tendency becomes, there is no danger so long as the elastic functions are fully discharged. The important question is rather what the elastic functions are.

In my opinion, both of the following conditions must be fulfilled for efficient discharge of the elastic functions.

1. A large amount of information.
2. A sufficient number of information processing functions.

A society with sufficient elastic functions should evidently be a post-industrial society. Therefore, from the functional point of view, a post-industrial society may be said to be a multi-channel society.

For what purpose does information exist? It exists for the purpose of being chosen. For instance, let us suppose that there are one hundred of separate pieces of information and that for Mr. M, information (a) is the most useful one, and for Mr. N. (b) is the most suitable. In this case the other 99 pieces of informations are treated as useless to Mr. M. and likewise, 99 are useless to Mr N. But they can be called useless only as a result of examining and comparing all one hundred, and this was how (a) and (b) were selected as being the most useful. However, had Mr M. and Mr N. been given nothing but (a) and (b) from the beginning, they could easily have become frustrated, since they would have expected to have better information, even though they were given the best. In this sense one may argue that the useless 99 pieces of information were necessary for both Mr M. and Mr. N.

This example shows how necessary it is to obtain a great number of alternatives, which eventually turn out to be useless for a specific purpose. It is easy to understand why a large amount of information should be available. The abundance of information makes it possible for the whole society to obtain the elasticity that will reduce the risks for frustrations.

No matter how much information is obtained, it still cannot be selected without efficient information processing functions. If information is over-abundant it could be a great public nuisance. Thus the more information we have, the more efficiently the information processing functions must be operated. The computer will be of central importance in the post-industrial society because it has an excellent information processing function. I believe that the computerization of society will increase the elasticity in the society. Some individuals believe that the computerization will increase the rigidity of society.

The reason for this is that the information processing function is now on the side of the information on supplier instead of information receiver. As Dr. Pierce has pointed out the quantity of information has increased very rapidly in Japan during the past decade. Many Japanese have begun talking about the "information nuisance". We must make every effort to transfer the information processing function from the information supplier's side to the information receiver's side if information nuisance is to be eliminated.

In this connection, the computer will contribute enormously in the coming 10 or 20 years. In the near future computers will be connected to the home telephone and exchange information by using ordinary language instead of a special language. When our society comes to this stage, a new value system will again be created because the innovations are mainly made in the homes.

I would like to draw your attention to the fact that the technological innovations taking place in our homes are the most important because they influence our character directly. Therefore, I believe that the most influential innovations in the post-war period are those of TV and electronic computer.

TV has become a new member of the family. Today, everyone is brought up with TV. When they were born, TV existed at their bedside already, and it takes an active part in the character building of the children and of their parents. Before the invention of TV, the process of character formation of children was dominated by listening to talk in the family or by reading a book. The traditional process is one-dimensional and linear, because the individual information is received in order and then, after a logical process one may understand and remember. Logic is the most important ingredient for binding individual information. The process of TV is quite different. It is a multidimensional process. Obviously pattern recognition depends on the senses instead of logic. Today, one of the most characteristic reasons for the generation gap is probably the difference in recognition processes between the old generation and the young generation. For the old generation it is made mainly by logic, for the young generation mainly by sense. One may talk about a confrontation between "Homo-logicus" and "Homo-sensus". I think this is a very important issue for education in future society.

Let us now consider the influence of the computer on our character. As I noted previously, during the coming 10 or 20 years, it will be possible to have a dialogue with a computer from the home telephones. In other words, we can be trained in a man-to-machine dialogue instead of only a man-to-man dialogue from the beginning of our lives.

The present society is often called the computer society or "computopia". As Dr. Pierce pointed out the spread of computers in Japan is very rapid too. I think that these are the most noteable signs for creation of new Homo-sapiens called "Homo-computer".

How will the generation gap be in the near future? Evidently this is one of the most pressing questions about the future society. Let us examine and evaluate the condition of our modern society from the viewpoint of the elastic function of society. For that purpose, let us macroscopically view our society as a whole in terms of systems theory, dividing it into three kinds of systems as follows:

1. The system of goods
2. The system of service
3. The system of systems

It goes without saying that a certain element can be part of various systems at the same time. A single element can be part of the system of goods on the one hand, and part of the system of service on the other hand. Here we must consider the system of goods from production to consumption as a coherent system. Hence this includes distribution, finance, sales and advertisement, elements which apparently belong to the service industry from the viewpoint of industrial classification. But when it functions to fulfill the totally individualistic desires of the person, it should be considered not as an element of the system of goods but as one of the system of services.

Thinking flexibly in this way, we can classify everything in our society in terms of the above three systems. And taking present-day Japan as an example, all three systems are operating quite satisfactorily as far as fundamental functions for non-individualistic desires are concerned, and the same can be said for all highly industrialized nations. We should know, however, that among developing nations, there are many in which even this kind of function is not sufficiently discharged. However, when it comes to the elastic function for individualistic desires, even very advanced nations, including Japan, are far from perfect. Taking the three above mentioned systems, these nations have usually a sufficiently elastic function concerning the system of goods, but when it comes to the system of services and system of systems, their functions are very incomplete. Here we find a large defect in modern society.

Let us consider for a moment the system of goods. Today, we are producing, distributing, and consuming various products. We can see that each of these products always has both elastic and fundamental functions, and that the conditions—the abundance of information and good information processing function—for the elastic function are quite satisfactory. Let's take a watch, for example. We can sell watches because they give us the time accurately. People must know this in order to function properly in daily life. The function of giving the time is such that every watch must necessarily have it. That is to say, among human desires, the desire to know the accurate time is a kind of non-individualistic one, and watches' function of giving the time (corresponding to that desire) is apparently a fundamental one. But most people have watches which differ from each other in design, size and price because they demand various watches according to their personal taste. That is, things like design comprise an elastic function for individualistic desire. Watchmakers display hundreds of watches in their windows and we can choose freely among them. Thus we have always a great deal of information, and when we buy a watch, we can use this information processing function at any time in order to choose what suits our tastes.

Today, computers are used to gather data rapidly as to consumer demand, and therefore wise producers can direct their production with regard to the market. Consequently the total cost of production of small amounts of various kinds may be cheaper than mass production of one kind. This may seem contradictory to traditional common sense. It is true that production of small amounts of various types of products cannot be economical, but instead, intermediate or indirect expenses can be cut down by a direct connection with the market, and in that case, the total cost is consequently lower. Here, computers contribute greatly to increase the elastic function of the system of goods by operating effectively in their information processing function. This phenomenon can already be seen in certain parts of our present industrial society. However, we have not yet reached the stage where we can say the same thing about the whole industrial society.

Especially with respect to the distribution of products, we must pay attention to the fact that the distribution of products and that of information are not fitted together well. Although information should be distributed before the distribution of products, they are not actually coordinated. This causes much waste in the distribution of products and consequently increases expenses. As for the distribution of information, such data communication machines as directly connected computers and telecommunication systems are going to be used practically. It can be of no good that the distribution of products is disconnected.

We now move on to the system of services. The elastic function of the system of services is far less efficient than that of the system of goods. This is because both the quantity of information and information processing, particularly the latter, function far less efficiently.

Before the war, services were performed manually by human labor. When a man offered his service to others, the fundamental function for non-individualistic desires and the elastic function for individualistic desires were bound so closely that it seemed even meaningless to consider them separate. It is a matter of course in personal relationship that, for example, when the other is in a bad mood, one pays attention even to his way of expression and when the other is in a good mood, one relaxes. Such immediate responses were possible because they have human minds. In other words, man can immediately perceive what the other selects according to his individualistic desire and can offer the suitable service. After the war, however, as the shortage of labor grew intense, machines were gradually introduced in the service industry. The most essential difference between man and machine is that machines have no mind. Therefore, machines have no elastic function corresponding to individualistic desire in the beginning. Machines are indifferent. In this sense, the expression "machines have replaced human labor" is mistaken. Though machines may have filled the fundamental function of human labor, they have had nothing to do with the elastic functions. If we have an incorrect understanding of this fact, we are missing more and more the elastic functions that we need most in our society. Apparently this will cause great frustration everywhere in our society, and accumulation of this frustration will produce social tension.

Are we not today committing this suicidal act unconsciously? This is why alienation of humanity is a common subject of debate. It means that inflexibility is actually a result of the fact that society has lost its elastic function. Thus, what is important here is to satisfy two conditions: namely an abundance of information and the establishment of an information processing function. Above all, the improvement of the information processing function will be an indispensable condition for the service industry.

And in this fact lies the answer to the question of what a service is. A service should be something that responds vigorously to the various demands of each individual. In spite of this, it is all too often that uniform services are offered today irrespective of customer's individualistic desires. After all, this is to deny humanity and to degrade man to the level of machines. No matter how much information we have, we must be able to process much more, even assuming the present capacity of computers. That is to say, we can improve more and more the consultative functions which today's service industry lacks most. Hence, we can get rid of the uniformity of service which is seen today.

When it comes to the system of systems, the situation is more pessimistic. What degree of inflexibility results from losing the elastic function! This can be seen everywhere. For example, systems of companies or government offices, legal systems, finance systems, taxation systems, education systems, community systems, housing development systems, or individual housing construction systems. I would like to point out that we are far from having a great deal of information but rather lack it in many social phases such as the above. Even if we have abundant information, it is apparent that almost none are processed. So it happens that we have no information about important matters when it is necessary. This is because our present social information processing function is not complete. And this fact is also the cause of our weak consciousness of participation in society. Thus we tend to be driven to despair, thinking "what will be, will be". This is partly because the flow of information in our society is not yet circular. Considering these facts we may eventually visualize the direction of the coming technological innovations.

Note

[1] Jantsch, E. Technological Forecasting in Perspective, OECD, Paris 1967.

The Advancement of Science for the Developing Countries

By Abdus Salam

International Centre for Theoretical Physics, Trieste, Italy

I shall be concerned in this paper with the possibilities of growth of indigenous traditions in basic and applied science in the developing world. I believe that the present situation as well as the future prospects of such a growth are bleak. The facts are easily stated. Of industrial science very little exists. This is because most industry in developing countries is based on processes bought from abroad; alternatively the industrial concerns belong to foreign companies, who prefer to undertake whatever new industrial research and development is needed in their own strong foreign based research laboratories. Among industries I am cynically including the one great source of scientific strength in any country—the weapons industry. The second area which one might have imagined would receive the topmost priority relates to sciences as applied to exploitation of indigenous resources. This includes agricultural sciences, soil sciences, mineral sciences, medical sciences in relation to local diseases and population problems. These are areas where the relevant scientific knowledge may not be available in the world supermarket and new knowledge needs to be created. Measuring scientific activity through the existence or lack of strong centres of research, barring a few outstanding examples of institutions internationally set up—and these I shall be speaking about later—there are unfortunately not many centres of outstanding worth. The reasons for this are well known. Basically they stem from the general apathy of those responsible for economic development to invest in local science; from the lack of trust in the capabilities of their own scientists, and reciprocally of the non-involvement of local scientific communities in the exciting problems of development. Finally, fundamental research in the universities or outside—again barring some very few exceptions in India, Argentina, Pakistan and Brazil—is weak for two well known reasons.

1. The towering men of science produced by most developing countries, finding the atmosphere in their own countries sterile, have tended to leave.

2. Those who are left behind are isolated and do not form part of the international world community. Thus the two promises of science, the one

relating to economic development and the second relating to intellecutal fulfilment, both remain unrealized.

The weakness of science and scientific institutions is not due to lack of lip
service paid to the ideals of science and need for its development by leaders
in the developing countries. Notwithstanding this lip service, however, the
fact remains that the scientific revolution of thought has hardly touched the
developing world. There is no comprehension of the scientific style of the
natural world, no intellectual transformation of society as a whole. The
energies of most intellectuals in developing countries are occupied either
with problems which arise from the local conflicts with those in the neighbouring countries or with problems arising from real or supposed economic
and other exploitation of their countries.

My thesis in speaking to a forum like this one is that the situation in the
developing world is so bleak that without active involvement of the international scientific community it will not change. My thesis is that indigenous
science in the developing world is weak, but that it should expect and
demand, as it were of right, fullest support from science abroad. We scientists pride ourselves as being the last of the idealists, our motives are not
politically suspect, we fortunately possess a fund of goodwill through the
work of the institutions which include private foundations, as well as the
scientific Agencies of the United Nations family.

The involvement of the world scientific community and the help it can
give to the weak scientific communities in the developing countries can take
many different forms. I shall describe only some of the possible ways. In
particular I shall concentrate on some of the institutional means the world
community may possibly use. But this is in no way meant to minimize the
importance of the other means which I shall not talk about. The crucial
point is a realization on the part of the world scientific community that here
is a sphere where they can directly help and they are expected to help.

But before we can make an assessment of what is needed today I feel it
is important to get an idea of the past, particularly of why it is that the
developing world, and particularly those parts of it with glorious traditions
of a scientific past, have been so tardy in achieving the modern scientific
transformation. Since personally I am most familiar with my own, the
Islamic civilization, I shall select my illustrations from its history.

Almost exactly twelve hundred years ago, Abdullah Al Mansur, the
second Abbasid Caliph, celebrated the founding of his new capital, Baghdad,
by inaugurating an international scientific conference. To this conference
were invited Greek, Nestorian, Byzantine, Jewish, Chinese, as well as Hindu
scholars. From this conference—the first international conference in an
Arab country—dates the systematic renaissance of science associated with

Islam. The theme of the conference was observational astronomy. Al Mansur was interested in more accurate astronomical tables than were available then. He wanted, and he ordered at the conference, a better determination of the circumference of the earth. No one realized it then, but there was read at the conference a paper destined to change the whole course of mathematical thought. This was a paper read by the Hindu astronomer, Kankah, on Hindu numerals, then unknown to anyone outside of India. Kankah had come to the conference to present to it copies of various Siddhantas—the Hindu manuals of astronomy.

Al Mansur's conference succeeded beyond all expectations. It laid the foundations of astronomical and mathematical studies in Islam; from this conference grew the idea of the founding of one of the world's first *international* Academies for Scientific Research, the Bayt-ul hikma. But even on the more practical, more pragmatic plane, from this conference date the architectural and engineering studies of Naubakht and Mashallah, both of whom attended its sessions and who were later responsible for some of the major monuments of Baghdad. From this conference dates the craft of instrument making in Baghdad, whose specimens still survive in the masterworks of Isa Asturlabi.

The fact that there was collected at Baghdad this concourse of scholars, forming an international gathering, was not purely accidental. The Arabs were building on the heritage of Greek science, the custodians of which at that epoch of history were the Nestorian Christians who, bitterly persecuted by the Byzantines, had emigrated to Mesopotamia, and later to South West Persia, from the sixth century onwards. They had made a home at Gondisapur, not far from Baghdad. They possessed, in Syriac, translations of works of Plato, Aristotle, Euclid, Archimedes and Hippocrates. The existence of this Nestorian Hellenistic centre of learning, Gondisapur, was Allah's gift to a new civilization, then bursting with youthful zest and fired with the Prophet's injunction to value science and learning above everything else. On this foundation, carefully nurtured, the Caliphs in Baghdad built, importing also Chinese and Indian scholars.

The next four hundred and fifty years saw the brilliant flowering of Islamic sciences and learning, both in Eastern Islam as well as in the West, in Spain.—What during this period was the attitude of Western Europe towards this outpouring of knowledge? In Charles Singer's words: "This attitude was the same which the Oriental now has towards the West. The Oriental recognizes that with the West are science and learning, power and organization and business enterprise, but the admitted superiority of the West does not extend to his sphere of religion. He gladly accepts Western standards of economics, technology, science and medicine, but repudiates and perhaps despises the religion, philosophy and much of the social outlook of the West. In the Europe of the tenth and eleventh centuries it was exactly the opposite. The West knew full well that Islam held the learning and science of antiquity. Muslim proficiency in arms and administration had been sufficiently proved." But with this longing for the intellectual treasures of the East, there was fear that Christian values and Christian culture would be deletereously affected. Thus no attempt was made to borrow or to make contact. An eloquent expression to these fears was given in a lament by Alvaro of Cordova writing in the ninth century. "Many of my co-religionists read the poetry and tales of the Arabs, study the writings of their scientists and philosophers, but where are those among us who can read the Latin commentaries on the Holy Scriptures? Among thousands of us there is hardly one who can write a passable Latin letter to a friend, but innumerable are those who can express themselves in Arabic and compose poetry in that language with greater art than the Arabs themselves."

This feeling of repugnance on the part of the West lasted some three to four hundred years. It then began to change. It is not commonly recognized how important the last half of the eleventh and the first part of the twelfth century are for the development of the European science and European civilization. For some reason there arose in Italy, France, Scandinavia and Britain a number of men who were willing to brave the disapprobation of the Church and its odium in order to make available to the West the learning of the East and the international intellectual treasures of humanity garnered and improved upon by the Arabs from Greece, India and China.

One of the most important among these men was an impoverished Scotsman who left his native glens to travel south to Toledo in Spain, some seven hundred and fifty years ago. For my second historical illustration I shall consider the life and work of this Scotsman. His name was Michael, his goal to live and work at the Arab universities of Toledo and Cordova. Michael reached Toledo in 1217. Toledo was an Arab town but not then in Arab hands. It had been captured by the Spanish Christians a hundred years before, but the tradition of Arabic learning, Arab teachers and language remained intact. One may note the parallel with the international centre of Gondisapur of the Nestorians five hundred years before, which had been captured by Islam but had retained its Christian identity. In Toledo, Michael the Scot formed the ambitious project of introducing Aristotle to Latin Europe, translating not from the original Greek, which he did not know, but from the Arabic translation of Aristotle then taught in Spain. Exactly one hundred years before, Adelard of Bath, an Englishman, had done a like service for geometry by translating Euclid into Latin, not from the original Greek, but also from an annotated Arabic translation.

Toledo's school, representing as it did the finest synthesis of Arabic, Greek, Latin and Hebrew scholarship, was one of the most memorable of international essays into scientific collaboration. To Toledo and Cordova came scholars, not only from the rich countries of the East—like Palestine and Egypt—but also from developing lands of the West—like Scotland. Then, as now, there were obstacles to this international scientific concourse. First, there was the political division of the world. In 1217 the wounds of the Third Crusade, fought barely thirty years before, were still not healed. And then there was the economic and intellectual disparity between different parts of the world. Men like Michael the Scot and his contemporary in Toledo, Alfred the Englishman, were singularities; they did not represent any flourishing schools of research in their own countries. With all the best will in the world, their teachers at Toledo doubted the wisdom and value of training them for advanced scientific research. At least one of his masters, despairing of his lack of grounding in science, counselled young Michael to go back to the clipping of sheep and weaving of woollen cloth.

Added to Michael's lack of background training, there was the disapprobation of the Church I have spoken about. Michael's countryman, Sir Walter Scott, in his "Lay of the Last Minstrel" has given expression to this disapprobation. The minstrel in Scott's poem tells us how Michael was accused of wizardry and other deadly sins:

In those far climes it was my lot
To meet the wondrous Michael Scot;
A wizard of such dreaded fame,
That when in Salamanca's cave
He lifted his magic wand to wave,
The bells would ring in Notre Dame!

The lay goes on . . .

When Michael lay on his dying bed
His conscience was awakened.
He bethought him of his sinful deed
He gave me a sign to go with speed.

But nothing could save Michael's soul. Dante found Michael in agony in one of the lowest circles of the Inferno—all for the deadly crime of learning Arabic and teaching Europe the Arab sciences of mathematics, biology and philosophy.

Another two hundred years were to pass. During these two hundred years, the devastation caused by the Mongols and Tamerlane destroyed all tradition of scientific enquiry in the lands of Islam. The tables were now completely turned; it was the Muslim scholar who had turned inward; inward towards the spiritual security afforded by his past cultural tradition; shunning all contact with newer thought which came now from the Western lands. One of the last of the great scholars in Islam, Ibn-Khaldun, whom Toynbee describes as a man who conceived and formulated a philosophy of history which remains the greatest work of its kind that has ever been created by any mind at any time at any place—even a man of such calibre, writing two hundred years after Michael the Scot, in 1400 A.D., about sciences in Christian lands expresses himself thus: "We have heard of late that in the land of the Franks and on the northern shores of the Mediterranean there is a great cultivation of philosophical sciences. They are said to be studied there again and to be taught in numerous classes. Existing systematic expositions of them are said to be comprehensive, the people who know them numerous and the students of them very many. Allah knows better what exists there but it is clear that the problems of physics are of no importance for us in our religious affairs. Therefore we must leave them alone." Ibn-Khaldun displays no curiosity, no wistfulness; just apathy bordering on hostility.

I could give parallels from the other two great world civilizations, the Chinese and the Hindu. As far as we know, the pattern is more or less the same; the initial borrowing from an *external* intellectual tradition—and I wish to stress *external* tradition—possibly at an international intellectual centre; the great diffusion of learning in the society, its wholesale acceptance of the scientific spirit of enquiry and then finally the closing in of mental barriers once again.

How can this situation be changed? I said earlier that a crucial initial role was played in building up science in Islamic and Christian civilizations by the essentially alien international centres of Gondisapur and Toledo representing traditions of living science in the midst of their own societies. I believe that something similar to these centres will have to be created in the developing world before it begins to enter into the spirit of a true scientific revolution. Nothing can give that instinct of what is credible and what is not, that fine sense of the scientifically genuine and the scientifically deceptive, as the direct experience of living science—living in your own conditions and environment and flourishing within your own cultural tradition. The problem which concerns us today is this: Can we capture or create the Gondisapurs and Toledos of today by our own efforts unaided within our countries? By and large, the answers appear to be: No! The reasons are simple. Science feeds on science. Men of science wish to work where other such men are and where they obtain facilities. We in the developing world cannot or will not afford these facilities, either through actual poverty, or through a poverty of spirit; far from attracting the foreign great men, we are likely to lose our own, retarding thereby still further the scientific transformation of our societies.

To re-emphasize my point, let us look more closely at the overall situation in the developing countries and ask ourselves what are the first-rate institutes there which have made the most impact intellectually or in terms of economic returns. Two such outstanding institutes immediately spring to mind. These are the International Rice Institute in the Philippines, set up with Ford and Rockefeller assistance, and the International Wheat and Maize Institute, similarly sponsored, in Mexico. One of the greatest revolutions, unpublicized so far, but potentially something as great as the industrial revolution itself, is the agricultural revolution which has been taking place in the last three years in parts of the developing world. This revolution we owe to the work done at these two institutes. As you are aware, the bulk of the gross national products of poor countries comes from agriculture. Unfortunately, the wheat and the rice and the cotton and the maize which we raise have had very low yields. This was not due to any sloth or perversity or incompetence on the part of our farmers. It simply was the result of the genetic varieties that throve without any diets of nitrogen. The introduction of a nitrogen-consuming Japanese variety of rice in India, for example, simply failed, for India, oddly enough, does not have the same long hours of sunlight as Japan.

The last few years have seen great advances in plant engineering. These advances have for the first time been purposefully applied to create new dwarf varieties of wheat and rice. The wheat research was carried out in Mexico, the rice research in the Philippines. The ideal rice plant, I understand, was literally designed on the drawing board; the roots of so much thickness, the stem, the stalk, the ears, the numbers of grain in each ear, the amount of sunlight it might receive. Likewise for rust-resistant wheat, with short, stiff straws to avoid "lodging" of heavyheaded plants, insensitive to differences in diurnal rhythms of sunlight and dark. The new varieties were tried on a large scale in India and Pakistan for the first time on some 30 million acres in 1967–68. The wheat crop yields went up by as much as 300%—the rice, in some instances, by 500%. This summer there was a shortage of agricultural labour in West Pakistan—the first time perhaps in history—there was so much to lift and reap. Wheat production in Pakistan has gone up from 3.8 million tons to 7 million tons; it is expected to increase at 10–15% per year for a number of years; Pakistan is worrying about a wheat glut.

Why were these international institutes able to work a miracle which no national institutes could? The reasons I think are not far to seek. The atmosphere of scientific pursuit as we understand it, the calibre of men that could internationally be assembled, the facilities that could be afforded, the contacts with the rest of the scientific community, the flow of information; all simple things which one takes for granted and which simply are not available or made available in the developing countries themselves.

Will the example of these institutes implant the true scientific ideals in the surrounding countries? Will they be imitated, their example followed? Will they bring the scientific revolution I have talked of before nearer? I believe so, I hope so. For one thing, for the first time the miracle wrought by the work at these institutes has convinced our hard-headed administrators that applied science is worth spending money on. To this symposium has been presented a proposal to establish an international centre on insect physiology and endocrinology in East Africa. I find it an exceedingly exciting proposal. It carries with it the promise of a scientific frontier field in a problem which is at the same time closely related to actual needs of the developing world. It promises to attract leading men of world science to work in the developing world and help to bring about the scientific revolution. Given thirty or forty such institutes around the developing world, I feel a real scientific transformation will come about.

I have spoken of the modern parallels of Gondisapur and Toledo, centres of scientific excellence set up in developing countries in conjunction with local universities or outside them, but backed strongly by the international science community. One of the important problems which arises in connection with such centres is: how should they be sponsored? The Wheat and Rice Institutes were set up by *local governments* with help from two of the highly respected scientific foundations. In addition to these foundations there is one other—and indeed potentially an even more important—non-political resource which we as a community have not fully exploited. This is the United Nations Organization and its scientific Agencies. The United Nations is a much maligned institution; most of us are conscious of only one side of its activities, the political, embodied in the Security Council. Very few of us know of its far reaching social, economic and scientific work. The scientific work is concentrated in its specialized agencies: the Food and Agriculture Organization, with an annual budget of $30 millions; the World Health Organization with a budget of $50 million, the United Nations Educational, Scientific and Cultural Organization, with a budget of around $30 million; and in a category by itself, the International Atomic Energy Agency, with a budget of $10 million. These are very modest sums, but in addition the United Nations itself dispenses some $100 million on science and technology through the United Nations Development Fund. These budgets are contributed by member nations according to a formula based on their gross national products. The specialized agencies dispense the funds for providing technical assistance to developing nations; they award fellowships and sponsor conferences and symposia. To co-ordinate the work of these Agencies, and to pinpoint newer areas where science and technology may make a direct impact, there is the United Nations Advisory Committee on Science and Technology, of which I have the privilege to be a member.

As an example of the exploitation of the United Nations machinery for pure science, I shall take the case of an international institute for the developing countries, in whose setting up I was personally associated. Unlike the other institutes I have spoken about, it is not an international institute located in a developing country, though it could have been. By speaking about it I wish to illustrate an important anti-braindrain device to end isolation of leading scientists from the developing countries which was pioneered at this institute and which may have applications throughout the scientific field. You may have noted that the scientific effort of the United Nations family has so far been mainly oriented toward applied science. A natural extension of this work would be to charge the Organization—with its unique inbuilt supranational structure and its collective use of available resources—with responsibilities also toward fundamental science, and this would naturally include responsibilities to the pure scientists from developing countries.

In September 1960 I had the privilege for the first time of attending the General Conference of the IAEA as a delegate from Pakistan. It seemed to me a good thing to try to make at least a beginning toward an international United Nations university, benefiting university scientists both from developing as well as developed countries, by proposing to set up a post-graduate Centre for Theoretical Physics under the IAEA auspices. With the cosponsorship of the Governments of Afghanistan, the Federal Republic of Germany, Iran, Japan, the Philippines, Portugal, Thailand and Turkey, we introduced a resolution on behalf of the Pakistan Government, suggesting that an international centre for research in theoretical physics should be set up under the auspices of the IAEA. In consonance with the standard UN practice, the resolution started with a preamble which stressed the unique virtues of theoretical physics for peace, prosperity and health of mankind.

Of the list of nations first sponsoring the idea, most were the less-privileged countries. It was clear that the setting up of such a centre was of interest to these nations, for the hope was that it might help in resolving one of the frustrating problems which their active university physicists face—the problem of isolation. Such men could come frequently to a centre of this type, not to stay permanently but to renew their contacts and then to go back refreshed after a period of concentrated research. This would not solve the problem of heavy teaching duties in their own countries, it would be no substitute for building up centres of excellence in their own countries, but it would certainly end one aspect of their disabilities—isolation from newer ideas.

Right from the outset the idea met with enthusiastic support from the IAEA's directorate, particularly from its distinguished Director General, Dr. Sigvard Eklund, whom you well know, as well as from the physics community. Two of our most ardent sponsors were Niels Bohr and Robert Oppenheimer.

After four years of intense behind-the-scenes effort, the Board of Governors agreed to set up such a centre, for a trial period of four years, provided the bulk of the finance for it could be found outside of IAEA funds. The reluctance of the Board of Governors was not unrelated to the fact that the IAEA's total budget of $10 million is itself an extremely modest one. Offers of financial assistance from interested Member States were solicited; of four received (from the Government of Italy for a centre to be located at Trieste, from Denmark for Copenhagen, from Pakistan for Lahore and from Turkey for Ankara) the most generous, and one which no developing country could hope to compete with, was the Italian Government's offer for Trieste. The moving spirit behind it was Professor Paolo Budini, Professor at the University of Trieste. This offer was accepted and the Centre started functioning in October 1964 with a mandate until October 1968. This has now been extended for a further six years; furthermore, from 1970 onwards UNESCO has decided to participate as a full partner with IAEA in financing and running the Centre.

Some of you may be familiar with the Centre and what it has achieved during the last five years. The Centre receives as visitors leading physicists; in principle from one hundred but in practice from around fifty nations— thirty of these developing. These men come to work on their own research problems in the milieu which they themselves create. In this the Centre does not differ from any other research centre in theoretical physics, except perhaps in the jealously guarded high standards it tries to maintain. Where it does differ is in the easy formality with which it can arrange long-term contact between physicists from the East and the West—this is possible because the Centre is a United Nations sponsored Institute and not a national one—and even more important, of physicists from developing countries. To break the barrier of their isolation, the Centre has pioneered what it calls an associateship scheme. I shall describe it, for, as I said it possesses wider applications outside the Trieste Centre. An associate in our terminology is a physicist working in a developing country who is simultaneously a member of the Centre's staff. Once elected he can come to the Centre every year for a period ranging from six to twelve weeks, with no formalities except a letter announcing his arrival. With a generous grant from the Ford Foundation the Centre pays the associate's fare and his expenses at Trieste; the associateship lasts for three to five years and is renewable. The intention is to try to cover all top active men in the developing world and to give them this financially-guaranteed possibility of remaining in touch with other leading men in their subjects. The crucial feature of the scheme is the stability of the three to five years which it provides a leading man in a developing university to plan his work and career. The one important pre-condition for remaining an associate is that nine months of the year must be spent in the developing country itself.

We received this year a generous grant from the Swedish International Development Authority to create twelve associateships for African professors. Our total at present is thirtyfive; I am hoping that some day soon my dream of being able to finance one hundred associateships for front-rank active theoretical physicists will be realized.

There is nothing special about theoretical physics so far as the associateship scheme is concerned. There is no reason why other institutes in other subjects may not start similar schemes to ours to end the problem of scientific isolation. Every university in the developed world can do this—by appointing five to ten associates in any discipline it may choose ending thus once for all the problem of isolation of scientists from developing countries. The United Nations Advisory Committee, at a recent session in New York, took the initiative to convene a meeting of US University Presidents and Heads of US private foundations to set up in conjunction with the United States Academy of Sciences and the Canadian Research Council a scheme catering in this manner for between 200 to 300 scientists. The Canadian Research Council has already started its own scheme of associateships or dual appointments of those leading men who have in the past received their research training in Canada. We are still waiting for the United States action.

The ideas I have spoken of form part of the greater idea of setting up a world federation of research institutions which may or may not have connections with the United Nations Organization but which could be affiliated to a world university about which Professor Lasswell will be speaking just after me. This is the idea to create a world federation of existing international postgraduate institutes for advanced study which may constitute a first step towards the achievement in the future of the bigger ideal of a fully-fledged world university. The essential element of the plan is to identify presently existing research institutions of first rate quality which are international in character and in terms of their faculties. All such institutions—if they exist in the developed world—may pledge to reserve perhaps 20% of their resources and facilities towards supporting the work of high grade

scholars from developing countries through associateships, dual appointments or other devices. Such Institutes, together with the International Institutes I have spoken about in the developing countries—both in pure and
applied sciences—as well as in Economics, Sociology and other studies of
man—would make up a Federation, enriching each other by contacts,
deriving strength from common ideals shared and practised. As I said I
would like to see such a Federation linked up with the United Nations
Organization or one of its Agencies in a loose connection. Most scholars
feel frightened of a possible deadening hand of the United Nations machinery. From personal experience with the Trieste Centre I can vouch for it
that their fears are exaggerated; on the other hand the advantages in terms
of true internationalism are very real and immense. In sciences, in scholar-
ships, when we speak of internationalism, most thought goes to contact between the East and the West. The thesis of my remarks today has been that
there is the third world, very much wishing and very much deserving to come
in as equal third partners. The United Nations system has the merit that it
constantly reminds one of this.

Before this Federation of World Institutes begins to look like the World
University in the sense most of us understand the University concept—and
this applies equally even if we limit our sights to a postgraduate University
—new Institutes, with tasks relating to universal studies relevant to man's
estate, will have to be created to link up with this Federation. But the first
step—the Federation—could perhaps come even within the next ten years.
In all my remarks I have throughout assumed that the scientific community
recognizes that it is part of its mandate to build up true internationalism.
We who pursue scientific enquiry as a profession find the international ideal
something bred, as it were, within our bones. The very exigencies of scientific creation demand that in this pursuit we recognize no colour, no creed, no
political persuasion. Most of us believe in this passionately, not just as one
more measure towards internationalizing this planet, but also for much more
practical reasons. We believe that science offers the one sure way of abo-
lishing the vast slum on this earth inhabited at present by two thirds of
mankind—a slum which no modern nation state would tolerate in its midst
but which we collectively do on the global scale. The international ideal was
never expressed better than by the seventeenth century mystic, John Donne:

No man is an island, entire of itself; every man is a piece of the continent,
a part of the main; if a clod be washed away by the sea, Europe is the less, as
well as if a promontory were, as well as if a manor of thy friends or of thine
own were; any man's death diminishes me, because I am involved in mankind;
and therefore never send to know for whom the bell tolls; it tolls for thee.

The Prospects of a World University

By Harold D. Lasswell

Law School, Yale University, New Haven, Conn., U.S.A.

Introduction

Imagine a world university in effective operation.

Most assuredly it will continue the historic commitment of every university to the advancement of knowledge, particularly in fields where interdisciplinary cooperation is the most promising line of advance.

In contradistinction to many contemporary institutions of higher learning a world university will play a responsible part in exploring the social consequences and policy implications of knowledge.

As a means of accomplishing its distinctive role the approach of a world university will be contextual and problem oriented. To be contextual is to take account of the continuing interplay between the world university and its social environment. To be problem oriented is to perform the intellectual tasks appropriate to any problem solving activity. We identify five such tasks: projecting the future development of knowledge and its social consequences; clarifying value goals of the university and the world community; describing historic and contemporary trends in the degree to which goals are realized; analyzing the factors that condition the direction and magnitude of significant trends; inventing, evaluating and selecting policy alternatives.

At any given moment the projection of events on a world scale calls for the mobilizing of all relevant knowledge. A world university will bring all the technologies of information storage and retrieval, and of simulation to bear, and the results will be shared with all who are sufficiently motivated to concern themselves with mapping the future.

A world university can be expected to assist in clarifying the overriding goals of the world community, no matter how confused or conflicting these may appear to be. Historically, differences of fundamental goal have tended to polarize mankind in two divisions: those who commit themselves to the dignity of *all* men, and those who are committed to the dignity of *some* men. The former are disposed to favor the realization of a world public and civic order in which value opportunities and realizations are widely distributed. The latter are disposed to support a self-perpetuating class or caste with overwhelming control of available values. The social structures and functions in harmony with the first goal seek to afford everyone an opportunity to discover and to exercise his latent talents and to mature them into socially acceptable expression; likewise, those who contribute effectively are rewarded above the minimum guaranteed to all. The social structures and functions in harmony with the second goal strive to perpetuate the control of elites over political power, scientific or technical knowledge or skill, economic resources, health, and other valued outcomes.

In coming years a world university will be challenged to assist in clarifying the goals appropriate to a world society whose science-based technology allows it to utilize genetic engineering, self-directing machines, and response conditioning. How is the conception of "human" dignity to be redefined under such circumstances? How is "freedom" to be re-defined, if indeed the conception is to be retained?

We take it for granted that the intellectual tasks relating to the description of trend, the improvement of scientific knowledge, and the invention and evaluation of policy options will be performed by a world university. The university will cultivate knowledge of the decision process itself, and of the ways in which knowledge can be effectively mobilized for current and upcoming problems of the world community. The institution will encourage acts of creativity that formulate novel yet realistic objectives, provide for the continuing feedback of observational data that make it possible in the future to evaluate the accuracy of forecasts and the suitability of explanatory models of social, biological and physical change.

Turn from this generalized picture of a functioning world university to the present situation. What trends and conditioning factors exhibit and account for the contemporary demand for a World University? What is the most probable course of future developments? What comprehensive goals, objectives and strategies are most appropriate for the growth and application of knowledge?

The demand for a world university

The world of our time is demanding new and renovated institutions of knowledge. Proposals for a world university are best understood as expressions of this demand.

When we ask who is launching these proposals it is not surprising to find that initiatives come from scholars and scientists of many levels of distinction in many disciplinary fields. Such proposals also originate in non-academic circles where they are champoined by individuals, young and old, who by no stretch of imagination can be called specialised intellectuals.

Probing into these initiatives one becomes familiar with justifying themes that frequently recur. Most often there is hope of doing something to liberate man from the nightmare of annihilation. A common remonstrance is that men of knowledge have for too long sought to evade their community responsibilities. The allegation is that they have abstained from contributing to public awareness of the social consequences and policy implications of the new knowledge of the atomic and sub-atomic world, of genetic codes, or the mechanisms of perception (and mis-perception). In more exalted terms we hear that our species is on the threshold of taking evolutionary destiny into its own hands, and of starting to penetrate and eventually to rearrange its solar habitat.

Whether the tone is hortatory, apprehensive, or querulous there is concern for shared access to an intensive, selective, and continually updated map of the past, present and future of the cultural, biological and physical realms. At every level of world community there is concern for having a voice in inventing, evaluating and choosing among value goals, intermediate objectives and strategic policies. If the Universal Declaration of Human Rights, for example, is to pass from rhetoric to reality, it is assertedly necessary to mobilize knowledge *of* and *in* the decision process. Whether we think of this as the restoration of commitment to the philosophic approach to government, law and politics, or as marking the appearance of a new conception of the policy sciences, the inference is the same: act to improve the functioning of the knowledge institutions of society.

Factors that sustain demand

It is not difficult to identify many of the factors that have combined to bring about the movement whose chief symbolic expression is the demand for a world university. As a living form "man" pursues "values" (preferred events) through "institutions" affecting "resources" (the natural environment). When ways of thinking and doing (institutions) are perceived as failing to yield expected value outcomes, or when they are experienced as accompanying value indulgences with unacceptable deprivations, changes occur. The world's institutions are today perceived as in whole or in part disfunctional; and men believe that something can be done to alleviate discrepancies. Many men believe that universities are among the institutions that are functioning unsatisfactorily to the extent that they fail to assist in appraising and re-planning the institutional network as a whole.

In reference to governmental institutions, for example, it is apparent that the system of nation states, bound together by an incomplete structure of obligation, is poorly adapted to the value goal of world security and peace. The institutions of production, distribution, consumption and investment are often alleged to be so warped in the service of colonial and ex-colonial economies that most of the population of the globe is deprived of access to the fruits of a science based technology. Similarly, the institutions of enlightenment and skill (of research, education and public information) are adversely criticized for their unbalanced state of development. The institutions of health, safety and comfort are assailed for failing to serve the needs of all mankind on an equitable basis. Structures of a more intimate kind— including family systems—may be experienced as failures for having neglected to provide an environment suited to the growth of integrated characters possessed of a realistic outlook on a changing world. At various places in the global community the institutions of class and caste are seen as deviations from the criteria of individual development and potential mobility. Ecclesiastical and ethical institutions are in manifest turmoil. Concerning the often devastating impact of social institutions on the natural environment it is unnecessary to go beyond the documentation provided by the present symposium.

The inference is that accelerated rates of interaction throughout the globe have contributed to the confusions of identity, of value priority and specification, and of reality expectations that affect—and are affected by—operational inadequacies throughout the social order.

The demand for a world university is at once symtomatic of distress and a symbolic tribute to knowledge. It demonstrates that the World Community of today is ambivalently aware of the two faces science: the menace and the promise to which Chairman Tiselius referred in his opening address.

Factors that limit demand

It would be erroneous to imply that initiatives on behalf of a world university have received the unreserved support of scholarly, scientific, or lay opinion. There is a sense in which every university properly conceives of itself as a world university. In the circumstances of today no establishment is so parochial that it can altogether escape the universalizing civilization of science and technology. This is true, for example, in the world of Islam at a venerable center of learning such as El-Azhar. It holds true of the principal sites of Buddhist scholarship. Although the universities of Western Europe are deeply affected by the Judeo-Christian tradition, or bear the marks of an emphatic reaction against many elements of this inheritance, they have generalized their norms until there are few ideological inhibitions against the advancement of verifiable knowledge.

If the proposal to inaugurate a world university is to win the cooperation of those who at first hold aloof, it must be perceived as a means of furthering the universal mission of universities and allied institutions. A world university must be accepted as a supplementary facility helpful in enabling present establishments to counteract whatever parochialisms of outlook are nurtured by expedient concessions of personnel or of emphasis to national or regional environments.

These limitations affect every knowledge institution. Every university or institute must obtain facilities from an immediate environment whose chief concern with the advancement of knowledge is not with the use of knowledge as a base for further knowledge, but as a base for obtaining political power, wealth, respect and other value outcomes.

The accumulated stock of knowledge available at a given moment is, in principle, universal. Fundamental propositions, findings and procedures are as verifiable in Stockholm as in New York or Leningrad. The assumption is that universities and institutes are concerned with universalizeable outcomes.

However, this assertion is subject to an important amendment. *Universal though a scientific or scholarly generalization may be, it is parochially introduced.* The immediate environment is circumscribed in space and time. A proposed generalization must run the gauntlet of evaluation by components of the environment who perceive it as a threat to their value position or as an opportunity to improve their knowledge, their political power, their wealth or other assets.

This analysis is not without application to the manner in which fellow specialists react to purported contributions reported by a colleague in the same field. The innovation may be so upsetting to traditional maps of knowledge that it is rejected out of hand as implausible. But some specialists may perceive it as a landmark contribution to the advancement of knowledge, the enterprise with which they identify themselves. Hence the innovation is totally incorporated, with appropriate recognition of its source. Or it may be partially, not totally, accepted by some colleagues, who incorporate part of it into their research, teaching and consultation. Actually, the incorporation may be total, save that the source is not acknowledged. Given all these conditioning factors, the sometimes erratic diffusion of knowledge along the routes of communication among specialists is not astonishing.

The factors that make for the diffusion or restriction of knowledge are, of course, more numerous than the predispositions of specialized colleagues. The colleagues are not the only significant participants in the social environment who assess an innovation according to its actual or potential impact on value positions. Appraisals by governmental, industrial, or other elites may influence rejection, acceptance or acceptance with modification. These appraisals affect the direction and rate at which knowledge spreads. Thus new knowledge may be kept secret or adapted to the military-political objectives, the programs of economic development, and the prestige-enhancing activities of a nation state or bloc of states, or of private organizations and groups. In this connection we must add that specialized men of knowledge are not without some degree of affirmative identification with the value demands and expectations current in the national, class and interest group environments in which they are reared or where they operate.

The interplay of universalizing and parochializing factors in the spread and application of knowledge has not escaped popular or scholarly attention. It is commonplace to recognize that European powers were able to utilize their precocity in the nurturing of scientific knowledge as a means of expanding their range, scope and domain well beyond their site on the European peninsula of the Eurasian land mass. More recently the ascendancy of European powers has been modified by the excolonial states who have partially incorporated the modes, findings, and technological applications of empirical inquiry.

The intensifying demand for a world university is influenced by the aspiration, shared by many men of knowledge and vision, to universalize the scientific enterprise, not as an instrument of onesided control by the West, or even as a tool of exclusively parochial aspiration elsewhere, but rather as a means of achieving shared participation in the evolution of planetary civilization. Many elevated minds would prefer to work directly for knowledge institutions that are explicitly identified as engaged in the advancement and appraisal of knowledge for *all* men, not for *some* men.

History of past movements

A glance at the history of past movements in support of institutions of higher learning shows that many of the factors influential now were significant then. We recognize the same intellectual excitement at new vistas and the same hope of contributing to human welfare. In the history of Europe we recall the great waves of university building toward the end of the Middle Ages. The enthusiasm for universities was fed by the curiosity of the young to transcend the prevailing world view and to recover the legacy of Greece and Rome. Furthermore, the new-old knowledge disclosed by the Revival of learning was understood to have great promise for human healing. It is not astonishing that medical faculties were occasionally the first faculties to take root in a center of learning, or that they were able to maintain a relatively independent identity (Salerno). As the number of physicians multiplied the most obvious impact of the new knowledge beyond education and research was on health, safety and comfort. Government and politics soon felt repercussions, since the revival of learning revived Roman law, whose relatively secular and centralized vision provided a ready instrument at the disposal of the rising system of nation states. Economic activities were affected by the recovery of knowledge of the modes of contract and settlement that had prevailed in a society whose economy was more complex. As the revival of knowledge by Renaissance scholarship changed into the pursuit of new knowledge by empirical procedures, effects were multiplied in every sector of society.

In considering the history of Western Europe we recall that the "wars of religion" reached a level of destruction that eventually generated an intense demand for the discovery of common interest, and for the use of knowledge on behalf of a European community that cut across traditional divisions. The concern for widening the market of peaceful buyers and sellers helped to provide the setting where a new wave of university building—in the low countries, for instance—underlined the common identity and the shared values and expectations of European man.

In antiquity a configuration similar to the pattern that led to modern universities had parallel results. The Greek world was held together by institutions that gave expression to a common identity, and to their expanding experience of the Mediterranean environment. It is not far wrong to treat the entire Greek commonwealth as a dispersed nation whose principal legislative and judicial institution was the network of oracles located at strategic places. The accelerating accumulation and application of knowledge gained recognition for a similar chain of centers that were devoted to learning and inquiry (Athens, Cos, for example).

The desire to transcend localism and to view the world in large untrammelled perspective were evidently factors that led to the evolution of institutions of advanced education and research in Buddhist, Hindu, and Islamic realms. The impetus to consolidate the world outlook of a vast domain occupied by people of many cultures helps to account for establishments (as at Nalanda in Northern India) committed to teaching, research and service. There is evidence that the heads of such establishments in Asia, like their European counterparts, became heavily involved in the political, economic and social policies of their areas. Responsive to, though not dominated by, ruling landholding or commercial families, Buddhist and Hindu monasteries and temples provided a site for famous teachers, or spun off the institutions mainly devoted to learning.

The possible future

This brief retrospect on past trends and conditioning factors is a stimulus to our vision of the future and particularly to the creative innovation of appropriate programs of institutional growth. It seems safe to assert that, barring disaster, many of the factors that have been favorable to world university movements in the past will gain strength.

(*a*) There is no solid ground for doubting that scientific and scholarly knowledge will continue to be perceived as of enormous importance to mankind. The knowledge revolution is likely to continue as long as man continues.

(*b*) Many scientists and scholars will demand of themselves that they act responsibly through institutions that enable them to contribute to the mobilization of knowledge for public policies that clarify and serve the common interests of mankind.

(*c*) Ambivalent attitudes toward knowledge and men of knowledge will continue among young and old in the world community, and among all who perceive themselves as in any sense value-deprived. The negative component of public attitudes need not destroy the institutions of enlightenment and skill. On the contrary it can prove an enduring challenge to the perfecting of a decision process that depends on consent rather than coercion.

It is highly probable that motives militating against a world university structure will gain in intensity as the factors in support of innovation come closer to making themselves effective.

It can be foreseen that as the idea of a world university gathers strength, opposing forces also gain support. Opponents will not necessarily declare themselves flatly hostile to the proposal. It is more likely that the conception will be dealt with in a more subtle manner. We referred above to partial incorporation of a proposal; and defense by partial incorporation is a means by which established modes of thinking and doing can look as though they were progressive and flexible at the same time that they nullify the fundamental thrust of an innovation. Partial incorporation implies partial rejection. It is, for instance, relatively easy to adopt the identifying symbol of a "world university" without changing anything else. Personnel, preoccupations and procedures remain as parochial as before.

Specifications of an acceptable university

What specifications of a world university are most likely to win immediate and long range acceptance? The specific details of a proposal must make it clear that *a World University is a timely extension of the existing network of institutions of higher learning. The aim is to facilitate the universalizing function of all the institutions of the knowledge revolution.*

That a proposal is to be taken seriously must be instantly obvious from the identity of those by whom it is initiated and sponsored. *Successful initiators will include world recognized contributors to specialized knowledge.* Given the present state of civilization this implies that the sponsors will be heavily recruited from Western Europe, Great Britain, and North America. In proportion to population Asia, Africa and Latin America are bound to be underrepresented. In recent decades, however, the trend has been toward universalizing the common culture of science and technology— a trend exemplified, for instance, in the rising eminence of Japan.

From the beginning it must be explicit that a world university initiative is intended to expedite the universalizing of access to science and technology by fostering *programs that aid in overcoming the barriers that presently handicap research, teaching and application in many parts of the underdeveloped world.* One suggestion is that the new technology of information storage, retrieval and processing can be utilized to make the world stock of knowledge instantly available to an inquirer sited anywhere on the globe (or beyond).

Analysis of recent trends and conditions would seem to warrant the conclusion that advanced modern societies have been passing through a phase in which the intellectual-managerial classes have been concentrated to an increasing extent at the centers of great cities. The high rise office building was evolved to meet the persisting demand of policy makers to communicate with one another in order to integrate their production, finance, marketing, public relations, research and development activities. The planner, advisor, promoter and decider needed a perch for his secretaries, his files, and his conferences. Unlike the chattering monkey in a jungle, the modern policy maker could not find a tree large enough to provide all the branches that were needed. It was necessary to plan his own perches. The office building is an arrangement of perches for symbol handlers and manipulators. These buildings have been jammed closer and closer together on Manhattan Island in New York City, in inner London, and so on. But the next development may be in a new direction. It may encourage dispersion by taking advantage of computerized information systems which allow the manager-intellectual to cut in on universal systems of storage and retrieval.

Proposals of this kind—looking to a universal information network— cannot at once be put into effect on a global scale. Aside from technical and economic difficulties they are likely to encounter the built-in restrictions characteristic of the world's political system, which is founded on the expectation of violence, the continuation of hostile groupings, the perpetuation of the arms race, and the prevention of free access to information either at home or abroad: in a word, the subordination of the sharing and utilization of knowledge to "security" considerations.

If the self-preference bias of established centers is to be moderated, it seems reasonable to assert that a world university must be *broadly represen-tative of the territorial areas which compose the world community*. Nothing as crude as a population ratio is necessary, since all the larger areas have already produced individual scientists and scholars of sufficient quality to deserve inclusion in a world wide structure. There is, however, a problem in providing prompt recognition by the intellectual community of the globe for those who contribute technological knowledge whose chief importance is perceived as pertinent to the needs of other than the advanced industrial eco-nomies. Is there, as is often asserted, a built-in bias against perceiving and acknowledging the intellectual significance of a contribution to varieties of plant and animal culture, for instance, that do not seem important to devel-oped economies?

A decentralized and pluralistic structure

If the potential of a world university intiative is to be fully realized, its basic structure must be relatively *decentralized and pluralistic*. What was said about the primacy of Western Europe and of those having long expo-sure to Western European civilization should not be allowed to obscure the point that the fundamental structure of the intellectual world is compara-tively decentralized and pluralistic. There is no simple hierarchy of accepted superiority—inferiority that covers every field of knowledge and stably dis-tinguishes one institution from another from one decade to another. At any cross-section in time we are accustomed to recognize a co-archy of several centers and sub-centers in every field. New centers occasionally rise with startling suddenness (as when the Massachusetts Institute of Technology in the USA rose rapidly from the status of an engineering school to a university with a special competence in, and emphasis on, the natural sciences). An old university may collapse with disconcerting speed. But it is more usual for the principal centers in national and transnational settings to maintain their acknowledged distinction for long periods, even though particular units rise or fall at different rates, depending on the fluctuating command of talent, timeliness and facilities. Every university or institute structure is a syndicate of pluralist concerns that fails to coincide neatly with territorial boundaries.

A world university that is pre-adapted to continuity and change *will identify primary units whose creativity is high, and whose interdisciplinary implications enable them to benefit, and to be benefitted, by more contact with units outside the immediate vicinity.*

Appropriate centers would need to be selected with an eye on the entire map of knowledge. There is, of course, little unanimity in the conventional terms with which many fields are designated. Luckily the initiators of a world university do not need to tie themselves in advance to any rigidly interpreted terminology if they allow the primary units to search for helpful connections wherever they can be found. Primary units are able to recognize one another, and to devise programs for dealing with particular problems. A cooperating center in microbiology, for instance, will work with other microbiological centers. It may also find it productive to work with units in other fields, thus encouraging the growth of highly differentiated co-operating chains. A world university that grows by allowing primary interdisciplinary units to evolve will of necessity interact with conventional conceptions of how the entire universe of knowledge is and ought to be divided. By beginning with primary units the evolution of new knowledge structures can be encouraged whose adaptation to the opportunities of the emerging future is at once flexible and stably continuous.

Whatever the variations of detail or terminology, it is generally understood that knowledge institutions are concerned with mathematics and physical nature, with life, and with culture. Within each realm the spectrum runs from primary stress on science and scholarship to primary stress on the arts of application to human objectives. In the first realm mentioned the range is from the science of the nucleus, for example, to the arts of nuclear engineering. In the second category—having to do with life—the gamut runs, for instance, from the science of genetic information to genetic engineering. In the category of culture, the span is, for example, from research on creativity to the cultivation of creativity in the arts of humanistic expression.

Distinctive concern for social consequences and policy implications

Analysis of the factors making for a world university implies that a proposal is likely to gain strength if it shows *concern for the social consequences and policy implications of knowledge.* Hitherto it has often if not usually been taken for granted that the working scientist would try to ignore, forget, or otherwise keep his focus of attention uncontaminated by any serious, systematic examination of the social consequences and policy implications of his specialty, or of the scientific enterprise as a whole. The assumption was that some members of the profession would be willing to take up the burden of inducing the social environment to provide the facilities which all scientists require, while abstaining from interference with research and publication.

The burdened few—destined by conscience or aptitude, or by unacknowledged ambition—were expected to constitute a corps of diplomats to negotiate with the "external environment" composed of the representatives of taxpayers or donors, or with teachers, writers, and others who concern themselves with pedagogical, philosophical and other ramifications of knowledge. In today's world this unexamined and self-segregated life of a scientist or scholar seems less possible, even less defensible, to more and more people who are both inside and outside the specialized realms of science and art.

It will not be denied, I think, that the intellectual community needs to devise a more profound solution to the challenge of relevance than the tactic of defense by attempting to keep the issue out of sight. In the past it has often been possible to take the heat off an official or private protest by relying on professional associations to invite a committee, with the aid of a staff, to give occasional attention to a burning topic ("birth control," "air pollution"). Or a committee has been authorized to draft a code of ethics and a declaration of social responsibility.

A more timely and compelling approach today is to bring to the study and practice of science and scholarship a continuing awareness of the social environment on which the whole enterprise depends for support, and which in varying degree it aids or imperills. It is hardly enough to include an occasional lecture or discussion in the curriculum of advanced professional training. If enlightened awareness of the social environment is to be nurtured in the scientific and scholarly community, the giving of thought to the interplay of knowledge-seeking activities with the other features of the social environment must become part of the ordinary routine of those who function in laboratories, research stations, or libraries. A world university provides a distinctive instrument for encouraging scientists and scholars to contribute to these investigations and evaluations. For instance, the sub-culture of the scientist can be modified to include a demand to participate in obtaining and revising a map of the role of knowledge in the society—past, present and prospective.

Mobilizing knowledge for primary problems

A further requirement would seem to be indicated for a successful world university program at this time in history. The proposal must *outline instruments and procedures for the mobilizing of knowledge for what are considered to be the primary problems of man.*

Continuing concern for social consequences and policy implications will develop a sense of timing for efforts to mobilize public attention on hitherto underemphasized issues, or a sense of priority among competing alternatives. Many discussions (such as those at conferences of the World Academy of Art and Science) have tended to underline two vast problem-sectors that emphasize the ineffectiveness of our present institutions of public order. The two problem-complexes are:

Security or the elimination of war and of scarcities attributable to imbalances of food, population and resources.

Freedom or protection of wide areas of responsible choice from invasion by biological or cultural engineering.

The proposal by the W. A. A. S.

I have said that a world university program that meets the criteria suggested above will have a favorable prospect of immediate and long term acceptance. As an example of a proposal along these lines permit me to summarize the plans of the World University presently in formation under the auspices of The World Academy of Art and Science.

The proposal is in harmony with the fundamental goal mentioned above: *The world university is put forward as an institution intended to supplement the existing structure of universities by providing a facility designed to strengthen the universalizing function of institutions of higher learning.*

The specific details meet the first criterion referred to above, since it is initiated by a representative sample of recognized contributors to their field of knowledge in the natural, biological and cultural sciences and arts. Further, the Academy is broadly representative of the large territorial areas of the globe, even though the present distribution of intellectual resources gives preponderance to Western Europe.

The plan is decentralized and pluralistic. It cherishes no dream of attempting to create a single, super-campus. The World University proposes to recognize the creative achievement and promise of primary units and to designate them as Cooperating Centers.

The plan is to supplement and to strengthen, not to supplant or weaken, the established institutions of learning and research. The distinctive emphasis, therefore, is in two directions: toward interdisciplinary frontiers, toward continuing examination of the social consequences and implications of knowledge. For instance, the World University's Fellows are to be chosen with particular regard to those who are concerned with the reciprocal impact of knowledge and the value institution environment—political, economic, and so on—in which high level research and teaching are carried on. The Fellows will be able to participate in continuing seminars on such problems at the various centers where they work.

The World University proposes to utilize the mechanism of the special commission to mobilize available knowledge for the clarification and creative resolution of the most urgent issues of public policy with special attention to matters that have been particularly complicated by the growth of knowledge, or that seem likely to benefit from the mobilization of existing knowledge.

The world university plans to supply auxiliary facilities, particularly in or for underdeveloped areas, for the furthering of investigation and the assessment of social consequences and policy implications. The specific services will presumably vary. Perhaps they will include joint laboratory, storage and retrieval, and consultation facilities. They may include daring educational prototypes intended to discover, motivate and develop creativity at all levels and in all environing circumstances.

We have said that in an important sense every major university is a world university, drawing upon the stock of knowledge common to man, and attracting talent from near and far. Nevertheless, biasses are found in every existing center that reflect the parochial setting in which it was conceived and from which it draws its principal support. Granted that it is out of the question to launch an institution that will be *fully* universal in outlook, personnel and procedure, the proposals and structures now taking shape are transitional steps toward mustering and enhancing the intellectual assets of man on a truly universal scale. Practically all of these initiatives are united in commitment to the dignity of man. They admire and seek to encourage his potential for enlightenment and skill, and for the integration of these capabilities with every facet of life. To value knowledge for its own sake, and also to come to terms with the problems connected with its responsible use, is to arrive at a harmonization of man, culture and environment at a level not hitherto within our grasp. This is the promise of contributing to the evolution of a truly world university for the latent nation of man.

At the very least the growing demand for a world university will foster the readjustment of existing institutions to fulfill the opportunities and to overcome the parochial factors that have operated to the detriment of their universalizing potential. The reconstruction of existing and emerging institutions will be sustained and encouraged by the innumerable initiatives now underway for a truly comprehensive, decentralized and pluralistic structure for the advancement of knowledge, and for the assessment of the social consequences and policy implications of knowledge.

STRATEGY FOR SURVIVAL

The Urge to Self-Destruction

By Arthur Koestler

London, England

From the dawn of consciousness until the middle of our century man had to live with the prospect of his death as an individual; since he unlocked the forces of the atomic nucleus, mankind has to live with the prospect of its death as a species. This is a radically new prospect; but though the novelty of it will wear off, the prospect will not; it has become a basic and permanent feature of the human condition.

One might even suggest that in the twenty-five years since it came into being, the novelty has *already* worn off—worn off before it has properly sunk in. "Hiroshima" has become a historic cliché like the Battle of Hastings or the storming of the Bastille. True, the explosions produced a kind of psycho-active fall-out which works unconsciously and indirectly, creating such bizarre phenomena as flower-people, drop-outs and barefoot crusaders without a cross. They seem to be products of a mental radiation sickness, which causes an intense and distressing experience of meaninglessness, of an existential vacuum, a search for the place of value in a world of facts. But in a world that refuses to face the facts there is no such place.

These symptoms, too, will wear off. We shall return to a state of pseudo-normality. But there is no getting away from the fact that from now onward our species lives on borrowed time. It carries a time-bomb fastened round its neck. We shall have to listen to the sound of its ticking, now louder, now softer, now louder again, for decades and centuries to come, until it either blows up or we succeed in de-fusing it.

I am concerned with the possibility of such a de-fusing operation. I do not mean by that disarmament conferences, nor appeals to sweet reasonableness. They have always fallen on deaf ears, for the simple reason that man is perhaps a sweet, but certainly not a reasonable being; nor are there any indications that he is in the process of becoming one. On the contrary, the evidence seems to indicate that at some point during the last explosive stages of the evolution of *homo sapiens* something has gone wrong; that there is a flaw, some subtle engineering mistake built into our native equipment which would account for the paranoid streak running through our history. This seems to me an unpleasant but plausible hypothesis, which I have developed at some length in a recent book.[1] Evolution has made countless mistakes; for every existing species hundreds must have perished in the past; the fossil record is a waste-basket of the Chief Designer's discarded hypotheses. It is by no means unlikely that *homo sapiens,* too, is the victim of some minute error in construction—perhaps in the circuitry of his nervous system—which makes him prone to delusions, and urges him toward self-destruction. But *homo sapiens* has also the unique resourcefulness to transcend biological evolution and to compensate for the shortcomings of his native equipment. He may even have the power to cure that congenitally disordered mental condition, which played havoc with his past and now threatens him with extinction. Or, if he cannot cure it, at least to render it harmless.

This is the kind of de-fusing operation that I mean. How it can be done, I do not pretend to know, although elsewhere I have ventured a few wild guesses; but I am convinced that it can be done. The first step towards a possible therapy is of course a correct diagnosis. There have been countless diagnostic attempts, from the Hebrew prophets to contemporary ethologists, but none of them sounded very convincing, because none of them started from the premiss that man is an aberrant species, suffering from a biological malfunction, a species-specific disorder of behaviour which sets it apart from all other animal species—just as language, science and art sets it apart in a positive sense. The creativity and the pathology of man are two sides of the same medal, but we prefer to look at only one. I am going to propose a short list of some of the pathological symptoms reflected in the perverse history of our species, and then pass from the symptoms to the presumed causative factors. The list of symptoms has five main headings.

First, at the very beginning of history, we find a striking phenomenon to which anthropologists seem to have paid too little attention: human sacrifice. It was a ubiquitous ritual which persisted from the prehistoric dawn to the peak of pre-Columbian civilisations, and in some parts of the world to the beginning of our century. From the Scandinavian Bog People to the South Sea Islanders, from the Etruscans to the pre-Columbian cultures, these practices arose independently in the most varied civilisations, as manifestations of a perverted logic to which the whole species was apparently prone. Instead of dismissing the subject as a sinister curiosity of the past, the universality and paranoid character of the ritual should be regarded as symptomatic.

The *second* symptom to be noted is the weakness of the inhibitory forces against the killing of con-specifics, which is virtually unique in the animal kingdom. As Konrad Lorenz[2] has recently emphasised, the predator's act of killing the prey should not be compared to homicide, and not even be called "aggressive" because predator and prey always belong to different species. Competition and conflict between members of the same animal species is settled by ritualised combat or symbolic threat-behaviour which ends with the flight or surrender gesture of one of the combatants, and hardly ever involves lethal injury. In man this built-in inhibitory mechanism against killing con-specifics is notably ineffective.

This leads to the *third* symptom, intraspecific warfare in permanence, with its sub-varieties of mass-persecution and genocide. The popular confusion between predatory and bellicose behaviour tends to obscure the fact that the law of the jungle permits predation on other species, but forbids war within one's own; and that *homo sapiens* is the unique offender against this law (apart from some controversial war-like phenomena among rats and ants).

As the *fourth* symptom I would list the permanent, quasi-schizophrenic split between reason and emotion, between man's critical faculties and his irrational, affect-charged beliefs.

Lastly, there is the striking, symptomatic disparity between the growth-curves of technological achievement on the one hand and of ethical behaviour on the other; or, to put it differently, between the powers of the intellect when applied to mastering the environment, and its impotence when applied to the conduct of human affairs. In the sixth century B.C., the Greeks embarked on the scientific adventure which, a few months ago, landed us on the moon. That surely is an impressive growth-curve. But the sixth century B.C. also saw the birth of Taoism, Confucianism and Buddhism; the twentieth of Stalinism, Hitlerism and Maoism. There is no discernable curve. Prometheus is reaching out for the stars with an empty grin on his face and a totem-symbol in his hand.

So far we have moved in the realm of facts. When we turn from symptoms to causes, we must have recourse to more or less speculative hypotheses. I shall mention five such hypotheses, which are interrelated, but pertain to different disciplines, namely neurophysiology, anthropology, psychology, linguistics, and lastly eschatology.

The neurophysiological hypothesis is derived from the so-called Papez-MacLean theory of emotions. Though still controversial in some respects, it is supported by twenty years of experimental research, and has for quite some years attained textbook respectabilty. The theory is based on the structural and functional differences between the phylogenetically old and recent parts in the human brain which, when not in acute conflict, seem to lead a kind of agonised coexistence. Dr. MacLean has summed up this state of affairs in a technical paper, but in an unusually picturesque way:

Man finds himself in the predicament that Nature has endowed him essentially with three brains which, despite great differences in structure, must function together and communicate with one another. The oldest of these brains is basically reptilian. The second has been inherited from lower mammals, and the third is a late mammalian development, which ... has made man peculiarly man. Speaking allegorically of these three brains within a brain, we might imagine that when the psychiatrist bids the patient to lie on the couch, he is asking him to stretch out alongside a horse and a crocodile.[3]

Substitute for the individual patient humanity at large, for the clinical couch the stage of history, and you get a dramatised, but essentially truthful, picture. The reptilian and primitive mammalian brain together form the so-called limbic system which, for simplicity's sake, we may call the old brain, as opposed to the neocortex, the specifically human "thinking-cap" which contains the areas responsible for language, abstract and symbolic thought. The neocortex of the hominids evolved in the last half million years, from the middle Pleistocene onward, at an explosive speed, which as far as we know is unprecedented in the history of evolution. Explosions, however, do not produce harmonious results. The result in this particular case seems to have been that the newly developing structures did not become properly integrated with the phylogenetically older ones—an evolutionary blunder which provided rich opportunities for conflict. MacLean coined the term "schizophysiology" for this precarious state of affairs in our nervous system. He defines it as "a dichotomy in the function of the phylogenetically old and new cortex that might account for differences between emotional and intellectual behaviour. While our intellectual functions are carried on in the newest and most highly developed part of the brain, our affective behaviour continues to be dominated by a relatively crude and primitive system, by archaic structures in the brain whose fundamental pattern has undergone but little change in the whole course of evolution, from mouse to man".[4]

To put it crudely: evolution has left a few screws loose somewhere between the neocortex and the hypothalamus. The hypothesis that this form of "schizophysiology" is built into our species could go a long way to explain symptoms Nos. 4 and 5. The delusional streak in our history, the prevalence of passionately held irrational beliefs, would at last become comprehensible and could be expressed in physiological terms. And any condition which can be expressed in physiological terms should ultimately be accessible to physiological remedies.

My next two putative causes of man's predicament are the state of protracted dependence of the neonate on its parents, and the dependence of the earliest carnivorous hominids on the support of their hunting companions against prey faster and more powerful than themselves; a mutal dependence much stronger than that of other primate groups, out of which may have developed tribal solidarity and its later harmful derivatives. Both factors may have contributed to the process of moulding man into the loyal, affectionate and sociable creature which he is; the trouble is that they did it only too well and overshot the mark. The bonds forged by early helplessness and mutual dependence developed into various forms of bondsmanship within the family, clan or tribe. The helplessness of the human infant leaves its lifelong mark; it may be partly responsible for man's ready submission to authority wielded by individuals or groups, his suggestibility by doctrines and commandments, his overwhelming urge to belong, to identify himself with tribe or nation, and, above all, with its system of beliefs. (Konrad Lorenz uses the analogy of imprinting, and puts the critical age of receptivity just after puberty. But there are two limitations to this analogy: the susceptibility for imprinting stretches in man from the cradle to the grave; and what he is imprinted with are mostly symbols.)

Now, historically speaking, for the vast majority of mankind, the belief-system which they accepted, for which they were prepared to live or die, was not of their own choice, but imposed on them by the hazards of the social environment, just as their tribal or ethnic identity was determined by the hazards of birth. Critical reasoning played, if any, only a subordinate part in the process of accepting the imprint of a credo. If the tenets of the credo were too offensive to the critical faculties, schizophysiology provided the *modus vivendi* which permitted the hostile forces of faith and reason to coexist in a universe of doublethink, to use Orwell's term.

Thus one of the central features of the human predicament is this over-whelming capacity and need for identification with a social group and/or a system of beliefs which is indifferent to reason, indifferent to self-interest and even to the claims of self-preservation. Extreme manifestations of this *selftranscending tendency*—as one might call it—are the hypnotic rapport, a variety of trance-like or ecstatic states, the phenomena of individual and collective suggestibility which dominate life in primitive and not so primitive societies, culminating in mass-hysteria in its overt and latent form. One need not march in a crowd to become a victim of crowd-mentality—the true believer is its captive all the time.

We are thus driven to the unfashionable and uncomfortable conclusion that the trouble with our species is not an overdose of self-asserting *aggression,* but an excess of self-transcending *devotion.* Even a cursory glance at history should convince one that individual crimes committed for selfish motives play a quite insignificant role in the human tragedy compared with the numbers massacred in unselfish love of one's tribe, nation, dynasty, church or ideology. The emphasis is on unselfish. Excepting a small minority of mercenary or sadistic disposition, wars are not fought for personal gain, but out of loyalty and devotion to king, country or cause. The theory that wars are caused by pent-up aggressive drives which can find no other outlet, has no foundation either in history or in psychology. Anybody who has served in the ranks of an army can testify that aggressive feelings towards the so-called enemy hardly play a part in the dreary routine of waging war: boredom and discomfort, not hatred; homesickness, sex-starvation and long-ing for peace dominate the mind of the anonymous soldier. The invisible enemy is not an individual on whom aggression could focus; he is not a person but an abstract entity, a common denominator, a collective portrait with caricatured features.

Equally unfounded seems the fashionable theory that the phylogenetic origin of warfare is the so-called territorial imperative. Territory means space, and while some wars were fought for actual occupancy of a given space, these were the exceptions rather than the rule. The rule is that the man who goes to war abandons his territorial home and fights for impera-tives which are not territorial but mostly symbolic or abstract: the true religion, the righteous cause, the correct political system. Wars are fought for words in semantic space. They are primarily motivated not by aggres-sion nor by territory, but by love.

We have seen on the screen the radiant love of the Führer on the faces of the Hitler Youth. We have seen the same expression on the faces of little Chinese boys reciting the words of the Chairman. They are transfixed with love like monks in ecstasy on religious paintings. The sound of the nation's anthem, the sight of its proud flag, makes you feel part of a wonderfully loving community. The fanatic is prepared to lay down his life for the object of his worship as the lover is prepared to die for his idol.

He is, alas, also prepared to kill anybody who represents a supposed threat to the idol. We now come to a point of central importance which is frequently misunderstood, and gives rise to endless confusion. Let me give you a naive example. You watch a well-acted film version of the Moor of Venice; you soon begin to identify with Othello or Desdemona or both; so of course you hate Iago and are quite prepared to strangle him with your bare hands. Your anger will produce all the physiological symptoms of a genuine emotion; yet the psychological mechanism which pumps adrena-lin into your bloodstream is totally different from that which operates when you are facing a real opponent. You know that the people on the screen are merely actors, not even actors but their electronic projections, and anyway the whole situation is no personal concern of yours. The adrenalin is not produced by any primary biological drive, it does not fit into Walter Cannon's classic hunger-rage-and-fear schema, nor into any behaviourist classification. The bemused spectator's hostile attitude to Iago might be called a *secondary* or *vicarious* type of aggression, devoid of self-interest, derived from a previous process of self-transcending identification. This process of identification must come first; it is the indispensable trigger or catalyst of the secondary aggressive reaction, its *conditio sine qua non*.

In a similar way, the violence unleashed in war and persecution is also a secondary or vicarious type of aggression derived from identification with a group and its system of beliefs. It is a de-personalised, unselfish kind of savagery, generated by the group-mind *which is largely indifferent or even opposed to the interest of the individuals which constitute the group. The* mentality of the group has its own pattern, and obeys its own rules, which are not the arithmetical sum of the rules of behaviour of the individuals which constitute it. Identification with the group always involves a sacrifice of the individual's critical faculties, and an enhancement of his emotional potential by a kind of group-resonance or positive feedback. The aggressivity displayed by the group against the supposed enemy is again an unselfish, impersonal, vicarious type of aggression: the egotism of the collective is nourished by the altruism of its members.

All this points to the conclusion that the predicament of man is not caused by the aggressivity of the individual, but by the dialectics of group-formation; by man's irresistible urge to identify with the group and espouse its beliefs enthusiastically and uncritically. He is as susceptible to being imprinted with slogans and symbols as he is to infectious diseases. Thus one of the main pathogenic factors is hyper-dependence combined with suggestibility. *If science could find a way to make us immune against suggestibility, half the battle for survival would be won.* And this does not seem to be an impossible target.

This brings me to my last but one point. Man is a symbol-making animal. The proudest and most dangerous product of this symbol-making is language. As a professional writer I need not sing the praises of language; but its dangers are generally underestimated. In the first place, language is the main cohesive force within a given ethnic group, but at the same time creates barriers, and acts as a repellent force between different groups. There exist between three thousand and four thousand human languages (according to the system of classification which you use), and this seems to be one of the main reasons why the disruptive forces have always dominated the forces of cohesion in our species as a whole. The stammering barbarian whose foreign tongue sounds like gibberish—bar-bar-bar—was never considered by the ancient Greeks to be fully human, and the same divisive forces are at work to this day between inhabitants of neighbouring Alpine valleys who speak different dialects, between Flammands and Wallons in modern

Belgium, or between the British upper and lower classes with their different accents. In the second place, quite apart from the diversity of vocabularies, the abstractive, concept-forming, categorising power of language enables man to formulate conflicting doctrines and belief-systems, each a potential *casus belli*. Recent field-studies on Japanese monkeys have shown that different groups of the same species are capable of developing different "cultures", different habits and fashions. Some groups wash their bananas in the river before eating them, others do not. Sometimes migrating groups of banana-washers meet non-washers, and the two groups watch each other's strange behaviour with apparent surprise. But they do not go to war, because they have no language which would enable them to declare banana-washing an ethical commandment, and the eating of unwashed bananas a heresy. In this context, one must once more emphasise man's suggestibility by emotion-rousing symbols, whether the Tricolor or the Swastika; but the most explosive symbols to trigger the chain-reactions of group psychology are words. Long before the media of mass-communication were invented, the prophet Mohammed got an avalanche going which was felt from Central Asia to the Atlantic. Without language there would be no poetry, but there would also be no wars.

The fifth and last pathogenic factor I shall mention is man's simultaneous discovery and rejection of death. The inevitability of death was the discovery, by inductive inference, of that newly acquired thinking-cap, the human cortex; but the old brain won't have any of it; instinct and emotion passionately reject the abstract yet deadly idea of personal non-existence. This simultaneous acceptance and refusal of death reflects the deepest split in man's split mind; it saturated the air with ghosts, witches, demons and other invisible presences, which at best were inscrutable, but mostly malevolent. They had to be appeased by offerings of human sacrifice or its symbolic derivatives; by holy wars, the burning of heretics, by castigation and self-castigation. Once more you have to look at both sides of the medal: on one side religious art, architecture and music in the cathedral; on the other, the paranoid delusions of eternal hellfire, the tortures of the living and the dead.

To sum up, I have listed five conspicuous symptoms of the pathology of man as reflected in the terrible mess we have made, and continue to make, of our history. I have mentioned the ubiquitous rites of sacrifice in the prehistoric dawn; the poverty of instinct-inhibition against the killing of con-specifics: intraspecific warfare in permanence; the schizoid split between rational thinking and irrational beliefs; and lastly the contrast between man's genius in mastering the environment and his moronic conduct of human affairs. It should be noted that each and all of these pathological phenomena are species-specific, that they are uniquely human, not found in any other animal species. It is only logical therefore that in the search for explanations we should concentrate our attention on those characteristics of man which are also exclusively human and not shared by other animals. Speaking in all humility, it seems to me of doubtful value to attempt a diagnosis of man entirely based on analogies with animal behaviour—Pavlovs dogs, Skinner's rats, Lorenz' graylag geese, Morris' hairless apes. Such analogies are valid and useful as far as they go. But by the nature of things they cannot go far enough, because they stop short of those exclusively human characteristics—such as language—which are of necessity excluded from the analogy, although they are of decisive importance in determining the behaviour of our species. There is no human arrogance involved in saying that dogs, rats, birds and apes do not have a neocortex which has evolved too fast for the good of its possessor; that they do not share the protracted helplessness of the human infant, nor the strong mutual dependence and *esprit de corps* of the ancestral hunters. Nor the dangerous privilege of using words to coin battle-cries; nor the inductive powers which make men frightened to death by death. These characteristics which I have mentioned as possible causative factors of the human predicament, are all specifically and exclusively human. They contribute to the uniqueness of man and the uniqueness of his tragedy. They combine in the double helix of guilt and anxiety which, like the genetic code, seems to be built into the human condition. They give indeed ample cause for anxiety regarding our future; but then, another unique gift of man is the power to make his anxiety work for him. He may even manage to de-fuse the time bomb around his neck, once he has understood the mechanisms which make it tick.

Notes

1 Koestler, A., *The Ghost in the Machine*. London and New York, 1968.
2 Lorenz, K., *On Aggression*. London and New York, 1966.
3 *Journal of Nervous and Mental Disease,* Vol. 135, No. 4, October 1962.
4 *American Journal of Medicine,* Vol. XXV, No. 4, October 1958.

The Future of Human Settlements

By Constantinos A. Doxiadis

Doxiadis Associates, Athens, Greece

Introduction

"Where is the wisdom we have lost in knowledge? Where is the knowledge we have lost in information?"

These questions as they are posed by T. S. Eliot strike us as particularly pertinent when applied to the sprawling, unstructured contemporary city, where we receive ever-increasing quantities of information from our environment, where we increase our knowledge in certain fields but at the same time lose the wisdom which would enable us to understand and enjoy it.

We know the contemporary city very little, and understand it even less. First, because it is growing larger and larger and therefore by necessity more and more complex, and second because, as in other fields of knowledge, we now have the means to study it in greater detail, and examine units or components of lower orders which are necessarily more numerous. In the study of our cities the complexity increases as the subject assumes greater dimensions and as we break it into smaller units.

Naturally enough we understand and know even less about the future. When we discuss it we get more and more confused because we can agree neither on the dimension of space, that is on the actual *size* of Human Settlements, nor on the dimension of time, that is on the chronological period covered by the word "future". In order to make our discussion meaningful we must define our position on these two questions.

The size of Human Settlements cannot be defined according to the extent of their built-up areas, as some people seem to think; nor can it be imposed according to the reach of administrative institutions. The size of a Human Settlement has always been defined by Man's ability to move around within a certain geographical space, in a practical (in terms of energy, time and cost) and productive way.[1] The built-up areas and institutions always eventually adjust themselves to this natural city of Man (fig. 1).

As for time, the future can be anything ranging from the next fraction of a second to cosmological eons. For Human Settlements however, whose components range from Man and house, with a life-span slightly longer than two generations, to roads, land-parcels and monuments with a life-span of several centuries or millenniums, a meaningful discussion of the future re-

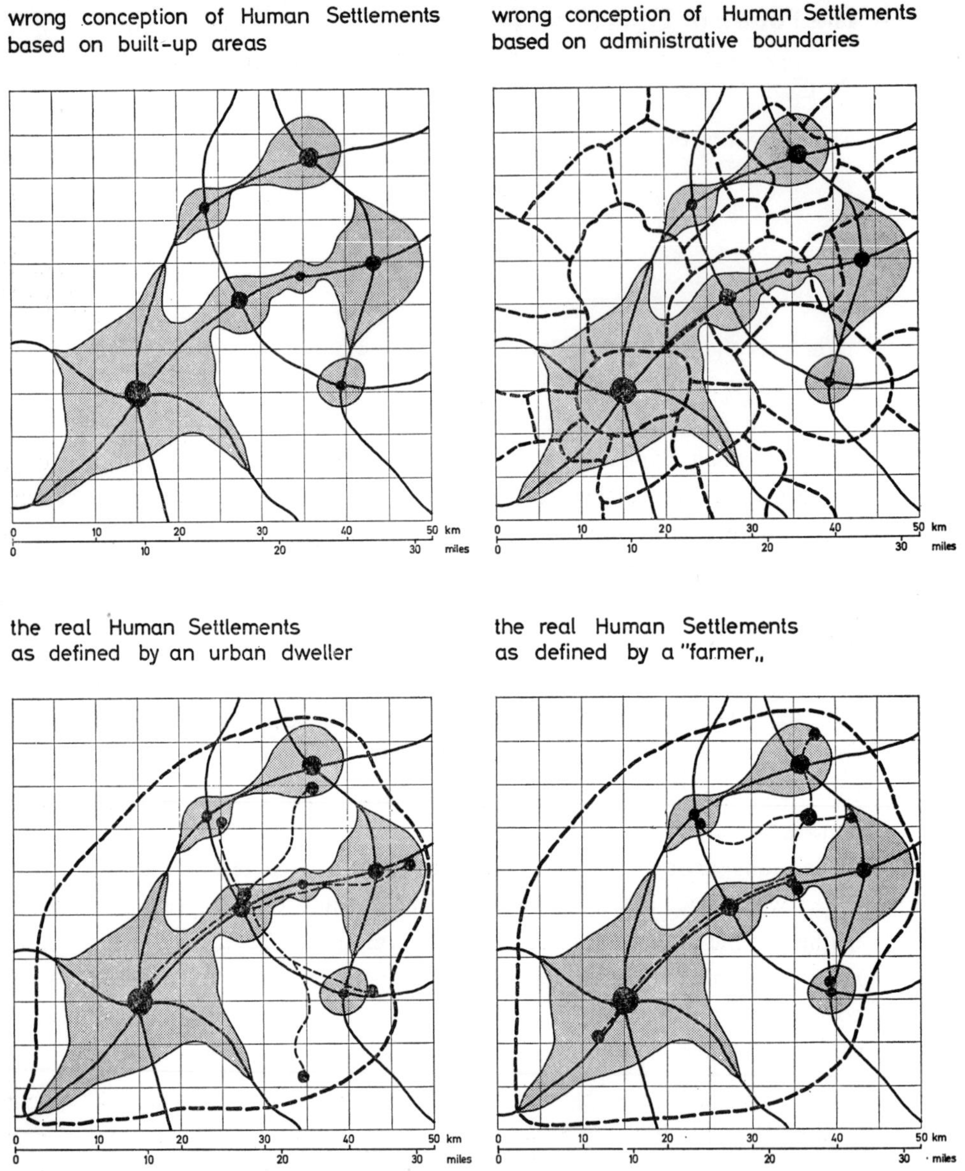

308   *C. A. Doxiadis*

wrong conception of Human Settlements
based on built-up areas

wrong conception of Human Settlements
based on administrative boundaries

the real Human Settlements
as defined by an urban dweller

the real Human Settlements
as defined by a "farmer„

Fig. 1

quires a projection from one to several generations, in our case from one to
five. A careful examination of the Human Settlements of the future, as we
can measure, conceive and imagine them, shows that they can be divided in
several ways into parts and aspects. Of these, the two which create the
greatest commitment for the immediate future are defined by actions which
have already been undertaken for them (fig. 2), leading to an inevitable
future, which is the real world of facts. The other future can still be shaped

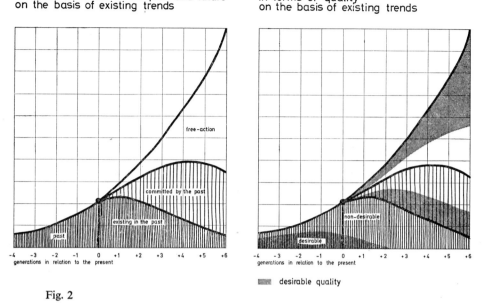

evolution of a city
in terms of forces of the past and future
on the basis of existing trends

evolution of a city
in terms of quality
on the basis of existing trends

Fig. 2

by us and it can be desirable or not, depending on the values defined by Man.

In proceeding to survey the future, I will deal first with the inevitable part of it and then with the part that is still open, dividing that into the inhuman and not desirable future which we must avoid, and the human or desirable one which must become our goal. I will end with some conclusions about the measures which can help us to work towards such a desirable future.

The inevitable future

Since we cannot be certain about the future of Man and his actions, about numbers and forces, about buildings and techniques, we cannot be certain about the future of Human Settlements. As a result we resort to utopias, and endless meaningless discussions, and more often than not end up taking no action for the future of our cities. In the meantime however we allow many forces to develop our reproductive processes, our economy and technology—and every passing day we make decisions on the construction of works ranging from cottages to highways, which commit our cities of the future. This method of avoiding confronting the whole while taking action on the parts, is completely inconsistent and unreasonable.

We cannot know the future, yet we are the agents who create it. The time has come to cease finding escape routes and instead shoulder our responsi-

the most probable future
defined by the Isolation of Dimensions
and Elimination of Alternatives (IDEA method)

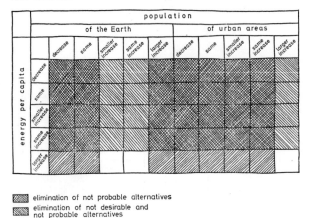

elimination of not probable alternatives
elimination of not desirable and
not probable alternatives

Fig. 3

bilities. In order to do this we have to make certain assumptions about what is the most probable future, and first of all about what part of it is inevitable.

The main forces which shape the Human Settlements are the people and the total energy they mobilize. If we make some basic assumptions about the possible combinations of these factors in the future we reach the conclusion that we will have to deal with settlements containing more people and greater quantities of energy than those of the present (fig. 3).

This conclusion is based on the theory about the formation of the Human Settlements as well as on assumptions about the probable evolution of population and energy in the next few generations. Now let us examine these three aspects.

The theory of the formation of settlements is a result of the observation of Man's actions from the time he descended from the trees into the great laboratory of the earth, in which he is both guinea pig and research director and has been tested wherever possible. According to this theory Man's actions on earth are guided by a total of five principles.

The *first principle* is the maximization of Man's potential contacts with elements of Nature (water, trees, etc.), with other people and with the works of Man (buildings, roads, etc.) (fig. 4). This, after all, amounts to an operational definition of personal human freedom. It is in accordance with this principle that man abandoned the garden of Eden and is today attempting to conquer the Cosmos.

The *second principle* is the minimization of the effort required for the achievement of Man's actual and potential contacts (fig. 5). He always selects the course requiring the minimum effort.

first principle :
maximization of potential contacts

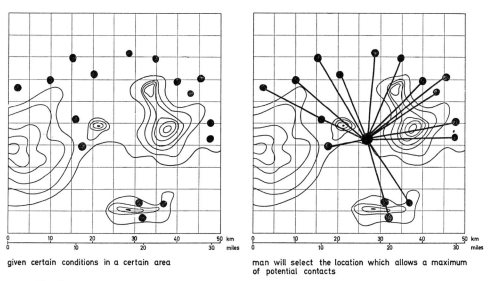

given certain conditions in a certain area

man will select the location which allows a maximum
of potential contacts

Fig. 4

The *third principle* is the optimization of Man's protective space at every moment and in every locality, whether it is temporary or permanent, whether he is alone or part of a group (fig. 6).

The *fourth principle* is the optimization of the quality of Man's relationship with his environment, which consists of Nature, Society, Shells (buildings and houses of all sorts) and Networks (from roads to telecommunications) (fig. 7).

Finally, man organizes his settlements in an attempt to achieve an optimum synthesis of the previous four principles; and this optimization is dependent on time and space, actual conditions, and man's ability to create a synthesis (fig. 8).

The probable evolution of the population in terms of numbers tends towards a levelling-off point but how this could and should be achieved is still debated. We are not sure yet how many people the earth can sustain. We can assume that, as in every similar situation there is a natural phase of levelling-off, that we will reach it some day but nobody yet can tell what this day is. On the basis of our calculations and assumptions we have arrived at the conclusion that the levelling-off of the population is going to be effected in the next three to five generations and that such an evolution will lead to a population of several more billions than the present one.

Even if we assume that we could do the impossible and effect an immediate levelling-off of the earth's population, the urban population would

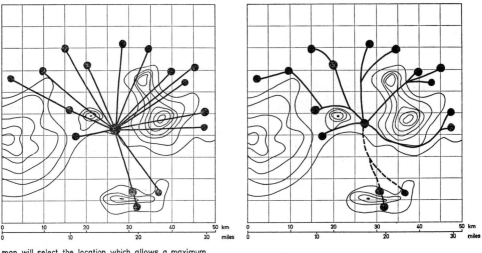

second principle:
at a minimum of effort in terms of energy, time and cost

man will select the location which allows a maximum of potential contacts

Fig. 5

still increase to three times its present size, first because of the operation of principles one and two, and second because of the greater energy which will be available to man, allowing him to inhabit larger urban settlements and to commute to his fields. There would only be one way of stopping this age-old trend, and that would be to surround the cities by walls, to paint the urban dwellers red and the rural ones green, and to have an autocratic government which will see to it that the green people leave the cities every night.

The natural attraction of the cities is going to be enhanced by the fact that although the genetical evolution of mankind is already preconditioned with slight intervention for the avoidance of some genetic defects, the total of the intellectual and social evolution of man can be immense (fig. 9) and can lead to a mankind which satisfies its age-old desire for more and better contacts with the world.

The probable evolution of energy available to man is going to be such that even if the size of the urban population were to be immediately stabilized—which is out of the question—the total Human Settlement would continue to grow in terms of activity and interaction of people, and would require a much larger area and result in a greater total potential of the city. We are not yet ready to measure this evolution accurately but the very fact that the energy consumed per capita today in the U.S.A. is 200,000 Cal. versus 4,000 Cal. in India shows what kind of development we must expect.

third principle:
optimization of man's protective space   or with others
if he is alone

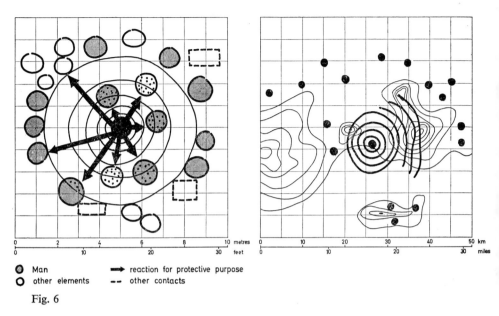

Man — reaction for protective purpose
other elements — — other contacts

Fig. 6

If these assumptions are correct we must expect the Human Settlements to continue to grow and to attain overwhelming dimensions. Even without any growth of the total population of the earth, the urban settlements will have three times their present population, cover six times their present area, earn income and expend many times more energy than the present settlements. If the population of the earth only doubles, and this is a very conservative and improbable assumption, then the urban settlements will have six times the population, at least twelve times the area, eighteen times the income and much more energy.

Continuous dynamic growth of the Human Settlements leads to new forms, since by necessity they will tend to interconnect and form systems of settlements[2] (fig. 10).

If we want to arrest the formation of larger urban systems the method is simple: we can always close the universities, stop any kind of research and close our industrial plants which produce different kinds of motor vehicles. If we do not choose this course, we have to accept as the next foreseeable phase the appearance of many megalopolises (fig. 11); and the dynamic evolution of Human Settlements in general into continuous urban systems, like the one in Greece (fig. 12) or in western Europe (fig. 13) or in the U.S.A. (fig. 14) and the final merging of all of them to form the Universal City or Ecumenopolis[3] (fig. 15).

This is the inevitable future of Human Settlements in the next few genera-

fourth principle:
optimization of the quality of man's
relationship with his environment

the five elements of Human Settlements
are now out of balance

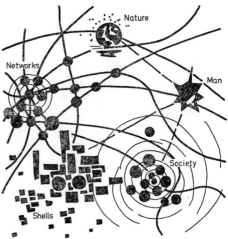

Fig. 7

tions, and we can well foresee that assuming we avoid any major catastrophe, we will have to deal with a universal city whose population will tend
to be stable in numbers but increasingly more developed intellectually and
socially, which will dispose of much greater quantities of energy and achieve
greater social interaction.

But what is going to be the quality of life in this city?

fifth principle:
optimization in the synthesis
of all principles

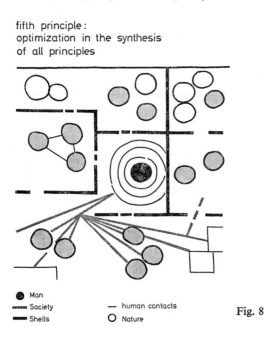

● Man
▬▬ Society   — human contacts
▬▬ Shells   O Nature

Fig. 8

the total potential
of mankind in the future

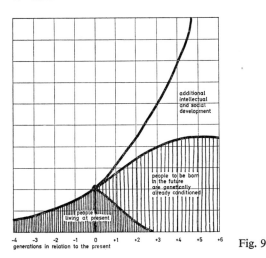

Fig. 9

The inhuman future

The inevitable future has already led and is continuously leading to a city which will provide more goods and services than at any other time; on the other hand it will be worse in the total quality of life it will offer, and it will create many new problems for its citizens, threaten many human values and lead to what can only be called the "inhuman future". To understand this let us examine the situation in the city in terms of the relationship of its elements, that is Nature, Society, Man, Shells and Networks, to Man who is the only measure for his city.

Man's relations with Nature, (with air, water, land, flora and fauna) are deteriorating, not only because the quality of the natural elements is becoming increasingly threatened, but also because the distance separating the average man from the location of any natural resources, forests, lakes or sea, is constantly increasing. The assumption is that this does not matter so long as we can purify the air in our buildings; this of course could not be more wrong. Let us only remember that the contaminated air is released into the streets where we breathe it as soon as we go out to get some fresh air.

The character of man's contacts with Man is changing completely. We can now communicate with others over great distances, but we cannot maintain our normal natural person-to-person contacts the way we used to. For example we do not allow our children to cross the street by themselves, and we hold them by the hand inside the city where in the past they were free to run; this is the type of problems of human development that we are creating. What kind of a man are we creating when we teach him to fear his city?

growth of a system
phase A: pedestrian kinetic fields only

phase B: pedestrian kinetic fields only

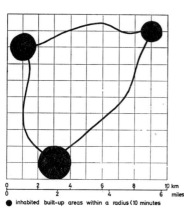

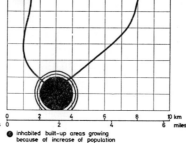

● inhabited built-up areas within a radius < 10 minutes

◉ inhabited built-up areas growing
because of increase of population

phase C:
pedestrian and mechanical kinetic fields

phase D:
pedestrian and mechanical kinetic fields

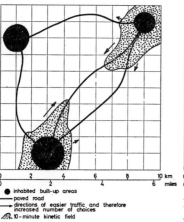

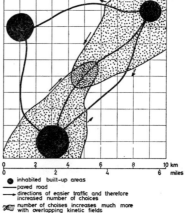

● inhabited built-up areas
— paved road
→ directions of easier traffic and therefore
   increased number of choices
🔳 10-minute kinetic field

● inhabited built-up areas
— paved road
→ directions of easier traffic and therefore
   increased number of choices
🔳 number of choises increases much more
   with overlapping kinetic fields

phase E:
pedestrian and mechanical kinetic fields

phase F:
pedestrian and mechanical kinetic fields

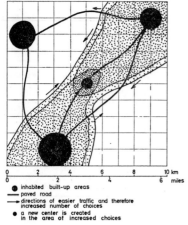

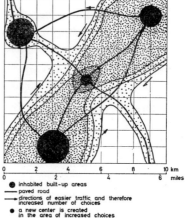

● inhabited built-up areas
— paved road
→ directions of easier traffic and therefore
   increased number of choices
● a new center is created
   in the area of increased choices

● inhabited built-up areas
— paved road
→ directions of easier traffic and therefore
   increased number of choices
● a new center is created
   in the area of increased choices

Fig. 10

Megalopolises 1960-2000 A.D.

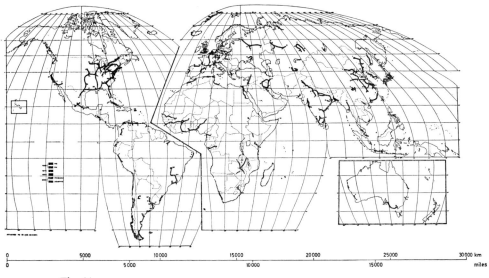

Fig. 11

The operation of Society is becoming more and more complex because more and more people are living closer together. In the past, the physical distances separating the groups of people living in villages and small cities reduced their choices for contacts because of limitations of energy, time and cost; in this way the problems of the operation of Society were by necessity simplified (fig. 16).

In the large settlements of today, people have many more choices for contacts and consequently many more differences and conflicts. In the big city the imbalances and disparities increase as man's mobility in space increases, and also become more apparent because of the proximity of greater numbers of people. In an isolated village man can be forgotten even if he is starving. In the big city this cannot be tolerated, not only for humanitarian reasons but also for operational ones. A reaction of people who try to avoid the contacts they do not like is the formation of segregated regions by the more affluent groups, and leads to the formation of ghettos by the weakest ones (fig. 17).

How such situations develop and how the complexity and the problems created by it increase can be understood if we think of the forces of growth in a big industrial city over the last hundred years (fig. 18). Where the population has grown 47 times, the area 62 times, the total income 397 times, and the total consumed energy 550 times the spatial complexity of people has to be reckoned in the thousands of times and this alone even without

Ecumenopolis in Greece

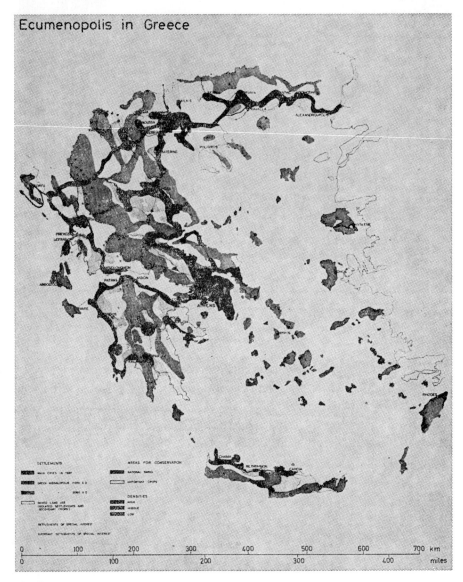

Fig. 12

further analysis explains many of the problems of a society which does not operate in a rational way.

The buildings that man is creating now in greater numbers, instead of contributing to the solution of the problems created by the growing settlements, lead towards situations which are less human, and help the operation of the city even less. The example of the multi-storey residential buildings is enough to demonstrate the intensification of the inhuman conditions. In these we pack people with families and young children (fig. 19) and isolate

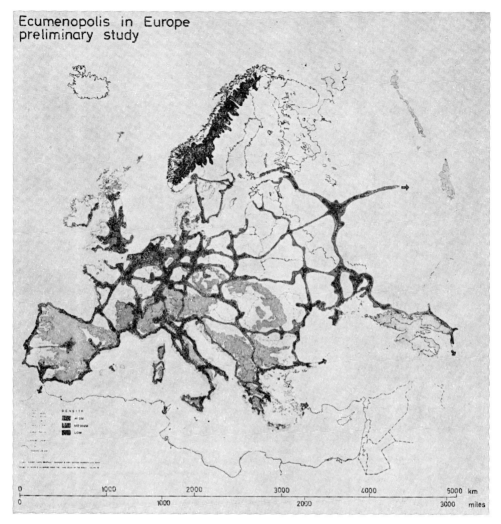

Ecumenopolis in Europe
preliminary study

Fig. 13

man from man, and man from Nature in sensory terms, whilst we leave
people exposed to one another's negative influences like noise, and we
multiply the stresses exercised on everybody, from child to mother.

The Networks which we create help people to achieve contacts over large
distances, but quite apart from disrupting the human scale, they increase
enormously the differences between people. In the past, even the richest man
in the world riding a horse could not travel at a speed greater than three
or four times that of the pedestrian and therefore his territory could only be
ten times larger than the poor man's. Today, as comparative studies in big
cities without proper mass-transportation systems have demonstrated

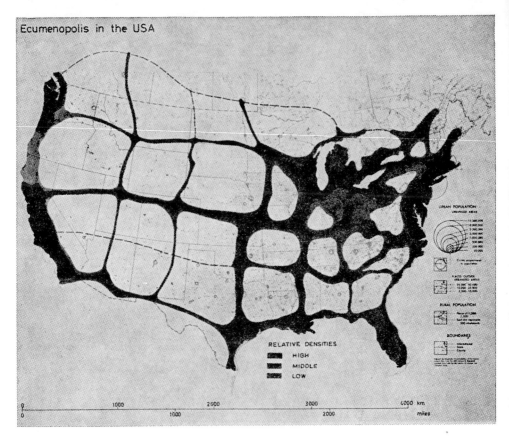

Fig. 14

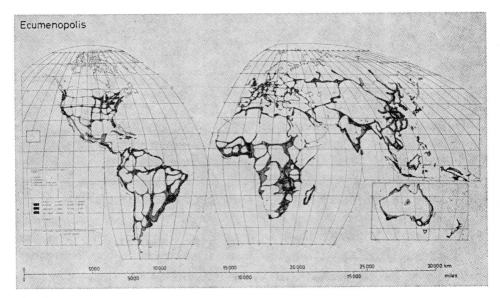

Fig. 15

a city of 50,000 people

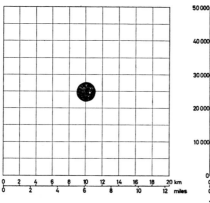

case of a citizen in a city
of 50,000 people

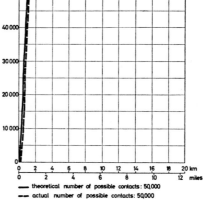

— theoretical number of possible contacts: 50,000
—— actual number of possible contacts: 50,000

a city of 10,000 people
in a region of 50,000 people

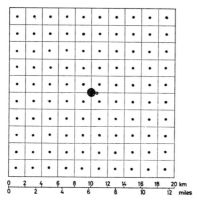

case of a citizen in a city
of 10,000 people in a region of 50,000 people

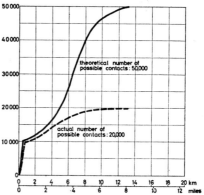

theoretical number of
possible contacts: 50,000

actual number of
possible contacts: 20,000

a city of 10,000 people
in a region of 50,000 people

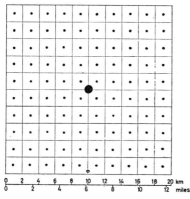

case of a "peasant"
in an outlying village
of a region of 50,000 people

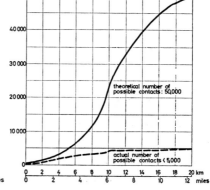

theoretical number of
possible contacts: 50,000

actual number of
possible contacts < 5,000

Fig. 16

the segregated city
first phase:　　　　　　　　　second phase:

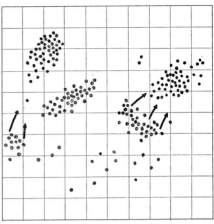
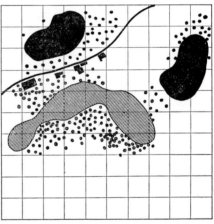

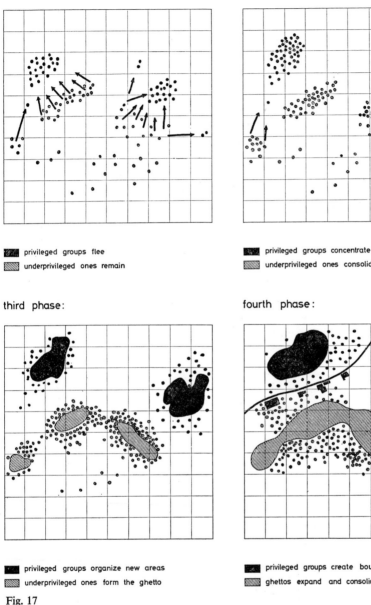

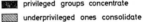

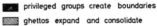

■■ privileged groups flee
▨ underprivileged ones remain

■■ privileged groups concentrate
▨ underprivileged ones consolidate

third phase:　　　　　　　　　fourth phase:

■■ privileged groups organize new areas
▨ underprivileged ones form the ghetto

■■ privileged groups create boundaries
▨ ghettos expand and consolidate

Fig. 17

(fig. 20), the man who drives a car has at least one hundred times more choices of movement within his area than the man who does not own a car.

The disparity between the spatial choices available to citizens increases with every day that passes. This is a case where technical developments magnify the existing differences between people. The modern transportation

increase of forces in a big western city

corresponding increase of complexity in the relations of people and space

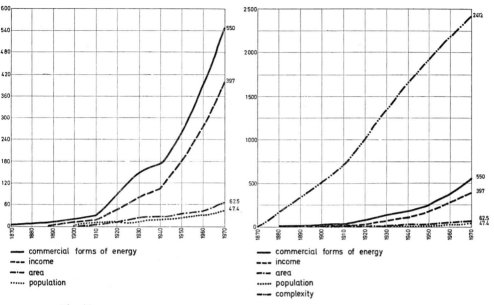

— commercial forms of energy
--- income
—·— area
······ population

— commercial forms of energy
--- income
—·— area
······ population
—··— complexity

Fig. 18

a multistorey residential building creates problems for the child and the mother

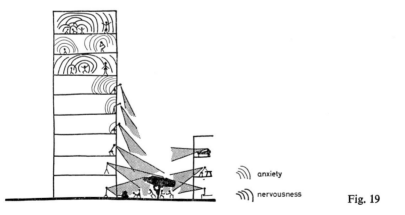

anxiety

nervousness

Fig. 19

networks have increased the mobility of man, but in general, have lowered the quality of the city and destroyed the equality between its inhabitants. In small settlements all people can interact in space in similar terms. In settlements larger than a certain size, some people are free to make the contacts they choose, and some are not (fig. 21).

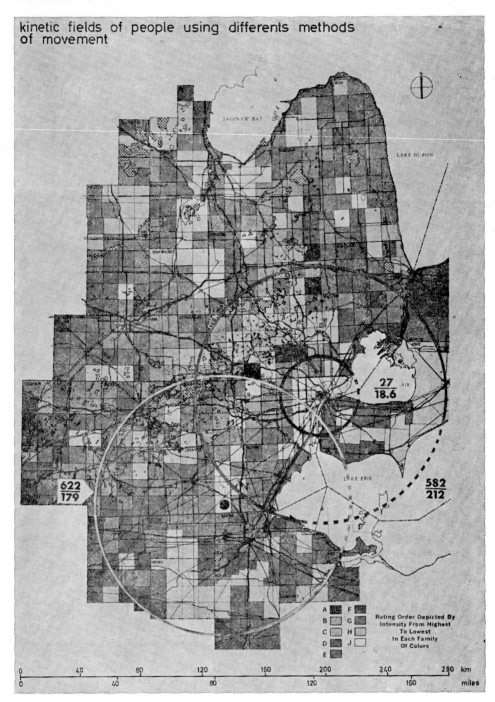

kinetic fields of people using differents methods of movement

Fig. 20

freedom for contacts in space
in the past everybody had the same
opportunities in his small world

freedom from contacts in space
now some people have the choice of
all contacts whilst others have very limited ones

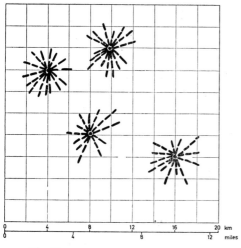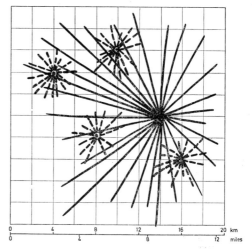

Fig. 21

Human Settlements of present
and future and the fulfilment
of Man's desires

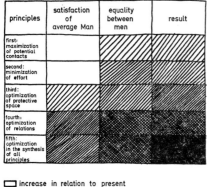

principles	satisfaction of average Man	equality between men	result
first: maximization of potential contacts			
second: minimization of effort			
third: optimization of protective space			
fourth: optimization of relations			
fifth: optimization in the synthesis of all principles			

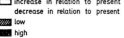 increase in relation to present
decrease in relation to present
 low
high

Fig. 22

Finally, the developing settlements keep man on the road for greater periods of time. So it has come to pass that whereas from nomadic days no man has tended to reduce the percentage of time he spends on the road, we are now reversing the trend.

"Where is the life we have lost in living?"

It is now becoming clear that people are tending to come together in larger and larger settlements (first principle); in doing so they are succeeding in minimizing the effort (second principle), however in practice only for those who can afford it. In the process they are tending to increase the distances dividing them from one another or to isolate themselves much more than required by the third principle, as much as pre-civilization man, and in doing so they are lowering the quality of the environment (violating the fourth principle) and the efficiency of the whole system (violating the fifth principle) (fig. 22). The Human Settlements are, and are becoming in many respects lower and lower in quality. Man is losing his scale and is adapting to an inhuman system where Society does not operate in a satisfactory manner and Nature is being spoiled. In this way we are entering a vicious circle where man is heading towards an inhuman future, a future which in its turn will condition an even more inhuman animal.

The human future

The trends which bring people together are inevitable since the first principle is the guiding one, and no force, present or future, which can reverse them can be foreseen. These trends are now leading to an inhuman future; yet this is something which can be avoided. The history of Human Settlements proves that man has the ability to create human environments; correct study and experimentation proves that while we cannot reverse basic trends towards larger sizes, we *can* guide the development of Human Settlements towards a completely different future, one which can best be described as human, a future which can be so different that it will be acceptable in the next few years, desirable in one generation's time, and more and more approaching the ideal from then on.

There is no technical reason why we cannot stop contaminating the air and water and spoiling land, flora and fauna resources. Air and water *can* be returned even more pure than when we take them into our cities; a more reasonable use of land can save its resources and regrafting of the skin of the earth has to become a goal. The real problem is an economic one since all these technical solutions will increase the costs of the city. This, however, is something that can be faced, first by a corresponding decrease in the total cost of construction and operation of the city, and second because of the rising per capita incomes. It is a question of time and regulations.

The second problem in the relationship of Man to Nature, that is the increasing physical distance dividing the two, can be solved with greater ease if we stop planning our cities and parks the old way, and begin to think of both as interconnected networks infiltrating each other (fig. 23).

Man's physical contact with man can be improved if we decide to separate the path of man from that of the machine. We made the mistake in the be-

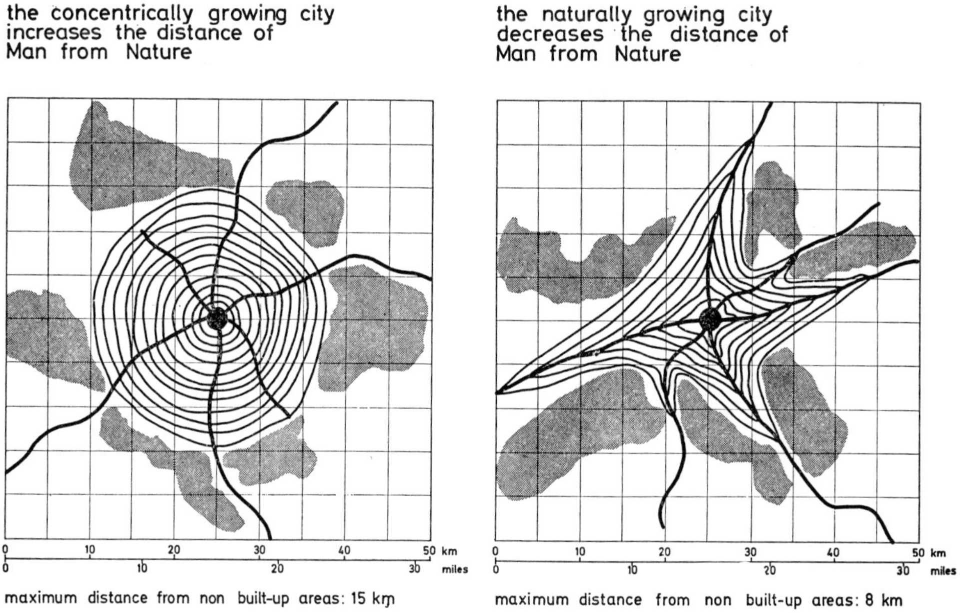
the concentrically growing city
increases the distance of
Man from Nature
0 10 20 30 40 50 km
0 10 20 30 miles
maximum distance from non built-up areas: 15 km
the naturally growing city
decreases the distance of
Man from Nature
0 10 20 30 40 50 km
0 10 20 30 miles
maximum distance from non built-up areas: 8 km

Fig. 23

ginning to bring water close to man in open ditches, then electricity through exposed wires. These mistakes have been rectified. Now we must convey the machines to a different level from that on which we function. This will be the ultimate solution. In the meantime we can separate the street of the motor cars from the path of man and re-establish the human scale (fig. 24). The moment has come for us to declare the cohabitation of man and machines as unhealthy as the open sewer in the streets of the old cities.[4]

Such a solution also lays the foundation for a much better spatial organization of our society. Problems are created because greater numbers increase the complexity of the system, but the solution does not lie in avoiding the greater numbers of people, facilities and potential contacts, since this would work against man's desires. The solution lies in simplifying the complexities, the way man has been doing for thousands of years by families and other social groups, and by structuring his city in physical terms (fig. 25) and leading towards higher degrees of simplicity.

Man is confused not by the size of a system but by his unstructured exposure to it, not by a speech of three thousand words but by a sentence of ten words if they are not structured, not by Florence of Michelangelo with fifty thousand people but by a nomadic camp of one thousand. There is no reason why we cannot structure our cities by using all networks as the dividing and connecting structures. We have to achieve it.

This can be meaningfully achieved for the unit of a group of dwellings, as

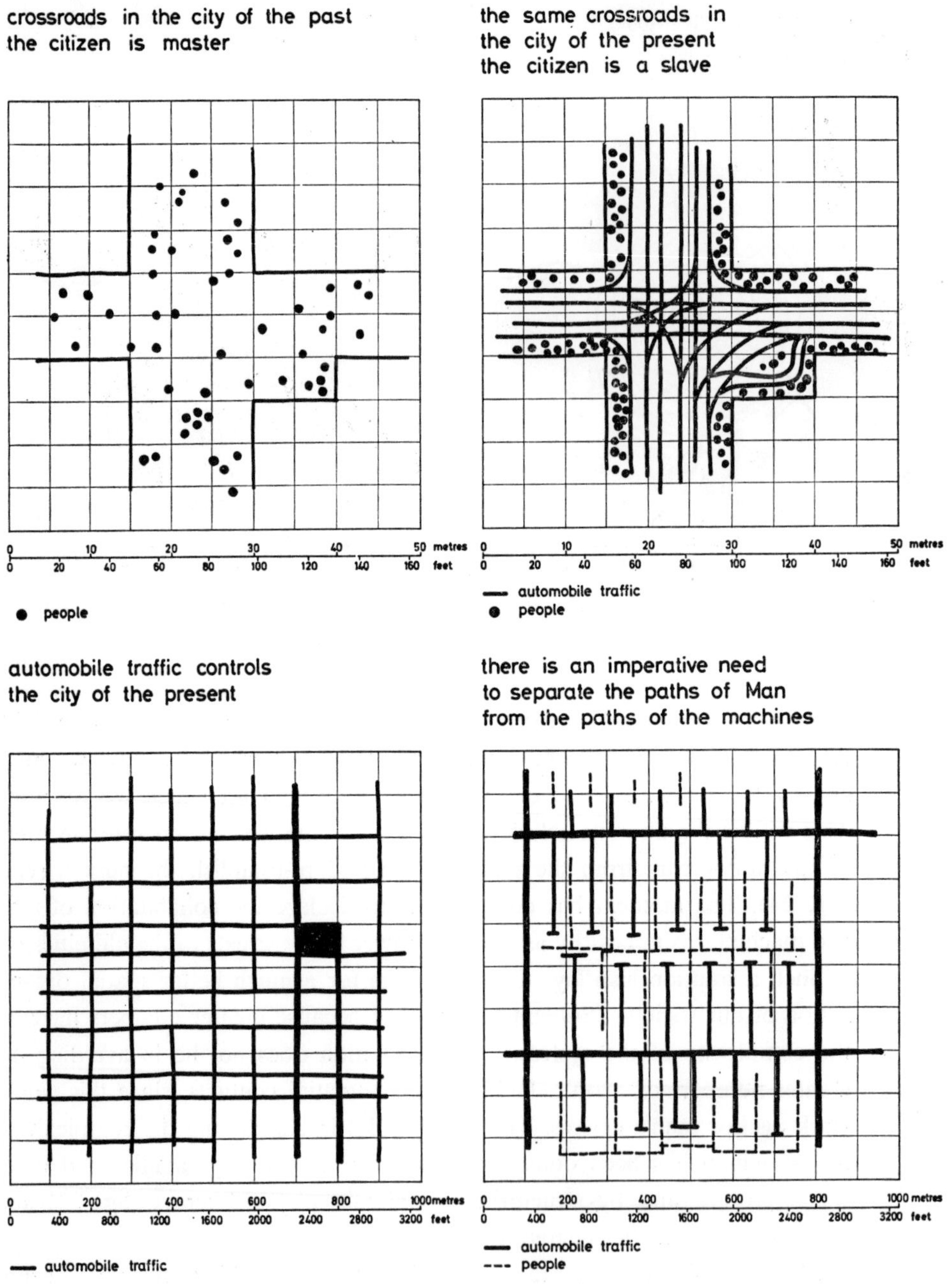

crossroads in the city of the past
the citizen is master

the same crossroads in
the city of the present
the citizen is a slave

```
0        10       20       30       40       50 metres
0    20      40      60      80     100     120    140    160 feet
```

● people

```
0        10       20       30       40       50 metres
0    20      40      60      80     100     120    140    160 feet
```

— automobile traffic
● people

automobile traffic controls
the city of the present

there is an imperative need
to separate the paths of Man
from the paths of the machines

```
0        200      400      600      800     1000 metres
0    400     800    1200    1600    2000    2400    2800    3200 feet
```

— automobile traffic

```
0        200      400      600      800     1000 metres
0    400     800    1200    1600    2000    2400    2800    3200 feet
```

— automobile traffic
--- people

Fig. 24

well as the very big units, with a special emphasis on the unit of the natural human city, which a long evolution has shown to be of particular importance since it has resulted from the natural use of the physical human scale. Islamabad, the new capital of Pakistan shows how this can be achieved (fig. 26); each one of its sectors corresponds to a natural city of the past

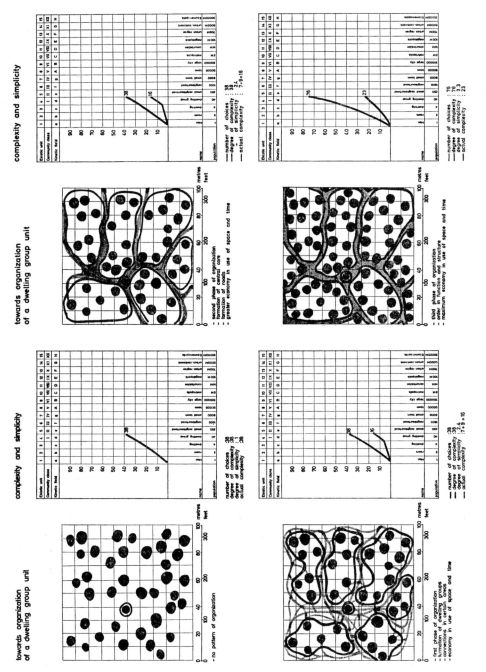

Fig. 25

Islamabad
a new dynapolis — 2,500,000

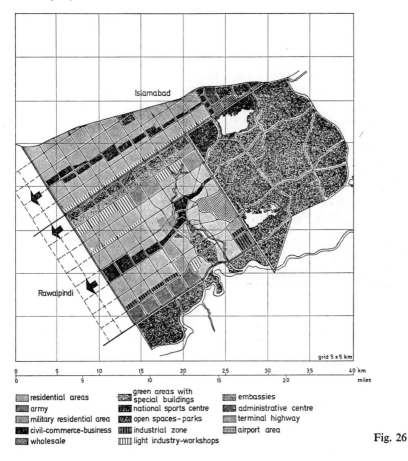

grid 5 x 5 km

residential areas	green areas with special buildings	embassies
army	national sports centre	administrative centre
military residential area	open spaces-parks	terminal highway
civil-commerce-business	industrial zone	airport area
wholesale	light industry-workshops	

Fig. 26

(fig. 27). In fig. 27 in the upper sector we have the whole Athens of the 5th century B.C. and Pericles. In the right-hand square we have Florence of Michelangelo, in the left-hand square London within the walls and in the lower square Paris within the walls. All these are in the same scale and the drawing shows that these famous cities are included inside one sector only of a modern city. The whole system is developed according to the forces leading to synthesis[5] in Human Settlements (fig. 28).

The problem of inhuman buildings can be dealt with more easily than most of the other problems. The relationship between neighbours can be strengthened by pedestrian paths facilitating communications and human development and facilitated by the creation of high compound walls around courtyards which would provide for everybody the necessary degree of isolation. By such conceptions we can help the operation of society from its second unit, towards the extended family which is more and more missed,

Dynanopolis in practice:
first sectors of Islamabad, Pakistan first planned in 1960

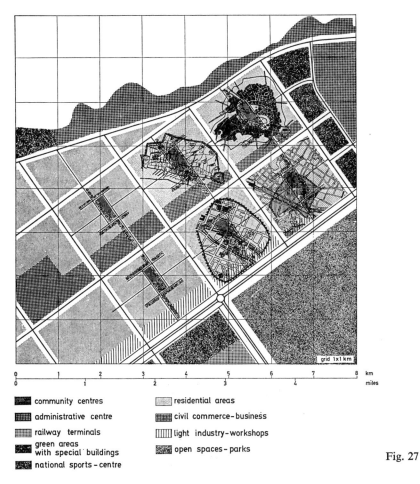

community centres

administrative centre

railway terminals

green areas
with special buildings

national sports - centre

residential areas

civil commerce-business

light industry-workshops

open spaces - parks

Fig. 27

and the larger units of organized neighbourhoods in all types of single-storey and multi-storey buildings.

The most crucial of all problems is the one created by the Networks, especially those of transportation, because they have led to the disruption of the city, facilitated the escape of some people and intensified the differentiation between others, destroyed many natural resources and increased the cost of the whole. In order to solve this problem we must revolutionize our approach. Only if we study the city as a total system and not merely as a transportation system, much less as a system of highways, can we find solutions which will enable us to economize in time, energy and total cost. Of course we must understand that the cost of the city is not the cost of construction of public facilities, but the sum total of costs of every type of construction plus operation of all services from transportation, to water and

probable validity of the forces
of Ekistic Synthesis
assumption one

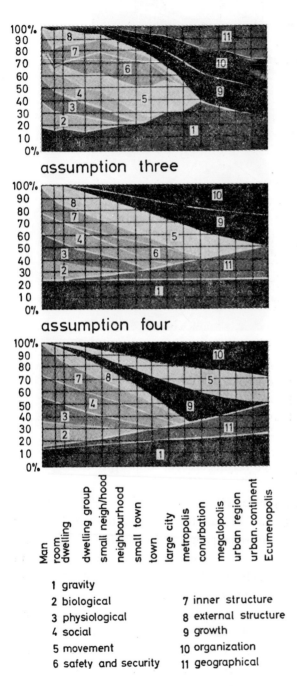

Fig. 28

1 gravity
2 biological
3 physiological
4 social
5 movement
6 safety and security
7 inner structure
8 external structure
9 growth
10 organization
11 geographical

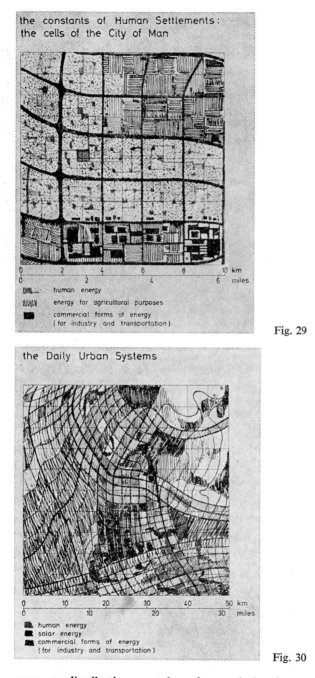

the constants of Human Settlements:
the cells of the City of Man

0 2 4 6 8 10 km
0   2   4   6 miles

human energy
energy for agricultural purposes
commercial forms of energy
(for industry and transportation)

Fig. 29

the Daily Urban Systems

0   10   20   30   40   50 km
0   10   20   30 miles

human energy
solar energy
commercial forms of energy
(for industry and transportation)

Fig. 30

sewer, to distribution, postal services and cleaning and maintainance plus the cost of human time invested in the system.

If we conceive the Human Settlements as the territorial expression *of our whole system of life* we can guide them gradually towards much better conditions and a future whose quality will be human. These new Human Settle-

the four futures
of Human Settlements

the human future
of Human Settlements

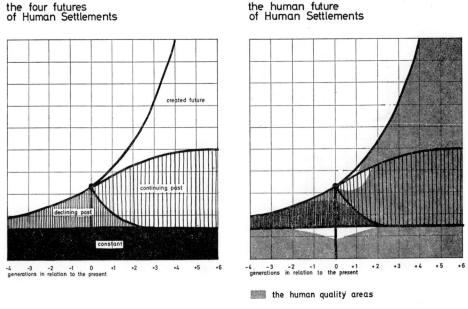

the human quality areas

Fig. 31

ments will consist of cells of human scale, which will be the basic units of life and human development (fig. 29), interconnected by the maximum use of technology and technically developed Networks to form smoothly operating systems which will allow Man to operate them in proper balance to the forces of Nature and Society (fig. 30).

In doing this we should not forget that calculations on the basis of quality of life based on averages can be useful if we do not forget that one prerequisite of quality in a Human Settlement is the equality of its citizens and this, in operational terms, means freedom for all to develop, to express themselves and to have access to all parts of the big city of man. Political democracy is a pre-requisite but not a goal in itself. Man needs a greater degree of equality than what we can offer at present when we still differentiate between rural and urban dwellers, between rich and poor, among races and among religions. These problems cannot be faced by the isolation of different people as in the past, but only by the creation of the Universal City of Man.

In the past whenever the energy available to man allowed him to operate easily within a certain territory, and this usually meant within one day at no unreasonable expenditure of time and energy, man would create institutions guaranteeing cooperation within this territory. Today, the energy available enables man to cover the whole earth within the same day. It is up to man to make the system operate!

Conclusions

The question which naturally arises at this point is: how can we help the future of Human Settlements? The answer is, I think, to understand the subject matter and to avoid the grave mistakes that we are making today. We must understand that the future of Human Settlements consists of four parts. The one is constant, for example the dimensions of our earth; the second is the declining past, for example the people living today; the third is the continuing past, for example the people to be born, who are a continuation of their ancestors. Finally, there is the created future and the degree to which every part is inevitable or not, inhuman or human, and, depending on this last, whether it should be changed or not. We can then reach the conclusion that within a period of two to three generations we can have settlements which are truly human (fig. 31).

The question which now arises is how we can facilitate the creation of the human future, and the answer lies in *action*, which is necessary and will involve that part of the future which influences us more than the others, and that is the conception that we have of Human Settlements (fig. 32). A careful study shows that the usual conception of Human Settlements is in numbers of people or of houses or of area. All these conceptions however are outdated, because they correspond to the era of one house per family and constant average activity and energy per person. Today, when the energy per person is constantly increasing and the activity is related to an enormously increasing complexity, only a proper combination of people,

forces of the present
as projected into the future

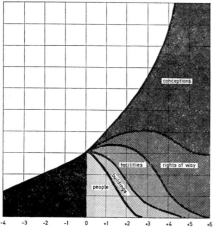

generations in relation to the present

Fig. 32

a static picture of a group of people as given in plans   the real picture of the same group as given by energy measurements

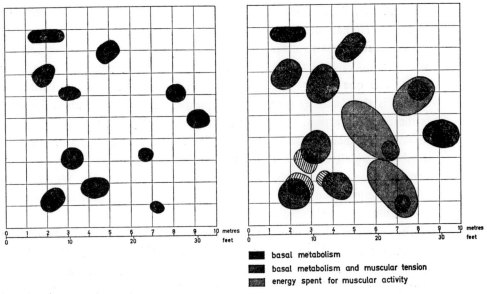

- ■ basal metabolism
- ▨ basal metabolism and muscular tension
- ▨ energy spent for muscular activity

Fig. 33

works, and area with energy, time, and cost can lead to an understanding of Human Settlements. As in medicine we move from anatomy to physiology; only we are a hundred years behind.

A comparison of a static picture of people with an energy picture, shows how we can have a more realistic view of man in space (fig. 33) and a few examples of the patterns of energy flow in Human Settlements show the great change that has taken place since the increase of commercial energy and that the task today is to understand and separate the human energy systems from the commercial ones (fig. 34).

In this way we conclude that we must influence the minds of people, inform them of the better ways in which they can live. In order to accomplish this we will need more knowledge than we have at present, which again means research, education and guided experimentation. Can we do it? The point was made that today our problem-solving capacity is greater than ever before; that is true in general, but we have to add that we have not used this capacity enough in dealing with the problems of Human Settlements. The reason is that they require a synthesis of views which we are not yet able to achieve and that the speed with which problems are created is very high and confuses everybody. There is no reason however why we cannot turn our total problem-solving capacity towards the solution of this problem. We only need the intellectual and moral courage to achieve this, the

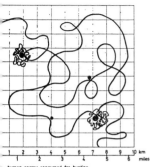

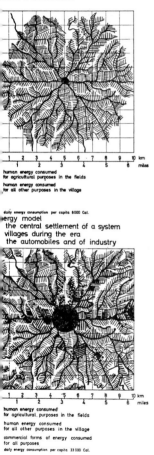

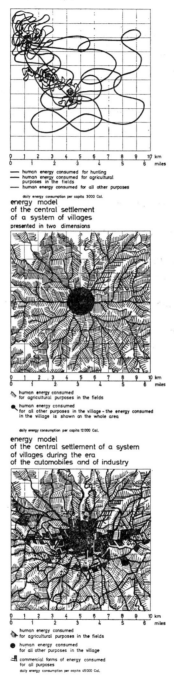

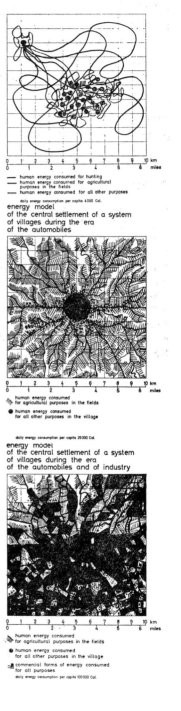

Fig. 34

courage which man had in the past when he was creating cities the size of the existing ones; a courage he has lost under the impact of the increasing problem.

Once however we are in the position to recognize this, we have the obligation to transmit the message in a meaningful, that is a scientific way, so that our society and our political leaders will see it as a problem which can be approached in a rational and objective way. When we reach this point the overall solution will be clear and we will not be afraid of the big city to come; instead of fighting it we will build it.

Notes

[1] Doxiadis, C. A., Man's Movement and his City, *Science,* Vol. 162, 18 October 1968, pp. 326–334.

[2] Doxiadis, C. A., Ecumenopolis: Tomorrow's City, *Britannica Book of the Year* 1968, pp. 17–38.

[3] Doxiadis, C. A., *Ekistics: An Introduction of the Science of Human Settlements,* Hutchinson Publishing Group, London, 1968; Oxford University Press, New York, 1968.

[4] Doxiadis, C. A., A City for Human Development, *Ekistics,* Vol. 25, No. 151, June 1968, pp. 374–394.

[5] Doxiadis, C. A., Ekistic Synthesis of Structure and Form, *Ekistics,* Vol. 26, No. 155, October 1968, pp. 395–415.

Conditions for a True Global Economy

By Jan Tinbergen

Netherlands School of Economics, Rotterdam, the Netherlands

I. *Introductory*

I.1. The subject which I was asked to report upon derives its significance from the disastrous consequences of nationalism and racism the world has been facing for centuries. The future threats are worse even than past clashes, since technological development has created weapons far more dangerous than ever. To overcome some forms of nationalism therefore is a condition for survival. In this paper the economic aspects of this problem will be briefly discussed. The meaning given to the concept "economic" will be taken in the widest sense conceivable, however, and actually covers a variety of social aspects as well. Economic science is rapidly learning from other social sciences and, moreover, has developed some methods which are useful to deal with wider social problems.[1]

The concept of a "true global economy" as chosen in this paper may seem hardly realistic, but should be seen as a frame of reference for present action, even if it is a far-away ideal only.

I.2. The intellectual tools used in this paper mainly derive from welfare economics.[2] This is the normative chapter of economic science whose main problem is what conditions must be fulfilled in order that a maximum of welfare be attained—in this paper world welfare—given a number of constraints mankind is subject to; these constraints are the laws of nature as reflected in technology and human learning processes.

As in every scientific process our thinking about welfare economics cannot be completely conscious and explicit but does rely on a good deal of intuition also. Intuition comes in wherever the explicit solution of a scientific problem has not yet been found.

The starting point of welfare economics is a concept of welfare, sometimes indicated by more pedestrian words such as wellbeing, utility or ophelimity. In this paper the concept will not be restricted to material welfare, however, but take into account spiritual components as well; among them the satisfaction derived from work and the fact that people make comparisons with other people while assessing their welfare. It will be understood that especially in these matters the element of an intuitive treatment is indispensable.

I.3. The structure of this paper is as follows. After the introductory remarks the conditions for a true world economy will be discussed in Section II; the institutions which are needed to let these conditions materialize in Section III and the road which may be followed to establish or strengthen these institutions in Section IV. Section IV therefore constitutes the link with present-day endeavours to move towards a unified world in which the dangerous aspects of nationalism are kept under control. The three following sections are subdivided according to some main aspects of the problem.

II. *Conditions for a true world economy*

II.1. One of the best-known conditions for maximum welfare is the condition of *price uniformity*. It says that all sellers should receive and all buyers pay the same price—except for transportation costs—for any commodity exchanged. If some buyers paid a lower price than other buyers, an increase in welfare could be attained by having the former buyers sell some of their purchase to the latter. A similar argument applies in the case of non-uniformity among the prices received by sellers.

II.2. The condition of price uniformity also applies to the prices of productive effort, that is *incomes*. For the same type of work the same price should be received everywhere. It is here that we find in reality one of the glaring deviations from the optimum. Unskilled workers, for instance, are paid very different wages in rich and poor countries. There are also large differences between incomes from qualified work of the same type in developed and developing countries.

II.3. Prices should be equal to the *marginal costs* of production. If they are higher, a larger volume of production of the commodity would raise welfare. If they are lower, a smaller volume of production would enhance welfare. This condition implies one price scale for all products to be optimal. Similarly an *income* (or wage) *scale*[3] for all types of labour can be derived, taking into account the marginal disutilities and satisfactions for each type of effort. Such a scale represents an optimum scale for incomes before tax (ef. II.5).

II.4. For the world at large, the preceding conditions define an optimum *"division of labour"*, or an optimum choice of industries (in the widest sense of that word) for each country. Such an optimum division of labour[4] will reflect the comparative advantages of each country in producing one or the other commodity. By way of example the concept may imply that countries with a hot climate produce tropical products, countries with large quantities of unskilled labour labour-intensive products, countries with high scientific skills research-intensive products, countries with relatively much capital capital-intensive products and so on. With increasing equalization of the endowments, production patterns will converge. Products with high transportation costs will have to be produced everywhere, also now already.

II.5. A less well-known condition for maximum welfare is that *marginal utilities* of consumption should be *uniform* among individuals and hence among countries. This implies a *redistribution system,* and consequently financial transfers from the well-endowed to the badly-endowed. Indeed in general one dollar transferred from a rich person to a poor person will raise welfare. The condition does not only imply social redistribution by taxes and social benefits within countries, but also among countries. There is no reason to confine such transfers to the financing of investments, and it should also imply transfers for consumption purposes. So far this principle has only been applied in cases of disasters, whether natural or man-made; it should be applied on a much wider scale. National autonomy stands in its way.

II.6. *Education* should be given primarily to these susceptible to absorb it,[5] that is, to the naturally gifted, but without discriminating between nationalities or races. This condition implies international transfer flows of educational activities much larger than the present.

II.7. Another activity where the actual international pattern is probably much out of line with a world optimum is the one known as R and D or simply *research*. As much as possible research should be directed at areas of knowledge where the largest benefits for the world at large can be expected instead of for a limited social or geographical area. Research benefitting some but damaging others, such as the development of synthetics competing directly with natural products has a lower priority than research for the development of synthetics complementing natural products, for instance the enrichment of the protein content of some food types.

II.8. A special dimension of the world optimum is its time dimension. Two types of conditions can be formulated here; loosely speaking they are that *stable and optimum growth* be attained.[6] Stability means avoidance of cycles or shocks or at least minimizing them. The optimum level of growth must reflect an equilibrium between the welfare of the present and future generations.[7] Under specific assumptions rates of growth higher than the prevailing ones have been estimated to be optimal.

III. *Institutions*

III.1. Among the institutions which will enhance world welfare some are in the field of *information* and *communication*. Lack of these two elements has made for much shortsightedness, in several respects, with loss of welfare as a consequence. We need not elaborate on these points.

III.2. A world order directed at a maximum of world welfare will be complicated, if only because of the fact that world population amounts to several billions and that innumerable decisions will currently have to be made, both by individuals and by groups in institutions for making a number of the necessary decisions. These institutions can be seen as a *pyramid,* with very many at "low" levels—local, enterprise, provincial, state, and industry level—and a certain number at *supranational* level. The distribution over the various levels poses an important problem. In all likelihood prevailing nationalist tendencies have led to too much emphasis on institutions at national level. Stronger and perhaps more institutions at the international level are needed. A non-economic example of extreme importance is a military institution—the U.N. Peace Force—but there is a need for stronger and maybe more supranational socio-economic institutions as well. Examples will follow.

III.3. Since many decisions can be taken by national institutions without damaging the interests of other nations, different socio-economic *systems* in different countries can coexist even in the optimum. Another question is whether it is in the interest of the countries themselves that the systems differ as much as they do to-day.

Since a number of world institutions are needed anyway, these institutions will have to be of the optimum type and nations will have to agree on that one type. Commodity agreements constitute an example. For these international institutions convergence of ideas is needed.

III.4. The condition of price uniformity (of II.1) *precludes impediments to trade,* except as a second-best solution for infant industries in developing countries. Trade impediments applied by developed countries stand at variance with the condition of price uniformity and can only be accepted for a *limited period* say a few years, in order to break shocks (of II.8).

III.5. The markets of many primary commodities are unstable because of low elasticities of demand or supply and of long reaction periods of supply.[9] In order to comply with the condition of stability (of II.8.) they must be regulated by *commodity agreements*. In order to comply with the research priorities (of. II.7) *synthetics* directly competing with natural products should be included in such agreements. Thus, synthetic rubber production must be subject to a quota system, even though the quota may be increasing. Some *processed agricultural products* may also have to be included. Wherever the danger of monopolies exists—which conflicts with condition II.3 that prices be equal to marginal costs—regulation is also needed.[10] Transportation markets are an example.

III.6. *Impediments to migration* are non-optimal too. While free migration constitutes the quickest way of complying with the condition of equal incomes for equal work, this condition may also be met by free trade in products only.[11] Since *rapid population growth,* especially in the poor countries, represents a special threat to the incomes of the less skilled, family planning is badly needed and free migration might be made conditional upon the extent and effectiveness of such planning.

III.7. The condition of *income redistribution* (of II.5) can only be met if there is a powerful *World Treasury,* with the task of carrying through such a redistribution among countries. The absence of such a Treasury constitutes the largest single deviation of reality from the optimum.[12] The establishment of such a Treasury may be made conditional on an increase in effectiveness of fiscal authorities in developing countries, somewhat similarly to what was said in III.6 on migration. The principal tasks of a World Treasury would be to collect taxes from all national governments and to allocate to countries entitled to support.

In order that both national and world taxes comply with optimum conditions indirect taxes and income taxes should be replaced by *lump-sum taxes,*[13] based on the capacity to produce rather than the outcome of that capacity.

Criteria for such allocation should reflect (a) the needs of the recipient countries, (b) their accomplishments and (c) the prospects for their economic development.

III.8. The optimal operation of the world economic system requires that the decision on the *creation of liquidities* be internationalized and no longer in the hand of national governments.

III.9. The redistribution of income mentioned under III.7 should be used to a significant extent for the extension and improvement of *educational* activities in developing countries.

III.10. Research programmes should be directed at wider interests. They can be influenced by government and international subventions but also, for instance, by extending commodity agreements to synthetics directly competing with natural products (of. III.5).

IV. *The road to a true global economy*

IV.1. As has already been pointed out (in I.1.) the conditions enumerated in Section II as well as the institutions described in Section III will be found "unrealistic" by many readers, since some basic preconditions for a true global economy, or rather society, are not fulfilled at all. National autonomy which, as a mental exercise, was assumed away, is precisely the fact the world is facing and suffering from.

It is useful to note that even under the assumption of its absence, the outcome of our exercise is that many tasks can and should be left to low levels of decision making, including national levels. For a few key decisions, however, the national level of decision-making is non-optimal and in a number of cases even disastrous. In the present section the roads open to the establishment of an international order will be briefly discussed. This assumes that there is some degree of political will to build an international order. Whatever willingness exists is based on the comprehension of the dangers ahead. This will exists with the most farsighted statesmen, but is is being thwarted continually by the hopes of some statesmen, partly the same, that their opponents will be eliminated. Most clearly and immediately this contrast comes up in the military field.

IV.2. We stated improved information and communication as a precondition (of III.1). While progress in the field of wider and *more objective* information has been made, there are still large numbers of "curtains" and walls, real and psychological, impeding better knowledge and understanding. There is still much scope for trying to overcome all these hindrances.

IV.3. The true optimal order of the world at large implies optimal orders in all countries. Sometimes cultural differences will make for different optimal orders in different countries. Even so we observe a convergence of *socio-economic orders,*[14] on the one hand because of converging cultural preferences, on the other hand because of increased understanding of what is really optimal. Thus, Western countries have shown an increase in central decision-making and centrally-planned societies an increase in decentralisation.

IV.4. Important activities have been developed into the direction of *freer trade*. Institutions such as the General Agreement on Tariffs and Trade (GATT) and the United Nations Conference on Trade and Development

(UNCTAD), together with individual governments meeting ad hoc, have been instrumental in this field. Even so, important programmes, especially of UNCTAD, still await acceptance by, above all, the developed countries.[15] Better access to the markets of the latter for both industrial and agricultural products is under discussion and likely to make some progress. Some reduction in monopoloid elements in transportation costs may also be attained.

IV.5. A few *commodity agreements* are in operation (wheat, tin, sugar, coffee), but a number of others still have to be concluded (cocoa being one example). Both the Food and Agricultural Organization of the U.N. (FAO) and UNCTAD are active in the field. Unfortunately the European Common Market (EEC) is not too co-operative.

IV.6. In the field of *income redistribution* most activities are taking place at the national level; but the International Labour Organization (ILO), for 50 years already, contributes to the spreading of social security measures over the world at large and recently started a programme for creating employment in a more systematic way. This will add to somewhat improving the income distribution. Much more forceful contributions in this field have been made by socialist countries, however defined, that is, either as communist-ruled or as social-democratic countries.[16]

IV.7. For the *international income redistribution* activities such as those of the International Bank for Reconstruction and Development (IBRD) and more specifically the International Development Association (IDA), administered by the Bank, are more important. New impulses can be hoped for if the Second Development Decade programme or the recommendations of the Pearson Commission be accepted by the governments of the prosperous countries.

IV.8. In the field of monetary policy the creation of the *special drawing rights* with the IMF has now become possible and may have a favourable impact on facilitating international trade and capital flows.

IV.9. In the field of *education* and *research* international activities in the direction sketched (in III.9 and 10) are being deployed by FAO, ILO, the United Nations Educational Scientific and Cultural Organization (UNESCO) and the United Nations Industrial Development Organization (UNIDO). As far as research policies are concerned, the U.N. Advisory Committee on Science and Technology gives general guidance to these efforts.

Notes

[1] One of the most active and interesting authors in this field is Mrs. Irma Adelman.

[2] I may be permitted to refer to some of my own recent publications on this subject; for instance Development Strategy and Welfare Economics, to be published in *Coexistence*, 1969.

[3] Cf. my forthcoming paper for the International Association for Research in Income and Wealth (1969 meeting): "A Positive and a Normative Theory of Income Distribution".

[4] Cf. my article "The Optimal International Division of Labour". *Acta Oeconomica Academiae Scientiarum Hungaricae* (1968, 3) p. 257.

[5] P. de Wolff estimated that around 1963 in the Netherlands 65 per cent more boys and 95 per cent more girls than actually had access to secondary education possessed the immate possibilities to complete such education. For university students the figures were higher even. (Weekblad v. h. Genootschap van Leraren aan Nederlandse gymnasia en lycea en de R.L.V. 57 (1963) p. 327, in Dutch.)

[6] The preference to avoid cycles is widespread and not shared only by the gambler type of people, who seem to be a minority. As a consequence anti-cyclical policies are generally preferred. Their possibility has been agreed upon ever since Keynes.

[7] An outstanding enrichment of theories on this subject has been formulated by M. Inagaki in a forthcoming book based on his dissertation (Rotterdam, 1967).

[8] Long ago already this proposition was defended in J. E. Meade: *The Economic Basis of a Durable Peace*, London 1939. Some doubts, however, have been expressed by J. Pinder, EEC and Comecon, *Survey,* London, January 1966, pp. 106, 107.

[9] An extensive body of econometric literature has dealt with this phenomenon; an early survey was given in J. Tinbergen, *Econometrics,* New York 1951: most of the concrete contributions have been made by the U.S. Department of Agriculture.

[10] Thus, the United States have their anti-trust laws the EEC Rome Treaty articles 85 ff.

[11] This is the famous factor price equalization theorem, extensively discussed in theoretical economics; the condition which has to be fulfilled can briefly be formulated that there should be less difference between the labour-capital ratios of the various countries than between the various production processes. This condition does, however, not (yet) apply in the present-day world.

[12] I made this point in my *International Economic Integration,* Amsterdam 1954.

[13] Lump-sum taxes do not need to be equal for all persons; they must be so as not to influence the marginal decisions on the increase or decrease of effort, however. Therefore indirect as well as income taxes are not lump-sum taxes and the income tax is a second-best only. Taxes on inherited wealth are closest to lump-sum taxes.

[14] Cf. J. Tinbergen, H. Linnemann and J. P. Pronk, "The Meeting of the Twain", *Columbia Journal of World Business,* Summer 1966; also in P. A. Samuelson, J. R. Coleman and F. Skidmore, eds., *Readings in Economics,* New York 1967.

[15] Cf. Report of the Second World Trade Conference, New Delhi, 1968, Geneva–New York 1968.

[16] Cf. G. Adler-Karlsson, *Funktionssocialism,* Oskarshamn 1967.

Resource Needs and Demands

By Harrison Brown

California Institute of Technology, Pasadena, Calif., U.S.A.

When man-like creatures first appeared upon the earth some two million years ago, individual needs for resources were very modest. Man needed food, water, protection and shelter, which he could obtain using the simplest of technologies. But as increasingly elaborate technologies were developed aimed at better satisfying these needs, demands for raw materials increased. The development of stone tools and weapons necessitated access to supplies of rock of the right kind for tool manufacture. The development of the controlled use of fire for cooking and warmth created the need for supplies of wood. The invention of agriculture created demands for land particularly suited to cultivation. The emergence of the great ancient urban civilizations led to the development of increasingly elaborate technologies and to the need for increasing per capita quantities of raw materials, notably stone, wood, clay, fibres and leather.

Copper was the first metal to come into widespread use on a substantial scale, not because it is particularly abundant (actually it is fairly rare), but rather because it can easily be reduced to the metal from its ores. Reduction temperatures are rather low with the result that the technology of producing the metal can be quite simple.

Metallic gold is actually easier to produce from its ores than is metallic copper, and indeed it often exists in nature as the metal. But gold is orders of magnitude less abundant than copper. Indeed, it is so rare in nature that it could never come into practical use on any truly substantial scale.

Iron is considerably more abundant than copper, but it is much more difficult to produce in metallic form. Higher temperatures are required and this necessitates in turn the development of a fairly elaborate technology. As a result, many centuries were required following the first substantial use of copper before the technology of producing metallic iron was developed.

The use of copper became widespread in the ancient urban civilizations and demands for the ore grew rapidly. Egypt, for example, quickly depleted her own local ore resources and began importing ore, primarily from Europe including the British Isles. Elaborate trade routes were developed for the purpose. But so rare is copper in nature, the price of the metal prevented it from coming into general use outside the cities. The peasants, who presented by far the greater part of the population, continued to depend upon the availability of rock and wood for their tools.

Once iron technology was developed, the use of metals could become truly widespread. The availability of new metal tools permitted Europe to be transformed from a vast forest to a fertile cropland. The great demand for metallic iron led to the emergence of a large iron industry in England where iron ore is plentiful and where there were ample trees for the production of charcoal.

Throughout the Seventeeth Century metallic iron was produced from the ore using charcoal as the reducing agent. Charcoal is obtained by heating wood at a sufficiently high temperature to denature it and drive off the volatile ingredients, leaving the carbon residue (or charcoal) behind.

Originally Britain had plenty of trees, but so great did the demand for wood become that in the latter part of the Seventeenth Century a serious wood shortage developed. Indeed, the iron industry of the island came close to shutting down. Attempts were made to substitute coal, abundantly available, for charcoal but the impurities in the coal gave rise to a product which was unusable for manufacturing purposes. Until the Eighteenth Century, little progress was made when by 1709 Abraham Darby had learned to drive off the volatile fumes from coal and produce "coke". By mid-century the right kind of coke could be produced in quantity for the blast furnaces.

Increased demand for coal led to the development of the steam engine and triggered a succession of technological developments. Demands for iron in the U.K. increased from 70 thousand tons per year in 1788 to 250 thousand tons per year in 1806. British coal production rose from 4.5 million tons in 1750 to 10 million tons in 1800 and to 16 million tons in 1829. Demands for many other metals increased equally rapidly. As the new technology spread to Europe and to North America, world demands for resources leapt upward and international competitions for their control developed, eventually to become severe.

The new technology was characterized by a sequence of technological competitions each of which gave rise to increased human productivity, but which inexorably gave rise to increased resource demands. As an example, in the middle of the Nineteenth Century the horse was the primary source of power on U.S. farms and the horse population grew about as rapidly as the human population. One horse was added to the population for every four persons. Had this trend persisted there would now be about 50 million horses in the United States. But the introduction of steam power to the farm about 1875, followed by the introduction of the internal combustion engine shortly after the turn of the century, produced a precipitous decline in horse population which is now little more than one million. Associated with this development we see greatly increased per capita demands for energy, steel and other metals. We also see greatly increased productivity, increased per capita and mass migration of workers from the farms to the cities.

Some of these changes which resulted from technological competitions proceeded with unprecedented rapidity. In a period of but 30 years (1870–1900), for example, the competition of the merchant marine of the United Kingdom was transformed from 90 percent wooden sailing ships to 90 percent iron ships powered by steam. In the process, of course, there was developed a greatly enhanced capability for transporting large quantities of materials and goods and greatly increased consumption of raw materials, in this case iron ore and coal.

In the Nineteenth Century, England became the dominant industrial power, eventually to be replaced by Germany. Following the First World War, the United States quickly became the giant industrial power. Today, the USSR and Japan are rapidly moving toward this position.

During the first half of this century steel production in the United States increased rapidly both on an absolute and on a per capita basis. By 1900 steel production was about 0.14 metric tons per capita. By 1910 it had reached about 0.3 tons per capita. For the past quarter century, however, although total steel production has continued to rise, per capita production has remained on the average virtually constant at about 0.55 metric tons per person per year. Only about 40 percent of this steel is generated from recycled scrap; the remaining 60 percent must be made up with new iron produced from ore.

The question as to why per capita production has flattened at this particular level is an interesting one. Studies of the consumption figures in other major steel producing countries suggest that for complex reasons this might represent the maximum rate at which new steel can be effectively absorbed by a highly industrialized society. In 1968 per capita steel production in Japan, Belgium , West Germany and Czechoslovakia were all higher than that of the United States but a considerable proportion of the steel produced in those countries is exported.

Were all of the metallic iron which has been produced in the United States in the last century still in existence, there would be in use some 15 tons per person. Actually a great deal of this has been lost as the result of production losses in the recycling of scrap, corrosion and other irrevocable losses. The figures suggest that we actually have in use some 10 metric tons of steel per person.

With respect to other metals which are essential to industrial civilization, some of the more important of them are used in remarkably constant proportions to steel. In spite of dramatically changing technologies, copper has been consumed during the last one-half century at a rate corresponding to 17 kilograms per ton of steel; zinc at a rate corresponding to 11 kilograms per ton and lead at a rate of 16 kilograms per ton of steel. By contrast, the proportion of tin to steel has been decreasing steadily, in part as a result of the rarity of the metal and in part as a result of technological developments which have given rise to substitutes. Also, by contrast, the proportions of aluminium to steel has been increasing steadily, in large part as a result of its abundance, its usefulness and rapidly changing technology.

These figures suggest that we now have in use in the United States for every person some 160 kilograms of copper, 140 kilograms of lead, 100 kilograms of zinc, 18 kilograms of tin and 110 kilograms of aluminum. Similar accumulations have been attained or are being approached in other industrialized parts of the world.

In order to meet our needs for steel and other metals together with the products derived from them in the United States, we transport each year for every person nearly 15,000 ton-kilometers of freight. Each person travels on the average each year some 8500 kilometers between cities, makes over 700 phone calls and receives nearly 400 pieces of mail. The population of private automobiles has reached 85 million corresponding to more than 0.4 cars per person. About 0.3 tons of packaging materials are produced and sold each year for every person, most of which enters the solid waste system, to be collected and disposed of.

Consumption of non-metallics in the United States is increasing considerably more rapidly than is that of metals. Since 1950 alone per capita consumption of stone, sand and gravel has increased from 3.2 tons to 7.7 tons—a factor of 2.4. Per capita consumption of cement has reached 350 kilograms and that of common salt has reached 175 kilograms.

In order to take care of all of the mining, production and distribution in the United States, we expend energy at a rate equivalent to our burning about 10 tons of coal annually per person. In contrast to steel, this level of per capita consumption is increasing at a rate of about 15 percent per decade.

Where are we heading?

Clearly man has become a major geologic force. The amount of rock and earth he moves each year in the industrialized regions of the world —a process which I have termed "technological denudation"—is already prodigious and will continue to grow, in part because of the spread of industrialization and in part because the demands of the industrialized nations of the world will continue to increase. When we add to this the fantastically high potential demand which would come into existence were the development process to be accelerated in the poorer countries, the total potential demand staggers the imagination. If by some magic the per capita inventory of metals in the world as a whole were to be brought up to the average level of the ten richest nations, all of the present mines and factories in the world would have to operate for more than 60 years just to produce the capital, assuming no losses. If we were to assume a world population of 10 billion persons (which I suspect is conservative) and a per capita steel inventory of 20 tons, some 200 billion tons of iron would have to be extracted from the earth. At the current rate of extraction, 400 years would be required.

With our present anarchical system of competing nation-states such levels of demand would place enormous strains upon the resources of the earth and would greatly intensify rivalries between nations. The richer nations already find it necessary to import increasing quantities of raw materials. Japan is virtually completely dependent upon imports. In 1950 the United States imported only eight percent of her iron ore; today she imports over 35 percent. A large proportion of these imports come from the poorer countries.

From a purely technological point of view man can in principle live comfortably off of the leanest of earth substances. He has always done the easiest things first. The first copper he used came from pure crystals of malachite which he picked up off the surface of the earth. This source gone, he dug deeper, went further afield and processed ore of lower grade. Even so, by the turn of the century we were still processing ore containing five percent copper. A few years later the average grade was three percent, then two percent, then one percent. Today we are processing ore which averages but 0.4 percent copper.

There are no technological barriers to our continuing this process and indeed it can be shown that man could, if need be, live comfortably off ordinary rocks. A ton of granite contains easily extractable uranium and thorium equivalent to about 15 tons of coal plus all of the elements necessary to perpetuate a highly technological civilization. Indeed, it would appear that we are heading for a new stone age!

Were I a cosmic gambler looking at the earth from afar asking where mankind is heading, I would probably write the following scenarios:

(*a*) The affluent nations will continue to become more affluent; the gap between the rich nations and the poor will continue to grow and mankind will eventually be completely divided into two groups. The smaller group will be well fed and rich and will live comfortably by applying technology to the leanest of earth substances. The larger group will be poor, hungry, and permanently miserable. It will have no advanced technology and will long before have been stripped of its high-grade resources.

But the rich groups, too, will face grave dangers. Being completely dependent for survival upon the perpetuation of its technology, it will be extremely vulnerable to disruption. And being made up of heavily armed nation-states, disruption will be highly probable. Sooner or later a nuclear war will take place and technological civilization will crumble. The poor will then inherit the earth and will live miserably everafter. With the earth's high-grade resources long ago having disappeared, technological civilization will be gone, never to rise again.

(b) My second scenario is really a special case of the first. Here the disruption takes place before high-grade resources have disappeared, the poor inherit the earth but eventually technological civilization once again emerges, preparing itself to experience the first scenario.

(c) My third scenario is the least probable one. Indeed, it verges on the miraculous. In this one, the rich nations arrive at a series of rational decisions. They eliminate vast nuclear weapons systems, thus lessening vulnerabilities. They control the flow of arms and develop effective procedures for the peaceful resolution of conflict. Even more important, they embark on a major program aimed at eliminating poverty in the world. A worldwide civilization emerges which can perpetrate itself indefinitely and in which all people can live comfortably and in peace with each other.

In the long run the two keys to the world's resources problems are politics and energy. Our present system of nation-states is not conducive to a healthy world resource economy perpetuating as it does gross inequities and inefficiencies.

Perhaps the greatest tragedy of the human experience is that our understanding of man and his behavior has not kept pace with our knowledge of how to control nature. We have now reached the point where from a technological point of view starvation and misery in the world are inexcusable. We can mobilize our genius to fly to the moon. But somehow we are unable to mobilize that same genius to build a world in which all people who care to do so can lead free, abundant and even creative lives.

The Task of the Commission on International Development (Pearson Commission)

By Wilfried Guth

Deutsche Bank AG, Frankfurt, Germany

Despite considerable development efforts during the past two decades, the gap between the rich and the poor countries is widening and we are facing a crisis in the commitment to development assistance due to congressional attitudes in some important donor countries. This is the situation to-day when the Report of the Pearson Commission is about to appear. Following an invitation of the President of the World Bank, Mr. Robert McNamara, the Commission on International Development was created in September 1968. Under the chairmanship of Lester B. Pearson, the former Prime Minister of Canada, it had seven members from seven different countries who all served in their individual capacity.

The task of the Pearson Commission was to clarify the development situation, to present and elucidate the facts of what has and what has not been achieved so far, analyze the present framework for aid, its possibilities and limitations, thereby trying to give a basis for an improved strategy of development for the coming decades. In a way this is part of a "strategy for survival", the subject under discussion here in our symposium. One might even speak of survival in a manifold sense—the survival of millions of people exposed to hunger and war (as we have seen recently in Biafra), the survival of our rich countries in a political sense and the survival of one of the basic values of mankind which is in danger of being lost, the commitment of the stronger to help the weaker, of the rich to help the poor.

In clarifying what has been achieved the Pearson Commission proved that the development aid of the past two decades in fact sustained an economic growth in the developing nations which is without precedence in economic history for nations in comparable stages of development. This is at the same time a promise that development aid is not a fruitless venture like pouring water into a broken jug. The aim of development aid is to put the emerging nations into a position where they can grow without help from outside. This self-sustained growth should be feasible for the majority of to-day's developing nations by the end of this century. If this goal is achieved development aid could be gradually reduced.

The basic rationale for development aid ought to be the moral commitment of the more highly developed nations to help their less fortunate neighbours. But this moral obligation has not proved strong or convincing enough. While the developed countries accept this obligation in principle they frequently argue that at first poverty and social injustice must be fought and abolished at home. This argument, however, is no longer tenable in a world where all countries are so closely linked. The poor of the developing nations are today as much a part of our world as our own poor. Mankind is moving together into a single community. The acceleration of history, which is partly the result of the impact of modern technology, has altered the whole concept of national interest. Who can ask where his country will be in one or two decades without asking where the world will be? This will be even more true in the decades ahead, for the generation of our children. If we wish that world to be secure and prosperous, we have no choice but to show a common concern for the problems of all people. In this sense, there is a very clear political rationale for aid, but one which is based on an entirely different kind of political thinking than that directed towards keeping positions or gaining allies in the Cold War. One might say it requires a more forward-looking political strategy. This is at the same time enlightened self-interest.

The same can be said in the economic field. The enlightened economic self-interest of the developed countries lies in the future possible utilization of all world resources, human and physical, which can only be brought about by international cooperation between the developing and the developed countries part of which is a new aid relationship. Intensified efforts to stimulate growth in the developing countries will lead to a general increase in international trade and investment, the prerequisite for adequate growth and welfare in almost all countries. Of course, the donors have also other and shorter term economic interests, such as for instance export promotion, but aid policies should have one primary objective: successful development.

The title of the Pearson Report: "Partners in Development" indicates that the Commission has laid much stress on the creation of a true partnership between donors and recipients based on a mutual understanding and an acceptance of reciprocal rights and obligations.

In this context a few words should be said on the Commission's attitude vis-à-vis the question of private foreign direct investment in developing countries. Contrary to the argument frequently heard nowadays in the richer countries that foreign private investment does not help the developing countries opinions expressed and memoranda submitted to the Commission indicated that most low-income countries welcome larger flows of foreign investment if foreign enterprises and entrepreneurs behave as true partners, i.e. convey their technical knowledge, provide ample opportunities for local talents on all levels, contribute to the fulfilment of national economic goals etc. The Commission has emphasized that multinational companies carry a great responsibility in this respect.

On the basis of the Commission's "philosophy" of a new constructive aid relationship many recommendations center on a request for more aid and higher quality of aid. But these points, crucial as they are, do not concern this symposium directly. What should be of particular interest here is the emphasis given in the report to the human factor in the development process.

Naturally, the Commission had to focus in this context on the question of population policy. Whether or not the excessive growth of population can be slowed down in the developing countries the outcome will in the longer run be crucial for the success of the international development effort. The only rational and human solution seems to be planning and control of population growth. But population planning is an extremely complex matter. There are certain dilemmas on moral, sociological, financial and even political grounds. To destroy suspicions existent in some quarters the Commission made two things clear: First, the industrial countries and the international aid agencies should not make the volume and terms of aid dependent on the introduction of population control programmes. This decision must remain in the full authority and responsibility of the recipient countries' governments. Secondly, aid for the solution of the population problems is in no way a substitute for the more traditional forms of development assistance, i.e. aid for economic infrastructure, agriculture, industrialization, trade etc.

Development aid should therefore render the developing countries all possible advice to conceive programmes and utilize methods of population control and give active financial support to those countries which have already established family planning programmes. This is the case in nearly 20 countries with a total population of about 800 million. Furthermore it is a task for scientists in all countries to improve methods of birth control and eliminate possible adverse side-effects.

Whilst in the past development assistance concentrated almost exclusively on financial and technical aid to foster industrial and—to a much lesser degree—agricultural development, in the future assistance should increasingly be devoted to education and research. This broadening of the aid spectrum is based on our growing knowledge that investment in education and research is perhaps the most important key to rapid economic growth in developed as well as in developing countries.

In the field of technical assistance much depends on the quality of the "envoys" from the developed countries which has tended to deteriorate as the demand from the developing countries has risen. One way out of this dilemma appears to be the creation of national or international career opportunities in the fields of technical assistance with the provision of adequate incentives. Yet, in the longer run developing countries should aim at "selfsupporting growth" also in this field, i.e. they should aim at educating their own experts and scientists.

A basic prerequisite here is the restructuring of primary education. Traditional forms of education—often imported from developed countries—do not correspond to the needs of the developing world to-day. They cannot reach optimal efficiency because they ignore the different set of values due to the different structures of societies. What is needed is more aid for basic research in educational systems fitting the low-income countries' necessities and recognizing their value systems. Recent progress in new techniques like programmed learning and the use of mass media in teaching give promise that much can be done.

The Commission spells out that aid for primary education should have high priority because it is one of the fundamental rights of man, as well as a necessary foundation for economic development. But the report also draws attention to the problems of higher education in the less developed countries. An evident outcome of insufficient possibilities for higher education and research facilities is the often cited "brain drain". The loss of skilled people was very often greater than the inflow of technical assistance personnel. For 1967 the UN estimated that 40,000 educated persons emigrated from the poor countries compared with an inflow of only 16,000 advisers. What the less developed countries need is first-class universities and research institutes providing the necessary professional environment, the social status and material incentives to their native scientists. University- and other research should in future be more related to possibilities of immediate application. For aid givers this means that more funds should be made available for the establishment of research institutes and development corporations for industrial research, tropical agriculture, fertilizers, tropical medicine, social research, housing and urban planning and demographic research. The Commission further recommended that developed nations should provide a fixed percentage of their official research and development expenditure to projects specifically related to the developing countries' problems.

As the Commission's general philosophy was that of a new partnership in the world community it might surprise some commentators that the question of coordination or even cooperation with the development aid effort of the communist countries has not been touched in the report. The main reason for this is lack of information and communication. But the Commission had no doubt that a joining of forces between East and West in the development effort could not only be highly desirable from a rationalization point of view but also and mainly because such cooperation would have a salutary effect on world peace and could be an integrating element in our world.

Youth and Its Rights[1]

By Henry D. Aiken

Brandeis University, Mass., U.S.A.

1

We live in a time of monumental paradoxes. When they occur in the mathematical and natural sciences, paradoxes represent a breakdown in thought only. But when they occur in the social or political, the moral or religious spheres, where by definition thinking concerns our existence as human beings, they can become mortally dangerous. However, paradoxes wear two faces: one a face of puzzlement, confusion, defeat or despair, the other of fascination, challenge, opportunity. The most stunning breakthroughs, whether in the sciences, in philosophy, or in social and psychological thought occur when some one discovers a new technique, invents a new tool, achieves a new perspective which, by enabling us to see around a paradox, makes it possible for us both to have our cake and eat it. Then we no longer need strive merely to shore up our ruins. Even tragedy is redeemed when we convert it into art. Now for the time being, we are once more out in the blue, and so having given form to chaos, we can press on to new reaches of human possibility.

Some of the contemporary paradoxes I have called human or existential may be witnessed (the selection is virtually at random) in the so-called "death of God" movement in religion, in the new moralities which at first look seem merely new forms of immorality or amorality, in the cult of anti-art, in the resistance and civil disobedience movements, in various student revolt movements which appear to threaten the very conditions of student existence.

This last paradox, which might be called alternatively, "the paradox of the student" or "the paradox of the university", is but one of a complex of "paradoxes of youth" or again alternatively, "paradoxes of maturity". In this essay I shall suggest some ways of coping with those which confront us all in our thinking about rights and responsibilities of young people in an age in which many youths view themselves virtually as a race apart while at the same time demanding immediate entrance into the ranks of adult citizens. On this score, the young people's position is merely a counter-image of their elders. We—and here I include many who still seek to preserve some identity with a tradition that calls itself liberal and democratic—subject our youth to a permanent Selective Service about whose existence, standards of selection or uses youth has little or nothing to say. Our economic and educational systems undoubtedly offer extraordinary opportunities for rapid advancement at least to well-off or gifted young men and women. For example, youths who have not cut their wisdom teeth are offered full professorships or placed in charge of research projects demanding the most intricate skills and the subtlest forms of understanding. Yet our legal and political systems still treat them as minors or semi-majors who cannot vote or else are unable to hold public office. Beyond all this our affluent society has fathered an affluent youth free to do and to possess many things of which a half century ago even the most extravagant member of the leisure class did not dream. Yet in matters of political judgment and social responsibility we treat them, especially in crucial situations, as children.

2

Political, social and moral attitudes, as I have come to think, are always correlated, directly or indirectly, with conceptions of human nature. Before trying to develop a new approach to problems about rights of youth, we must therefore ask whether certain traditional ideas about human development do not stand in need of revision. The classical view, inherited with little modification from the Greeks, is that man's nature is largely fixed, and that as in the case of all other natural kinds, there is a certain mature human character which every unthwarted human being seeks to actualize. About a half century ago, however, a fascinating inversion of this theory, identified largely with the name of Freud, began to take its place. According to this view (vastly over-simplified), the fundamental psychological problems of adult life are set in infancy or early childhood. From the moment he is thrust into the world, each individual is subject to certain characteristic traumas, complexes, forms of repression and compulsory release or compensation, which largely govern his behavior for the rest of his life. And liberation comes, for a very few, through a lengthy and usually costly process of analysis, devoted to uncovering of archetypal forms of maladjustment, based on the same infantile traumas and complexes.

More recently some ideas have been broached about man's nature, which provide bases for a more subtly differentiated account of the phases of human development, according to which the child is to be viewed neither as father to the man, nor as the man in embryo, but on the contrary each child, like the aging individual that will one day replace it, is in certain respects a creature unto itself. In particular, I have in mind the work of psychologists such as Erik Erikson (who, significantly, came to his work as a psychoanalyst after a career as an artist) who now talk very compellingly about a number of distinct life-stages, each with its own qualities of being, its distinct forms of creativity and sterility, its corresponding fulfillments and failures, its characteristic crises and ways of coping with them. From this point of view, as it were, none of us is a single, developing person, but as it were a sequence of related persons. In an important sense, two adolescents may in fact have a closer, more intimate identity with one another than either has with the strange oldster that will one day bear its name.

My own interest here is in a conception of youth which overlaps but does not exactly coincide with Erikson's notion of the life stage of adolescence. Yet much that he has to say about adolescents as "transitory existentialists by nature because they become suddenly capable of realizing a separate identity", has direct bearing upon the ideas I have come to in developing the ideas about rights of youth which I wish to offer for your consideration. The conception of youth I have in view also overlaps the next stage in Erikson's "epigenetic cycle", which he calls "young adulthood". At this stage, as he describes it, the individual youth, having made a start in coping with his problems of personal identity, now moves on to issues created by interpersonal relationships, particularly such interiorly personal ones as friendship, love, and sexual intimacy. But this is also a time when the crisis of identity, as Erikson calls it, partly resolves itself in the form of a special sense of "intimacy with oneself, one's inner resources, the range of one's excitements and commitments". And just as the adolescent, actively seeking his own identity is subject to special problems concerning the social roles he is expected to play, which he often resolves through some sort of generalized religious or ideological conversion, through identification with some larger presence to which he can give his loyalty, so the young adult becomes involved in distinctive problems of isolation which he tries to resolve, for example, through marriage and, according to his talents and interests, through some form of dedicated work. The period of adolescence and young manhood is thus a time both of passionate searching for independence and of striving for ideal attachments and forms of unselfish achievement.

Much of this spells out what we already know intuitively. Who can fail to perceive the extraordinary precocity, the energy, and capacity for sympathetic involvement in great (as well as less great) "causes" which are so characteristic of human beings in this marvellous springtime of life? And who can be unaware of the special forms of vulnerability, the yearning, restlessness, loneliness, and unspeakable unhappiness to which young people are liable?

Now it seems to me that if thinkers like Erikson are even half right, we must question all approaches to problems concerning rights and responsibilities of youths, inbred in us since the time of the Greek philosophers, which treat youth as merely a potential something else and the time of youth as merely a bridge-passage between childhood and manhood. A youth is already something, with a form and an identity of its own. And if, from one point of view, he is not fully mature, the same can as well be said, from another, of the man "at the (supposed) height of his powers" who has yet not attained to that distinctive ripeness and wisdom of life one finds in the works of such incomparable, self-rejuvenating old men as Dewey and Russell and Freud, as Verdi and Stravinski and Yeats, or as Tillich and Martin Buber.

Indeed, the very word "rejuvenate" itself suggests that in restructuring our thinking about the problems of youth, and the rights pertaining thereto, we may find clues to a reconstruction of our attitudes toward the problems of later phases of the human life cycle, and so discover good reasons to modify uninflected and uniformitarian doctrines about the rights of man which we have inherited, like pieces of old furniture, from another era when the pressing needs of men in societies created problems of equality and fraternity, as well as liberty, in many ways quite different from our own.

3

Our problems about rights of youth would remain formidable even with the help of the best available psychological theories about this extraordinary period of life. Unfortunately, the very terms in which the topic is discussed —youth, adulthood, maturity, above all rights—are subject of misconceptions that cause us to falter in the very act of thinking about them. Worse, these are not terms employed in sorting out natural objects that help us to play a neutral animal vegetable and mineral game with members of the human race. Through them, on the contrary, we contemplate roles, assign functions, and articulate decisions central to all political, social, and moral life. How can we answer one of the great and pressing questions of our age, whether youths should share the rights of adults, if because of misconceptions and preconceptions about what a right, a youth, or an adult is, we cannot clearly envision the possibilities which the question demands us to consider? I fear there is nothing for it, then, but to refurbish some parts of the conceptual apparatus with which we must work.

Our notions about the concept of a right are perhaps the most confused. By this time moral philosophers have done some part of the job of removing the accumulated dust that overlays our conceptions of good and evil and moral right and wrong. Legal and political philosophers are making progress with such terms as law, authority, revolution and, save us, ideology. But the elusive concept of a right, which has such important applications in every sphere of human action is still covered with a dozen coats of ideological varnish which are nearly impossible to remove.

For example, since the advent of utilitarianism and pragmatism in the 19th century, influential thinkers everywhere have tended to conflate the ideas of a right and a good. This error is egregious. Granted that many, though by no means all, rights are among our most precious political or human values, there are many goods, as matters stand, to which we can claim no right at all. The task of a doctrine of rights is to specify, and hence to restrict, those goods to which we can meaningfully regard ourselves as entitled. That is why a true bill of rights is of such immense importance to a society. For only after making sure that no relevant rights would be seriously infringed can we consider whether a good is justly to be pursued. The "pragmatic theory" of rights, as I shall call it, encourages its advocates, governmental officials as well as private citizens, to treat rights as merely one set of values among many which therefore may be thrown indiscriminately into the pot of deliberation where prospective policies are cooked. This is its overwhelming fault. For it returns us, in effect, to a Hobbesian state of nature where the liberties of each man, subject to no constraining bills of entitlement, are unlimited.

I am not suggesting here that it is never proper to abridge or alter rights. But anyone who would do so has his work cut out for him. For it is the abridgment, not the right, that needs justification, and the good achieved by abridging or abandoning it must be at once overwhelming and at least as palpable as the right in question. This is why many young people, often deeply conservative in their basic attitudes toward the American system, are moved to rebellion by pragmatic political and military policies which, in the name of an impalpable something called "the national interest", ride roughshod over their rights both as youths and as young citizens of a supposedly liberal-democracy. It is also why black men, not ill-disposed to the principles of a free society, are maddened by pragmatic realists who calmly ask them to wait indefinitely for substantive enjoyment of their rights until, say, the cold war has been won, until the city planners have cleared the slums, or the political parties have been made response to something other than their own interests.

Two other misconceptions are worth mentioning here, for they also are prevailing sources of confused thinking and acting. One is the "gift theory" of rights. According to it, rights are happy benefits bestowed upon us by some beneficent person or institution: a relative, God, the state, the university. This will not do. All of us, I trust, are grateful for the gifts we receive from known or unknown donors. But unless we are mad, we do not on that account claim them as rights. The trouble with the gift theory, as we shall see more clearly presently, is that it ignores the correlative notion of responsibility, without which the concept of a right is meaningless. One of the things we perceive intuitively to be wrong with even the most benevolent of dictators is that the privileges they bestow are merely gifts. For what is given according to one's pleasure may be withheld for the same reason. Those radicals who profess to despise liberalism would do well to ponder the fact that one of the immense strengths of the liberal tradition of John Locke and of his followers among our own revolutionary founding fathers was their grasp of the confusions implicit in the gift theory of rights.

But now we have to consider, all too briefly, another theory which, while it contains much truth, still does not provide an adequate *general* conceptions of rights. This I shall call the "juristic" or "legalist" theory, according to which, following the model of the law, a right (roughly) is to be understood as a recognized social practice. From this point of view, for example, the right to be at liberty amounts in fact to a system of social or legal permissions which a society or its government recognizes and for violations of which it provides acknowledged remedies. Accordingly this theory advances a great step beyond those previously considered. For by implication it clearly recognizes that when somebody has a right then some other person or persons have a responsibility to observe or protect it.

Two other merits of the juristic theory deserve mention here; one concerning the concept of a law and hence, by implication, that of a legal right; the other, at least in its contemporary forms, concerning its view of the general relation of law to morality. As to the first point, because the juristic theory contends that a law as such cannot be fully understood as "a command of a sovereign", as realist utilitarians and pragmatists have contended, but only as a rule tied umbilically to a general rule of law, to which any rightful sovereign is also subject, it helps to protect us from indiscriminating forms of cynicism, to which young people in our time seem particularly prone, which treat legal rights as nothing more than *de facto* permissions of those who hold power.

I am not unmindful here that all existing legal systems including our own are very imperfect approximations to a true rule of law. Every black man, every migrant worker, and many, many youths have learned to their sorrow that our own legal system is full of unpardonable lapses from the commonest principles of justice inherent in a rule of law. All the same, to vary a thesis of David Hume, the first rational act of those driven to overthrow an existing legal-political system must be to establish another more equitable, surer, and closer to the principle of a true rule of law. Nor, important as it is, need we make a sacred cow of the idea of a rule of law; for no matter how excellent it may be it does not exhaust what we understand by justice. And justice is not the only good we require of a politically organized society. A rule of law, in short, is a necessary but by no means a sufficient condition of tolerable government or even of an acceptable legal system. For we must ask not only that justice be done but that the justice done, however impeccable, is adequate in all the spheres of life which law and government affect.

But this leads directly to the other merit of the juristic theory: its recognition of the distinction between the law as it is and the law as it should or ought to be. This distinction, which provides the indispensable leverage for responsible demands for rightful changes in regard both to particular laws and to the legal system as a whole, is ignored both by sentimental exponents of "the law" as the embodiment of a system of ideals, and by legal realists and pragmatists whose distaste for moralism spills over into contempt for moral criticism itself.

My purpose, then, is not to raise questions about the need for qualification of the theory of law underlying modern versions of the juristic theory of rights. And for the sake of argument, at least, I am prepared to accept it as a working hypothesis about the law itself in dealing with issues concerning rights of youth that are only in the second instance legal. I contest only the thesis that a legal right, viewed as an established practice within a system of law, affords a suitable model for a general conception of rights, especially those of the sort we call moral or ethical. On the contrary, it turns out in its own way to be prejudicial to a study of rights of youth which, although very real, are not yet embodied in any established social or legal practice.

In the following paragraphs it is possible to give only a bare outline of a general theory of rights for which I have argued elsewhere. First, let me say that in the widest sense a right is not definable as a kind of rule or practice, even though it may afford the basis for establishing a practice. It is entirely meaningful, for example, for one person to say to another, "I grant you the right to make a practice of walking over my land". The right in this case isn't a practice; rather does it provide the ground for a practice. Furthermore, it is meaningful to say, "I grant you the right, on this occasion, to walk across my land." This, note well, is no mere gift. For if I grant such a right then in so doing I hold myself responsible either to respect the freedom of him to whom it is granted or, conceivably, to guarantee that he will not be molested either by myself or others when he takes his walk. In short, in granting a right, I *create* a claim whose terms I thereby obligate myself to honor, even though by the terms of the grant it may lapse when a single action has been performed. Thus, whereas a legal right is not merely the basis of a practice or an action, but a practice in its own right which correspondingly imposes a recurrent duty toward those who may claim the right in question, a moral right, on the other hand, exists whenever a claim may be made that some person or other obliges himself to respect, whether or not a practice of any sort exists.

A second feature of significant ascriptions of rights, especially those of the moral sort, is that since they implicitly involve assignments of responsibility, they are never correctly understood simply as statements of fact. For ascriptions of rights impose responsibilities and therefore are always intended to dispose those to whom they are addressed to be ready to perform (or refrain from performing) an act or acts of a certain kind when the circumstances warrant. Ascriptions of rights, in short, belong to the domain, not of what philosophers (misleadingly) called theoretical, but of practical reason. And reason functions practically, only when it means, to vary a famous thesis of Karl Marx, not simply to describe reality but to change it.

But here we have reached a place where the liberal tradition must take its own licks. For, since the time of Locke, that tradition has been concerned largely with rights, whether moral or legal, that pertain only to so-called negative liberties. Such rights permit us to do as we please in certain circumstances—say, save our lives, enjoy and protect our property, or follow our own way to happiness—but permissions entail no primary obligation on the part of others save to refrain from interfering with the actions of those who possess them. If they elect to go to hell in a bucket, we pledge only not to stand in their way. The idealist and socialist traditions, which in this respect go back behind Locke to the Greeks, remind us that there is more to the rights of civilized life than entitlements to do as we like. Some rights lay claim to what are sometimes called "positive freedoms". These rights are not simply permissions, but on the contrary require all responsible persons actively to aid and support those who possess them. Rights of this sort are of particular importance in the case of young people who even when they already possess powers of judgment and discrimination, are commonly without the means of realizing their ends. And it is precisely with respect to rights of this sort that liberals, as John Stuart Mill for one came eventually to see, have had much to learn from the socialist and idealist tradition.

Now, as I have indicated, the concept of a right is inescapably correlated with that of responsibility. No one can significantly claim a right unless there is someone who is obliged to honor the claim. Before ascribing rights, therefore, it is essential to inquire who, if anyone, may be held responsible for their observance. And in the case of rights of youth, this point is also of particular importance, since it is commonly, though by no means always true, that those who must assume the primary burden of responsibility no longer enjoy exactly similar rights. Efforts to enlarge or modify rights of youth thus impose great problems of understanding and sympathy. For most of us, not unnaturally, find it easier to acknowledge another's right when we ourselves also possess it. These problems are further complicated in societies like our own where simplistic uniformitarian doctrines of justice prevail and where, especially in the economic sphere, people are still left so largely to their own inadequate devices. At the theoretical level it is widely taken for granted that if all rights entail responsibilities, then all rights and responsibilities must be mutual. This is plainly false. For example, aged persons have rights which entail no mutual responsibilities. But this is not all. For in principle rights and responsibilities need not be reciprocal. Insane or senile persons (I should hope) have rights, though virtually by definition they can assume few or no responsibilities. But even when some form of reciprocity is just, it can by no means always be established by appeal to a principle of equality.

In sum, a tenable general theory of rights must make allowance in advance for many possibilities of differential treatment among human beings according to their various circumstances and powers. This does not mean that we should abandon entirely the principles inscribed in doctrines that speak of the rights of man. Nor does it mean that we renounce altogether libertarian doctrines about rights which are essentially permissive in character. It means, rather, that such principles and conceptions be amplified, amended, and supplemented by others in terms of which the generosity and good will of man's ethical consciousness, at its best, may be more discriminatingly inflected and extended.

4

In preparing this essay, I already had a fairly clear idea of what I wanted to say about rights as such. The terms youth, adulthood, and maturity, which have been little studied by analytical philosophers, turned up some surprises: connotations I assumed to be straightforward turned out to have some curious angles, and both affinities and disaffinities I had taken for granted faded on closer scrutiny. As a preliminary exercise I have as usual consulted the *Oxford English Dictionary,* a book which, if not always profound and often imperfect, is useful when one wants to see in outline the lay of a conceptual land.

Youth, we are told, has three main connotations, some of them more perplexing than they may seem at first glance: (a) the fact or state of being young and, more figuratively, newness and recentness; (b) that phase of life between childhood and adult age, and again more figuratively, any early stage of existence and (c) the qualities characteristic of the young, for example, freshness, vigor, vitality, creativity and (more pejoratively) wantonness and rashness. What shall we say of all this? To take the last point first, I think we must say, rather firmly, that though many youths do appear rash or wanton in the eyes of their elders, and some of them doubtless are so by any standards, rashness is endemic to the human species, and that every stage of life presents its own forms of liability in this regard.

The much discussed movie, *The Graduate,* whatever may be said for its artistic merits, certainly suggests that middle age is a time of immense hazards in both directions especially among the affluent. It also raises the question whether some of the rashness and most of the wantonness ascribed to youth may be functions of the examples set for it by people in the life-stage ahead. More interesting, however, is the likelihood that those forms of rashness and wantonness to which youths as such may be prone are merely deviant expressions of their other, more positive powers of freshness, vitality, vigor, imaginativeness and creativity. In any case, what the potentially rash and wanton of all ages need are not so much laws that restrict their liberties as knowledge to inform their vigor and vitality, and better opportunities for significant love and affection. More positive freedoms, not fewer negative ones, are the primary cures for these faults where they exist.

The second connotation, which distinguishes youth as that phase of life between childhood and adult age, raises many questions. Plainly it does not refer merely to a specific term of years. Many people retain the qualities and powers, as well perhaps as the vulnerabilities mentioned above, until well beyond their middle twenties; and some precocious youngsters enter upon the age of youth before their teens, just as others remain children, in effect, all their lives. Clearly the age of youth turns less upon questions of time than upon qualities of being, and for the most part I shall so treat it in what follows.

More puzzling are the relationships between youth and adulthood. If, for example, one understands by an adult one who is mature in a purely biological sense, then obviously many youths are as adult as they will ever be, and a great many fortunate adults are still youths. Evidently biological factors cannot be decisive here. On the other hand, if by an adult one refers to a person who is entitled to enjoy legal or other rights, not in potency only but also in act, then, from the perspectives we have now reached, some youths are fully adult and others not—and vice versa.

Evidently it is time to take a closer look at the notion of an adult itself. The central entry in the *Oxford English Dictionary* tells us that a person is adult when he is "fully developed in mind and body" or else possessed of full powers of "thought, deliberation and judgment". On the one side, an adult is somebody who is mature in a certain respect. On the other he is one who possesses certain psychological qualifications. Let us leave the notion of maturity aside for the moment. Certainly the powers of thought, deliberation and judgment, as here understood, are not empirical concepts at least in the sense of the term currently employed in the so-called behavioral sciences. For while they do indeed have to do with questions of behavior, these are questions of intention and conduct, not of mere bodily movements or changes. And it is for just this reason that contemporary behavioral psychology which attempts to correlate forms of bodily "inputs" and "outputs" (as the jargon goes) avoids like the plague all such intentional verbs as "deliberate" and "judge". Given their purposes they are right to do so. Unfortunately those concerned with problems about rights of youth cannot settle for input–output correlations, but must deal with psychological concepts of a wholly different sort. What are these?

We may get some leverage by observing that definitions of an adult make reference to a *person* who is developed in certain powers of mind. The concept of a person presents many problems. Still, enough is known about its use to make it clear that powers ascribed to persons are not the same sort of thing as the dispositions imputed to mere things or objects of a certain sort. Now as its etymological root (*persona*) suggests the concept of a person is normally employed in speaking of someone or something to whom (or which) certain desirable roles or functions are ascribed. (This point becomes obvious enough when we recall what is involved, for example, in the concepts of legal, moral, or religious persons.) Accordingly, a person is one who is assigned particular offices and duties, prerogatives and rights. And the psychological powers imputed to him are those required in order to perform the roles and fulfill the functions in question. Hence in speaking of an adult as a person who is fully developed in mind (and body) we are at the least of it ascribing to him mental powers not pertaining to individuals of a certain age, but those necessary to certain forms of achievement, in virtue of which he is entitled to perform relevant actions and, in some circumstances, may be held liable if he fails to perform them.

Adulthood is therefore not just any sort of maturity, and so far as youths and their rights are concerned, this is a matter of great importance. Thus, while we may speak of mature lions, elm trees, or parsnips, we would not, I believe, ever regard them as adults. The mature lion must meet certain specifications, but they do not suffice to make him adult, and this for the reason that, as such, they give him no status as a person. What is required of adults, unlike merely mature creatures of a certain breed or species, are mental powers pertaining to the fulfillment of roles pertinent or perhaps indispensable to the aims of some institution, society or way of life. And in such matters, questions of age in particular seems entirely secondary.

5

But are they? Up to this point I can well imagine that both young and old readers may feel, from their respective stations, that hitherto my remarks about the concepts of youth have been too abstractly functionalistic. What has been left out are the sheer unalterable facts of age and aging. The first entry on youth in the *Oxford English Dictionary* reminds us that youth is the fact or state of being young. Thus, while Leonard Bernstein still may be the most youthful of middle-aged Americans, he is no longer a youth, whereas the teen-age supporters of Eugene MacCarthy who were beaten by Mayor Daley's cops are youths, whatever the quality of their political wisdom or moral rectitude. From the standpoint of the older generation, it may be argued further that although conceptions of adulthood are indeed tied to social practices or attitudes, there remain basic universal functions of adults in all historical societies, to which the thoroughly exoteric powers of judgment, deliberation, and thought have always been indispensable. In short, adults are and must be people of mature age who must share the primary responsibilities of ordinary social life: the responsibilities of earning a living, parenthood, citizenship, performing the tasks essential to keeping of the basic institutions of society in working order. Thus older people, by and large, have and must continue to set the standards of adulthood, for their judgment, however fallible, is what we finally have to rely upon.

This sounds very concrete. Unhappily (or happily, depending upon your attitudes) other things are also concrete. I can imagine many intelligent, well educated, and dedicated young people replying as follows: if youth connotes not only the fact or state of being young but, more figuratively, also newness and recentness one thing is clear: we indeed live in a society whose institutions are not only run by old people, but which is itself old, and like most old things arthritic, incapable of making the freshly-conceived decisions and adjustments essential to the survival of the very society and its institutions which our putative adults cherish. For example, in our system it is next to impossible for any but dodos to be elected President of the United States. And much the same holds with respect to the major managerial jobs of the great corporations, the great universities and foundations, and the military and police forces. In most important situations, our young people are indeed treated not as adults but as occupying ambiguous positions between childhood and adult age. In practice they are at best merely pre- or potential adults who may one day become adults *if* they behave themselves and submit to the forms of judgment and thought of those who effectively control the policies and activities of our major institutions. But what about those who resist or radically dissent, those who, as the phrase is, opt out? Will they be allowed to become adults? Business is indeed business, and the more unconventional the youth the more systematically is he excluded from its decisive transactions and operations.

But let us, as friends of youth, continue to play the game of connotations according to Hoyle, only demanding like the greying eminences themselves, that all concrete realities be taken into account. Speaking thus as presumptive youths therefore, we will accept, subject only to qualifications that *"our"* experience shows to be realistic, the conditions of adulthood that existing adults regard as *sine qua non*: judgment, deliberation and thought. In passing we may observe that most existing institutions, political, legal, educational, and religious are systematically calculated to delay our acquisition of the powers of judgment necessary to established ways of adult life. And if from our elders' point of view we are too often rash and wanton, is not the fault theirs as much as ours? Or rather is it not owing to a prevailing social order that compels us, even from our own point of view, to take long shots, to take our fun where we can find it and to make up our own games as we go along? But speaking as soberly and concretely as we know how, we already possess powers that entitle us to the sort of adulthood which a decent contemporary society would accept as a matter of course. Take the matter of thought, essential to sensible deliberations and judgments in affairs of government. We know more about the world, human and otherwise, possess more finely honed conceptual and intellectual skills than all but a handful of our elders. However, let us not only concede, but insist that knowledge of matters of fact is not the only thing essential to sound deliberations and judgments. What is wanted also is the capacity for emotional development, powers of imagination, sympathy and affection, the capacity for idealism and of identification with great causes, such as are inscribed, for example, in our own *Declaration of Independence* and our *Bill of Rights*. These surely should be the auxiliary powers of adult persons capable of making the great decisions upon which not only our well-being but our very lives depend.

Yet (speaking now in my own person) if the freshest, most imaginative of your contemporary psychologists are to be believed, it is in the age of youth that men possess these powers more abundantly than at any other time of life. And surely our own experience during this troubled and immensely troubling period in our history confirms this. I am not forgetting the contributions of some young people to the disorders that have made repression the great theme of both political parties in the current presidential campaign.

But surely if adult Americans have learned anything from history it is that repression—call it "law and order" if you prefer—is the last response which creative minds would make to the general disorders to which our youths have contributed their own destructive bit. Repression is the response, not of wise adults, but of men who have lost the powers of reflection that can enliven the judgments, political and otherwise, our people so desperately need. Our great trouble is not lawlessness but something far worse: the loss among our law-abiding leaders of that saving "sweetness" of spirit (the word of course is Matthew Arnold's) which in calling men to order, conveys at the same time a sense not of hardness but of care, not of a desire to hang on to one's own but to share it, not of a demand for "justice", which here becomes another word for retribution, but of need for rehabilitation and reunion.

I am not unaware that, so far as our contemporary youth are concerned, Matthew Arnold can hardly be regarded as our man in the 19th century. That is partly why I have mentioned him rather than, say, Nietzsche or Kierkegaard. But he is also worth remembering here, not only because he himself tried in his own unflinching Victorian way to find a way toward understanding and meeting the responsibilities of adulthood in a time which was after all a prelude to our own, but because he himself, as he all too well knew, was afflicted in his own phrase with "this strange disease of modern life", an illness from which another writer, closer in style to ourselves, William James, also suffered throughout his life. What is the disease? It has many names, but scepticism will do.

What does scepticism mean in the sphere that here concerns us: the sphere of judgment and deliberation and hence not of purely theoretical but also of practical reason whose aim is choice and action? Here, where James like Arnold knew whereof he spoke, scepticism means on the one side loss of faith, of concern for loyalty and trust, and on the other a failure of will. Judgment is listless, spectatorial, and therefore pointless unless it moves the will. And it is sporadic, desperate, merely compulsive, unless it is infused with faith and the vital urgency which is the offspring of faith. Yet if Erikson is even half right, it is in the age of youth that these qualities of being still exist as actualities, not as something to be recovered for a dying moment through someone else's rhetoric. As every teacher knows, he needs his students more than they need him. For they enable him first of all to perceive that *his* scepticism is not the result of uncynical wariness and experience but all too often of a disabling, self-protective, loss of heart. It is our students and our children who bring us back to life by showing us the preciousness and precariousness of all significant human being, without which ordinary adulthood, with all its flim-flam of "judgment" and "deliberation", and indeed the whole business of practical reason become a dreary farce which we run through each day for want of something better to do. It is youth, by forcing us to reconsider our "principles", which for the most part are merely the routine responses of party men, professional men, members of a social class that help us to recover a significant, functional scepticism out of which—who knows?—even we might come up with a new idea or a fresh hope for our kind.

How little do we know ourselves, we adult Americans, managers of the world's greatest novelty shop? What do we sell there that could make us new men? We are masters of gadgetry. But we have let our institutions, once examples to all mankind, become rigid and lethargic, unresponsive to serious demands for rapid social change. In our fear of the outside world we outdo the Russians themselves. Who are our statesmen and preceptors? They are, quite literally, creations of cosmeticians, ghost writers, image-makers, pollsters. Thought, deliberation, judgment: what an incredibly sad joke it is that at the circuses where major parties pretend to conduct the deliberations that are supposed to enable a great democracy to make reasonable judgments, by whom and how it shall be ruled, these balding eagles can find no visible way of demonstrating their manhood except to surround themselves with flag-waving children, pin-up girls, rosy-cheeked daughters and handsome sons, and (slightly less obviously) cadres of sleek, well-groomed young bodyguards. Youth: only its circumambient image seems able to prove, either to themselves or to their audiences, that they even exist. But all they really want is the image; the presence, the actuality scares them stiff. And real youths, serious youths who have proven their adulthood, are held at bay by Mace, tear gas and night sticks. How can this tragedy be stopped? And how can a democratic people renew its strength? Only, I am convinced, by enabling all youths to participate fully in forming the judgments of our common social and institutional life. Only, that is to say, by enabling them to view themselves as adults. If some of them are not yet mature—as I realize—then we ourselves can match them two for one. But, young or old, one learns to walk by walking and until our youth walks, our society will remain in a wheel chair.

6

Thus, by pondering the meanings and applications of the terms of our discourse in some of the concrete circumstances of their contemporary use we are brought directly around to the immense problem of this essay: rights of youth. Notice, however, that I have spoken only of "rights" not of "the rights" of youth. Here I propose to begin by asking in the form of an imaginative experiment, not what rights young people may claim of some abstract entity called "mankind", but what sorts of rights enlightened young people may ascribe to and claim of one another, when viewed as members of a certain moral community.

Let us suppose them to be reflective, tolerably informed and generously inclined yet disposed also to give a certain primacy to the claims of their own community: call it, for convenience, "the league of youth". This sense of priority, as they themselves recognize, stems partly from a sense of exclusion and hence of alienation from the prevailing institutional and social life of the American system. More positively it stems also from a sense of their identity with one another as youths, as well as from an awareness both of stress and of opportunity which distinguish them not merely from their elders but in some measure from previous generations of young people. Owing to the existence of the various media and forms of transportation which make possible virtually immediate communication with other youths, both at home and abroad, they realize that community for them (as well as for others) is no longer a function of geographical closeness, of superficial cultural similarities, of ties owing to accidents of birth and nurture in a particular town or country or social class. For this and other reasons, they feel themselves to be the bearers of a new culture which, were it allowed to spread, could help toward the rejuvenation of the whole race of men. Perhaps it is not too fanciful to say that they view themselves as filling an historic role in our time somewhat analogous to the roles which other reformist and revolutionary classes believed themselves to be filling during the great revolutionary ages between the 18th and early 20th centuries in America and Europe. And if this imposes upon them special responsibilities it also disposes them to regard one another as possessing certain correlative rights. Analogously they feel a kinship with contemporary revolutionary movements in Latin America, in Africa, and in Asia, and consider all disenfranchised and disadvantaged people as having transnational and transcultural rights which it is their right as members of the league of youth, to defend as advocates.

Some have called them "anarchists" because they talk of "participatory democracy", because they engage in seemingly unorganized, isolated and gratuitous acts "against the system". This, I think, is a shallow view. For though militant they abhor all military and para-military forms of organization and unity. Actually they are trying out forms of organization, inspired in part by men like Gandhi, that require both extraordinary selflessness and self-discipline. Perhaps they will fail in this but what a pity if they do. For, if I understand them, their view is that the alternative is not gradual piecemeal progress through "legitimate" institutional channels, but very conceivably a dead planet. And more generally, in a time of unique danger not for themselves alone but for *their* successors—their children and their students—it is not their task only but a right which they bestow upon one another, to serve as agents of a general spiritual and social reformation. And it is in terms of this right that they justify their continuing resistence to "the system" and their exemplary acts of extreme refusal and defiance. What appear from a conventional, moral or legal point of view to be acts of immorality or rebellion are consequences of collateral obligations which their rights as active members of the league of youth entail.

Some foolish spokesmen for the league of youth profess to be contemptuous of the liberal tradition. Yet in some ways our youths strike me as reaffirming a fundamental contention of that tradition, which views rights primarily as permissions or liberties to do as one pleases without interference, particularly in the sphere of personal life. In fact, I should argue that one of the salient characteristics of their community is their insistence on extending the range of such permissions, in matters not only of taste, including such things as dress, manners, and modes of speech, but also more importantly, of sex. However they do not equate personal freedom with privacy. And whereas the Victorian liberals and their Bloomsbury successors were often very free indeed in sexual as well as in other matters of personal life, they performed their rites behind closed doors in thickwalled houses well back from the road. Here I think we must see that in the classical liberal tradition there was a deep connection between the rights or permissions, associated with personal liberty and the rights pertaining to private property. I have a right to do as I please in my house or in houses where I am invited, in such affairs as sex because this is the proper sphere of personal life. I have no such right—just the contrary—in public places where, presumably, my roles are no longer purely or primarily personal. On this score the league of youth, less concerned with private property and possessions, are at once more permissive about what may be done in public and less observant of rights of privacy. What shouldn't be done in public simply shouldn't be done at all, and what is permissible in private is in effect permissible anywhere. In this respect in short, their sense of community like that of the socialists, is so strong that they can scarcely understand why anyone should claim rights to privacy, where in the name of liberty, the individual for the time being cuts himself off from his kind.

This of course creates an impression of vulgarity, of callousness, of plain indecency among solid citizens who, in their carefully guarded penthouses and suburban homes feel free to do just as they please, however debased or debasing. And I have no doubt that there is here a profound generation gap. But it is closely tied to different primary attitudes, regarding both the sense of community and something entirely different: the institutions belonging to a social system. Accordingly, that generation gap is accompanied by radical differences in regard to the moral claims which people may lay upon one another in the names both of negative and of positive freedom. Solid citizens quite properly from their point of view begin their deliberations concerning their own moral responsibilities toward other members of society by reflecting upon their various institutional rights which they assume at the same time to have a *prima facie* moral claim upon themselves and others. The members of the league of youth, enjoying only a modicum of such rights, and thinking of themselves in the first instance as members of a community which the society does not even realize to exist, attach no such moral significance to the institutional rights in question. And so what are virtually indefeasible rights to their elders are for them functions of social policies whose worth appears to them entirely problematic.

The implication is plain: if youths are to think as solid citizens, attaching an inherent moral significance to the institutional rights of the social system, they must be transformed into solid citizens. This can only be done by treating them as full-fledged adult members of the system who can therefore make some identification with its institutions. They must possess these rights, moreover, not merely potentially, but also actually and in full.

But now we have to consider briefly another dimension of the moral outlook of the league of youth which is, as I have observed, profoundly at variance with a deep stratum in our cultural tradition and which has been reinforced in recent years by the advent of the graduate university and the commanding position of the university among the primary institutions of our emerging national society. For want of a better term, I shall call this aspect of our tradition "rationalism", and indeed it does derive, as an ideology, largely from the writings of the great classical philosophers beginning with Plato and Aristotle. From this point of view, human normality and maturity are derived from a conception of man as "the rational animal" whose highest good is knowledge, and whose highest knowledge is of the sort we nowadays call "scientific". Further, possession of the intellectual powers and skills necessary to the achievement of such knowledge is itself an evidence of wisdom and hence of a *prima facie* right to leadership, if not to rule, within the society. A democratic society like our own professedly denies this intellectual elite the right to rule, but increasingly it bestows upon it an informal but nonetheless powerful right to be heard, to advisory positions of immense prestige and power, and of course to leadership and governance within the university itself. Let me quote a recent candid formulation of this point of view by Professor George Kateb in an essay, "Utopia and the Good Life".[2]

In his defense of the life of the mind, Kateb acknowledges the importance of "educated feelings" and the significance of play in that life. He speaks of the values of "playing at life", and of its virtue in the "enrichment of character" and in enabling people to "experience the higher pleasures" which however, must be kept under control by the higher faculties. What are these faculties? Kateb's answer is revealing:

> ... play is play: there must be some steadiness, some seriousness in the midst of this release and fluidity. Once again, the cultivation of higher faculties provides the answer. Greater in seriousness than even the making of beautiful objects and the doing of glorious deeds is the life of knowing ... We would compound the intellectualist heresy and say that man possessed of the higher faculties in their perfection is the model for utopia and already exists outside it ...

Kateb, a very up-to-date Plato, makes it clear that no "metaphysical theory of the world" underlies this contention. He is talking as a plain scholar in behalf of the plain factual knowledge to which the contemporary university professor and researcher aspire, which decidely does *not* include such *outré* things as, say, the knowledge of God, the playful knowledge of the lover of Mozart, or the presumptive wisdom of sages and prophets.

It must suffice to say that Mr. Kateb, no doubt happily, does not belong to what I have called the league of youth. For one thing they conceive the life of the mind in very different terms from the tradition which he represents. They do not despise scholarship certainly. But they are more sceptical of the undisputedly supreme worth of investigations of which the sciences provide a paradigm, and of the tendency, from the Greek philosophers on, to view the arts either as inferior vehicles of knowledge or else as expressions of emotion and feeling which are therefore of secondary value. The new youth tends to view man's higher faculties and indeed the whole life of the mind itself in less abstractly intellectualistic and hierarchical terms. Accordingly they regard the prerogatives of science in the educational sphere and the rights of scientifically oriented youths as in no sense primary or preemptive. The love of truth, particularly as the scholar-scientist views it, is only one of the major passions of the mind. In a certain way indeed, the deep vein of equalitarianism which is elsewhere such a persistent theme among members of the new youth, also shows itself here in the equal respect it pays scientists, poets, painters, dancers and philosophers.

Beyond this, however, they find distasteful the whole mentality which so delights in ranking "glorious deeds" below (or above) other forms of action. Imaginative works of love and affection are as wonderful and often as difficult as any others. Why should we not accept them with the same regard as we accord other manifestations of human genius? But this brings us finally to corresponding differences between their religious attitudes and those of many exponents of the Judeo-Christian tradition for whom the supreme, not to say the only authentic religious act, is comprehended exclusively in such phrases as "the love of God". Most of them are unorthodox. But I am impressed both by their sustained religious seriousness and by their tolerance for all genuine expressions of the sense of the holy and the wonderful. And in fact, among no group in our time is the sense of the *profane* in our common social life a source of greater sorrow. Indeed, it is the absence of any authentic religious spirit in the routines of conventional institutional activity which makes them despair of their human worth.

7

In bringing this discussion of youth and its rights toward its conclusion, I now propose to shift perspectives, moving outside the league of youth to a conceivably wider community of human beings of which the members of that league may well (and as I think rightly) regard themselves as members. In the first instance however, I shall continue the discussion in essentially ethical terms. It is for this reason that I have stressed the term "community" here rather than "society" or "social system". As here understood a community is not itself an institution or network of institutions, though it may establish institutions that serve in various ways as its agencies. (By an institution here I have in mind such things as banks, courts of laws, electoral colleges and universities.) An individual can be the member of a society against his will; he may also unwittingly and in some measure fulfill the functions of a class or perform the functions assigned to him by a social system while feeling little or no sense of moral obligation in doing so. Or like many of us, he may be selfdivided in this respect. And so he may proceed by stages from dissent to resistance, and from thence to rebellion and revolution according to the equality and direction of that self-division. But one cannot revolt against a community; one can only leave it, cease to acknowledge oneself as one of its members. This is because a community is by definition like a "congregation" of religious worshippers: it has no reality or meaning save insofar as its members conceive themselves as belonging to one another in continuing relations of mutual trust and respect. In short one cannot be the member of a community without feeling a basic moral responsibility to it and to its members.

But while it is impossible to conceive anyone as being the member of a community, in the sense I have in mind, without enjoying certain rights, which are among the conditions of membership, there seems to me no reason in logic to suppose that every member of a community should have exactly the same rights and responsibilities. Accordingly, I shall make a distinction between two sorts of communal rights, one generic, the other more special. Thus for example, while as one may well imagine, every member of a community might properly claim a right to life and to as much negative freedom as is compatible with the survival and the pursuance of other primary ends of the community, it might also be argued that certain rights are to be enjoyed only by certain members of classes thereof. Thus for example, elderly persons no longer capable of fending for themselves, might properly claim rights to certain forms of protection or to comforts to which other members of a community have no rightful claim.

Now let me emphatically assert that if youths are to be regarded as members of the wider community of men of which I have spoken, their youth does not exempt them from responsibilities pertaining to the generic rights of all of its members. Thus they must (let us assume) respect or even be obliged to protect, in many situation, the lives of their fellows. And they must at the same time respect the negative freedoms of other members. (Here as elsewhere we may also reasonably assume that rights like responsibilities are rarely, if ever, absolutely unconditional; they hold as we say, *ceteris paribus,* so that it may on occasion be necessary to perform acts that radically limit or override a particular right.) But in this essay our concern is primarily with rights of youth. And it is their special rights within the community of men that now concern me, and in particular those rights that derive not from their common powers of judgment and deliberation, nor even from their capacities to acquire or develop such powers, their potentialities, that is, as "adults", but from the qualities of their youth itself. Here our earlier psychological and conceptual analyses, provide indispensable clues. Thus specifically, I have in mind among the special rights of youth in the wider community of men those necessary for them to fulfill themselves as youths: their enormous capacities for learning, invention, and creation. But also quite unsentimentally, I believe it all the more necessary to stress in these days, when pundits talk endlessly of "law and order", their extraordinary problems of love and companionship, identity and self-discovery, in virtue of which they should have rights to a special tolerance, patience, and quiet assistance that are more extensive than older members of the wider community may decently claim for themselves. And if this tolerance and patience are not forthcoming, and they are not accordingly protected against the thuggery of police and the retributive justice of benighted administrators of the draft, the price in alienation and dissociation from the wider community will be a calamity, not for themselves alone but for us all.

But the preceding sentence places the accent in the wrong place. For the proper emphasis here should be on the positive endowment of young people, not potentialities from which other presumably more mature powers may come if they are to be accorded liberties "we" would not claim for ourselves. This endowment, in the age of youth, is already at flood tide, in some respects as strong and mature as it will ever be. Save for unconscionable accident, a Keats or a Schubert, a Pascal or a Frank Ramsey might have gone on in later years to fulfill a genius at which the rest of us could only marvel. This in no way blunts my point. At eighteen or twenty or twenty-five many men are more "mature" than they will ever be again and have already done things—performed "glorious deeds", created "beautiful objects", discovered theorems—and paradoxes—which are as splendid, as lovely, as true as the human spirit and mind can ever achieve.

From this I conclude that in certain directions rights of youth are not in the least like the rights of "minors": the rights that is, of potential adults or the potential rights of adults. They are rights in full being that belong to youth itself. And if these rights carry with them subsidiary rights to forgiveness and excuse, this only proves the greatness and the wisdom—the adulthood—of the great community of men which I have in mind and to which I aspire to belong. This is not to suggest that every youth is a genius, or every young person just because he is young, is a great benefactor of the human race. It is to say rather that there exist dimensions and possibilities of experience as fully realized in youth as they are likely ever to be again, and hence that the great community of men owes them special consideration in the form of rights of youth which by the nature of the case can involve no corresponding obligations on the part of youths to other members of that community. I have argued that generically rights are not practices. But now powerfully I can use the point in saying that such rights ought, as far as possible, to be translated into social practices in the form both of economic supports and of continuing educational aid, fellowships, grants in aid, and the life which will afford them the leisure necessary to fulfill themselves as youths. Too often in our society youth is treated either as a period of rapid preparation for adult life or else as a time in which, if they have no special intellectual or artistic talents, youths should be put to work at jobs that are menial, less interesting and less rewarding than those of their elders. Older people we sometimes think have thereby earned the right to an increasingly early retirement, a time of leisure, in which to do as they please. But an affluent society, were it wise, should, as it could, extend to the young comparable periods or intervals of prolonged leisure in which they too could follow their bent as youths. In short, an inconceivably wealthy society like ours might well turn its immense economic and technological resources to the liberation of all young people from the full necessities comprehended under the phrase "earning a living". One can even look forward to an age in which it will be time enough to start earning a living after one has lost the bloom of youth. Nor is there any need to view such a period of leisure as a period either of idleness or of more extended preparation for the rigors of later life. Just the contrary. It is possible, moreover, to envisage forms of education, artistic, intellectual or cultural activity, in which instead of being taught by elders who seek to pass on skills, forms of knowledge, technical or otherwise, which they as elders greatly prize, young people would do better to teach one another in ways that are appropriate to their own perspectives and interests and that develop powers which youths as such find worthy of cultivation. Institutions of higher learning of and not merely for the young need not be separated entirely from existing institutions. And multiversities which contain schools of dentistry and departments of home economics, not to mention the burgeoning cross-departmental area studies that enlist the energies of teachers trained in widely different disciplines, might very well establish "colleges" in which, at the same time, the young could engage in forms of study whose content, modes of instruction and personnel they themselves largely determine. Well, why not?

Finally a word must be said about those more generic human rights which, at present, youths possess to a large degree only in potency. The odd thing about the present situation is that although we like to pretend that owing to their immaturity they are also exempt from many of the responsibilities of adult persons, many harsh and dangerous responsibilities are now borne mainly by young people that require of them skills, understanding and judgment at least as complex as those possessed by their elders. Further, when we consider the subtle problems of conscience which must be confronted, for example by youthful dissenters and conscientious objectors, it is evident that we expect of them forms of moral development and powers of religious and ethical discrimination at least as advanced as those which we oldsters fancy ourselves as possessing. However, the age of youth especially in our time, has proved itself to be an age of moral idealism and dedication which fully entitles our youths to enjoy in act most, or all, of the generic rights we claim for ourselves. As I have elsewhere remarked, a young person mature enough to understand what it may mean to die for his country is also old enough to decide or to help to decide, whether the cause is worth dying for.

It is a fact that, despite various breakdowns in our school systems, including our institutions of higher learning, many young people in virtue of their extraordinarily extensive informal as well as formal educations, are vastly more developed as persons than either the youths of twenty or thirty years ago, when I myself was young, or the middle-agers the youths of that time have now become. Like many of my academic colleagues, I find to my acute embarrassment, that many of my students are not only more sensitive and imaginative than I am—that I take for granted—they are also more cultivated and in some respects by my own standards, wiser. For among other things, they know in the fullest sense how near to death is all mankind. I am astonished both by the gentleness of their manners and by the simplicity of their lives. And if drugs are a problem for them, they or their analogues are problems for us all. It goes without remark that in the face of all the forms of suffering, mental as well as physical, with which our society and its institutions have threatened them or else inflicted upon them over and over again, their courage shames us all. Neither dismissal from college, social harassment and ostracism, jail, injury or murder, deflect them from their determination to see not only that justice is done themselves, but also that our whole society commit itself to that reawakening of the community of spirit which begins with justice but ends with great-heartedness and love. By any standards that we, their elders, may in reason apply to ourselves, they have attained adulthood.

This being true, the problem of their political and legal rights in principle pretty well takes care of itself. The state and the legal system, so far as they strive to be just and to serve the common good, deserve respect from members of the party of humanity. But the state and the legal systems are not ends in themselves, but serviceable agencies of human communities. Or if they may sometimes be more, then this is so only insofar as they become primary carriers and symbols of man's communal life. Hence no political and legal order that deserves our loyalty can be repressive or deny to any member of the human community which it serves and symbolizes any right relevant to the maintenance and progress of that order. There can be no quarrel with the thesis that the state, as an agency of that community, may properly be viewed as a guardian that in effect holds in trust the rights of children, of the senile or the insane. But despite Plato, it cannot be a guardian to adult citizens. Thus if, as I claim, our youth is adult and already belongs to the human community in the most active sense of the term, then it is entitled to every legal and political right required for participation in the political process.

Such rights we must remember cannot include merely negative liberties, permissions to vote, run for office and the rest. For important as they may be, they do not remotely suffice for effective citizenship. Hence such negative liberties must be implemented by rights that enable their full and proper exercise. In the case of youth particularly, this means above all more and better education. For in the modern age education is virtually the condition of all the other positive freedoms, economic and political, as well as intellectual and spiritual. But education decidedly is not enough, even if our educational system were, as it so tragically is not, up to its own responsibilities. Youths must therefore be entitled to all the forms of social security as we call it, required for realization of their powers, not now simply as youths but as citizens.

These, I have been told, are utopian dreams. Are they? Well then, as the poet has said, responsibilities begin in dreams, and unless someone holds himself responsible, as we have seen, rights do not exist. With all possible emphasis I say it: they had better not remain dreams forever. For youth is not only restless; it is also knowledgeable and determined. As never before it has reached an understanding of its own identity, its strength, its indispensability to any advanced social system like our own. But this is no reason to be afraid. Rather is it a reason for us, not their guardians but their advocates and friends, to make certain that the league of youth remains part of the good society of which the word "America" was once a symbol. For only we ourselves can finally drive them out.

Notes

[1] Another version of this paper will be published by the University of Georgia Press, Athens, Ga.

[2] Kateb, G., Utopia and the Good Life in *Utopias and Utopian Thought,* ed. by Frank E. Manuel, The Dedaelus Library, Houghton Mifflin Company & American Academy of Arts and Sciences, 1966, p. 257.

The Enmity between Generations and its Probable Ethological Causes

By Konrad Lorenz

Seewiesen, Germany

1. *Darwinian approach and the question of adaptation*

"Ethology" is simply the application to the field of behaviour study of all those methods of approach which, since the days of Charles Darwin, are regarded as obligatory in all other branches of biological research. In other words, ethology regards behaviour as a *system* which owes its existence and its special form to a series of historical events which have taken place in the course of phylogeny. The purely causal question *why* a living system happens to be structured as it is and not otherwise, cannot be answered except by investigating the history of its evolution, in other words its *phylogeny*.

Investigating behaviour, including human behaviour, from the phylogenetical viewpoint has brought ethology into the center of an ideological controversy which is still going on. The doctrine that human behaviour is entirely determined by processes of conditioning which are brought about by environmental influence, originated from an immoderate generalisation and simplification of the findings of I. P. Pavlov. It became the basic theory of American behaviorism, yet it would imply injustice and even slander to call it the "behaviouristic" doctrine, because many intelligent scientists who consider themselves "behaviourists" have never believed in it. I therefore suggest the term "pseudo-democratic" doctrine. This is justified by the fact that the doctrine derives its world-wide distribution as well as its moral weight from the rather insiduous distortion of a democratic truth: it is a truth and indubitably a moral postulate that all men should have equal opportunities to develop. But an untrue dogma is easily derived from that truth (if only by those that reject logic, as Philip Wylie has pointed out): that all men are potentially equal. The doctrine carries the premise one step further by asserting that man is born as a tabula rasa and that all his behaviour is determined by conditioning.

Ethology has run foul of this doctrine by demonstrating irrefutably that all behaviour, exactly like all bodily structure, can develop in the ontogeny of the individual only along the lines and within the possibilities of species-specific programs which have been mapped out in the course of phylogeny and laid down in the code of the genome. "Biology", says Philip Wylie, "has proven that men are not equal, identical, similar or anything of the sort, from the instant of conception. Common sense ought to have made all that evident to Java man. It didn't and still doesn't, since common sense is what men most passionately wish to evade." This passion has the character of truly religious zeal. The pseudo-democratic doctrine has indeed become a world religion. Like many religions, it is the simplification of a truth, as such easy to understand, and it is welcome to those that are interested in manipulating great masses of people. It would indeed be of equal advantage to capitalistic producers and to super-Stalinistic rulers, if men, by proper conditioning, could be moulted into absolutely uniform and absolutely obedient consumers or communistic citizens. This explains the otherwise surprising fact that the pseudodemocratic doctrine rules suppreme in America as well as in the Soviet Union and in China!

Like all devout supporters of a religion, the doctrinaires of the pseudo-democratic doctrine do not stop at anything when it comes to silencing the heretic. The approach to human behaviour as to a phylogenetically evolved system has been rejected on a large number of pseudo-rational reasons and branded as immoral in a large number of ways, of which the book *Man and Aggression* edited by M. F. Ashley Montagu offers a rich choice of examples, of which one is sufficient to demonstrate the near-religious bias. "There is", says Ashley Montagu, "not the slightest evidence or ground for assuming that the alleged 'phylogenetically adapted instinctive' behaviour of other animals is in any way relevant to the discussion of the motive-forces of human behaviour. The fact is, that with the exception of the instinctoid reactions of infants to sudden withdrawals of support and to sudden loud noises, the human being is entirely instinctless." More modern representatives of the pseudo-democratic doctrine take another and more subtle attitude. While conceding that ethology is, in principle, correct in trying to separate phylogenetically evolved and ontogenetically acquired programs of behaviour, they contend that ethologists attribute an exaggerated importance to this distinction, in other words, that the question "innate or acquired?" is no more than a quibble. It isn't and I shall come back to this point at the end of this paper.

For the moment it suffices to say that most of the properties which we encounter in the structure as well as in the behaviour of organisms owe their specific form to that oldest and most efficient of cognitive processes which we call *adaptation*. The fact of adaptedness entails a question characteristic of biology and unknown to chemistry and physics, the question "what for?". When we ask "what for has the cat crooked retractile claws?" and answer "to catch mice with", we are not questing for the ultimate teleological meaning of the cat's claws, we are only using an abridged way of expressing a truly scientific *causal* question which, fully stated, should read: "what is the function whose survival value exerted the selection pressure *causing* cats to evolve that particular form of claws?".

A lifetime spent in asking this question (to which I shall refer to henceforward as Charles Darwin's question) with reference to a great many morphological structures and behaviour patterns, results in great support for Darwin's theories, for the simple reason that so very, very often a clear-cut and convincing answer can be found. In fact, we have grown so accustomed to receiving such an answer that we find it hard to believe that there *are* any highly complex and differentiated patterns or structures which do *not* owe their specific form to the selection pressure exerted by their function. The more bizarre they appear on their face value, the surer one may be of discovering such a function.

2. Creative integration and the method of approaching systems

Before expounding the methods obligatory in the approach of complex systems, a few words must be said about the way in which unprecedented systemic properties spring into existence when two pre-existent but independent systems are linked together; if, for instance, two systems of electric circuit, one running over a coil, the other obstructed by a condensor, are linked together, the new system will possess the property of oscillation which is not to be found, on principle, in any of the two subsystems in their unconnected state. This kind of event obviously has happened and is happening whenever phylogenesis makes a step forward. The term "evolution" as well as the German word "Entwicklung", implies etymologically that something *preformed* is merely being unfolded in the process. None of our western languages possesses a verb for the coming-into-existence of something entirely new, because at the time of their origin, the only process of development known was that of ontogeny for which these terms are indeed etymologically adequate. Sensing its inadequacy for the creative events of phylogeny, some philosophers used the term "emergence" which is still worse as it implies that something which was invisible only to a literally superficial view, becomes visible by surfacing. In my paper "Innate Bases of Learning" in which I discussed these matters in detail, I suggested to use, in a new sense, the term "fulguration" which had been introduced by medieval mystics to describe acts of creation, implying, of course, that it was God's own lightning that caused something new to spring into existence. For the scientist, lightning is an electric spark like any other, and if he notices an unexpected spark within a system, the first thing it brings to mind is a short circuit. This makes the term fulguration strangely appropriate. That which constitutes a step forward in the sequence of creative phylogenetic events regularly consists in the coming-into-existence of a new systemic property which is caused by a new causal relationship springing up, within the living system, between two of its pre-existing subsystems, integrating them into a new one of higher order. As we refuse to believe in miracles, we are convinced that it is always a structural change that brings about such a new integration and causes new laws of nature which had not previously existed, to come into existence.

The new lawfulness arising out of new structures never abolishes the laws of nature prevailing within the living system previous to the new event of integration. Even the systemic properties of the newly-united sub-systems need not be entirely lost. This is true of every step taken by evolution, even of its greatest and initial step from the inorganic to the organic. It is quite particularly true of what we, in admitted pride, are apt to consider the second-greatest step, the one leading from the anthropoid to Man. The processes of life are still physical and chemical processes, though, by virtue of the complicated structure of chain molecules, they are something very particular besides. It would be plain nonsense to assert that they are "nothing else but" chemical and physical processes. An analogous relationship exists between man and his pre-human ancestors: man certainly is an animal but it is simply not true that he is nothing but an animal.

3. *Cumulative tradition as an example*

The fulguration of those properties which are essential of man and which do not exist, at least not together and not to any appreciable degree, in any other animal, furnishes an excellent example of the way in which new systemic properties come into existence with new connections of pre-existing systems. Exploratory behaviour leading to a considerable degree of objective knowledge of objects exists in many animals and so does true tradition of individually acquired knowledge. In Man alone they are brought together into an integrated system.

Self-exploration which had been dawning in the anthropoids, must have progressed by leaps and bounds as our forefathers proceded from tool-using to tool-making. The working hand, as a part of the own body, together with the manipulated object in the same visual field could not fail to draw attention to the fact that one's own subject is also an object, and one extremely worthy of consideration! By the consciousness of his own self, by "reflexion", a new objectivity was forced upon man's attitude to the objects of his environment. Originally, and for the majority of all animals, one object possesses entirely different meanings dependent on the different psychological and physiological states in which the organism happens to be at the moment. A potential prey animal has entirely different "valences" for a hungry lion and for a satiated one. Once we have realized that we are ourselves "real things" participating in an interaction with the other "things" in our environment, we have automatically gained a higher and altogether new level of objectivity trandscending by far that which had hitherto been possible by virtue of the abstracting function of Gestalt perception and by the effects of exploratory play. Not being hungry, we might be totally disinterested in a food object and pass it by as the sated lion does, but knowing ourselves as we do, we are able to take our own momentary state into consideration and abstract from it, rightly foreseeing that the object in question may and will become highly interesting in a short while.

It is only together with and on the basis of all the other objective functions which already pre-existed in higher animals, that true reflection could come into being. Self-exploration could never have happened except on the basis of a pre-existing, highly developed exploratory behaviour. The comprehension of a concept could never have been achieved had it not been for the observation of the own prehensile hand taking hold of and interacting with environmental objects.

Tradition existed before that. Rats can pass on the knowledge concerning the deadly effects of a poison over many generations without any individual repeating the personal experience leading to that knowledge. Jackdaws can hand down, to the unexperienced young, their knowledge of dangerous predators and monkeys have been known to pass on the tradition of certain acquired motor skills, for instance that of washing sweet potatoes in sea water. However, all these processes of the handing down of acquired knowledge are dependent on the presence of their object. Without it, the rat cannot tell its young what poison not to eat, nor can the jackdaw teach its progeny what predator to avoid, nor the monkey demonstrate its skill. Even so, we cannot quite explain why traditional knowledge does not tend to accumulate in any species of social animal beyond the degree to which we actually find it developed. Thus, right up to the fulguration of cumulative tradition in man, the genome remained the only mechanism capable of an accumulating long-time storage of knowledge.

With the coming-together of conceptual thought and tradition, unprecedented systemic properties sprang into existence. The continuity of tradition made it possible for concepts to become associated with the free symbol of the spoken world. The growth of syntactic language was thus rendered possible, and, in turn, opened a new avenue to an accumulation of traditional knowledge, ever increasing with the number of generations following one another. The new system is that which is generally called culture and its unique systemic property consists in its being able, like the genome, to store practically unlimited quantities of information and, at the same time, being able, unlike the genome, to acquire knowledge worth storing, within minutes instead of millenia. If a man learns how to make or invents a bow and arrow, not only his progeny but all his culture will henceforward possess these tools, nor is the likelihood of their ever being forgotten any greater than that of a bodily organ of equal survival value ever becoming rudimentary. The new systemic property is neither more nor less than the famous inheritance of acquired characters and its biological consequences are hard to exaggerate. It was the selection pressure of accumulating tradition which caused man's telencephalon to grow to its present size. It is bodily structures, such as the forebrain and the various speech areas in the dominant hemisphere which make man *by nature* a creature of culture. Without cultural tradition, these structures would be as devoid of function as the wings of an ostrich, only more so. Yet all these tremendous changes which certainly do make man something that is very different indeed from that which we would describe as "just an animal", were wrought by the rather simple integration of two sub-systems of behaviour, none of which is exclusively characteristic of our species.

Our knowledge of the way in which, during phylogeny, systems of higher integration came into being by a series of unique and unpredictable historic events, has far-reaching consequences in two entirely unrelated respects.

4. *The axiomatic scale of organismic values*

The first concerns our philosophy of values. We cannot help feeling that organic systems are the more valuable the more highly integrated they are, in fact our accustomed way of calling some animals higher and some lower is the immediate outcome of this inescapable value judgement. Its axiomatic nature is easily demonstrated by the following thought-experiment. Visualize yourself confronted with the task of killing, one after the other, a cabbage, a fly, a fish, a lizard, a guninea pig, a cat, a dog, a monkey and a baby chimpanzee. In the unlikely case that you should experience no greater inhibitions in killing the chimpanzee than in destroying the cabbage or the fly, my advice to you is to commit suicide at your earliest possible convenience, because you are a weird monstrosity and a public danger.

The scale of values extending between lower and higher organisms is quite independent of that other which stretches between all the degrees of less and more successful adaptation to environment. The chances of disadaptation and illness are roughly the same on all levels of creative integration; if anything, the higher creatures seem to be more vulnerable than the lower. A man or, for that matter, a whole culture may be in direct danger of disintegration and yet be of higher value than another which is in the best possible state of health and superlatively viable. We are apt to become aware of the independence of the two parameters of value judgement when we come to consider our own moral responsibility. Obedience to the moral law within us, as Immanuel Kant has called it, may often exact a behaviour which is far from healthy and not too rarely human beings are faced with the alternative of either behaving immorally or making the great sacrifice of martyrdom—which may as well be entirely in vain.

5. Methods obligatory in the approach to integrated systems

The second all-important consequence which is forced upon us by the realization of the "stratified" structure of organic systems concerns the strategy of their analysis. For obvious reasons, the first step to the understanding of a system which consists of a whole hierarchy of sub-systems, integrated into each other level by level, must be to gain some provisional survey knowledge of those subsystems which, on the highest level of integration, are immediately subordinate to the whole. To begin with this first task is the more obligatory, the more complicated and the more highly integrated the system under investigation actually is. In other words, the chances of gaining insight into the make-up of a system by atomistic and operationalistic methods decreases in proportion to its complication and its level of integration. We must be successful in quite a few inspired guesses in order to arrive even at that pre-hypothetical stage of vague suspicion which allows us to sift our observations sufficiently to arrive at a workable hypothesis as to what are the greatest and most widely embracing subsystems to approach. In this task, plain observation and the free play of our own Gestalt perception are the most promising methods. I wish to assert seriously and emphatically that in our first tentative approach to the understanding of complicated living systems, the "visionary" approach of the poet—which consists simply in letting Gestalt-perception rule supreme—gets us much farther than any pseudo-scientific measuring of arbitrarily chosen parameters. I do not mean that a man who is "nothing else but" a poet has a better chance of understanding integrated systems than a scientist has. What I want to express is that a scientist, with all the scientist's methodological and factual knowledge at his disposal, has no chance of ever understanding a complex living system such as that underlying human social behaviour, unless he utilizes his

Gestalt perception to the utmost, giving it an absolutely free rein while at the same time feeding into its ample hold as many pertinent observational data as he can get hold of. There are people who seem to be able to do just that. One of them is Erik Erikson who, in my opinion, knows more about the deepest roots of human behaviour than anybody else I could name.

6. *Pathological disturbance as a source of knowledge*

Even so, Gestalt perception would not lead us far enough in the understanding of really complex systems like that of human behaviour, to make it possible to begin applying the quantitative methods of verification, were it not for the help from a rather unexpected side.

There are cases in which Charles Darwin's question "what for" fails to get an answer. In captive animals and quite particularly in civilized men we find regularly recurring behaviour patterns which are not only devoid of value but even demonstrably detrimental to the survival of the individual as well as of the species. If one asks Darwin's question with regard to a military parade, a voodoo ceremony in Haiti, a sit-in of students at Vienna university or modern war, one finds oneself unable to obtain an answer—at least as long as one applies the question in the simple and unsophisticated way in which, as biologists, we are accustomed to put it.

When confronted with such a puzzling and disturbing behaviour pattern, my late friend Bernhard Hellmann used to ask another question: "Is this as the constructor intended it to be?" Though this question was asked half jestingly, it implies a deep realization of the existence of a borderline which, though extremely difficult to define, plays an all-important role in biological and particularly in medical thought: the borderline between the normal and the pathological, between health and illness.

When, in respect to some crazy pattern of human behaviour, we fail to get an answer to Charles Darwin's question "what for?" as well as to Bernhard Hellmann's question "is this how the constructor meant it to be?" we need not lose confidence in normal biological approach, though we have to resort to additional questions belonging to a different way of approach, to that of the medical man. In one of his last letters to me, my late friend Ronald Hargreaves, psychiatrist at Leeds, wrote that he had schooled himself to ask, in approaching any sort of mental disorder, two simultaneous questions. The first is: what is the normal survival function of the process here disturbed? The second is: what is the nature of the disturbance, and, in particular, is there an excess or a deficiency of the function in question?

At first sight it might seem that the unpredictable pathological disturbance of a system which is superlatively complicated and, therefore, most difficult to understand in any case, would add yet another and unsurmountable obstruction to the endeavour of its analysis. However, physiologists have known for a long time that this is not so. So far from being an additional obstacle to the analysis of a system, its pathological disturbance is, as often as not, the key to its analysis. In fact, the history of physiology has recorded a great number of cases in which the very existence of an important physiological mechanism or system was not even suspected until an illness caused by the disturbance of one of them drew the scientists' attention to it. The history of the discovery of endocrine glands and of the progress of their analysis offers an excellent paradigm of the method obligatory in approaching systems. When E. T. Kocher, in the attempt of curing hyperthyroidism had removed the thyroid gland, he found that he had provoked what he termed 'cachexia thyreopriva'. From this he deduced correctly that the function of the thyroid gland stood in a relation of balanced antagonism with that of other endocrine glands and that Basedow's disease, or hyperthyroidism, consisted in the disturbance of this equilibrium in favour of an excess of thyroid function.

The rationale of this approach is most strictly applicable to the majority of the disturbances nowadays observable in the social behaviour of human beings. Indeed very many of them consist in the loss of equilibrium between two or more behavioral systems, the word "system" being used in the sense of the excellent definition Paul Weiss has given in his paper "Determinism Stratified": a system is everything unitary enough to deserve a name. Ronald Hargreaves' double question ought to make everybody realize how inane it is to attribute the adjectives "good" or "bad" to any mechanism of behaviour, such as love, aggression, indoctrination, ritualisation, enthusiasm and so on. Like any endocrine gland, every one of these mechanisms is indispensable and, again like a gland, every one, by its excess or defect function, can lead to a destructive desequilibration. There is no human vice which is anything else but the excess of a function which, in itself, is indispensable for the survival of the species.

I shall now proceed to illustrate the application of Ronald Hargreaves' double question to certain phenomena which are obviously threatening our culture and which, in my opinion, can be attributed to the desequilibration of two important behavioral systems. The first is the mechanism which ensures that which Sigmund Freud described as the balanced economy of pleasure and displeasure. The second is the rather complicated system whose function it is to transmit traditional knowledge from one generation to the next, while at the same time making sure that obsolete items of tradition can be discarded and new ones acquired.

7. The disequilibration of pleasure-displeasure economy

I begin with the description of some symptoms which I believe to be caused by the disturbance of pleasure-displeasure equilibrium. Perhaps the most telling of these symptoms is the *urge for instant gratification*. In a considerable percentage of present-day humanity, and not only among the younger generation, there is a demonstrable decrease in the ability and willingness to strive for aims that can only be achieved in the future. Any goal that cannot be attained *at once* ceases to appear worth striving for. Even large business concerns refuse to look more than a very few years into the future. In science the unwillingness to undertake long-term programs has led to a deplorable neglect of *descriptive* branches in which a patient and protracted gathering of knowledge is obligatory.

Although it is not clear which is cause and which is effect, there is certainly a close connection between the current loss of patience and a general *inability to endure any kind of pain or displeasure*. The excessive consumption of anodynes and tranquillizers bears witness to this intolerance. Once I observed my nephew swallowing an enormous spoonful of pyramidon powder, and commiseratingly asked him whether he had got a bad headache. No, he said, but he was somewhat afraid that he might get one. Kurt Hahn tells a story about a pupil coming to school carrying with him a package of tablets which his parents had given him and which were guaranteed to be an unfailing cure against any onset of homesickness.

A third symptom, closely allied to the two already mentioned, is a general *unwillingness to move*. Any exertion of striated musculature has become unfashionable, to the point of changing the facial expression of large numbers of people: a tired, languishing, bored look, occasionally slightly overlaid by an expression of reproach and sulkiness is observable in all-too-many young people. Between the twenty-year-old of, say 1920 and those of 1969, there is a very considerable behavioural difference in the quantity of walking performed to enjoy nature. In the Vienna Woods which were teeming with young people in 1920, one rarely meets walkers, and if one does, they are over 60. Amongst young people who consider themselves as very sporting, there may be a certain willingness to perform muscular labour, but only for its own sake, and not in pursuance of any other goal. This would be considered as "work". Therefore, young people can be seen queuing-up for 40 minutes at a ski lift in favour of walking uphill for 20.

Technological production caters for the growing unwillingness to perform muscular work, a prosperous citizen cannot be expected to walk upstairs or to turn a crank to open a window or the sliding roof of his smart car: to press a button is the utmost he will condescend to do.

It was Kurt Hahn who called attention to the disquieting fact that this type of physical laziness is very often correlated with an accompanying *sluggishness of emotion*. A weakness of ability to feel *compassion* is, according to the great expert, a frequent concomitant of the typical laziness of blasé adolescents. I do not think I need mention examples, everyone knows many instances in which people have been tortured, killed or raped in well-frequented streets of big cities in the presence of hosts of inhumans who refused to "get involved" by assisting the victim. Inability to feel compassion also plays an important part in the acts of open hostility against weak old people of which adolescents often are guilty.

Now let us ask, in respect to the phenomena just described, the first of the two questions proposed by Ronald Hargreaves. What is the normal function which is miscarrying in each of these cases and what is the nature of its miscarriage? I think we can give a fairly probable tentative answer to these questions, and what is more, the same applies to all four of the phenomena mentioned.

All organisms capable of true conditioning possess a built-in mechanism whose function it is to mete out reward and punishment, reward for behaviour achieving survival value for the individual or the species, or both, and punishment for all that is contrary to these interests. "Reward" and "punishment" are terms here used only as shorthand for the functions of *reinforcing or extinguishing* the preceding behaviour. Pleasure and displeasure are the equally real subjective experiences which accompany these learning processes.

Many otherwise profound theories on learning have overlooked a fact which is of supreme importance to our consideration, namely that this highly integrated computing mechanism must possess in its program phylogenetically acquired information, in fact *knowledge of what is good and what is bad for the organism*. This mechanism "knows" all the values of reference which all the homoeostatic cycles within the organism are supposed to keep constant, it administers the punishment of making us feel lousy if anything is out of order in any of these regulating cycles, for instance if we have too little or too much oxygen, glucose or whatever else in our blood, if we are too hot or too cold etc. It rewards us by making us feel good whenever our behaviour has contributed to correct these values, as we do when we ingest the right kind of food ect. It puts a premium on performing any of the typical species-preserving activities in the biologically "right" manner.

This great teaching mechanism, the "innate schoolmarm" as I have jestingly called it, could, theoretically, work with reward (or reinforcement) alone, or with punishment (or extinguishing) alone. We have introspective knowledge, however, that it uses *both* principles and there are objective criteria supporting the assumption that the same is true of animals. It could be that it is just a case of assurance being made doubly sure, a procedure of which there are many examples in evolution. Another tentative answer, which I thought sufficient until quite recently, lies in the fact that it is difficult to make organisms behave in a very *specific* manner by the exclusive use of repellent stimuli. It is very hard to *drive* a bird into a cage, as one would have to use a large number of stimuli impinging from all spatial directions, with the exception of that of the cage door, to do so. Thus it would seem preferable to put some reward into the cage and thus entice the creature to enter it. We find that evolution has learned that trick and "applies" extinguishing procedures, if the biological aim is just to keep an animal away from noxious environmental influences, but "uses" the allurement of reinforcement in cases in which the organism is requested to do something more specific.

A further difference between reinforcing and extinguishing processes lies in the manner in which external stimulation is evaluated. In appetitive behaviour, in which the organism is endeavouring to reach the source of stimulation, any increase in the quantity of incoming stimuli acts as a reinforcement while, in avoidance behaviour, any decrease in stimulation reinforces the preceding mode of behaviour.

These considerations are quite correct, as far as they go, yet they do not contain the real answer to the question why the conditioning apparatus of higher animals is constructed on the basis of two opposing principles. The antagonistic effect of two independently variable motivations is necessary to uphold an *economic* equilibrium between certain biological advantages gained and the expenses incurred in gaining them. By virtue of conditioning, the organism is made capable of going straight for the achievement of some goal which has survival value and which offers a *future* reward, in spite of the fact that it has to begin its activity in the teeth of a *present* stimulus situation acting as a strongly extinguishing deterrent.

It is this element of *foresight* that constitutes the most important function of conditioning. It enables the organism to pay a price for something to be gained later, the price consisting of the expenditure of energy, of incurring certain risks and other disadvantages. The balance of pleasure and displeasure, all the phenomena which Sigmund Freud called "Lust-Ökonomie", represent the subjective side of that kind of deal.

If this negotiation is to yield, to the organism or its species, a net gain in terms of survival value, the price paid must be in proportion to the gain in gross which it purchases. It would be bad strategy for a wolf to go hunting, regardless of the cold, in a particularly bad winter's night, he simply could not afford to pay for one meal with a frozen toe or two. However, circumstances may arise, for instance a dire famine, in which our wolf would indeed be well advised to go hunting regardless of costs and risks, playing a single, last chance.

This example serves to illustrate that there is no constant relationship between the values of the goal achieved and the price paid for its achievement. Exactly as in commercial economy, the price which is to be considered as adequate in a given situation, is determined by the laws of supply and demand. The varying strength of the motivations causing appetitive behaviour is to a great extent determined by the *needs* of the organism or the species—very often indeed in a most direct manner by the tissue needs of the individual. The effectiveness which the achievement of the goal develops *as a reinforcement* of the preceding behaviour, varies in proportion to the strength of this motivation. The readiness to tolerate punishment which is unavoidable in the conquering of obstacles, does exactly the same. It is an immensely complicated and finely adjusted system of adaptively variable reinforcing and extinguishing mechanisms which achieve a balanced equilibrium in the organism's economy.

I believe that we can unhesitatingly answer Ronald Hargreaves' first question concerning the survival function of the disturbed mechanism by saying that the symptoms hitherto discussed, the inability to wait, the inability to bear displeasure, the unwillingness to move and the weakness of compassionate emotion are all caused by a disturbance of the mechanism achieving the balanced equilibrium of pleasure-displeasure-economy.

I proceed to Hargreaves' second question: what is the nature of the disturbance? In order to make my tentative answer intelligible, I must say a few more words about the physiological as well as about the historical properties of this balancing mechanism.

Like many other neuro-sensory functions, the mechanism under discussion is subject to habituation or "sensory adaptation". This term, though generally accepted by sense physiologists is not a happy choice, because the effect of the phenomenon need not necessarily be adaptive in the sense of survival. The *waning* of the response to an often-repeated stimulus—or combination of stimuli—is advantageous only on the premise of the statistical probability that an ever-recurrent stimulus is not likely to denote something really important. Whatever it signals is likely to be rather "cheap" economically. In some respects, habituation may be similar to fatigue and it may even have evolved phylogenetically from certain forms of fatigue. Its function, however, is entirely different. Also, habituation is not localized in the peripheral sense organ, but, as Margret Schleidt has shown experimentally, in the central nervous system itself. Habituation is not always specific to one particular stimulus, but often to a highly complicated combination of stimuli. It is only the threshold of this particular stimulation that is raised, or in other words, it is only the response to this that decreases, while all other responses to all other stimulus situations, even for very similar ones, remain unaltered.

The second physiological property, also common to very many neural functions, is that of *inertia*. Any time-lag in a regulative cycle leads to the effects of rebound and oscillation. If a deviation from the "Soll-Wert" is caused in any homoestatic cycle, the restitution of this value is hardly ever reached in a direct dampened curve, but in most cases *overshoots* the reference value and only reaches it at last by way of one or several oscillations above and below the value. This overshooting of the mark set by the regulating system constitutes what is generally called a rebound or a contrast. Among other more complicated causes, contrast is one of the factors which makes activities appear in bursts or bouts, instead of "dribbling" constantly. In the constant presence of food, for example, an animal does not eat constantly and very slowly, but eats its fill and then stops for a considerable time. This is because the regulating cycles of food uptake overshoot the mark both ways: first the animal continues eating by virtue of inertia, slightly longer than it ought to, then, having slightly overeaten, it remains refractory to the constantly present food, because the stimulation emanating from the latter, by "creeping in", elicits a response again slightly later than would exactly correspond to the threshold of the reference value.

Lastly, in order to understand the function of the pleasure-displeasure-equilibrating apparatus, it is necessary to consider the circumstances, under which it originated historically. At the time of its probable origin humanity eked out a precarious existence. Hence it bears the earmarks of a selection pressure working in the direction of the utmost economy. At the dawn of humanity, men could not afford to pay too high a price for anything. They *had* to be extremely reluctant to make any expenditure of any kind, of energy, of risk, or of possessions. Any possible gain had to be greedily seized upon. Laziness, gluttony and some other present-day vices were virtues then. To shun everything disagreeable, like cold, danger, muscular exertion and so on, was the most advisable thing they could do. Life was hard enough to exclude all danger of becoming too "soft". These were the circumstances to which our mechanism balancing pleasure and displeasure has been adapted in evolution. They must be kept in mind in order to understand its present miscarriage.

For obvious reasons, our apparatus of pleasure-displeasure-economy is prone to disfunction under the conditions of modern civilisation. Man has been all too successful in evading and circumventing all stimulus situations causing displeasure, and all too clever in devising more and more rewarding "super-normal" enticements. The inevitable consequence of this has been an ever increasing sensitisation to all stimulation eliciting sensations of displeasure, accompanied by a corresponding waning of the responses to formerly pleasurable stimulus situations. It is an old hackneyed truth that there is no joy, however great, which does not become stale with constant repetition, yet modern humanity seems to have forgotten it. Furthermore, in all his alleged wisdom, man does not seem to understand that the highest levels of happiness which are accessible to him at all, can only be reached by exploiting the phenomenon of contrast. There is no path to the peaks of bliss except through the valley of sorrows and modern man is so pampered and coddled that he shrinks from paying even the moderate toll of discomfiture and toil which nature has set as a price for all earthly joy. It is as simple as that!

To expend any joy down to the point of full exhaustion, is outright bad pleasure-economy and still worse, to push that point of heightened threshold still further up by finding supranormal stimulation. Such a procedure is comparable to driving a cart with a permanently tired horse which, by continuous flogging cannot made to go faster than a rested animal would go without the whip. Besides being unhealthy for the horse, this precludes a maximum performance which can occasionally be attained by whipping the well-rested horse. One should think that the stupidest human being on earth should see through that error, yet people don't. There are many sides to civilized life in which intelligent people commit faults analogous to that of a silly mother who thinks that she can increase the food-uptake of a weak child by feeding it exclusively on delicacies. In regard to the economy of pleasure, this is just as stupid as that which has frequently enough happened in commercial economy. The whaling industry, for instance, has exhausted the whale population to the point of leaving hardly anything worth exploiting, and *keeps* it exhausted, because the exploiters lack the intelligence and foresight, as well as the financial reserves necessary for the only sensible strategy of letting the whale population recover to the extent at which it would furnish a maximum yield. This is a perfect commercial model of that which happens in human pleasure-economy.

The inability to wait, to hold back for the period necessary to let the threshold of pleasurable stimulation recover their normal values, has, of course, pernicious consequences for the *rhythm* in which consummatory activities are repeated. As I have already explained, the apparatus which balances the price to be paid against the advantage to be gained, is also responsible for the important function of making activities appear in bursts or bouts, instead of "dribbling" continuously. This, however, is exactly what happens as the consequence of the disturbance here under discussion. The subject afflicted by it is unable to put up, even for a short period, with the slightest need. Like my young nephew, he may even be so afraid of the mildest pang of any want that he has to anticipate it even before he feels it. The normal rhythm of eating with enjoyment, after having got really hungry, the enjoyment of any consummation after having strenuously striven for it, the joy in achieving success after toiling for it in near-despair, in short the whole glorious amplitude of the waves of human emotions, all that makes life worth living, is dampened down to a hardly perceptible oscillation between hardly perceptible tiny displeasures and pleasures. The result is an immeasureable *boredom*.

If you have eyes to see, you will perceive this boredom in a truly frightening multitude of young faces. Have you ever watched young people courting, kissing, petting and all-but-copulating in public? You need not be a peeping Tom to do it, you cannot help observing if you walk in the evening through Hyde Park or ride on the Underground in London. In these unfortunates, the fire of love and the thrill of sex are toned-down to the intensity of emotion to be observed in a pampered baby half-disgustedly sucking an unwanted lollipop. The bored juvenile is in a particular hell of his own, he must be an object of sincere pity and we must not be deterred from our commiseration by the fact that he hates us more than anything in the world.

The causes of this hostility consist only partly in the disturbance of the pleasure principle of which I have spoken hitherto. To a greater part they lie in a disfunction of the mechanism which transmits cultural norms of social behaviour from one generation to the next. Of this I shall speak anon, but first I must discuss the arousal of hate by effects already mentioned.

The "going soft" is a rapidly progressive process, therefore the younger generation is automatically more severly afflicted by it than the older. Parents are therefore easily tempted to play the role of the "Spartan father" and to sermonize on the merits of a hard, frugal life. This of course is the worst thing they can do. The therapists who have successfully combated the phenomenon of "Verweichlichung" (the German word is the most descriptive by far, "pampering" or "coddling" seem to apply chiefly to the bringing-up of children and "effeminate" is a libel to women!) are unanimous in the opinion that the circumstances counteracting it must emanate from the impersonal environment and not from any human agency. Helmut Schulze, in his book *Der progressiv domestizierte Mensch* has pointed out some very interesting possibilities of therapy, and long before him Kurt Hahn has applied the same principle.

The nature of the therapy illuminates the primary root of the disturbance: the essence of all countermeasures consists in getting the "patient" into *real* trouble, which, if possible, concerns not only himself but is strongly evocative of social responses. The most effective therapy for "blasé" adolescents which Kurt Hahn could devise, was setting them the task of saving life at some danger of their own. Helmut Schulze came to identical conclusions on the basis of the paradoxical observation that some of his patients who had lived in concentration camps and who had, under these dreadful circumstances, proved to be heroes of courage and altruism, became neurotic or went to pieces in other ways as soon as they had regained the security of a soft civilized life. Another illustration of the same paradox is furnished by the not infrequent cases of young people who find the softness of modern civilized life boring to the point of attempting suicide, succeed in hurting themselves badly and afterwards, amazingly, go on living happily with a broken back or with their optic nerves shot through. Now they have a real trouble to face and to conquer, they find life worth living.

To sum up: the cause of the symptoms hitherto discussed is, at least to a great part, to be found in the fact that the mechanisms equilibrating pleasure and displeasure are thrown off balance because civilized man *lacks obstacles* which force him to accept a healthy amount of painful, toilsome displeasure, or alternatively perish.

8. *Disequilibration of mechanisms preserving and adapting culture*

I now turn to the description of another set of symptoms, those which I believe to be caused by the unbalancing of that system of behaviour whose function it is to transmit tradition from one generation to the next, and, simultaneously, to eliminate obsolete and to acquire new and adaptive information. All these phenomena add up to a most alarming hostility which the younger generation bears the older and which is characteristically reciprocated only halfheartedly and only by a small proportion of the adults. A very small part of this hostility may be caused by the ill-advised attempt on the part of the older generation, to act the part of the proverbial "Spartan father" in regard to the softening process already discussed. The young might forgive us our admonitions to take some exercise, they might even condone our earning the money on which they live. They hate us for other reasons and I am afraid they hate us very deeply indeed. It is not only the "rockers" who do so, though others do not go to the extremes of torturing people just because they are old. An ambivalent element of hate is noticeable, to the initiated, even in the behaviour of sons who are overtly and consciously quite fond of their parents. Their hate is not *personal,* it is directed at *cultural* properties of the older generation. They hate our mode of life, our attitudes, the way we dress, wash and shave, they distrust us and refuse to believe anything we say. They think that they are gloriously free from parental influence while in reality they are copying the preceding generation slavishly, if with a negative sign. When Hippies wear elaborate velvet waistcoats and long, gloriously curling locks, skin-tight trousers and chains round their necks, they don't do it because they really like it, but because *we dislike it*. All this is done to spite us, and the horrible thing is that we react exactly in the way we are expected to do. At least, I myself, have to confess to a desire to kick the behinds of the languidly pretty young men, and slightly less of the bearded unwashed type. I am very angry with myself because I cannot prevent myself from getting angry, which is quite unworthy of the initiated ethologist—but there it is! Other old men, more dignified than I am and less prone to subject their own motives to a self-ridiculing ethological analysis, simply get uninhibitedly furious with the younger generation and this mutual hostility, by a process of escalation, can reach dangerous levels wherever the younger and the older generation are thrust upon each other, as they are, for instance, at schools and universities.

The enmity which so many members of the younger generation bear the older has a lot in common with that which can be observed between two hostile ethnic groups. The term "ethnic group", is here meant to describe a very wide concept: that of any community whose individuals are kept together by their *regard for common symbols* rather than by personal friendship. The budding of an ethnic group begins with the first occurence of *culturally ritualized norms of behaviour* which are specific to the group. These ritualized norms may consist at first of quite inconspicuous mannerisms, in an accent, in ways of dressing etc., as can be observed in schools, small military units and similar small communities.

These group-specific ritualized norms play a most important part in keeping the group together. They are *valued* by all its members. "Good manners" are, of course, the manners of one's own group, its ways of dressing are those that are considered "elegant". Deviations from the rules set by these ritualizations are regarded as contemptible and *socially inferior*. Therefore, two comparable groups of this kind, each being aware of the contempt in which it is held by the other, will show a quick escalation of hostility. Hostile contact of this kind enhances the value which each group attributes to its specific ritualizations. Ethnologists have known for a long time that the etiquette and the old modes of peasant dresses which otherwise are rapidly disappearing all over Europe, retain their traditional force in localities where different ethnic groups are in direct contact with each other, for instances in Hungary wherever Slovakian and Hungarian villages are bordering on each other.

Ethnic groups developing independently of each other become more and more different with the lapse of time. In other words, their distinguishing properties permit deductions concerning their age and history much in the same way as the genetically fixed properties of animal and plant species permit the reconstruction of their genealogical tree. The *comparative* method is equally applicable in the elucidation of cultural and of phylogenetical history. Of course, one must be conversant with the subtleties and the pitfalls of this method, in particular one must know how to exclude convergent adaptation as a source of error. Of these methodological necessities, few ethnologists seem to be aware. Divergent cultural development erects *barriers* between ethnic groups in a very similar manner as divergent evolution tends to separate species.

It was Erik Erikson who first drew attention to this phenomenon and coined for it the term of *cultural pseudo-speciation*. In itself, it is a perfectly normal process and even a desirable one, because a certain degree of isolation from neighbouring groups may well be advantageous to a quick cultural development, analogous to the reasons why geographical isolation facilitates the evolution of species. There is, however, a very serious negative side to it: pseudo-speciation is the basis of *war*. The group cohesion effected by the common esteem of group-specific social norms and rites is inseparably combined with the contempt and even hate of the comparable, rivalling group. If the divergence of cultural development has gone far enough, it inevitably leads to the horrible consequence that one group does not regard the other as quite *human*. In many primitive languages the name of the own tribe is synonymous with that of Man—and from this viewpoint it is not really cannibalism if you eat the fallen warriors of the hostile tribe! Pseudo-speciation suppresses the instinctive mechanisms normally preventing the killing of fellow-members of the species while, diabolically, it does not inhibit intra-specific aggression in the least.

There is no doubt that the younger generation responds to the parent generation *of the same community* with all the typical patterns of hostile behaviour which are normally elicited in the interaction with a *strange and hostile* group. Our deplorable familiarity with the phenomenon prevents us from realizing what a bizarre distortion of normal cultural behaviour it really represents.

At this point let us ask Ronald Hargreaves' first question: what is the mechanism which we find disturbed and what is its normal function in the service of the survival of the species? Obviously, the functions concerned are those which normally ensure an ethnic group's continuance in time. I have already said that, in the continued existence of a culture, all those mechanisms which preserve and hand down from one generation to the next all the culturally ritualized rites and norms of social behaviour, are performing functions which are closely analogous to those which the mechanisms of inheritance perform in the preservation of a species. They *store* knowledge (*not* simple information in the sense of information theory) and passes it on from generation to generation. In my paper "Innate Bases of Learning" I explained what happens to a species or a culture when stored knowledge gets *lost,* and I shall try to sum up what I said there as concisely as I can. If details drop out of the genetic "blueprint" of the general, large-scale structure of an organism, the consequence is a malformation; if the loss concerns the microstructure of tissues, the result is very often a regression to an ontogenetically or phylogenetically *more primitive* type of structure. Between these two, all kinds of intermediates are possible. If the loss of knowledge goes so far that, in the body of a multicellular organism, some cells altogether "forget" that they are parts of an adult metazoan, they will naturally revert to the behaviour of unicellular animals or of embryonic cells, in other words they will begin uninhibitedly to multiply by division. This is how a tumor originates and, for obvious reasons, its malignity is in direct proportion to the extent of the regression, to the *immaturity*—as pathologists call it—of its tissue.

If only in parenthesis, I must here mention an old hypothesis of mine which contends that some of the phenomena under discussion have a *genetic* basis. In all these alarming symptoms I cannot help feeling a strong undercurrent of *infantilism*. Diligence, long-term striving for future goals, patient bearing up with hard labour, the courage to take the responsibility for calculated risk and, above all, the faculty of compassion are all characteristic of the *adult,* in fact they are so uncharacteristic of children that, in them, we all are gladly ready to condone their absence.

We know from the work of Bolck and others that man owes some of his specifically human properties to what he has called "retardation", in terms of common biological parlance to neoteny. In my contribution to Heberer's book on evolution, I myself have tried to show that this permanent retention of infantile characters in man has its parallel in many domesticated animals, also that one of these characters retained, infantile *curiosity,* has been one of the essential prerequisites for the genesis of man. I have a shrewd suspicion that mankind has to pay for this gift of heaven by incurring the danger that a further process of progressive self-domestication might procedure a type of man whose genetic constitution renders him incapable of full maturation and who, therefore, play the same role in the context of human society which immature cells, by their infiltrating proliferation, play in the organisation of the body. It is a nightmare to think that disintegration of society may be caused by the genetic disintegration of its elements, because education, which is our hope otherwise, would be powerless against it!

Still I believe that the bulk of the disintegration phenomena here under discussion are "only" cultural. A culture however, is nothing but a living system and a highly complicated and vulnerable one at that! As I have already pointed out, its structure is, in many points, analogous to that of systems of less high integration. The blueprint of the programme which, in pre-cultural systems is stored in the genome, is contained, in the case of human culture, in all the ritualized norms of social behaviour, in all the symbols on which the cohesion of a culture is dependent, in the logic of language, in adherence to certain values, in short in everything that is handed down in tradition from one generation to the next. While genetical knowledge is present in coded form in every single individual of a species so that, in the case of a catastrophe, one survivor is, in principle, in possession of all the knowledge necessary to build the species up again, cultural traditional knowledge depends on a far more extensive and more vulnerable repository. Cultural knowledge—and with it a whole culture—can be snuffed out in the interval from one generation to the next. The individuals who have foregone the traditional knowledge of the culture from which they stem, very often behave in a manner analogous to that of tumor cells. Being unable to fend for themselves, they fall back on parasitism.

It cannot be my task here to convince readers of the fact that our culture is in immediate danger of extinction. I can refer them to the work of people like Kurt Hahn, Max Born, John Eccles, Paul Weiss and many others. That a sudden collapse of culture has not happened in previous history is no legitimate reassurance. There is no more blatant untruth than Rabbi be Akkiba's alleged wisdom that everything that happens has happened before. Nothing has, and I am setting out to demonstrate that the sudden break in cultural tradition is threatening just *now*. With that I proceed to Hargreaves' second question, concerning the causes which effect a malfunction, or even the cessation of function, in the mechanism of passing-on tradition.

I must begin by describing a few functional properties of this mechanism. Though human intelligence and inventiveness "enter into" its results, the growth of a human culture produced something that is not "man-made" in the sense a bridge or an aeroplane is. Like a forest, a culture needs a long time to grow and, like a forest, it can be annihilated in one short holocaust. Unlike a forest, however, it does not leave behind it fertile soil, on which new plants can grow quickly, but a barren land devoid of all fertility. To believe that a culture can be "made", starting from scratch, by one generation of men, is one of the most dangerous errors, not only of juveniles, but of many adult anthropologists. As Karl Popper has pointed out, the total destruction of our world of culture, Popper's "third world", would set us back to the Palaeolithicum.

The ritualized norms of social behaviour which are handed down by tradition represent a complicated supporting skeleton without which no culture could subsist. Like all other skeletal elements, those of culture can perform their function of *supporting* only at the price of *excluding* certain degrees of *freedom*. The worm can bend wherever it wants to, we can only bend a limb where a joint is provided. Any change of structure necessitates dismantling and rebuilding, and a period of increased vulnerability intervening between these two processes. An illustration of this principle is the crustacean which has to cast its skin-skeleton in order to grow a larger one. The human species is in possession of a very special mechanism providing the possibility of change in cultural structure. At the approach of puberty, young people begin to loosen their allegiance to the rites and social norms of behaviour handed down to them by family tradition, and, at the same time, to cast about searching for new ideals which to pursue and new causes which to embrace. This "moult" of traditional ideas and ideals is a period of true crisis in the ontogeny of man, it implies hazards quite as great as those threatening the newly-moulted soft-shelled crab.

It is at this phase of man's ontogeny that changes are wrought in the great inheritance of cultural tradition. The puberal "moult" is the open door through which new ideas gain entrance and become integrated into a structure which otherwise would be too rigid. The culture-preserving and, therewith, species-preserving function of this adapting mechanism presupposes a certain balance between the old traditions that are to be retained and adaptive changes which make it necessary to discard certain parts of traditional inheritance.

In my opinion it is certainly this mechanism which sifts and hands down tradition and whose disturbance creates all the symptoms just described. We can proceed to Hargreaves' second question concerning the nature of the disturbance, before putting a third one: what are its causes?

The essence of the disturbance indubitably lies in the fact that the process of *identification* by which the younger generation normally accepts and makes its own the greatest part of the rites and norms of social behaviour characteristic of the older, is seriously impeded or entirely obstructed. Excellent books have been written on this subject by Erik Erikson, Mitscherlich and others, so I need not enlarge on it. However, I think it is necessary to add that this failure to identify with the traditions of parental culture enlarge on it.

However, it must be emphasized that this failure to identify with the social norms of the parental culture is the direct cause of truly pathological phenomena. The urge to embrace some sort of cause, to pledge allegiance to some sort of ideal, in short to *belong* to some sort of human group, is as strong as that of any other instinct. Like any other creature which, under the imperative drive of an instinct, cannot find its adequate object, the deracinated adolescent searches for and invariably finds a *substitute object*. Here, the pathological disfunction is particularly significant for the analysis of the underlying phylogenetically programmed mechanism. The diagram of the social situation for which the unrequited instinct is pining, appears to be simple, as all those stimulus situations tend to be which form the goal of appetitive behaviour. The adolescent must have at his disposal a group with which to identify, some simple rites and social norms to perform, and some sort of enemy group to release communal militant enthusiasm. If you have seen the psychologically excellent musical "Westside Story", you have a perfect illustration of how all the social virtues of courage, unselfishness, friendship and loyalty reach the highets, most glorious peaks in a gang war, entirely devoid of any higher aims or values, in an absolutely senseless orgy of mutual killing.

Art representing these deplorable disfunctions would not move us as deeply as it does if it did not strike a chord which is still responsive in most of us. The very simplicity, the almost diagrammatic character of the sketch constitutes an appeal to very deep layers of our souls, to neither more nor less than the phylogenetic program of tribal warfare. What we observe in practically all the juvenile groups which break with tradition and take a hostile attitude to the older generation, is the more or less complete realization of this program. The Hamburg rockers who declare open war on older people, represent the most clear-cut paradigm, but even the most emphatically non-violent groups are constituted on essentially the same principles. All of them are constructed as surrogates to assuage the burning need of adolescents who, by the processes described, are deprived of a natural group whose causes they can embrace and for whose values they can fight.

Considering all this we are, I think, justified in our assumption that it is quite particularly the failure of normal identification which causes the alarming break-down of the mechanism whose important survival function lies in the sifting as well as in the handing-down of cultural tradition from one generation to the next.

We now come to the question what are the causes contributing to erect an apparently unsurmountable obstacle to normal identification. We can name a number of them, but we cannot be sure that we know all of them.

Optimists who believe that men and women are reasonable beings, tend to assume that rebellious youth is impelled by rational motives. There are indeed many good reasons to revolt against the older generation. It is perfectly true that practically all "establishments" on all sides of all curtains are committing unpardonable sins against humanity. I am not only speaking of actual cruelties, of political suppression of minorities, like the Czechoslovakians, or of the mass murder of innocent Indians by the Brasilians, but also of the deadly sins against the biology and ecology of mankind which are consistently being perpetrated by all the governments: of the exploitation, pollution and final destruction of the biosphere in and on which we live, of the constantly increasing hustle of commercial competition which deprives man of the time in which to be human, and of similar phenomena of dehumanisation. The youthful do indeed have good reasons to take issue at the goals at which the majority of the older generation is striving and I think that they do indeed recognize the intrinsic worthlessness of utilitarian aims.

There are several circumstances which tend to raise our hope that there is an element of intelligent rationality in the rebellion of youth. One is its ubiquity: the youthful protest against Stalinistic orthodoxy in communist countries, against race discrimination in Berkeley, against the utilitarianistic and commercial "American way of life" all over the United States, against antiquated tyranny of professors at German universities etc. Another reason for optimism is that never, as far as I know, have the youthful exerted their powers in the wrong direction, never have they demanded a more effective commercial system, better armament, or a more nationalistic attitude of their government. In other words, they seem to know—or at least feel—quite correctly what is wrong with the world. A third reason for assuming that there is a considerable rational element in the rebellion of youth is a very special one: rebelling students of biology are far more accessible to intelligent communication than are those of philisophy, philology and (I am sorry to say) of sociology.

We do not know how great a part of the rebellion of youth is motivated by rational and intelligent considerations. I must confess that I am afraid it is only a very small part, even with those young people who profess—and honestly believe—that they are fighting for purely rational reasons. The main roots of the rebellion of youth are to be found in wholly irrational, ethological causes, as I hope to demonstrate. Many adults have found, to their cost, that it is useless to try reasoning with rebellious young people. In many countries, left-oriented professors have attempted, rather pathetically, to propitiate rebel students by making all possible concessions to their demands. As the German sociologist F. Tenbruck has pointed out, this endeavour led, in every single case, to a concentration of attack on the would-be peace makers who were insulted with particular rancour and actually booed in exactly the same manner as a bull who refuses to fight is booed in the corrida. Political opinions play no role at all: Herbert Marcuse, extreme communist and advocate of completely scratching all tradition, was insulted by Cohn-Bendit and his young people, not because he held other opinions—which he did not—but because he was nearly seventy years old. Anyone familiar with ethological facts needs only to observe the hate-distorted faces of the more primitive type of rebel students in order to realize that they are not only unwilling, but quite unable to come to an understanding with their antagonists. In people wearing that kind of facial expression the hypothalamus is at the helm and the cortex completely inhibited. If a crowd of them approaches you, you have the choice of either to run, or to fight, as your temperament and the situation may demand. In order to avoid bloodshed, a responsible man may be forced to do the first—and be accused of cowardice in consequence. If he sees fit to fight, he will be accused of brutality, so whatever he does will be considered wrong. Yet it seems nearly hopeless to argue, as it appears impossible to reach the cortex across the smoke screen of hypothalamic excitation.

However, we must face the sad and highly alarming fact that, whatever the rebelling youthful *say* concerning their reasons for rejecting everything the older generation stands for, their *actions* prove, to anybody with some knowledge of neuroses, that their real motivation is to be sought in much deeper and more archaic disturbances. When rebelling students resort to defecating, urinating and masturbating publicly in the lecture theaters of the university, as they have been known to do in Vienna, it becomes all too clear that this is not a reasoned protest against the war in Vietnam or against social injustice, but an entirely unconscious and deeply infantile revolt against all parental precepts in general, right down to those of early toilet training. This type of behaviour can only be explained on the basis of a genuine regression causing the recrudescence of ontogenetic phases of earliest infancy, or, from the historical viewpoint, precultural states of affairs far below those of palaeolithic times. This alone is a sufficient reason to suspect strongly that the foundation of this type of neurosis is laid very early in life. The alarming fact is not that this type of mental illness does indeed occur, but its overt symptoms evidently pass unnoticed or at least unrebuked by intelligent and otherwise responsible young people.

We are safe in concluding that a large part of the factors which, by preventing normal cultural identification, cause hostility in the youthful, is strictly non-rational. We may divide these factors roughly into three groups. The first are those which enlarge the gap which is to be bridged between two generations, the second are those which impede the process which normally effect the bridging, the third and most interesting are those which make the present-day young people of different cultures more similar to each other than to their own parents.

The rapid change which the explosion of technology, enforced by irresistible technocracy, forces on human ecology and sociology has the unavoidable consequence that cultural norms of social behaviour are becoming obsolete at an ever increasing rate. In other words, the proportion between those traditional norms which are still valid and those which have become obsolete, is changing, with increasing velocity, in the direction of the latter.

Thomas Mann, in his marvellous historical and psychoanalytical novel about Joseph and his brothers, has shown most convincingly how complete the identification of a son with his father could be, could afford to be in biblical times, for the simple reason that the changes necessary to be effected between one generation and the next were negligibly small. I believe that humanity has just now reached the critical point at which the changes in social norms of behaviour demanded within the time period between two generations has begun to exceed the capacity of the puberal adapting mechanisms. The ever increasing gap between the social norms which circumstances dictate to each generation, has suddenly attained a size which the powers of filial identification fail to bridge. From the point of view of the young, the parents are hypocrites and liars. In a rapid escalation of hostility, they are even now beginning to treat each other as enemy groups.

The discrepancy between the rapidity of ecological change which technological development forces on humanity, and the relative slowness of the adaptive change possible to traditional culture, would, all by itself, be a sufficient explanation for the breaking-off of tradition. There are, however, a number of further causes contributing to the same effect. The indispensable process of *identification* is severly hindered by the *lack of contact* between the generations. Lack of parent-child contact even during the first months can cause inconspicuous but lasting damage: we know, by the work of René Spitz, that it is in earliest infancy that the faculty to develop human contacts passes through its most critical period. It is one of the functions that are dangerously prone to *atrophy* if not thoroughly used. The horrible syndrome which Spitz has called "hospitalization" consists of an "autistic" unwillingness to form human contacts at all, accompanied by a complete cessation of exploratory behaviour, as well as by a "negativistic" response to external stimulation in general. The child literally turns its back on the world, lying in its crib with its face turned to the wall. This awful effect can be caused by the seemingly innocuous change of personnel which takes place in most hospitals. The baby begins, at the age at which it becomes able to recognize persons, to form a personal bond to one of its nurses and would be ready to enter into a near-normal child-mother relationship with her. When this bond is severed by the routine change of personnel, the infant will try to form a second attachment and, halfheartedly, a third or even a fourth, but finally it resigns itself to an autism which is in its external symptoms very similar to infantile schizophrenia—whatever that may be.

Mothering a baby is a full-time job. The silly baby games are the beginning of cultural education and very probably its most important part. I do not know the English equivalent to "Bocki, bocki stoß", or "Hoppe, hoppe Reiter", "Guck guck—Dada" could, I think, be translated by "Peek-a-boo". Have you ever seen a baby's face light up when it has just grasped the *communicative* character of such a game and starts to join actively in it? If you have, you will have grasped the importance of this first establishment of mutual understanding on a cultural basis. Nowadays young mothers all too often have no time for this kind of nonsense, many of them would feel self-conscious in doing such a silly thing as gently butting a baby with her head or hiding behind a curtain and popping out again, crying "peek-a-boo". I think they are afraid of treating a small baby too anthropomorphically.

It may seem surprising to some, though it really is not, that this early education is obviously indispensable. It represents the infant's first introduction to *ritualized forms of communication,* and it would seem that, if this is not effected at the correct sensitive phase of the child's ontogeny, permanent damage is done to the development of its faculty to communicate at all. In other words, we have to face the fact that the majority of present-day babies are slightly, but noticeably "hospitalized". They talk later and they become toilet-trained much later, as is witnessed by the huge, diaper-distorted behinds of quite big children. On the principle of distrusting anybody over thirty, their mothers flatly disbelieve me when I tell them the age at which my children were toilet-trained. Today's children are literally "uneducated", they do not "know the first things". How should they, as nobody takes the time to tell them? So the basis for later phenomena of dehumanization is laid down at an early age, by diminishing the readiness for contact and compassion as well as by dampening the natural curiosity of man.

I am aware that the precept that all young mothers should spend most or all of their time with their babies is one that cannot be followed. The scarcity of mother-child contact is a consequence of the scarcity of time which, in turn, is caused by intraspecific competition and ultimately by crowding and other effects of overpopulation. The same fundamental evils have, with equally disastrous results, wrought profound changes in the sociological structure of the family. The preindustrial family was lucky in respect to several prerequisites of the successful handing-down of tradition. The family worked together striving for common aims intelligible to the children. These helped their father at his work and, doing so, not only learned his craft but also developed a healthy respect for his powers and abilities.

Mutual help engendered not only respect, but love as well. Very little disciplining and certainly no thrashings were needed to impress the children with the superior position which the parents held in the social rank order of the group. Even the gradual taking-over of the leading position by the son was a frictionless ritualized procedure which generated as little hostility as possible. Except in certain lucky, old-fashioned peasant families in some parts of Europe, I do not know where these happy circumstances prevail any more. This is just too bad, because they are the indispensable prerequisites for the younger generation's readiness to accept the tradition of the older!

How many children of today ever see their father at work, or help him in such a manner as to be impressed by the difficulty of what he is doing and his prowess in mastering it? Tired Pa, coming home from his office, is anything but impressive and if there is anything he wants to do less than talk about his work, it is to discipline a naughty child. He may even irritably shout at Ma when she—with full justification— thinks it necessary to do so. There is nothing to admire in her either, in fact she is the lowest-ranking creature within the child's horizon, because she is evidently rank-inferior to the char-lady whose favour she is currying in an abjectly submissive manner for fear that this all-important person might give notice.

In addition to these hardly avoidable evils, the parents may have heard the "environmentalistic" theory that human aggression is only engendered by frustration and may try to spare their unlucky offspring the necessity of overcoming any kind of obstacle, including, of course, any kind of contradiction from their parents. The result are intolerably aggressive, and, at the same time, neurotic children. Quite apart from the fact that trying to raise unfrustrated human beings is one of the most cruel deprivation experiments possible, it puts its unfortunate victim in a position of tormenting insecurity. Nobody, not even an all-loving saint, can ever *like* a nonfrustration child, and the latter, with the great sensivity which young children have for non-verbal expression, are very receptive to the suppressed hostility they arouse in every stranger with whom they come into contact. Defended by two despicable weaklings who do not even dare to slap back at a tiny child when slapped by it, and surrounded by a multitude of strangers who dearly would like to give them a sound thrashing, these children live an agony of insecurity. Small wonder if their world breaks down and they become openly neurotic when they are suddenly exposed to the stress of public opinion, for instance on entering a college.

Young people are able to accept tradition only from a person or persons of the older generation whom they respect *and love*. It is as simple as that! When the family environment fails to produce these conditions, which very often coincides with a degree of early hospitalization, there is only a small chance that the adolescent may find a father figure in some other person, for instance in a teacher, with whom to identify himself. If this tenuous chance, too, is lost, the unlucky juvenile, in the phase of searching for new ideals, is completely at a loss, more than a little demoralized and highly vulnerable to all the dangers of accepting an unworthy substitute object of his or her loyalty. From this, there are all possible gradations to outright neurosis.

A third set of factors which, while enhancing the cultural break between generations, might nevertheless prove beneficial in the end, consists of all those which tend to minimize the differences between cultures. The mass media, the increasing facility of transportation, the all-embracing spread of fashion and others, all tend to make the representatives of the young generation more similar to each other than their parents had been, and indeed more similar to each other than to their widely divergent parents. Those that were reared after the last war, were reared under circumstances and in an athmosphere entirely different from that of their parents' childhood. In this respect, their relation to their parents has been rightly compared to the one existing between the children of immigrants into a new country and these immigrants themselves. This, in fact, represents a silver lining in an otherwise very dark cloud: if the break of traditional knowledge is not so complete as to cast humanity back to a pre-cultural state of affairs, one might cherish a faint hope that the youthful of the whole world, while waging war upon the older generation, might become less prone to do so on each other.

9. *Conclusions and outlook*

Our culture is in an unbelievably paradoxial situation. Here, on the one hand, we have an established culture, assiduously committing suicide in seven different ways. First, there is the population increase which will soon suffocate, if not our species, still all that is really human about it. Second, the rat-race of modern commercialism threatens, in a truly satanic vicious cycle, to accelerate to the point of insanity. Third, man is progressively destroying nature, devastating the biotope in and on which he lives. Fourth, there is the progressive "Verweichlichung" of which I have spoken which is the death of human emotionality and, therewith, of all truly human relationships. Fifth, an imminent danger of genetic deterioration of mankind is due to the fact that common decency in every civilized community is at a negative survival premium. Sixth, and quickest, is nuclear warfare, yet I believe it is the least dangerous, because of its obviousness. Everybody understands the threat of the atom bomb, but who cares about disintegration of culture, genetic deterioration and who will even believe that insecticides can endanger the world in which we live?

The powers that be flatly ignore all these dangers—except where soil erosion or other consequences of over-exploitation become financially disturbing. Yet any man of average intelligence and tolerably good education cannot fail to see them. This irresponsibility of the responsible is due neither to their being stupid or immoral, but to their *indoctrination*. Indoctrination may be regarded as public danger number seven. Fundamentally identical with superstition, it is camouflaged under pseudo-scientific terminology and grows apace with the absolute number of people that can be influenced by the so-called mass media. The function of all doctrine, as Philip Wylie puts it, is to explain everything. Where doctrine rules, all possibilities of truth is gone, and, with it, all hope for an intelligent consensus. Indoctrination is, I think, the very worst of humanity's deadly vices!

On the other side, there are the rebelling youthful. At least some of them, and the best among them, are gloriously free from indoctrination and commendably distrustful of all doctrines; also, they are yearning for a just cause for which to fight, for real obstacles to overcome. There is no dearth of dangers to humanity which must be fought and our attempt to save mankind meets with a number of great obstacles which ought to be quite sufficient to keep the most ebullient militant enthusiasm of the young happily occupied for a long time.

The youthful *say* that they want to save mankind. We may be convinced that they are honest about this, and I even believe that some of them even have a real understanding for the predicament of man. But do they, collectively, show and promise of ever accomplishing their great task?

At present, they are indulging in the archaically instinctive pleasure of tribal warfare. The instinct of militant enthusiasm is not a whit less seductive than that of sex, nor less stultifying. And hate is the most absolutely stultifying emotion of all, as it precludes all communication, all acceptance of that kind of information that might tend to abate it. This is why hate is "blind" and why it is so dangerously prone to escalate.

We must face the truly horrible fact that the hate which the young bears us, is of the same nature as national or tribal hate. It bears all its earmarks, the haughtiness of only regarding the own party as quite human, the tendency to discredite and vilify the enemy ("Never trust a man over thirty"), the honest conviction that it is a moral duty to stamp out the enemy's culture as completely as possible, etc. etc. All these are attitudes and slogans which we know only too well as the tools of demagogues well-versed in the technique of sicking one nation against another.

Of course, there is a certain danger that the older generation might reply in kind, in other words that there might be an escalation of the enmity between the generations. It is a fact that the young revolutionaires are actively striving to be as revolting to the older generation as they possibly can contrive to be. I know a number of highly intelligent and altogether admirable old gentlemen who are neither hide-bound nor etiquette-ridden, but who would find it absolutely impossible to take seriously what a man dressed-up as a hippy or a communarde has to say. I myself confess I should find it difficult to listen to M. Cohn-Bendit in his pretty blue blouse, or to suffer having flowers heaved at me by flower-power. I honestly feel I should be in greater sympathy with Papuans throwing spears at me, and all this in spite of the fact that I know about my own instinctive responses and do my very best to suppress them. Professionally disciplined not to bite back when being bitten by a subject of my studies, I still doubt that I could keep up my readiness to communicate with APO students when fully hit in the face by a paint-bag, as an 80-year-old colleague has recently been in my presence in Göttingen.

Yet I do not think that there is any danger of the old ever hating the young in the manner the young hate the old. We of the older generation are prevented from doing so by the most archaic of instinctive responses, by those of parental care. Among the rebelling young there are our own children or grandchildren, and we find it impossible to cease loving them, let alone to hate them. This creates a queerly unbalanced situation of being hated and quite unable to reciprocate hate, and it seems to be human nature to react to the conflict thus produced in a very specific and unexpected manner. If somebody we love dearly suddenly flies into an apparently justified rage against us, we automatically and subconsciously assume that we have inadvertently given good cause for that rage. In other words, we react by feeling *guilty*. Highly social animals, such as dogs and certain species of geese show an analogous response. When unexpectedly attacked by an otherwise friendly companion they act "as if" it were their own fault, or else a mistake. In other words, they "react by not reacting" submitting to the attack by simply ignoring it whereupon the attacker regularly ceases to be aggressive. In terms of observable behaviour, the human "guilt response" is strictly analogous, whatever the accompanying emotions may be. I am sure that part of the feeling of guilt which at present is weighing down many people of the older generation, has its source in the paradoxical reaction just described, and that this is particularly true of the almost masochistic attitude assumed by some university teachers towards the rebelling young.

To sum up: our culture is threatened with immediate destruction by a breaking-down of cultural tradition. This threat arrises from the danger of what amounts to a tribal war between two successive generations. The causes of this war, from the viewpoint of the ethologist as well as from that of the psychiatrist, appear to lie in a mass neurosis of the worst kind.

This diagnosis, though matter-of-fact, is pessimistic only in appearance, because any neurosis can, in principle, be cured by raising its subconscious and unconscious causes above the threshold of consciousness. In respect to the neurotic war between the generations it should not be too difficult to do just that. It ought to be quite easy to make those among the rebelling students who are neither hopelessly indoctrinated nor stupid, understand the few biological facts of which I could give some idea even in one short presentation. The young *have* already grasped the one fundamental fact that humanity is going to the dogs at a rapid rate if some vicious cycles like population growth, destruction of biotope and accelerating commercial competition are not stopped and *soon* at that.

They still have to understand a few further truths. One is that even if their whole generation consisted of nothing but blessed geniuses, they could not build up a culture from a scratch, but would be back at Neandertal if they followed Marcuse's precepts of destroying all tradition: tradition is to a culture what the genome is to a species. Another fact they must comprehend is that they should not give way to hate. Hating the older generation prevents them from learning anything from it, and there is a lot to learn. It is hate that makes them so stupidly haughty, that creates, in them, that exasperating inverted "mother-knows-best-attitude" which makes them impermeable to advice and renders them actually paranoic because everything one tells them is automatically interpreted as an attempt to uphold the so-called establishment. (If one criticizes establishment one is suspected to be a particularly insiduous and clever supporter of it.) Finally they should come to understand in fairness that, if we of the older generation on being hated don't reciprocate hate, this is not because we are guilt-ridden having perpetrated nameless crimes against them, but because, being their parents, we cannot help loving them.

I am admittedly an incurable optimist and I believe that the youthful can be made to understand all this, and that, if they once have grasped the simple ethological facts underlying it, they will not only be able to save and retain everything worth preserving of our present-day culture, but that they might do more: they are, as I said, even today loosening their allegiance to their several established cultures and they are becoming increasingly similar to each other, independently of their provenience. Provided they do not, by jettisoning the accumulated knowledge of their culture, relapse to Neandertal, provided they attain power when they attain maturity, provided they do not then forget their present aims and provided they do not get caught, as they are all-too likely to be, in the orthodoxy of some doctrine or other (it does not matter in the least which), they really might be successful in getting mankind out of the horrible mess it is in at present.

All these high hopes depend, of course, on education, and if I have seemed overly optimistic just now, I have occasion to counteract that impression at once. One of the ugliest facts in the social life of present-day humanity is that the decision concerning what to teach to the young and what to withhold from them, still rests almost exclusively with those who are in power politically. What is to be taught to the youthful and what is to be witheld from them, is therefore mainly dependent on what the politicians deem advisable in the interests of their own, shortlived political aims and not on any consideration of what will be necessary for the present-day young people to know when, a few years hence, they will have to shoulder the responsibility for the survival of mankind. The teaching of Charles Darwin's discoveries is still legally prohibited in the state of Indiana, a few miles from Chicago. Biology, and particularly Ecology and Ethology, are regarded as subversive sciences in many parts, the teaching of biology in German middle schools has been cut down to a ridiculous minimum.

Furthermore, the technique of all teaching, particularly in the United States, is still founded on the assumption that the pseudodemocratic doctrine is absolutely true. This results in a purely utilitarian teaching which leaves entirely out of consideration the fact that man possesses certain species-specific programs of behaviour, the suppression of which inevitably leads to neurosis and contributes to the horrible mass neurosis with which we are confronted nowadays. In other words, the usual kind of education intentionally or unintentionally ignores the fact that the realisations of certain phylogenetically evolved programs of human behaviour constitute unalienable human *rights*. So far from being a mere quibble, the question whether a certain pattern of human social behaviour is determined by a phylogenetically adapted program or by cultural ritualisation becomes of suppreme importance the very moment we have to deal with a pathological disfunction. Its correction requires entirely different steps in each of the two cases. If the disturbance has its source in cultural tradition alone, education alone ought to be capable of dealing with it. If the central cause of the disturbance lies in a phyletic program which, by remaining unfulfilled, causes malaise and even neurosis, educative measures will only serve to make matters worse by destroying what faith in the educator is still left. One cannot *teach* a man to remain happy, to retain his love for his neighbour, to avoid developing neuroses, high tension and heart attacks under the stressful conditions of crowded commercial city life. Which is exactly what present-day education is persistently and unavailingly trying to do.

Even from the full recognition of the *cause* of certain pathological phenomena it does not follow that a means of combating them is automatically apparent. There are many examples in medical science demonstrating this sad fact. However, I believe that an increased emphasis on teaching biology, in particular ecology and ethology, on teaching young people to think in terms of systems rather than in those of atomism, together with a certain amount of tuition in pathology and psychopathology would help enormously to make young people understand the real predicament of mankind. This considered opinion of mine is founded on what I regard as a highly suggestive fact. Among the rebelling students there is a clear positive correlation of their knowledge of biology and the constructiveness of their demands. The deepest malaise, the most uncompromising enmity against the teachers, the deepest confusion of the intentions of the teachers and those of the politicians in power, in short the greatest amount of general disorientation is to be found among the students of sociology, of a science which I reproach for being still too much under the influence of the pseudo-democratic doctrine. In a discussion of three hours duration which I had late at night with APO students in the streets of Göttingen, a discussion which began in hostility and ended in friendship, I could not offer any better suggestions for the solution of the problems of education just mentioned than I have to offer now. Politicians can only be influenced by the pressure of public opinion. There is only one way to gain their attention for our problems, and that is by *infiltrating public opinion* with the knowledge of the real causes of man's predicament and trust the public to force politicians to do the right things. It is an error common among scientists to underrate the intelligence of the public, and that is why all-too few scientists regard it as their duty to write generally intelligible books, leaving this task to popularizers who rarely accomplish it in a satisfactory manner. If science is ever to gain that kind of influence on politics which is obviously necessary to save mankind, it can only do so by educating the public independently of accepted political doctrines.

Note

Some of the essential problems dealt with in this paper, particularly those concerning the methodology of approaching systems, mainly discussed in 1. *Darwinian Approach and the Question of Adaptation,* as well as those treated in 9. *Conclusions and Outlook,* cropped up, for the first time, in the discussion of the so called Frensham Group, a number of scientists meeting semi-annually on the subject "The Predicament of Man". I am indebted for many thoughts expressed in this paper to the members of the Frensham Group, particularly to André Cournand, Father Dominique Dubarle, Robert K. Merton, Pierre Piganiol and Paul A. Weiss.

Education for Humanity

By Margaret Mead

The American Museum of Natural History, New York, U.S.A.

My mandate is to discuss "Education for Humanity", which might be taken to mean either Education for all of Humanity, seen as all of the human race, or Education for Humanity, that is, an education that increases the humanity of those who receive it. The second sense of the word, as it has been applied, in English, to the *humanities* has too often been exclusive and elitist and arrogant. But I believe a fair case can be made today for the coincidence of any education designed to increase the humanity, literally the humane outlook, of its recipients with the need for universality. Any education that takes for granted the superiority of any group, national, continental, racial, religious, or ideological, over others, contains within it the seeds of "man's inhumanity to man". As the world has been explored and all peoples have been put into communication with one another, *man* now includes the inhabitants of the most remote islands of the sea. No country, therefore, however ancient and honorable its tradition, or however advanced its contemporary technical or political development, is justified in considering either reinforced perpetuation of its former systems of education, or innovation in the field of education, without including the effects of such activities in other countries. However far apart in technical development, however opposed in ideology, however contrasting in ethos different countries may be, what happens anywhere in the world today is significant for the whole world. Those who innovate, whether in a technical or social field, in taking responsibility for the foreseeable effects of their innovations, now can do no less than to take into account the whole world—and all the inhabitants of the six continents and the islands of the sea.

Planning for the planet can be modelled on responsible national planning only to the extent that there is no distinction made between internal and external influences. Today most national planning considers only such matters as trade, possible military attack, and rivalries which assume that, in a sense, nations are not part of the same system. Therefore even the most complete national planning, whether in small homogeneous advanced societies or in great conglomerate societies like the USSR, the US, India and China, cannot provide the kind of model we need. To date, the activities of

United Nations commissions have implicitly assumed standards developed in some particular part of the world, usually Euro-American, as the standards to which other peoples should conform. The inclusion of particular religious philosophies has been limited to veto positions, as in the case of Roman Catholic views on birth control, but it is rather as exponents of particular styles of modernity that countries from the world outside Europe have spoken. We have at present no mechanism by which the traditions of the entire world can be included on anything like an equal basis. This means, in effect, that responsible bodies like this symposium are continually planning for other people, but not with them.

The recognition that we represent only a small and differentially articulate part of the human race alive today on this planet, and that everyone here has been educated within a single tradition, however much that tradition may be predominant in the world's current scientific and technological advances, imposes certain limitations on our deliberations here. They must necessarily be tentative and cast in such a form that other peoples can systematically be included within the development of any particular feature of the plan or of the very direction of the plans themselves.

So while it is true that we may be, in information terms, somewhat ready to think about the rest of the world, this may only make our plans the more destructive, just as the ethnologically trained missionary is more efficient in the destruction of the local religions, the practices of which he not only abhors, but is equipped to ferret out for abolition.

Including the entire planet has other implications. Each step we may inaugurate, assuming that some recommendation of this symposium were to be accepted effectively, somewhere, within the part of the world that we represent, will have effects elsewhere, as it is observed, disseminated, copied, reacted against or rejected by the rest of the world. No experiment of consequence can be conducted in secrecy today. Those who would attempt such secrecy are themselves injured by what becomes, inevitably, a lack of generosity. No ideological division prevents groups theoretically opposed to each other from watching each other's procedures very closely. So, in any serious attempt to think and to plan, the inclusion of all forseeable results includes not only such matters as differences in scale, the state of the existing culture, the sources of previous changes, as South American countries looked to Spanish and French models of higher education, or Japan, at an earlier period, looked to China, but also the nature of the response that is likely to occur, slavish imitation, irresponsibly poor copying, violent rejection couched in religious, nationalistic or ideological terms, or symmetrical types of nominal rivalry, as when the United States tailors its scientific education to a supposed model of scientific education in the USSR.

In this paper I shall use the word education as inclusively as I know how to include *purposeful* teaching and learning on any subject and at any age, and conducted within any institutional setting. Such an inclusive definition overrides the traditional type of discussion in which education is something that is done to children, or young people, or adults who have been poorly educated and must be brought up to the standard attained elsewhere by children. It also overrides the frequent distinction between education and training. Most uses of the idea of training treat human beings as objects, training them, as one would a race horse or a sheep dog, to perform some specialized task, in contrast to educating them as whole beings. On the other hand, it is possible to speak of educating an animal, as the puppies who are to become guardians of the blind are educated in the United States by being reared in a family of children—a purposeful attempt to produce the kind of upbringing which an Eskimo husky puppy receives among Eskimo children in an igloo. It is also useful to distinguish education from two other social processes: socialization, the adaptation of a human child to a social environment; and enculturation, the adaptation of a human child to its particular cultural environment. Socialization and enculturation are descriptive terms for processes that occur in all known societies. Neither term implies consciousness on the part of teacher or learner, nor specific and articulate goals. Education as I am using it here, is a goal-directed conscious process on the part of the teacher, or learner, or both, in which a change is envisaged in the learner. We have not, historically, envisaged a change in the teacher, except as greater proficiency came from something loosely defined as "experience" or "practice". We have usually been willing to call any system educational in which there was a stated goal for the learners, whether or not those goals were achieved or shared by the learners themselves.

It is also useful to realize to what extent teaching is peculiarly characteristic of man. With the use of words and the conception of distant goals, man can consciously impart information or behaviour patterns to those he wishes to teach, while among animals, the invocation of future or non-visible actions has to be built into face-to-face procedures, or into genetically transmitted mechanisms.

Every known human society however simple conducts some education, that is, there is a conscious attempt to teach certain things to the young, and this is sometimes extended to the stranger, the immigrant, or the married-in adult. What is taught varies widely. It may be formal gender, in a language which has multiple noun classes; it may be large amounts of rote material which include ancestral myths, or genealogies; it may be the names of plants; or a repertoire of hundreds of different color distinctions. Whenever there is differentiation of the behavior of any class of persons in a society—between the sexes, between age groups, between occupational groups—these differences bring into consciousness the associated behaviors so that behavior tends more to be taught and learned consciously, than to be simply absorbed without conscious attention. Such educational procedures can be treated as the precursors of schools, with occasional occurrence of institutions with the attributes which we at present associate with schools, where a group of identified learners are gathered together in an identified place and taught some identified body of materials, or skills, by individuals designated to do so. So periods of initiation of an age grade, by an older age grade, have been called "bush schools" in describing traditional African societies, and the ancient Polynesians, intent on preserving their traditions, had recognizable schools among the Maori of New Zealand and in old Hawaii.

All schools that we know of, whether in our own tradition, reaching back through the Mediterranean to the Middle East, or the schools of the ancient civilizations of Asia, Africa and pre-Columbian America, have been based on the assumption that the learners were being taught something that was already known to the teachers. The addition of script gives further emphasis to this position; what is known is written, and the teacher having learned to read it, and possibly to interpret it, teaches the pupil to read it, and possibly to interpret it. Such exercises in the mastery of the known may also include exercises in mental agility, in working out new philosophical or ethical problems, or those postulated but not solved by the traditional material. It has also been characteristic of the existence of schools, now taken in the widest sense of the word to include universities or lifelong centers of religious learning, that there was the possibility of a pupil becoming a greater teacher than his master, but the classic assumption was that the pupil who excelled, understood better or engaged in more brilliant exegesis, or had access to more reliable sources of inspiration from some authoritative supernatural source.

What we are facing today is a later stage of the changes in education which have been introduced wherever science has been included, and the idea of the production of something new incorporated within the traditional educational structure. But because scientific education has had to operate within a structure designed to communicate only what was known and accepted, and that primarily with the use of script, even scientific education has been heavily imbued with the idea that those who know, teach what is known to those who do not know. The process of discovery has been masked by a system of learning within which experiments, the answers to which were known, were repeated over and over again by generations of students, and often the search for the new has masqueraded either as comparable to the traditional contribution of a historian who discovers a new fact, or as research stimulated by practical demands for technological application. The unwillingness to view science and technology as a single process, and the attempt to dignify science as one of the pure scholarly traditions in which men sought truth for its own sake, has further obscured a reality of modern education—the fact that in a world in which we can consciously state un-solved but soluble problems, education has changed. The old system de-signed to teach what is known to those who do not know, is no longer viable. What we now need, in recognition of this changed milieu, is a changed form of education itself but that form has not been invented. There have been sporadic recognitions of the need, the search for ways of identifying the particular idiosyncratic and age-connected capacities of individuals, especi-ally of young children, begun by Binet and pursued by Piaget, Lowenfeld, Inhelder, and Bruner; the attempts to build curricula in which ex-ploration and discovery will supplement the present emphasis on rote learning; and the emphasis on the university as the scientific center of modern society responsible for innovation, experiments in teaching skills and materials taught to children and, in some societies, to adults in an adult form. All of these small exploratory attempts have, in one sense, been attempts to widen education but at the same time to contain it within a pro-liferating institution, with its heavy weight of traditional practice and vested interests. Very seldom is there any question raised as to whether indeed there should be a class of people called teachers, whose life-long occupation is to impart selected materials to identified learners, nor has there been any very thorough questioning of the position that education consists of an interchange between those who know and those who do not.

Yet these are two assumptions which the contemporary condition of society on this planet calls severely in question. In highly traditional coun-tries, and in countries where literacy is rare or non-existent, teachers are trained to impart very special bits of knowledge or proficiency; the whole thrust of what they do is a function of their not deviating in any marked extent from the way they were taught themselves. New subject matter may, of course, be introduced, provided that it is completely absorbed within the old system of teaching. But any attempt to introduce new subject matter which brings into question the old method of teaching, produces trouble. I believe the position can be supported that when the teacher is able to teach as he or she was taught, children, and adults, learn successfully whatever it is the school sets out to teach, regardless of the method of teaching. Children learn to read by chanting in unison, by learning to sound the alphabet, by drawing letters in the air, by associating words and pictures, generation after generation, as long as there is no marked discontinuity between the world in which the teacher learned and that in which the pupils or students live.

Even the teaching of science survived its assimilation to the traditional dependence upon print and verbal demonstration, and its failure to incorporate first hand observation, exploration and discovery. The educational system firmly embedded in a cultural tradition in which the major premises were unquestioned, worked. It did not, it is true, produce a literate public who understood the science that was transforming the world about them. It did not produce legislators or civil servants or military men who understood the new scientific ideas and the new technology. It educated groups of young scientists who were able to tolerate the rituals to which they were exposed, and who became on the whole alienated from many of the "humane" values to which they were exposed in the rest of their education. The split between appropriate scientific education and the rest of the educational process has now produced, in the most scientifically advanced countries, a reaction against science and technology. We have the situation of a decided reduction in the proportion of young men who wish to go into physics, with outbreaks of anti-rational cults, in which individuals who were never taught what science is really about confuse it with the mistakes of irresponsible and uncontrolled technical development leading to worldwide dangers of scientific warfare, pollution, population explosion and famine.

This rejection can be, at least in part, attributed to a split in our educational procedures in which methods appropriate to replicating the past were applied in fields where the main purpose is to expand and thus change our view of mankind and the future. If a student wishes to be a scientist, he is still required to exclude a good deal of relevant human life from his consideration, and the average person feels he can reject the findings of science the way he could reject the words of some religious leader recorded hundreds of years ago.

These confusions so conspicuous currently in those areas most touched by science and technology, and among those who go on to so-called higher education, are multiplied in attempts to extend specific styles of education designed for the members of particular classes, within particular historical traditions, to the members of other classes, or other cultures. These extensions have not, of course, always been from an elite to a group of less standing and power—the attempt to educate illiterate governing groups by specialized scholars has also occurred—but the typical extensions in this century have been from imperial peoples to colonial subject peoples, from the town to the country, from superordinate racial groups to subordinate racial groups, from the skilled and the more well off to the less skilled and the poor, from men to women, and paradoxically, from the up-to-date young to their behind-the-times elders. In all of these cases, the dependence upon the past as a model has been combined with an assumption of superiority of those who taught, or whose culture was taught, to those who were taught. So to the hierarchical superior status that past knowledge held over present living was added the assumption that knowledge, inaccessible to one's forebears of the same race, sex, age or status, made those who received the new education, in some sense, both superior to their forebears and inferior as parvenus. With all of these extensions has gone a whole set of attendant circumstances, the attempt to train, rather than educate, a sufficient number of teachers; the recruitment of teachers who had not received the same type of enculturation as teachers in the past; the downgrading of teachers; and the perpetuation of a variety of exclusionist stereotypes, ranging from beliefs about the innate capacity of people of different "races" to handle abstractions to an insistence that women learn typing rather than mathematics. The more the egalitarian demand grew for previously dispossessed groups to share in the education that had been associated with elite status, the more distorted, unreliable and muddled the educational system became. Today, in many parts of the world, including the United States and parts of Europe, the very educational practices that were designed to bring a large proportion of the citizenry of a country into fuller participation in the society serve instead to isolate them; schooling designed for those who are believed to be less capable or less appropriately aspiring, conveys, sometimes almost with conscious intention, lower aspirations and lower self-esteem. In reaction against such educational systems we find the types of symbolic egalitarianism in which students in countries that have recently acquired Euro-American types of education, write theses which are meaningless caricatures of what a thesis should be. Conversely, there is the demand in the United States that black students be admitted to higher education regardless of their preparation or intellectual level, finally completing the transformation of the degree from a certificate of special educational attainment into a badge of social and economic acceptance.

A third feature of the present day worldwide scene is found in the changes accompanying the definition of education as age-related. Schools have traditionally discharged the role of mass child care as well as education. They were places where the young of elite groups could be protected, and the young of people of all ranks could be cared for, during a large part of the year. They have become, in some technically advanced countries, ways of protecting trade unionism by keeping the young out of the competitive labor market, and, as such, a late school-leaving age and compulsory retirement complement each other. They have provided a means for the entire child population to be given minimal health, and sometimes, dietary supervision. All of these primarily caretaking functions replace the family and kin group and are not primarily educational at all. The greater the emphasis on these caretaking functions, the more complete the emphasis on education as something that is done to and for children and early youth. Attempts to extend the school-leaving age are joined not with the educational needs of the young but with worthy attempts to reduce child labor, protect young people from corrupting circumstances, and supervise their health. Only in those countries where there is an ideological emphasis upon giving greater power and prestige to some new elite drawn from the peasantry, the proletariat, or some primitive political hierarchy, is this association between education and childhood and youth temporarily set aside, and then the educators discover that adults can sometimes learn in a few weeks what it takes a child a year or more to learn, or that appropriate motivation enormously short cuts the kind of learning traditionally insisted upon for the captive young.

Yet the conditions of the contemporary world, with the tremendously accelerated rate of change and worldwide interaction by mass communications and transportation, actually mean that where once children, and later, in more complex societies, adolescents, and still later, young people in their 20's, could be taught, once and for all, what they needed to know, there is now a demand for continuous education and re-education for people of all ages. Unlearning is becoming almost as important as learning. If this condition is once realized, schools will have the potential of being transformed from centers where a few adults, officially committed to teaching, teach a mass of children and youth, committed to learning simply by age status, to centers where many people will be learning from those younger than themselves, and where possibly the most effective form of learning will be teaching across age lines in both directions. Under such circumstances, possibly some of the other contemporary functions of schools, as caretaking institutions for children and early adolescents, as weaning institutions for late adolescents, may be minimized or shifted to other institutions. Or, alternatively, education may be diffused throughout the society, and apprentice-type learning, but with the added possibility of the younger teaching the older, may replace its current forms.

With these other shifts, we may expect that the pre-occupation of educational institutions with the written word, which has characterized them since script was invented, may give way to other forms of education, in which visual and auditory experience may replace the peculiarly linear nature of learning from script. Both ease of communication and ease of travel are producing a demand for more simultaneous and wholistic experience and for the kind of thinking in which the entire individual is involved. If this occurs, the present hierarchical position given to script will vanish, and other forms of learning, whether it be of a painter or a dancer or a programmer, will be given recognition. The tremendous dependence upon script that has characterized all the high civilizations and molded our forms of thought and determined the limits within which we could develop, can now be broken. This will admit individuals with many different kinds of minds into full participation in building a new kind of culture. It will overcome, probably in a variety of ways, including a second worldwide spoken language, and possibly a new idiographic system with multiple linguistic reference, comparable to the present notation system of the sciences, the present divisions among peoples due to differences in mother tongues, but without destroying those mother tongues.

The new humanity, toward which we are struggling, is essentially based upon valued diversity and absence of hierarchies among peoples, races, ages, sex, the senses, and the traditions within which mankind has flourished. It is based upon placing the unknown future in the forefront, and seeing the pasts of different peoples, as routes, none of which is to be discredited, to a present in which we can work for a shared future.

A Strategy for Human Survival

By J. R. D. Tata

Tata Industries Private Ltd., Bombay, India

History

Throughout recorded history, crises have been the lot of the human race. With the relatively rare exception of natural catastrophes—earthquakes, floods, famines, drought, pestilence—these crises were usually caused by man himself, by wars of conquest, or religion, by periodic revolts against tyranny and oppression and other forms of human conflict. The impact of these man-made crises was usually confined to the parts of the world where they occurred, for instance, where a war was waged. Rarely did it spread beyond adjacent countries or groups of countries.

The conditions of living in terms of means of livelihood and economic standards were relatively uniform throughout the world. When man changed from the nomadic life of a hunter and settled on land to grow his food, there was little to differentiate a farmer or a fisherman in China from one in Europe. The values which governed his life and attitudes were also basically similar.

The industrial revolution, following the discovery of steam and electrical power and the means of making steel on a large scale, brought about a dramatic and global change. Had the industrial revolution spread from the start to all parts of the world, a fairly even balance in the living standards of the people of the world would have remained unaffected.

Because, however, the immensely increased economic and military power of the new industrial nations gave them the opportunity to conquer and exploit others with impunity, a new colonial era coincided with the industrialisation of Europe and America; and because the value system of those days saw nothing wrong in such colonial conquests and exploitation, the fruits of advancing science and technology were deliberately denied to the colonies. As a result, by the time European colonialism melted in the fires of the Second World War, an enormous gap had developed between the wealth, productivity and living standards of the West and those of most of Asia and Africa.

On the Indian sub-continent, the rapid increase in the population growth resulting from a sharp fall in mortality, combined with economic stagnation through lack of industrialisation, aggravated the relative as well as absolute deterioration in the living standards of its people. Denied the benefits of modern technology which would have enabled them to modernise their age old industries and agriculture and to create the wealth with which to pay for the education and other essentials of a modern, creative life, the people of the sub-continent gradually sank into poverty, lethargy and despair.

It has been argued by some observers that even had the benefits of modern technology been made available to Indians from the start, their caste ridden system of values and their superstitious and fatalistic philosophical attitude to life, would have in any case prevented them from taking advantage of the opportunities created by industrialisation.

The evidence of the last twenty years of industrial growth in India, the remarkable skills shown by all sections of society in the establishment and management of modern industries, including quite sophisticated industries, refutes this argument. There can now be no doubt that had India and other similarly placed countries been allowed or encouraged to develop their economy as in the countries of the West, by the application of modern science and technology, they would today be in a situation comparable to, or not far behind, that of Japan.

During this colonial period, and until the First World War, Europe and America enjoyed a remarkably stable period free from any serious political or economic crisis. Busy with their industrial growth and the exploitation of their colonial empires, they basked in the sun of their mounting wealth, power and glory. Forgetful of the lessons of the French Revolution, ignorant of, or impervious to, the new forces and the inevitable changes in human values created by their unprecedented economic progress and the spread of education to the masses, they drove headlong and unseeing into a catastrophic era of change for which they were not prepared.

Crises before us

Is it surprising that, after two decimating world wars, the violent revolutions of Russia and China, the collapse of empires, the population explosion, the discovery of nuclear power and weapons of total destruction, the exponential advance of science and technology, the peoples of the world today find themselves in a state of deep crisis, the complex causes of which they do not fully understand but which, they sense, threaten not only the survival of age old and cherished values of a civilization built on the labours, sufferings and blood of centuries, but even their physical survival?

The present world crisis is a complex and multiple one, but for convenience, although admittedly an oversimplification, it may be divided into two main sub-crises. First a crisis of the spirit amongst the more affluent peoples of the world, as evidenced by the deepening dissents, the confrontations, the growing rejections of old values and previously accepted national goals and policies, the alienation of youth, and other manifestations in Europe, America and elsewhere.

While some of the causes of this crisis are still to be fully understood, it is clearly a crisis of change. Never before has man been faced with the need to adapt himself in so short a time to such drastic changes in his environment, his way of life, his thought processes, and his scale of value. Bewildered and devoured by the galloping advance of his own scientific, technological, productive, managerial and marketing skills, haunted by fear of the use his leaders might make of the cataclysmic powers which control of the atom had placed in their hands, indignant at the diversion to military purposes and senseless wars of a disproportionate part of the world's income and wealth which could be used for the benefit of mankind, revolting against the excessively materialistic nature of present day civilization, man finds himself unable to keep pace, socially or spiritually, with the traumatic changes wrought in his life.

Whereas in the past, in times of stress and danger, he could, and did, derive strength, comfort and reassurance from religion, from trust in his leaders or from an unshakeable faith in age old values, today's educated man, although free from want, finds himself bereft of guidance and succour and, like a sailor in a crippled ship drifting in mountainous seas, feels lost, abandoned and in mortal danger.

This sense of a doom, although shared by a surprisingly large proportion of educated people and particularly the younger generation throughout the world, is clearly an exaggerated one, with the obvious exception of the justifiable fear of nuclear annihilation. Even there, the realisation amongst nuclear powers that any atomic war would inevitably lead to the total destruction of both participants, and death or irreparable genetic damage to hundreds of millions of innocent people throughout the world, provides a reasonable certainty that there will never be a resort to such mass suicide.

All the other main problems created by technological change in the last half century, the pollution of air and water, the ghettos and the slums, the population explosion, the waste of resources, the organisational and managerial deficiencies, the social, racial and economic inequalities and inequities, are clearly within the powers of modern man to solve within the next few decades, provided he does not destroy himself in the meantime. In science and technology, which have been the principal causes of the present day threat to his survival, will he find the solutions to the problems they have created. Thus, in resolving the crisis threatening Western civilization, the problem is largely one of finding the means of harnessing and co-ordinating the abundant scientific knowledge, human skills and material resources required for the task. It is not the purpose of this paper to attempt specific suggestions in this regard. In his thought-provoking paper, "What We Must Do", a copy of which has been distributed amongst the participants in this symposium, Dr. John Platt has dealt in considerable detail with this very problem and made valuable and constructive suggestions.[1] From these and others will, it is hoped, emerge an effective worldwide programme of analysis, planning and action.

The other dominating element in the global crisis which threatens civilization today, while encompassing some of the elements mentioned earlier, is a crisis of want amongst two-thirds of the peoples of the world. This crisis, if unchecked, will not only condemn hundreds of millions of human beings, along with their children and children's children, to continued poverty and mental darkness, but will have calamitous repercussions on the rest of the world. For the peoples of the under-developed countries, the problem of survival is concerned with securing the basic essentials of life—food, shelter, education, clothing and above all employment—rather than with the frustrations and doubts now afflicting their more affluent brothers in the West. Those of us who come from one of such countries are naturally primarily concerned with the problems of this crisis of want.

Treats and opportunities

Except for the threat of nuclear war, this crisis is, in the writer's view, the more serious of the two. For, failure to meet it, to solve the problems which caused it, and to fulfil the tasks which will overcome it, will have disastrous consequences for the whole world.

It is no longer possible to expect from the afflicted peoples of under-developed nations the patience and resignation to their miserable fate which they have shown for centuries. Today, with the phenomenal development of mass media for the dissemination of news and information, with radio, television, newspapers, illustrated magazines and films spreading the image of Western prosperity throughout the world, even illiterate people in the poorer countries have become conscious of the staggering difference between their conditions of living and those of the peoples of Europe, America, Russia, and now also Japan. They want a piece, however small, of that affluence for themselves; they want it not only for their grandchildren but in their own lifetime. Here in the making is a revolution of rising expectations, tremendous in its potential for good and evil. Unless, within the next decade or so, there is a visible and sustained improvement in the miserable conditions of life of the people in the under-developed world, two-thirds of mankind will revolt with increasing violence against the grossly inequitable distribution of the world's wealth and opportunities.

Already in the last fifty years, humanity has faced two such upheavals—in Russia and in China—which have engulfed directly or indirectly a billion people. At this critical juncture in human history, when the explosion of science and technology has strained to breaking point our capacity to adapt ourselves to the changes it has wrought in our environment, we just cannot afford another even greater upheaval if we are to save our democratic civilization, painfully built up over the centuries.

Thus, one of the great challenges of the age is the two-fold one of bringing up the living and educational standards of the under-developed or developing countries to an acceptable minimum, and, as an essential part of this task, to halt the population explosion which today nullifies most, and in some cases all, of the economic progress they are able to achieve on their own.

We know that there are people, some of them highly knowledgeable, who feel that the magnitude of the economic problems of countries like India, combined with the growth of their population, are beyond solution or that the cost would be far beyond the capacity of the developed countries to finance even in part. They thus foresee, within the next few years, an inevitable Malthusian catastrophe with famine and death stalking large areas of the world. In this writer's view there is no justification for such pessimism. Much progress has already been made and is being made today in the planned economic development of India and similarly placed countries, while the population problem is being tackled with vigour, on an unprecedented scale and with distinct signs of timely success. The annexed charts give some indication of the action taken and the progress made in the current decade.

The main obstacle to accelerated growth is a lack of adequate resources available for development investment from internal savings, which creates a vicious circle in which inadequate savings lead to inadequate investment which perpetuates poverty, which in turn ensures inadequate savings. Just as within individual countries the small savings of the poor are bolstered by larger savings extracted from the rich by escalating taxes, the inadequate savings of poor countries in the initial decades of accelerated development need to be supplemented by aid, loans or investment from rich countries.

The quantum of such supplementary support to internal savings and investment is within the means of the richer countries of the world. Many studies by the World Bank and other agencies, and now the Pearson Committee's Report, have shown that the allocation for a decade or two of one percent of the G.N.P. of a group of nineteen countries would enable underdeveloped and developing countries to accelerate their development and to reach a self-sustaining rate of growth within a relatively short period of time.

Because, of all the under-developed or developing countries (other than China), India has the largest population and possibly the lowest per capita income, the task of bringing up its standard of living to an acceptable minimum and of ensuring its self-sustaining growth, would be the heaviest of all. Therefore, India provides the best possible test of the viability of any worldwide programme of assistance to under-developed countries. If it is shown that the objective can be attained in India within a reasonable time and at reasonable cost to aiding countries, it can undoubtedly be attained more easily, quicker and at less cost elsewhere. In addition, a country like India, where the centuries still co-exist, where man travels by bullock cart as well as by jet aircraft, uses wooden ploughs and handlooms as well as tractors and the most sophisticated automatic machine tools, uses both muscle and atomic power, would provide a unique workshop or proving ground for experimentation, for planning and achieving development in the full knowledge and understanding of possibilities and consequences.

India, a challenge

Using India as a prototype, the remaining paragraphs of this paper will be devoted to a brief exposition of its present economic status, the progress it has made in the last decade, and to a projection of future growth backed by adequate foreign aid. This shows that the challenge can be fully met well before the turn of the century.

Indian development during nearly two decades of planning serves, perhaps, both as an example and as a warning. In any global strategy of development its significance cannot be ignored for at least three reasons:

1. At $77, India's "per capita" income is possibly the world's lowest. This indicates the leeway it has to make up to bring up this figure to somewhere around $250, now enjoyed by several other developing countries.

2. Nearly 30 percent of the population of the non-affluent world is Indian. Thus, on a quantitative basis alone, India's success or failure to achieve a minimum standard of living must be a matter of deep interest and concern to the whole of mankind.

3. From the viewpoint of liberal values, the achievement in India of sustained economic progress within the framework of political democracy

cannot but inspire and encourage other developing countries of the world to make similar efforts and achieve equal or greater success.

Since planning began in 1951–52, the Indian economy has scored an annual growth-rate of about 3.2 percent. Other developing countries, it is true, have achieved higher growth-rates but it needs to be remembered that in the first fifty years of the present century, the Indian growth-rate was less than 1 percent. However, the fact remains that, set against the population growth-rate of 2.1 percent during the planning period, the "per capita" income has risen at an annual rate of barely 1.1 percent. This figure, however, seriously underestimates substantial achievements, particularly in recent years. For instance, in the provision of infrastructure facilities like power and transportation, the record is impressive. Thus India is now adding each year to its power capacity more than the total capacity it inherited at the time of its independence in 1947, while the current level of industrial production, accompanied by a conspicuous measure of diversification, is three times higher than in 1950–51.

Even in erstwhile weak areas—Agriculture, Exports and Family Planning —the spurt in the last five years has been sizeable.

In Agriculture is emerging a "Green Revolution" which, breaking through food production, long stagnant at 2.5 to 3 percent per year, has now begun to forge ahead at 5 percent. Fertiliser consumption has increased from 650,000 tonnes in 1963–64 to 2.2 million tonnes at present, while tractor production—which was 1,632 in 1963–64—thouched 18,000 units in 1968. During this same period, the number of irrigation pump-sets energised leapt from 300,000 to over 1.1 million.

In Exports India is now emerging as a major exporter of even sophisticated engineering products, the value of which increased five times in the last five years. Steel exports increased nearly eight times; these two items alone annually earn the country nearly $165 million in foreign exchange.

In Family Planning there are unmistakable signs of a significant advance. Whereas over the first five years of this decade India spent only $35 million, during the next five years it intends to spend $400 million. Where there is determination to deal with this problem, the reward is swiftly forthcoming. Thus, in the two industrial towns of Jamshedpur in the east and Mithapur in the west, within a five-year period the birth-rate has been drastically reduced to below 25 per thousand against 40 for the nation as a whole. And throughout India the number of sterilizations performed—1.8 million a year—are twentytwo times higher than the number performed in 1960–61.

Perhaps, what is even more crucial to an evaluation of India's future potential is the sharply accelerated utilisation of inputs of modern technology. Thus in tractors alone, not only has the demand risen over four-fold to 24,000 (internal production accounts for 18,000), but it is estimated that in another five years the demand will rise to 90,000 units. Similarly, in fertilisers, the demand is estimated to increase by two-and-a-half times by 1973–74—such is the gathering tempo of the Indian economy.

This tempo can be sustained, and even stimulated, if a relatively small amount of foreign aid for a relatively short period is ensured during the process of accelerated development. To prove this point, a model of Indian economic growth can be built around three major assumptions:

(*a*) that the annual rate of population growth now at 2.5 percent will, in successive stages as indicated in the attached table, be reduced to 1 percent by 1990;

(*b*) that the annual rate of savings will likewise be stepped up in successive stages from the level of 11 percent to 25 percent by 1990; and, finally,

(*c*) that India's *per capita* income currently at $77 will rise to at least $220 by 1990. Any level of individual income below this limit would fail to ensure a reasonable standard of living in terms of food, clothing, shelter and education.

It is, therefore, necessary to assess at this stage India's foreign aid requirements during these two critical decades, in which it is sought to treble its *per capita* income from the current level of $77 to the minimum level of around $220. Doubtless, in constructing such a model, any number of permutations and combinations are possible, but for the sake of simplicity, only one assumption needs to be made to drive home the point that India can reach a self-sustaining and self-generating stage with only a limited amount of foreign aid for a limited period of time.

The attached table shows that were foreign aid to be assured to India at the rate of 2.5 percent of its GNP during the decade of the 1970s, and then be reduced, in successively lower proportions, to 1.5 percent during the first five years of the 1980s, and to 0.7 percent during the last five years, by 1985–86 India could reach a point of self-sufficiency in its foreign aid programmes.

Briefly, the position that would emerge is as follows:

| Time period | Annual rate total savings | | End-year estimates foreign aid | | |
	Domestic (%)	Foreign (%)	Gross (Mn. $)	Net (Mn. $)	Per capita ($)
1971–72 to 1975–76	11.5	2.5	1,386	778	2.26
1976–77 to 1980–81	15.5	2.5	1,811	899	2.70
1981–82 to 1985–86	20.5	1.5	1,560	192	2.17
1986–87 to 1990–91	24.3	0.7	1,172	−880	1.55

In absolute terms, India's foreign aid requirements during the 20-year period of rapid development would be $26.2 billion, but significantly by 1985–86, its repayment liabilities would start exceeding its foreign aid inflow. In other words, by 1985–86 India would cease to be a *net* foreign-aid receiving country. This process would continue upto and beyond 2,000 A.D. By this year, India would have repaid most of its aid liabilities.

Such a global programme of world aid would have a two-fold advantage. The advanced countries of the world would not only be giving aid which in terms of their GNP would be a small fraction,[2] but would by the end of the century have recovered most of the capital they would have loaned, together with the interest thereon. This would be so because, unless there is a distinct shift in the composition of foreign aid towards outright grants, the overwhelming proportion of foreign aid would continue to be in the shape of long-term credits. Thus, by 1990 India would have repaid about $25 billion out of the $26 billion received as foreign aid over the two decades of development.

Moreover, India would be bearing, as indeed it should be bearing, the main brunt of the resource-mobilisation necessary for this sharp increase contemplated in the *per capita* income of its inhabitants. Out of the total savings of $369 billion required during these two decades, $342 billion or 93 percent would come from India's own resources.

Thus, a scheme of global strategy based on India as a proto-type of a developing country with a markedly low initial standard of living would secure the following achievements of deep significance to world peace and stability:

(a) *By 1985–86,* India would cease being a *net* foreignaid receiving country;

(b) *By 1990–91,* India would reach a *per capita* income level at which its citizens would be ensured a reasonable standard of living; and

(c) By 2 000 A.D., the developed countries of the world which would have aided India to the extent of $26,2 billion during its two critical decades of development will have recovered through India's repayment most of their capital with interest.

In conclusion, no strategy for civilised survival can be meaningful unless it includes the objective of making it possible for all the people of the world to live a life free from want and fear. The means and the resources for achieving this great task are available in abundance. There is also much evidence of man's capacity to mobilize aid and to co-operate with his neighbour anywhere and whenever disaster strikes. What is now wanted, therefore, to solve the crisis of the spirit and the challenge of want which threaten our survival, is the mobilization of these material and human resources and their application to a bold and sustained programme of global co-operation.

Notes

[1] Platt, J., *What We Must Do*. Mental Health Research Institute, University Michigan, Ann Arbor, Michigan, U.S.A., 1969.
[2] Thus, the total GNP of the OECD countries would currently be in the vicinity of $1,650 billion; whereas the total aid extended to India over the next two decades beginning from 1971–72 would in our scheme be hardly $ 26 billion.

Projections of Indian economic growth

	Units	1968-69 Anticipated	Base year 1970-71 estimates	1971-72 to 1975-76		1976-77 to 1980-81		1981-82 to 1985-86		1986-87 to 1990-91	
				Annual rate of growth (%)	End-year estimates	Annual rate of growth (%)	End-year estimates	Annual rate of growth (%)	End-year estimaies	Annual rate of growth (%)	End-year estimates
I. Population	(Mn.)	526	550	(2.2)	613	(1.8)	670	(1.4)	719	(1.0)	755
II. GNP	($ Mn.)	40,736	44,485	(4.5)	55,436	(5.5)	72,452	(7.5)	104,013	(10.0)	167,512
III. Per capita GNP	($)	77	81	(2.2)	90	(3.7)	108	(6.1)	145	(8.9)	222
IV. Total savings[a]	($ Mn.)	4,888	5,338	(14.0)	7,761	(18.0)	13,041	(22.0)	22,883	(25.0)	41,877
Of which:											
a) Domestic savings[a]		3,870	4,226	(11.5)	6,375	(15.5)	11,230	(20.5)	21,323	(24.3)	40,705
b) Foreign aid[a]		1,018	1,112	(2.5)	1,386	(2.5)	1,811	(1.5)	1,560	(0.7)	1,172
Repayment[b]		520	540		608		912		1,368		2,052
Net foreign aid		498	572		778		899		192		−880
V. Per capita foreign aid	($)	1.94	2.02		2.26		2.70		2.17		1.55

[a] Figures in brackets represent percentages of GNP.
[b] After 1975-76, the average annual repayment liabilities are assumed to increase by 50 per cent per quinquennium.

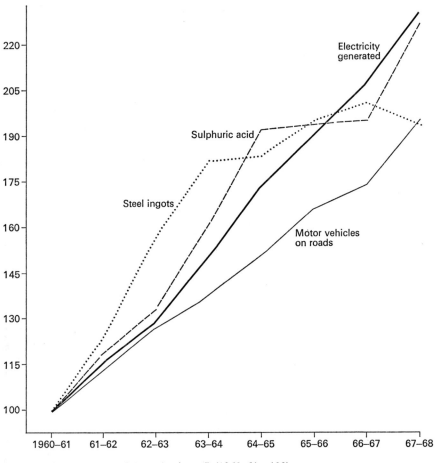

Fig. 1. Indices of Industrial Production—I (1960–61 = 100).

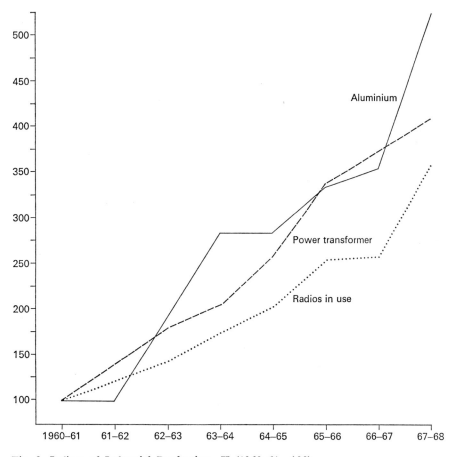

Fig. 2. Indices of Industrial Production—II (1960–61 = 100).

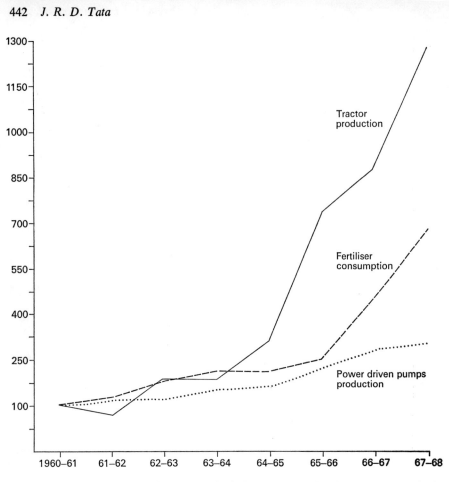

Fig. 3. Indicators of Modernisation of Agriculture (Index Numbers: 1960–61 = 100).

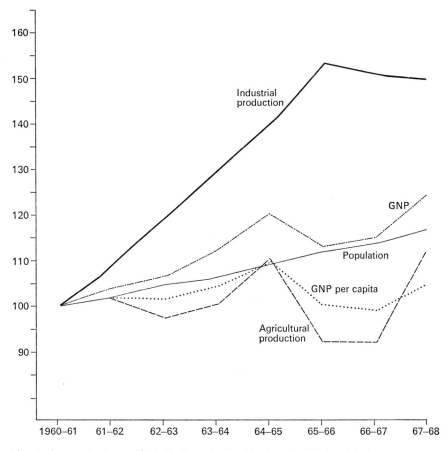

Fig. 4. Aggregate Economic Indicators (Index Numbers: 1960–61 = 100).

SUMMARY OF DISCUSSIONS

Discussion

I. *The menace and the promise of science*

On the papers by Monod and Lederberg a number of interventions were made on the role of science in formulating new value systems and particularly the role of research in biology.

The paper by Pierce caused Doxiadis to draw the attention to the social gaps created by the tremendous difference in development between different fields in science and technology. Koestler was convinced that in the near future we will have a new kind of neurosis, contactile deprivation, caused by the gradual disappearance of physical contacts.

1. *Lorenz* agreed with Monod that biological research will have to take a great responsibility but he did not believe that it will be of such an importance in formulation of new values as Monod thought. Lorenz meant that there is a great danger in using scientific analysis in formulation of values. The danger with the scientific attitude is that some traditional values, which are extremely valuable for society, are defined as inconsistent.

Monod agreed with Lorenz on most of the points but was convinced that we cannot any longer postpone the decision on new values. We have to go back to a complete revision of the value system. On a remark by *Lederberg* Monod claimed that animistic anthologies cannot serve as a social cement because they stand in conflict with scientific thought.

Koestler (as a "hybride" between the two cultures according to his own definition) took up the distinction by Monod between ethics on the one hand and knowledge on the other. He thought that there is a third element that enters into both ethics and knowledge, namely the esthetics of science and esthetics of ethics. By esthetics of science Koestler meant the familiar, spontaneous feeling of beauty which comes to most individuals around the age of 15 when they first discover the proof by Euclid. This proof is of incredible elegant shortness and by finite means it tells us something about the infinite. This kind of experience plays an essential part in the persuit of science. Ethical experience in science can be a reward but Koestler did not think it can be a *source* of ethics. Nor can knowledge be a source of ethics. "I think ethical insight or intuition in validity and fallibility comes from somewhere else. Where they come from is anybody's guess", said Koestler.

Waddington took up the statement by Monod that language has evolved only once and that it might very well not have evolved at all. Waddington thought that language is a staggeringly efficient way of transmitting information from one generation to another. There has been a number of what might be called evolutionary inventions, the first one of which was to find some way of getting a recombination between genetic factors. Most of the animals and plants have deployed an organism that they contain in two representatives in each gene and a mechanism for recombination, which usually is based on a sexual process. But there are alternatives. Many bacteria have invented alternative ways of recombination, which again is a way of speeding up the evolution. Any new way of speeding up evolution, if it occurs at all, is going to have an enormous natural selective advantage.

Some way of increasing the speed of evolution by conceptual transmission of information as opposed to material transmission seems to be something very likely to have occurred in some way or another. It has occurred in the world by the invention of language. A question of particular interest at this symposium is the relation between language and value. The operation of a language involves participants in the system who accept some sequence of noise or some marks on papers as meaning something. This acception of meaning is closely connected with the acception of value. Then you can ask yourself: Is there a way to persuade yourself that certain sounds have meaning other than authoritatively, that you are told they do by your culture?

One of the things the human infant has to do is to learn that the world consists of relatively definite objects, that all this mass of colours, lights, pains, and defrauding can be discriminated into things you can pick up, with an outline surrounding them. And this seems to be quite a difficult lesson to learn from what we can make out of people who are born blind and got their sight later on. It takes them years to acquire this ability. That acquisition seems to be important enough to be tied up with the convention that certain sounds and certain marks have meaning and can be used for transmitting information. However, we have not employed that. We have employed a parental or social authority to say: "These things are meaningful". This suggests that in the first place some system of rapid transmission of rapidly variable information might have been evolved by any living system. Secondly, the way we have done it may be arbitrary—there may be other possible ways in which you could have done it, and the other possible ways might not have evolved anything. "I believe that our language does have relations to ethical value", said Waddington.

Harrison Brown took up the question "Is life on earth a miracle or not?". Most of those who have thought about these problems would conclude that it is not, that if you were to make the earth again as it was in the beginning about 4 000–5 000 million years ago, the same kind of chemical evolutionary processes would take place, given the same sequence of both chemical and physical environments, and that life would inevitably emerge as the end product of a rational series of chemical events. Given the proper degree of chemical flexibility—by which is meant an environment in which the complex sequence of chemical reactions can take place with the right ingredients—life would emerge anyway, assuming things were not too hot and not too cold and assuming you had the mediums.

It is interesting to speculate on how wide-spread such phenomena have been in our universe. There is now increasing evidence that stars and planets can exist in co-stars. Multiple starsystems are the rule rather than the exception. Planets outside our own solar system are very difficult to see, as they do not shine for one thing, but you can detect at least the large ones as the result of perturbation of the proper motions of stars. And already, as the result of painstaking work that has been done mainly in the United States, eight companions to known stars, all of them quite close to the earth, have been discovered. The picture that seems to be emerging is that in some way co-stars of astronomical bodies are formed when one of them gets large enough to support the starting of the reactions that ignites. Quite often in such co-stars, two will ignite together and become large enough to ignite three, four and five. We know at least of one system—Castor—where six bodies, looking like a planetary satellite system, have actually become large enough to ignite.

In the case of our own solar system, we have one body which is ignited, namely our sun, and one body which, had it become somewhat larger, would have ignited, namely Jupiter, which is essentially a cold star. Statistically, it would appear that planetary systems in our own galaxy are rules rather than exceptions. Most stars probably have cold bodies of planetary dimensions associated with them. You may ask what proportion of those will be close enough to the center of radiation, so that it is not too cold for chemical reactions to take place and not too hot for very complex compounds to associate, and further which of those planets are not too small, like the moon or Mars, to support the medium in which chemical reactions can take place. On our own planet the medium is water. Statistically it would appear that something in the order of 5 % of such bodies (5 % of the visible solar systems) might well have cold bodies associated with them which fit these overall conditions. The conclusion is that life may very well be an extremely abundant commodity within the universe. One can then go one step further and ask. Here on earth one first went through the chemical and then the biological evolutionary sequences. What are the chances that this might have happened elsewhere with the emergence of the power of conceptual thought, which then results in cultural evolution replacing biological evolution as a major force.

One can go still further and ask. Given the emergences of the power of conceptual thought, what are the chances that creatures endowed with this power elsewhere have gone through a sequence where they too have learned how to harness large concentrations of energy? Here on earth we have what may be called a high energy civilization, characterized by the concentration of very large quantities of energy per person. Conceivably it has emerged elsewhere. By its very nature, a high energy civilization is basically unstable. It will exist for a while. It might well be—this applies to what is going on on the earth at the present time—that it is not possible to stabilize the situation. And sooner or later something rocks the boat in United States, the Soviet Union or China, so that one no longer is capable of supporting that kind of an activity.

It is interesting to explore what our own attitudes are of man as a part of a much larger whole of creatures possessed of the power of conceptual thought, which might exist elsewhere. Harrison Brown felt that such suppositions could be cited mainly to complement discussions where we tend to look at man in an isolated way. It may be preferable to think that man is part of a very much larger whole.

Monod responded that speculations on the probability of the emergence of life are almost meaningless. It is anybody's guess whether the probability is almost 1 or, given enough time, tentatively 70. Modern knowledge of the structure itself has not made the probability greater but, if anything, smaller. It is exceedingly difficult to tell, for instance, how the genetic features evolved. One can fairly well understand how the very primitive replicating of the nucleic acids might have appeared—that is not too difficult—but the next step which is the formation of what we call cells with a modern soul with all its apparatus is very difficult. Specialists on the origin of life seem to agree that nothing can be said about this. We cannot say anything about the probability of life having appeared at all or not. Again, it is anybody's guess. But there is one important event in evolution which we are very interested in, namely the emergence of language. This happened only once and it might just as well not have happened.

A student asked Monod how safe we could be in extrapolating our belief and faith in science to the domains of values. Will it for instance be possible to take into consideration alternative values in the system proposed by Monod?

Monod answered that the essential thing is to make a clear distinction between science—that is to say the knowledge which has been gathered by the adoption of the scientific attitude—and the attitude that we take, in the adoption of an epistemology which decides, more or less automatically, that true knowledge can only be gained through the systematic confrontation of logic and experience. An important articulation in the system proposed is that *you cannot derive a value system from scientific knowledge.* You cannot accumulate scientific knowledge without having chosen an epistemology and therefore also a scale of values to begin with. You have to decide, that in fact objective knowledge (this is a prevalue) is part of your soul. Therefore, it is not right that adopting the scientific attitude means getting rid of the soul. Not at all! It is in fact part of your soul. One of the greatest works that established modern scientific methods— *Discours de la méthode* by Descartes—is in fact, not as it is generally presented in schools, an essay in epistemology but a long meditation on ethics.

Pauling thought—contrary to some of the statements in the discussion— that ethics should properly be a scientific subject. He presented what he called the principle of the *minimization of suffering.* As one example of how one can apply the principle of choosing from among alternative courses the one that corresponds to the smallest predicted amount of suffering— he took the problem of how long one should keep old or ill people alive by repeated heart transplants or other methods. One has to ask how much suffering is involved for the person himself by being kept alive as compared with dying and how much suffering is involved for his family through his being kept alive rather than dying. This is probably what physicians and other people do for the most part in deciding whether use will be made of a kidney machine or available transplants. Pauling was much troubled by these questions, because in the city of Seattle a committee of non-specialists had been set up to make the decision, and in this case, the decision depends on whether the person in question has a big enough income, $15 000 a year or something like that to pay for it, whether he goes to church regularly, whether he has been a boy scout leader, whether he belongs to a good solid conservative political party or is a radical, and so on.

Pauling did also comment on Lederbergs statement that it is very difficult to know how to improve cerebration by any biological or technological method. He thought that it is possible to improve cerebration and that it has to be done for the affluent people as well as for the poor and undernourished people who are clearly deficient mentally in part because of malnutrition in the infancy and childhood. He thought that it is possible to improve cerebration by improving the molecular environment of the mind or, as we may say, by providing the optimal molecular environment of the mind. Pauling took vitamins and essential amino acids as examples.

Human beings suffer from a score of two genetic diseases that their ancestors long ago learned to cure by diet. It turned out that it was beneficial to suffer from these diseases and to control them by diet. The mutants which had defective genes could compete better just because of having these in-born errors of metabolism. Every vitamin, every essential amino acid in-dicates a genetic disease of this sort that we control by diet, for example vitamin C, which man and a few other animals require while other animals manufacture it for themselves. But it was only about 30 million years ago that the mutation occurred that evolved the loss of the ability to manufac-ture vitamin C. The dog, the rat, the cat, the horse, and the cow all manufac-ture vitamin C for themselves, but Man and the anthropoid apes and monkeys cannot. We have all lost the ability, a mutation that occurred before the separation of the recessed monkey and Man took place.

Why did the mutants survive? The mutants survived because there was a supply of the drug, vitamin C, available for him, and he was relieved of the burden of the machinery that other animals use to manufacture their own vitamin C. The same thing is true for vitamin B_1 vitamin B_2, vitamin B_3, and so on for the other vitamines and essential amino acids. You are better off physically and mentally too if you do not have to manufacture these substances for yourself.

Pauling then raised the following question. Why do the nutritionalists tell us that somewhere around 30 or 60 milligrams is the proper amount per day of ascorbic acid for a human being? He believed that it is the result of a misunderstanding. You get in bad shape if you are getting only 30 to 60 milligrams of ascorbic acid per day and you come down with scurvy and die. Now, how much do you need to function really well? Pauling thought that the maximum is perhaps 3 000 milligrams per day, 50 or 100 times as much as is recommended. In fact, it is very hard to find any evi-dence in the literature as to what the maximum is, but there is also a lot of indications that people are really significantly healthier and "smarter" if they get 3 000 milligrams of vitamin C per day than if they get only the conventionally recommended amount. The division of clinical research of the National Institute of Mental Health carried out an investigation a few years ago in Texas of several hundred school children. It was found that the IQ was quite a well-defined function of the ascorbic acid concentration in the blood of the school children. When one devided the children into two groups, one with low ascorbic acid concentration and the other with high, and gave them an extra 50 milligrams of ascorbic acid a day, a glass of orange juice, the IQ of the lower group went up by five points. This was statistically significant. The other group of children also received the orange juice, but they were already high enough up on the curve so their IQ did not change by a detectable amount.

We have the problem of protein starvation. One usually says that the minimum amount of protein required to prevent diseases from protein starvation is half a gram protein per day. The reason for this is that some of the essential amino acids are not contained in the proper amount in the food and there is evidence that if there was a proper distribution of the essential amino acids, then 10–12 grams of protein a day would be enough. Pauling thought that it might well be that the cerebration of even well-fed people could be increased by 10%—ten points higher an IQ—by providing a better diet. Having a good income does not mean that you are well-fed, because ignorance of one sort or another is involved. Therefore when we come to the malnourished people, in addition to the *quantity* of food that they need we should also think about the *quality* of food. Pauling believed that there is a real possibility that by adding lysine and other essential amino acids to the green protein something really significant could be done and improve the mental health as well as physical health of people.

2. *Doxiadis* brought up the impact that telecommunications can have on our relationship with other people compared with person-to-person contacts. He did not think it was right—and hoped that Dr Pierce would agree—to make the statement that it is only now when we communicate through telecommunications that we can communicate with minds that are miles away. Socrates for instance certainly had much stronger intellectual connections with the philosophers on the other side of the Aegian than with his neighbours. Whether these philosophers influenced his wife Xanthippe and his neighbours who condemned him to death, we do not know. We only know that this dual type of connection existed in very early times and that it is not directly related to telecommunications. Doxiadis came to one tentative conclusion, namely that telecommunications, as many other technologies, have added dimensions to our life but without reducing the age-old dimensions of person-to-person contacts.

Doxiadis did also take up the great progress in telecommunications explained by Pierce and the even greater one anticipated. We can expect that telecommunications and computers will take care of for example the delivery of our goods to our homes very soon. This would be possible thanks to a perfect organization of the information in the delivering systems. But it was not clarified how we were going to *get* the goods we need or want. Doxiadis meant that this may serve as a good illustration of the weakness of our modern civilization and technology. We make huge progresses in some fields, like in transmitting information, but we make no progress at all or very little in others. We must develop much better means of communication between different scientific and technological fields so that huge gaps are eliminated or diminished when progress in a certain field is far ahead of that of other fields.

Pierce pointed out that he consciously simplified matters in attributing contact over a distance to telecommunications. In the time of Socrates people were, in a somewhat slower way, known over what was then the civilized world. What telecommunications has done is to make this a commonplace of almost everyone's life. In America, the people you know and the people you work with are not the people you live next door to, and you do not have to have a worldwide reputation such as Socrates had to participate. Certainly, telecommunications are extended to everyone or to a large group of people. It was earlier reserved for a small elite or perhaps the wandering sailors.

Telecommunications and computers organizing a delivery system were not meant in terms of people and crafts, but were given as examples with a somewhat broader view in mind. Today, we are faced with a situation in which science and technology have greatly improved the output of man in manufacturing automobiles, chewing gums, and almost anything else. There is another service sector which includes the performing arts as well as plumbers repairing your plumbing, where technology has not much improved the output or the effectiveness of the people. The only area in which it has done so is in the area called telecommunications. This has been largely achieved by using automatic switching instead of human telephone operators.

At a time when we have so much goods, we find it difficult to get good education, good health services, good delivery services and good repair services. We are going into pieces in the midst of plenty, because no way has been found of increasing the productivity in these areas of human activity. Pierce agreed with Doxiadis that it would be nice if we could transmit goods through pipes and sit down at our offices and homes to solve the problems by the use of telecommunications. Science and technology are doing what they can to that end. Some wonderful things have happened. We have the nuclear power generation, we have television in our homes and we developed radar during World War II. On the other hand, we do not understand very well the relation between science and technology and the economy in general. We do not know what to do to make things better to be to the service of man.

Koestler could visualize that from telecommunications would almost automatically follow a neurosis which he thought would be very prevalent in ten years time from now. The next development is that not only board room meetings will be conducted by telecommunication networks but that quite a number—perhaps the majority—of big business firms and government departments will have their members conduct their business from their desk at home through closed circuit television. In the two biggest cities in Australia—Sydney and Melbourne—already today 90% of the two million people live in suburbs. There is no night life in the cultural sense because getting home from the office and then getting back and home again would mean 6–8 hours commuting. A recent social survey showed that only 2% of the suburbanites go out in the evening during the week. Some of the others go out on Sundays visiting their relatives but there is no social life any more, because everything is piped into the house, television, radio, and so on.

We have executives now who meet regularly at airports and this has become a problem for the development of the airports. But it is much simpler to conduct business meetings and symposia by closed circuit television. This development is unavoidable, as there is no reason why administrative business should not be conducted from the desk at home.

And now comes the new office. Your boss becomes a superman or phantom, standing there in three times natural size projection. He talks to you, but you cannot pat him on the shoulder or punch him or pull him, he is real and unreal. There will be a neurosis called contactile deprivation and this neurosis is unavoidable. We know from experiments how very quickly the nervous system goes sleigh-riding if one or several parts of its ties is cut off. In order to avoid this deprivation the analyst will suggest: "Keep in touch! Don't lose the grip on reality! Don't try to grasp what I am telling you! There will always be tactile simulators."

Tiselius commented on *Chagas* paper about the difficult matter of priorities in science. He found that Chagas had mentioned as particularly worthy of priority the biological studies taken in the widest sense. There is a very striking example of this in the successful work on the improvement of rice and wheat and some other plants, which have proved extremely important to a number of countries such as Mexico, Pakistan and India. This work can chiefly be ascribed to the support by the Rockefeller and Ford Foundations. It was the result of about 10 years' very patient and persistent work. Some people claim that this is perhaps the greatest contribution that science has made to the solution of the problems of the developing countries. The total input has been in the order of 15 million dollars while the result has been estimated to several billion dollars. Tiselius meant that this has actually demonstrated that very much can be done if a concentrated effort is made. This ought to be applied to other problems of similar kind.

The environmental problems and the ecological problems are good examples. It is encouraging that most governments now realize the importance of these problems and that to a certain extent they are ready to start organizations to solve them and to invest large sums of money for this purpose. Tiselius claimed that there is still lacking an organized collaboration on an international scale on these problems. We must remember that in most cases we already have the tools and the background of fundamental research for attacking these problems. He felt that the way these problems are being approached now is highly inefficient. In most countries they are treated as a local national affair. For mission oriented research of this kind it would seem natural to have an international organization of a rather firm character with a dictatoric leadership that would just tell people—research workers and technologists from different countries—to do this and that. There should also be a master plan of the whole undertaking. Tiselius could well foresee that there would be objections to this. One objection would probably be that this is incompatible with the freedom of research. To speak of a "dictator" in this connection is not very popular. But it should be stressed again that it is not a question of basic research—which must be free of course—but a problem of applying results and tools which already exist. There are several examples of what can be achieved by such a strong and planned mission. Take the nuclear energy field and the space programmes for example. Great things can be done if a concentrated effort is made. So far, however, these results have been achieved mainly on the national level. Suppose one could initiate a mission on environmental control on an international scale. Only then something of significant value could be achieved and time is short.

In Sweden the mercury poisoning has created serious problems and much research has gone to this, especially to research with regard to the mercury poisoning of fish. Tiselius concluded that since the mercury problems in Sweden must be roughly the same as the mercury problems in say Holland or Canada an international collaboration is both needed and desirable. He did not believe that the objections from the research workers themselves would be a problem. Tiselius expressed his desire that the participants of this symposium would oppose to all political and commercial resistance to establish such a collaboration.

II. *The teaching of knowledge and the imparting of values*

A vivid discussion took place on the role and kind of creativity in arts and science. Engelhardt elaborated on the interrelation between freedom and necessity in social development. Klineberg meant that it is a false interpretation of history to think that the development follow a smooth curve. For most individuals and societies today's changes are very drastic. Based on the paper by Lambo, Mead was convinced that in today's help to developing countries we tend to underestimate the potential engagement and effort by the people themselves in these countries.

Tiselius expressed his view on the creativity in arts and science. He did not believe that there exists any fundamental difference in the act of creation but eventually in the ways of presentation. Scientists are human beings and suffer from all the weaknesses which are typical for human beings. Moreover the results of the creative work by scientists are published in special journals, where everything is presented and organized in a certain uniform style. There is no space in these journals to tell how things really developed.

Tiselius drew the attention to Koestler's book *The Sleepwalkers* in which science, scientific method and scientists are followed through history of modern man. The scientists are here not presented as individuals full of cold facts but as human beings with all their weaknesses, and mistakes. Tiselius meant that if one looks at the scientist in this way the difference between them and the artists would not be as marked as is generally believed and it would probably be possible to bridge the gap of understanding between the scientists and the artists, poets and humanists.

Gombrich agreed on this with Tiselius and emphasized that he did not say anything to the contrary in his paper. However, there is a very important difference between art and science, Gombrich meant. If you say to anybody that some lines and figures on the blackboard is art there is very little to argue about. It is not possible to "measure" if you are right or not. But if you publish a scientific result in a paper, you and the scientific community can tell whether it is or not of required standards.

Tiselius said that when you talk about the act of creation you should not compare say a painting with a scientific paper because the latter does not expose anything of the creative mind. The scientific paper can be characterized as a kind of "after-rationalization", of course without distorting the facts reported.

Koestler pointed out that his book *The Sleepwalkers* was only the first part. In the second book called *The Act of Creation* he took up the verifyability in art and science and it was maintained that verifyability and fortifyability is a matter of evolution.

Chagas told that about 30 years ago he was visited by a famous poet who was exiled in Brazil. After a visit to Chagas' laboratory and a thorough discussion about how scientific research is undertaken the poet expressed his views as follows: "I never thought that you were undertaking science in the same way I am doing poetry."

Chagas further said that he had recently in a paper explained his ideas on the similarity between scientific and artistic creativity. He believed that in both there are two elements in different proportions. The first one is called *accumulated* intuition and the second one *instantaneous* intuition. Both can be found in scientific and artistic creation, according to Chagas.

Pierce was very much struck by Auden's *Secondary world* of limestone and lead mining, which lead him to think that science is a secondary world which we all share. It must correspond as nearly as possible to the primary world in which we all live. Consequently the secondary world must be continuously revised when we find out that we have made it imperfectly.

Engelhardt meant that the suggestion by Auden in the summary circulated before the symposium to classify people in labourers and workers was excellent. It pointed to the ultimate goal of mankind as formulated in "Maximum happiness to the maximum number of people". In Auden's classification this would mean a society with a maximum number of workers and a minimum of labourers.

Engelhardt did also comment on the words "Freedom and Necessity" standing side by side in the title of Auden's paper. Freedom is one of the few human values which may well be called a cardinal value, because it was introduced by the great French revolution. Engelhardt regarded the coupling of freedom and necessity as highly significant. According to most philosophers in modern times up to Spinoza, freedom can be considered as recognized necessity. This definition is excellent. It implies that freedom must be pertained to sacrifice to a certain degree in accordance with what necessity requires. Probably no other value is so liable to changes as freedom to prevailing conditions. The changes go almost exclusively in one direction namely that of diminishing, delimiting and sacrificing step by step. Freedom decreases hand in hand with increasing complexity of the social structure of society. It is only by recognizing the necessity of these limitations that we can avoid a feeling of dispair and frustration. It is an insufficient re-cognition of the relation between evil and necessity that to a large extent is responsible for the adolescent trouble, characteristic of our time.

Engelhardt then took a very pragmatic example to illustrate the relation between freedom and necessity. "You walk along a street, you come to a crossing where the red light is on and you stop. Nobody prevents you from going on, only a signal with a certain meaning has reached you. You are free to go on but you sacrifice part of your freedom, and decide to stand still instead of risking the catastrophe of finding yourself under the wheels. The price you pay is negligible, just two minutes stand still or being late at dinner. The value you obtain is infinitely great compared to the price which may be infinitely small. You have recognized the necessity to sacrifice part of your freedom. Your sense of philantropy is first rate."

Engelhardt apologized for choosing this naive example to illustrate one of the most precious human values around which there are also the hottest disputes going on. In his opinion freedom has a peculiar resemblance with a concept from the very remote field of physics, namely entropy, which has the universal tendency in nature to increase with disorder. Organization, which is always accompanied by an increase in order, counteracts the universal tendency of entropy to increase.

In society we can witness similar conditions so far as freedom is concerned. With increasing order brought about by increasing complexity and efficiency of the social structure, freedom is reduced and necessity increased. Freedom is at maximum for a man staying in singularity beyond the constraint and the responsibility (necessity) imposed by society. It is the case of Robinson Crusoe before the appearance of Friday.

Different elements of social order bring restraint to the behaviour, and freedom is reduced just as entropy decreases with the appearance of order and form of biological systems.

The following question may arise: "Is the decrease of freedom a partial sacrifice which is an inevitable condition for the progressive improvement of the social structure? If so, how long can this decrease proceed without leading to an exhaustion of the 'total' available supply of freedom?"

Engelhardt was convinced that an improvement of the present social structure can be achieved only by increasing the element of order and by imposing more responsibility on each member of the society. In the long run this will lead to a situation where the previously necessary elements of order and restraint one by one are getting obsolete and superfluous. This would mean that the dimension of freedom, instead of decreasing, will gradually increase. Like the phenomenon of entropy the increase of freedom may acquire the properties of a driving force instead of being a mere consequence of the change of social order.

Lorenz took up the concept chreod as it was introduced by Waddington. He was disappointed to find that Waddington when talking about cybernetics did not use an English word for "Sollwert". Lorenz concluded that chreod in Greek or English must be equivalent to the German word Sollwert.

If evolution is a chreod, and Lorenz believed it is, then it might be possible to find an explanation for purpose of evolution. We have reached a consensus that purpose is nothing but an internal chreod which somehow gains just above the threshold of our conscience. Value must be something very similar, it is also a chreod. Value is a particular sort of purpose or chreod. Lorenz did not think that in using the chreod we could avoid the reproach of being animistic. He would not be disappointed to find his own ideas on evolution depreciated and expressed in a complete, mechanistic way, a chreod for evolution. It would still retain its upward tendency or direction, he thought. Perhaps our appreciation of the value of this direction is purely a prioristic, that is to say necessary, because we are part of the Universe which produces this.

The mechanics of evolution is very similar to the one of human creativity so accurately described by Gombrich. However, evolution is an entirely misleading word. The Western languages have no word for what really happens when something entirely new comes into existence. Development, Evolution, Entwicklung are all terms which involve reformation.

In culture, invention and intellectual research play the same role as selection and quotation and recombination of genes play in evolution. Evaluation of constant values constitutes the retarding, stabilizing factor which is necessary in order to store and keep what the intellect and learning have acquired. Every stabilizor, every structure is bought at the price of lower degree of freedom. All culture rests on a skeleton of very slowly evolved social norms of behaviour and the rigidity of this structure is necessary but may be an obstacle to further evolution. In every process in which the structure is changed one has to break down parts of the skeleton. This will always involve a period of failures. Lorenz finished by saying that he believed that evolution does not consist of one chreod but is a succession of different chreods.

Klineberg took up the extent to which a ratchet can develop during a cultural development if there is no automatic "slipping back". He illustrated what happens when a cultural tradition "arises and disappears" by taking some examples from the scientific literature.

The first was in a group of Japanese investigators who worked with Japanese makaks. They found an interesting phenomenon. One of the makaks took off one day into the water with a jam—sweet potatoe—and washed the dirt off in the water. Then there was a chreod in the colony —all of them were taking jams, washing them in the water and then eating them. But then they also took enough to wash even when they were clean, and the process itself became the object of the activity.

The chimpanzees developed two types of activities. For example, one of them could be an activity in which they would find a new use for an object. They would take that object and put it in as many contexts as possible. For example, they first got into the "stick phase". In the "stick phase", they tried to use the stick to get things into a cage. Then they would dip the sticks into a fruit and eat these very tasty fruits, which seems to be a chimpanzee habit. Around the chimpanzee enclosure there were chickens and one of the games the chimpanzees played, probably to relieve the dullness in the cage, was to lure these rather stupid chickens over and swoop them, and the chickens would fly away. They introduced the stick into that game too. They would lure the chickens over and then stick the chickens with the stick. That was one form of activity.

Then they developed another form of activity that would be a chreod *within* the colony. In this case the chreod took the form of recognizing that you may climb up things that are extended and rigid, so they would climb up sticks, they would climb up the keeper, they would climb up the wall, a ladder and forget all about the process of getting the fruit that was hung up there and that became the object of the task.

What was quite striking in each one of these activities, was that the behaviour that the chimpanzees had developed and which they were imitating within the colony became de-sociated from the objective. In every case it ended within a month, because of habituation. Habituation—or fatigue or whatever you want to call it—would take place and there was no way of transmitting. Once habituation went into operation, it just disappeared from the colony, so that you almost had the feeling that here was truly what a ratchet is, a basis for making record.

You can have an old tradition and some way of making a mark. You can make a mark with a gene, you can make a mark on a piece of paper and you can make a mark in an old tradition. However, in order to somehow have this next step where you speak of an increase of information it is necessary to hold it almost an order of magnitude larger. The container has to be there.

Mostly, the leaps that we see in human development are drastic changes. You just lay a whole bunch of the leaps next to each other, take an average and you will get a smooth curve. This is one of the greatest lies in human history, Klineberg meant.

Aiken was struck by the contrast Bruner saw between the truth and the knower and by the demonstration of how difficult it is for the knower to get to know the truth as a consequence of all the phenomena in the central nervous system that Bruner described. Even when we deal with phenomena that are very close to our hearts, minds and passions, there seem to be tremendous variations between individuals in the degree to which they can approach the knowing of the truth. Aiken took an example from daily life, the way in which we look upon our own children and grandchildren. There are not many of us, said Aiken, who can be objective and see the truth as distinct from the knower's view. Some of us can see our children much more clearly and objectively than others. This variation in the extent to which the knower ignores or distorts the truth gives rise to the following questions. "If there is this large difference and if some people can see very clearly even in areas that are usually considered passionate or emotional and other not so clearly, how do we know whether there are any limits to that possibility? If there is already a marked variation, can we not hope or assume that the knower and truth cannot come together?"

Bruner answered that he took the design of education to provide exercise in ways of knowing, and he would like to see education in that respect start much earlier than at the point when one happens to get into school. Presumably the capacity to view objects from different perspectives to a whole commitment of action is larger then. It is precisely what one would hope to design exercises for in the process of growing up. It is a question of what would be the proper education for a human being, who is naturally equipped with so much biasing in his nervous system, to achieve techniques in order to see the world in ways that accounted for the bias.

Aiken took up the distinction between "is" and "ought" raised by several of the speakers and particularly by Waddington. He thought that there is another distinction that is of very great interest, the distinction between the notion of the value and the notion of obligation. He put it in the following way. You use the wording "to value" or "he values". This is rather like saying "he likes" or "he wants" or "he desires". But when one uses the word "ought", when one enters upon the notion of morality, the propositions do not express themselves as equivalents to "he likes", "he wants" or "is required". Kant put it in another way when he said that our obligations have as their function the limitation of desire, not the expression of desire. The pragmatists—like John Dewey—think of moral principles as if they were instruments or tools. Aiken did not think that this is a good view. There are many, many models, but the point here is not that we have ethical principles and then interpretations or models for conceiving them but that these models infiltrate our thinking i.e. put a bias on the manner in which we reflect. For that reason Aiken thought that we ought to be very careful about the models we adopt in talking about the moral principles.

Waddington agreed that there is a distinction between value and obligation. There are many sorts of values, esthetical values and values of pleasure for instance, which are not ethical values. It is from the command to do things, to take actions, and from that aspect of early language that the ethical values come, whereas other values come from other more communicative purposes of languages.

Gombrich thought that among the problem solutions, both in evolution and even in art or in culture, there are some of great complexity which we would not necessarily regard as evil. Cruelty—there *is* such a thing as refined cruelty—may be such a problem solution which works and which we do not identify with a value. He thought that in that respect it remains our choice what of development and of problem solutions we regard as valuable.

Margaret Mead pointed out in relation to the problems of the developing countries that there are some experiments that are too expensive to make, and this is the point where models and simulation come in. There are some experiments that are remade by history but we might not be able as analytical scientists to analyze in detail what technical changes in scientific education would best fit Nigeria or Burma or some other part of the world. This is an exceedingly expensive, long-term and rather stupid way of arriving at the answer, when we have Nigerians or Burmese to work with. Using the cultural background and education of each country as much as we can with any knowledge that we transfer, means that we include the whole of possibly 10 000 years of specific cultural experimentation in its behaviour. Mead mentioned as a very brief demonstration that during World War II they were asked to devise ways in which exceedingly unpalatable and nutritious foods could be made palatable for different countries. They found after considering that they might do an analysis of each country and decide whether the Yugoslaves or the Greeks or the Norwegians would handle these foods in particular ways. One decided that a much more economical thing was to get a group of cooks from each country and let them cook, and in each case they developed quite different foods that fitted the diet of the natives in the specific countries. It is probably going to be long before we can handle these things out of Lilleput, but if we include the most gifted, the most imaginative from each culture, we will be able to handle them in this fashion of *living models*.

III. *The new republic—scientist, humanist and government*

Lederberg, in view of Máleks paper, expressed his opinion that for the liberation of the intellectually developing child an "a priori" reasoning is hardly a scientific method for trying to elaborate the educational system. He would have thought that greater emphasis should be laid not on "a priori" courses of action of education but on the need for experimental and pragmatic investigation of those aspects of the educational system that can meet the creativity.

Bruner agreed with Lederberg that the amount of empirical evidence we have about the different techniques for education is very small. There are reasons for this, however. First of all, it is quite evident that education as such turns out not to be a simple technical enterprise. One of the most important things about the nature of hypotheses that form the experimentations in education is *that they represent idealizations of what the nature of man is as such.* It is not something stated ex hypothesis if you say: "Let us assume the following to be relevant for releasing creativity in the human being", but rather it takes a value system and from it derives a particular image and a particular process by which you produce a kind of human being. Here is a beautiful occasion in which we can take intrinsic or inherent values that shape our experiments and try to make them explicit. Bruner had heard several things that were implicit in this, for example the notion that challenge and opportunity to see one's capacity for bettering the challenge makes a more selfconfident human being. This may be true, but it would then be interesting to make a careful analysis of what kinds of activities in the life of a child can embody that challenge and also how the child would be given knowledge of the results of its coping with the challenge. Bruner meant that we have here a classic instance of a presentation of a point of view that comes not only from the head but from the heart, something that moves us all. But now, if we really mean what we say about making our values clear enough so that we could examine how to instrument them and how to analyse the consequences of seeking values of that sort—this is precisely the kind of matter we ought to take as a program for analysis to find out what specifically we have in mind and how many changes it would take in the nature of the society to do it. Bruner did agree with Lederberg's view that we keep our sceptical spirit but he would also like to urge that we keep innocent as babies and say right at the outset: "Let us go ahead and take this as seriously as we can and convert it into an experimental program, look at it and not stay just as a preference for a kind of human being but as an experiment."

Gombrich agreed that "the creativity of birth" of course is a noble chreod but he thought that when we talk about creativity in the context of this symposium, the idea of value and the idea of standards should not be omitted. His interest is in the arts and poetry and here the word creativity has certainly been tremendously misused. The idea that anything that goes and anything that is done is creative is surely misleading. Gombrich emphasized that the purpose of his lecture was to point to the existence of standards, and when you come to consider standards, rather than random mutations, then the optimism about the widespread character creativity in children is not so easily supported. Children's paintings are charming and we all enjoy looking at them but perhaps not for a very long time, but if we only liberated it, everybody would be an artist or a scientist which does not seem to be supported by the facts we know. Gombrich did agree that one should try to liberate as much creativity as possible but he thought that one should not pin one's hope on getting a complete information of man.

Lorenz had intended to say much of what Gombrich said but from the biological point of view. He did also agree with everything that Málek said except his antithesis of stability and creativity. When in evolution something new evolves—he did not like the word "emerge"—it stays the same thing while becoming something additional. A bird is a reptile and man is an ape plus cumulative tradition. Lorenz meant that Gombrich had given some very nice examples in his beautiful exposition of the relationship between craftmanship and art. Art is craftmanship plus something else. What he wanted to oppose was the entirely erroneous supposition that creativity implies the complete change and reorganization of everything else it builds upon. He did not think that Málek meant that but that people often believe that one can wipe out everything and start from scratch. Artists have had a history of art before them which must have lasted—judging from the slowest of cultural evolutions of time—about 10 000 years. Then Lorenz wanted to say something as a consolation. He was quite aware that, of course, Málek was right in saying that everyone of us can realize only a minimum of possibilities. But then these possibilities may exclude each other. He felt that perhaps he himself might have become a great actor but this might not go together with being a biologist.

You have to limit yourself in the vast possibilities. You have to decide, which Man has within himself. Lorenz thought that indeed creativity has some of the properties of a chreod and pointed out that Málek himself had mentioned that it is helpful to become creative in order to survive obstacles Lederberg said that obstacles are necessary to enhance and challenge creativity. It has been said that the best works of art have been produced in unheated and unpleasant localities. Even if Lorenz did not quite agree with that, he admitted that there was something in it. Creativity in people who have it is very difficult to suppress and the obvious fear of the manipulation and the indoctrinability of the human society was something that Lorenz did really share. There is the greatest danger that manipulators of all kinds, of all possible political denominations will manipulate people. But this would only be possible if the doctrin, which says that man has no instinct and is completely dependent on the environment was true, which it is not.

Málek agreed fully with Lederberg that we must use some hypothesis in connection with creativity and education. There are two possible hypotheses. Either that there exist very narrow potentials of genetic character on which we have to concentrate, or that there is an immense quantity of creative talents among the population which represent themselves by scientific thinking or by a variety of excursions in other fields. The educational system must be constituted in such a way that all kinds of creativity can be developed.

He also agreed with Lederberg that we have to experiment. Málek did agree with Engelhardt that the exploatation of creativity must be coupled to responsibility imposed upon the individual.

One of the *students* took up Segerstedt's paper on the values and the future. On the one side we have facts and experience and on the other there is the purpose for development. He would have expected to hear a lot more about the purpose to guide the action. He was also very critical to the fact that most of the methods for futurology today have been developed by the military-industrial complex, and this should not be what we would like to see determine our future. To whom are we willing to give the possibility to direct our future, he asked.

Another point in connection with futuristic predictions which he took up was the reluctance of the politicians to use scientific methods in studying alternative changes. Their interest rather seems to be to obscure the real direction in which they wish to see the change go.

The student finally expressed his scepticism about reaching international agreements on some kind of common values.

Another *student* expressed his scepticism on cooperation between different scholars. He was afraid that this would lead to a new elite structure. Instead one should emphasize the cooperation between scholars and public opinion.

Tinbergen thought that Segerstedt had indicated some very important elements. As an economist he was very much hesitant to focus the interest on the year 2000. We are forced to do some exercises and from now to the year 2000 is a very long period to base something definite on. Economists are really very satisfied if they can say something about the next ten years. Tinbergen agreed, however, that it is fundamentally right that we ask questions about the next 30 years or so, but we are lacking methods for this work. Today two approaches are used. One could be called forecasting and it is an analytical approach, the other is more connected to planning and could be called a policy approach. From the book "The Year 2000" by Kahn and Wiener it seems as if the forecasting method is used more than the planning method. Tinbergen felt that in economy the uncertainties with the forecasting method are larger than with the planning method.

In the latter case we set out a program based on certain goals and the uncertainty about all the parameters involved are automatically reduced. Therefore, Tinbergen did also agree with Segerstedt that we have to get an international set of values that we can use for our planning in a first phase. The values are then adjusted and revised before a second phase of a plan and in this manner the development proceeds in an iterative manner. Tinbergen agreed with one of the students that an agreement on international values is not easy. He had seen the difficulties in the United Nation's work for development planning. He thought that at least in social and economical matters we can formulate values by using five or six indicators, which can be such as national income, employment, educational targets and health targets.

Segerstedt meant that one of the great problems in defining social indicators is that we have done very little to measure them. We are reforming our schools and we say that we will improve the possibilities for children to learn foreign languages but we never make any kind of operational determination about how to measure these things. We have to start by defining ways to make measurements in an operational way. When we plan a reform we should at the same time try to tell how far we intend to reach. Only then will it be possible to ask: "Why are we not reaching the goal we had in mind?"

Segerstedt also pointed out that the presentation of alternative future developments with regard to priorities in certain scientific fields would make it easier for people in responsible positions to make decisions.

Segerstedt then took up the formulation of values and said that he thought that we will probably never come to a consensus in a direct way but in an indirect way. If we say that the consequence of alternative A is that and that the consequence of alternative B is that, and so on, we would probably find some common values. Simply because some of the consequences are not desirable for anybody.

Tinbergen was delighted to listen to Pauling but he thought that there is quite a distance between the thinking of an "idealist" like Pauling and himself on the one hand and the average politician on the other hand. The difficulty is to find the best tactics for making the progress in the direction given by Pauling, and on which we all agree. Tinbergen thought that he as an economist is probably somewhat closer to the politicians than Pauling and his tactics are therefore closer to compromise even if he always is inspired by the same feelings as Pauling.

To illustrate his point, Tinbergen gave some examples from his experience in the United Nations. About ten years ago he began to advise the government of Turkey. He suggested, after careful analyses, that Turkey should strive for a 7 % economic growth rate in its first five year plan. The program was accepted but only after heavy criticism by a social democrat and former finance minister for being unrealistic. Turkey succeeded in reaching 6–8 % growth and Tinbergen saw this result as very encouraging since Turkey is a very conservative country.

Recently in Bangkok Tinbergen had a discussion with the United Nations planning committee about the possible growth rate of India during the period 1970–80. Tinbergen went in for 6 % but before he got agreement in the committee he had a difficult dispute with one of his economist colleagues from India, who meant that it was too much. Tinbergen added that it was quite remarkable also from the viewpoint that this economist could be characterized as a radical on the left side politically. The economist based his scepticism on the bad experience from the past when the western countries reduced their aid to India. This was particularly the case with USA who made this decision on the motivation that India was neutral. Tinbergen argued that the option is quite different now because we plan for a world wide effort during the second development decade. You have to ask yourself: "What can we do if we agree to do something together?" The greatest danger we face here is that most governments and their politicians stick to an unconditional autonomy of their country.

In contrast to what some participants at the symposium had said about the threats and opportunities in biological sciences, Tinbergen was convinced that the greatest danger we face today is the ambitions for national autonomy. We are also in bad need for improvements in joint decision making. Tinbergen agreed with Pauling that the end point should be some sort of World order. However, we are very far from that goal and the best we can hope for during the next few years are *commitments* by the various governments for the future.

In United Nations it is tried very hard to reach these commitments and also to set certain norms for the commitments. Even if the goal 1 % of the GNP amounts to only 15 billion dollars a year, Tinbergen would be happy if that commitment was reached by all countries in 1972.

Aiken was doubtful about the possibilities for scientists to succeed in formal politics. The experience from the last 25 years shows that they are not more qualified to occupy public offices than ordinary men. Nevertheless, there is an enormous amount of informal politics and co-operation on the part of scientists at many levels. Aiken wanted to include also those scientific technologists who implement and follow policies and practicies established by their own governments who make possible the very military activities which Pauling so profoundly and sensitively deplored.

There is also a large class among the scientists, the class of the acquiescent, who neither run for office nor council in governments where the priorities have already been established for the rest of the scientists. Aiken suggested that each scientist must decide to discriminate in his act of cooperation with nations, states and even with international agencies, and to be ready to refuse cooperation when it is obvious that it leads to the appalling results Pauling described. Aiken thought that this continuing resistance in all countries on part of scholars and men of learning could do a great deal to reduce and to block the nihilistic activities among our governments.

Monod also expressed his sympathy for Pauling's courage and viewpoints but he believed that good feelings alone are not enough to find an ethical system. We have a central nervous system, genetical conditions and condition by selection, which require something stronger and firmer than simply good feelings as a foundation for ethics and for action. Monod did strongly believe that the kind of ethical system that we must try to reconstruct and which will have to replace the various animistic systems which are dead or almost dead will gradually lead to much stronger principles. We need borrow something from Nietsche.

The main danger of war comes from fear, fear between nations, and Monod thought that the ethologists would agree with him. Most animals including predators are not really dangerous unless and until they are afraid and concerned. The fear is the reason that nations today, including the two largest nations of the world, are mortally afraid of one another. You may argue that they are afraid because they have a stockpile of weapons. Monod thought that they have a stockpile because they are afraid, even if he could agree that this is an autokatalytic process. This process must be attacked also at the psychological level. The virtually total lack of true relationship between the two worlds is one of the elements which nourishes most dangerously this fear. Monod was convinced that the actions by USA in Vietnam and by the Soviet Union in Hungary and Checho-Slovakia, exemplified by Pauling, have been dictated by fear and nothing else.

Doxiadis did also agree fully with Pauling and he was convinced that unless we have these ideals and the courage of Pauling's expressing them, we cannot go anywhere. On the other hand Doxiadis thought that Monod and Seaborg were right by saying that we have to translate the ideals to operational terms.

Doxiadis referred to his experience as a city builder. At the beginning of his career he was always referring to Aristotle's ideal that the goal of the city is to make people happy and safe. These are the two basic issues debated at this symposium, Doxiadis said. By that time people used to smile when he referred to happiness and almost laughed when he referred to safety in connection with city building. The crises in the cities today make people less inclined to laugh at the notion of safety and the danger of a nationwide war does not make them laugh either. Doxiadis had learned from experience that we have to express every plan or idea in very specific terms and took the popular issue equality between people in our cities as an example. It is easy to define equality in political declarations, it has been done for centuries and it will be repeated, said Doxiadis. But let us see what we are doing to our citizens in our cities. We help them to be segregated more and more with every day that passes because of progressing technology. If one cathegory has 5 000 dollars and another 10 000 dollars per year we draw the conclusion that their relationship to practical life in the city is 1 to 2. However, our analysis shows that it is rather something like 1 to 50 or 1 to 100, because the person who can afford to buy and use a car can reach positions in most cities within a radius of 50 kilometers and thereby have a number of choices in selecting a job, visiting friends, going to schools, theatres and entertaintments which is about hundred times more than a person without a car. Speaking to people in operational terms and measuring the phenomena and making them specific is an imperative necessity.

Doxiadis mentioned other segregations we are consciously or unconsciously promoting and he referred to his paper for details about specific cases. He thought that the worst segregation today is that between the farmer and the urban dweller of a central city. We are not entitled to speak as civilized people if we allow anyone to live in a rural village unless he or she, given all choices of the big city, prefers the isolated life in the beautiful countryside.

Doxiadis then made some remarks about the gaps between generations. Most of us here at this symposium represent a declining past, he said. In three generations time nothing or very little of our work will exist in life or memory. When the forces of the past have declined enough the responsibility will be in the hands of the next generation, if we want it or not. Biologically, our children represent a continuing past. They have inherited almost everything from us, and their sector of the development of the society which diagrammatically is very small today will grow enormously into the future. We have to take into account the forces of a declining past but we must also learn to measure the forces. Only then will it be possible to express everything in specific terms. There are some "forces" you cannot get rid of, for instance the young generation cannot kill us. It cannot impose on the majority of the mature people its wishes, even if they are right, because then democratic principles are violated.

However, sooner or later the moment will come at which the young people have the majority, no matter what we say or if we are the establishment. Be prepared for the moment when you will be in charge, Doxiadis said to the young generation.

Mead asked Doxiadis if he really meant to tell the young that if they just prepare themselves for the moment when we die, they could take over and manage things well. It was Mead's impression that the young are not content to wait and only prepare for the decease of their parents.

Doxiadis said that if this was the impression of what he said, he had

transmitted his message badly. What he meant was that the young generation has two possibilities. The first one means immediate contribution by their
suggestions, by dialogues and by influencing those sectors of society which
will be changed or created anyhow. This can be an intellectual contribution
or a moral contribution. The second one is related to the evolution of society
and man. No matter what will be the outcome of today's disputes and
dialogues, biology tells us that one day, which is fairly easy to estimate,
they will take over so they should be prepared for that task as well.

Hedén was encouraged by Doxiadis pleading for operational terms. The
participants of this symposium all agree on the importance of international
contacts for the improvement of mutual understanding, he said. But there
is another group, the statesmen, who are charged with making decisions
which influence us all. Their working day is dominated by briefings, hear-
ings and short memos flooding them with facts in an abstract "think-tank
atmosphere". When heads of states occasionally meet it is under the onus
of expectations for results, and every smile and movement is subject to
serious interpretations in mass media. Hedén directed a question to Seaborg
on how long he thought that we could afford to let the statesmen judge their
"opponents" on the basis of evaluations by middle-men and not on normal
personal contacts. Hedén suggested the establishment of a recreation club
for statesmen and their families, ideally on an extra-territorial island, far
away from the tentacles of mass media. This place may also be developed
to a platform for education of decision makers about facts about such things
as exploitation of natural resources, environmental problems, human ecology
and all other things that require comprehensive long range planning.

Seaborg agreed that the political leaders should get their information
more directly somehow. He found the suggestion of an informal statesmen
club a very intriguing one. He would be in favour of it if it could be effected. However, he was not very optimistic that something like that would
be forthcoming in the near future due to the complexities involved and the
great changes that would be entailed in such an operation compared to
the way that our leaders of state meet occasionally at present.

A student asked Seaborg to clarify what he meant by talking about anti-
intellectualism and anti-rationalism as a danger and a power in the world
today. He would also like to know what Seaborg meant by a distrust of
technology today.

Seaborg answered that he used the term anti-intellectualism as a broad
description of certain groups that are becoming very vocal in their opposition to technology. He meant that this is brought about for instance by their
observation of the environmental problems that technology has caused as
a result of productivity running so far ahead of our ability to dispose the

pollutants and the general area of pollution. There are also in the American universities tendencies among those on the faculty in non-science areas to try to convince in some cases the students not to enter the scientific fields. The distrust in technology applies to many other areas than only the environmental problems created by the industrial production. Certain criticism of the role of nuclear power, the increasing role and the fear of encroachment of computers, such areas as electronic surveillance, the advances in biology and genetics that we fear may try to dictate the future composition of the human race and of who is going to decide it. This, Seaborg meant, is just a short list of areas where much distrust in science and technology as such is met.

Harrison Brown was satisfied to hear Tinbergen's comments on Paulings paper and he was himself convinced that unless all nations of the world mobilize their efforts to the solution of the problems of the developing countries they are simply not going to get solved. Brown was inclined to go along with the one per cent goal but with some modifications. If the nations of the world were to say: "All right, we will invest on the average one per cent of our gross national product, and we will provide this in the form of capital transfers to those nations which have a low average per capita income."—Fine! But he believed that there ought to be some kind of a graded scale, even if it is difficult to tell how to do it. Perhaps like most nations handle income taxes. Brown said that during the last few years he had spent quite some time in developing countries and in particular he headed a study that was made of US Technical Assistance Programs Overseas in South America. The more he travelled in these areas, the more he became convinced that the main limiting factor to development is the production of people who have the education to solve the kind of problems and to make the kind of decisions which have to be made. At the moment, the rate is probably capital-limited in the sense that more money could be absorbed than is being transferred at the present time and absorbed reasonably effectively. But not much more. What you might call technical assistance is in the long run fully as important as capital assistance. We must mobilize our efforts for technical assistance as well as for capital assistance and again on a scale which far transcends anything that is being done today.

When you compare what is happening in the general area of armaments and the way in which the cold war has resulted in our providing armaments to developing countries in the interest of our own political outlook Brown agreed completely with Pauling. This is evil and criminal. Brown believed that in any overall agreement that might be reached concerning ways and means of accelerating development, one must concentrate on those areas where one has the greatest chances of producing a significant effect. This means eliminating those areas which invest unduly much in armament. It also means eliminating those areas which have an unusually large dissipation by corruption and concentrating on those areas which are really making plans which stand a chance of being carried through.

The next point Brown made was that the more we can channel capital assistance through the international organizations and strenghten those international organizations in such a way that they can handle the expanded capital assistance properly, the better off all of us are going to be. In other words, it is very important that we get the business of capital assistance out of the political arena as rapidly as we possibly can.

With respect to technical assistance. Brown thought that also this to a certain extent can be given effectively through the international organisations. However, he suspected that a great deal of technical assistance can be better given on a bilateral basis, provided one can avoid political connotations and political crushes.

Brown said that he did not believe that we are going to be able to carry on a program which is commensurate with the need as long as the cold war exists and he completely agreed with the Russian scientist Sakharov that a d'entente between the USA and the USSR is absolutely essential. If we do not have this, we are going to continue to spend money in the way we are spending them now, where we and the developing countries themselves spend much more on arms than on development. As long as the developing countries become ponds in the cold war there will be no real help. Brown meant that one of the most important explorations this symposium could make was to ask the question and attempt to answer it: "What constructive steps can be taken to create the kind of a d'entente where we do not necessarily have to agree with each other's politics and economics but where we can agree upon certain basic common goals which involve the limitation of armaments and of arms traffic and which involve a considerable acceleration of the business of development?"

Pauling took up the comments by Tinbergen and Harrison Brown to his discussion of the possibility of transferring a considerable amount of the world's wealth—eight per cent of the world's income—from the very rich to the miserably poor. He meant that their comments dealt with just what he had proposed, namely that there must be a study made as to how this can be achieved in a practical way. Pauling was also pleased to hear Tinbergen talk about the possibility that by 1972 there would be a contribution made by the more affluent nations of one per cent of their GNP to assistance in developing other nations. Pauling felt that there is one danger in the world today, that we have to attack, and it is the increasing ownership—as apart from income—of the wealth of the world by a small number of people. The profits are becoming greater and greater—they have gone up from 8 per cent to 14 per cent on investments in the USA, which means that the small group of people who have these large incomes achieve a greater ownership of the wealth of the world. A rather small group of people in the USA receive some 43% of the income of the world, and they own over 60% of the wealth of the world, with this fraction increasing. Pauling had made a study of Canada when he gave an Expo–67-lecture and found that the profits of $1 500 million of the Canadian corporations were transferred to the extent of $900 million to USA investor and only $600 million to Canadian investors. It is no doubt worse now. It would not really cause a great amount of human suffering if these rich people were not so rich. The amount of money involved is incredibly large.

Pauling then took up statements that scientists are not free of blame because there are scientists who work for the Atomic Energy Commission on weapons or who work on the development of chemical and biological methods of warfare and so on. And then there are also scientists in the universities who are acquiescent in co-operation with the government, in carrying out research with government money, often from the armed forces. Pauling pointed out that there are many scientists who work for commercial companies and who, despite their interests in social, political and economic affairs, are prevented by their companies, by unwritten conditions of employment, from expressing any radical ideas or voting for a somewhat radical candidate. He wanted to advocate that scientists make personal decisions for themselves about where they want to work but emphasized that he never advocated that the scientists of the world or of the USA should refuse to work—as a body or a whole group of scientists—on nuclear weapons or an anything else. He meant that this would represent the operation of a sort of oligarchy of scientists, and thought that these are problems that need to be decided by the people as a whole and not by the scientists just because they would have the power, assuming that they would have the power to stop operations by going on strike in this way. Pauling admitted that he might be wrong about this emphasis of democracy and the involvement of the people as a whole. It is clear that it is contrary to the policy of the US government, but he approved of scientists refusing individually to work on projects of this sort.

However, he thought that the matter of war research done in the universities had been exaggerated somewhat. Even the contracts made by the armed forces have in a good number of cases—the majority—been in support of pure science, unclassified work with no military application and this has sometimes been good.

Pauling then turned to Monod's doubt that the principle of the minimization of suffering would be enough; that we need something stronger and firmer than good feelings. He supposed that we do need something in addition to good feeling, in addition to morality. Enlightened selfinterest could operate very effectively. The people of the world are able to see that it would be better to have a world government; better for every nation and for almost every human beeing, if we could leave out the professional soldiers and other people in the military-industrial complex who make careers for themselves there, and constitute the analogue without such powerful stimula—the excessed profits—as are involved in the military-industrial complex in the United States. Everybody, or almost everybody, would be better off and the whole world would be better off if we could save the money that is involved in military projects and abolish the suffering associated with war. Pauling felt that we should emphasize self-interest. Bertrand Russel once said that if everybody worked as hard to make himself happy as he does to make other people unhappy, this world would be a paradise.

The second point was that we should attack the problem of the stock piles of nuclear weapons from the psychological side. It is fear that has caused USA and USSR to take the actions that they have taken. Pauling thought that this is right. In his address in Oslo on the 11th of December 1963 he made a proposal about nuclear weapons, namely if we were to destroy the stock piles of nuclear weapons, then almost surely ordinary war would start up again, so we need these stock piles of nuclear weapons, but we must have greater assurances that they will not be used, even though they remain in existence. Let us therefore put every stock pile of nuclear weapons under joint control of the national government that possesses it and the United Nations or another international agency, so that these weapons cannot be used without the permission of this international agency with dual agents—controllers—in every center: the United Nations representative and the national representative. There may be some other way of handling the problem of fear of nuclear war, the fear that one side or the other will make some development that will enable it to win a nuclear war without being itself completely destroyed. He had the feeling from analyzing the situation that with respect to the cold war it is USA that leads and USSR that follows, and essentially for a practical reason. In USSR they are trying very hard—and succeeding—to improve their economy, to use available money for developing the civilian economy. And they spend the amount of money that they feel they must spend in order that USA will not get out of hand, that is to preserve this balance. Pauling did not mean to place the whole blame for the cold war on USA, but he hoped that scientists would be able to exert greater political pressure there and that some of his visionary ideals would find expression in reality.

Seaborg took up a question by Aiken about situations where scientists might become resistant. He admitted that such situations exist. There are many examples of this and he thought to great advantage. Seaborg hoped that, at situations like this symposium, it would be a matter of the scientists gathering to present their arguments and support facts in a way that would convince those in the positions of political power and the people and not just rely on the fact that they speak in the name of scientists.

Klineberg had a comment on Segerstedt's paper. When he referred to the future and the attitude towards the future, Klineberg was reminded of a substantial amount of psychological and sociological research in what is called "technically future time prospective". People differ tremendously in the extent to which they are future-oriented, in the extent to which they are willing to give up certain things today in order to get more tomorrow. Some are and some are not. Klineberg had heard it been suggested that some of the problems connected with development in certain areas of the world may be due to very marked differences in this respect. In certain areas, where the techniques take time to show themselves in terms of results, like building a factory or introducing a new form of agriculture, one of the great stumbling blocks is the insistence on getting something today and not waiting till tomorrow.

IV. *Free or directed research—a choice for the individual and for society*

Bruner took up Hayashi's definitions of the human activity sectors, the productive system, the service system and the system of systems. Bruner chose the field of medicine and meant that as we move along towards progress we make certain kinds of things non-selective for individuals. We no longer have the question of selecting a dentist according to our taste because we put fluorine or something else in the water and we get rid of caries. The question then arises: "What do we do with the freed talent in manpower?" We can eventually put it to some new use we invent, a new profession or occupation to meet the needs and the values of society. If this is the case it should be with progress, Bruner meant. You could take lots of other examples. For instance, if you made an instructional language you could free the language tutors to teach poetry more to taste. Bruner would like to see as one of the most important measures of economic progress in general the invention of new occupations to meet human needs. It puzzled him that this is never discussed by economists. We talk about industries going out of existence. "How do we reallocate, is there enough problems of the reallocation of talent and resource in order to meet the new needs and is not that one of the ways in which we keep refresh the purposes and the values of the society?"

Monod directed his question to the social technologists and futurologists whether they have any idea of how much science will or should not grow in the future. It is well known from the statistics that 90% of all scientists that ever worked in research are alive today. This is one way of expressing the enormous growth of science. In all advanced countries the fraction of total national income going to research—fundamental research and development—has been increasing financially since the late fourties and perhaps even before. Monod was convinced that it is quite clear that it cannot go on growing financially. He asked the question: "Is there a reasonable figure on what fraction of the total national income may go to fundamental research and development—technology excluded?" It will be very important, in particular for education. We should be able to plan, to know how many students in pure science should be admitted in the science schools, not only now but in 10 years or 20 years. In France there is at least a tendency among science students in particular to go into science even before they have any experience of what science is and even less what research is. They decide that they want to do research and they do not want to do any teaching. Monod said that it is perfectly clear that we will need more and more science teachers, probably more than researchers. But we must have the figures before we make our ambitious plans.

Tata thought that the voice of a business man or an industrial executive, as he preferred to call himself, must sound pretty different from the voices heard up to now. When he was invited to participate in the symposium he was struck by a number of thoughts. He first thought that it must be a mistake. He could not imagine that in a scientific symposium of this kind a man of his type could contribute anything that could be worthwhile. Then when he read more carefully the aims and objectives of the symposium, and found the announcement made by the Nobel Foundation in a paper, which was published in his own country and in which it referred to the hope that the participants coming from east and west might help to set a new course for humanity and discuss a strategy for human survival, it struck him that perhaps it was not meant that this symposium would deal entirely with highly academic matters, but that there was an aim and objective to deal, in a scientific way of course, as far as possible with the practical problems which are today plaguing societies in several parts of the world. Tata said that he had spent the most exhilarating days that he ever had, because in the past he had not attended any symposia of this nature. He had listened with a mixture of fascination and awe to some of the lectures. He had learned words that he had never heard about before and also realized that the meanings of some words are different from those that he was taught when he was young. At the same time, however, he had got a feeling that with the exception of the interesting paper by King this symposium would wish to come to grips with some of the real basic problems of this century and this decade, and also a need of some kind of a follow up. Considering the tremendous stature of most of the participants, something more than merely a fact report and a book containing the papers and discussions must follow. Tata thought that in countries where the problems are particularly serious and particularly down to earth there would be some expectation that out of this symposium would emerge some improvement in some direction or the other. "We have now reached the fourth day of discussions but so far as I am concerned we don't yet seem to have come to a definition of some of the problems we were going to deal with", Tata said. Coming from a part of the world where survival is largely a question concerned with the necessities of life, Tata meant that the main problems are economic and social, though the social ones undoubtedly follow the economic ones and not the other way. He wondered whether, in this part of the world, and amongst the top scientists who are so well represented at the symposium, it is realized the urgency as well as the seriousness of the crisis that is facing us, and not only today. It is going to face us in at least 10 or 15 years. For a thousand of years, people in places like India have accepted the unbelievable conditions there. But under the impact of science and particularly the dissemination of news, films, magazines, newspapers and television, you would be surprised at the extent to which even ignorant people in a country like India have come to realize the almost unbelievable different standard of living that exists between countries. The temper of the people, the feeling of the people as you can see expressed in a number of demonstrations, confrontations, is no longer one of the patience and resignantion of the past. People of countries like India do not want a little of the prosperity of economic growth for their great grand children; they want some of it now! Unless some means of accelerating the economic growth—we must start with the economic growth in a country like India before anything else—are mobilized now, unless we find some means of controlling the growth of population, not in 25 years from now but within the next 10 years, we might face within the next 10 or 15 years an upheaval in India or on a similar continent in South East Asia or in Indonesia, which would have tremendous percussions throughout the world. Tata did not think the world can afford another upheaval in a part of the world like South East Asia and possibly also in parts of South America. Therefore he would have hoped that some of the great scientific talents that have been assembled in this symposium could have been asked to apply their minds not to an immediate *solution* of the problems that are facing us but at least to those very practical and immediate *problems* which, if they are not solved, are going to make the solution of almost all other problems in this world hardly worth achieving. He could only suggest at this stage that there might be a follow up from this, perhaps the creation or expansion of some institutions. We have heard of the United Nations economic planning committee, and Tinbergen is a distinguished member of it, but Tata was sure that we really need some institutionalized form of applying modern scientific thought to the basic problems he had been referring to, which unfortunately are largely concentrated to the underdeveloped parts of the world. Throughout the course of the symposium we have heard little with reference to the population explosion. Tata had hardly got the impression that this was considered anything of immediate importance in the sense that something has got to be done now and not 10 or 15 years from now. It is probable that the biologists feel that the greatest and quickest advance might be made in finding a quicker and more practical means than has been found up to now to control the growth where there is a population explosion. Tata stressed that "explosion" is only a political term. In India, for instance, the rate of growth is only 2.4%, but because it is 2.4% on 550 millions, we get a result which means that every seven and a half month we add to the population of India the whole population of Sweden. But we are not adding eight million educated Swedes, we are adding eight million mouths to feed, children to educate, children who from the start only have the chance to achieve a fraction of the life that they would achieve in Sweden.

Tata had nothing specific to propose but he believed that the solution of the problem would come from scientists. Therefore he hoped and prayed that scientists would occasionally—even those with highly sofisticated subjects to deal with—deliberately try to apply their enormous knowledge to the practical solution of the problems he had touched upon.

Some people say: "What can you do about the population problem of India? It is an impossible one. You grow 15 million people a year." The answer is that something *can* be done, and Tata gave an example. Today the birth rate is around 40 a thousand. The population explosion in India is exclusively due not to a growth of the birth rate but, as everybody knows, to a reduction of the death rate from about 36 down to 16, thanks to medical science. Maybe it would have been better if medical science had come later to India, said Tata. But there it is! The aim and object is to reduce the population growth of India down to about 1 per cent. In order to achieve that the objective is to reduce the birth rate to 25 per thousand. It may be of interest to know that a company with which I am connected has been heavily engaged in a family planning program in a town in India which had a population approaching 500 000. It is now 450 000 and the town is entirely based on heavy industry. In four years it has been possible to reduce the birth rate to 25 per thousand owing to a sustained and intelligent campaign of family planning and birth control, and it has been achieved also on a smaller scale in another smaller town— which is built around a chemical plant. There the birth rate has been reduced to below 25 per thousand. These examples only show that things can be done, but they have to be done on an enormous scale. It is easy to do something like that in concentrated groups of largely literate people. The problem is of course that you have to tackle the 75 per cent of the people who live in the villages but even there are certain ways of doing it. We can no longer afford to have a constantly widening gap between the under-privileged countries and the affluent societies. Tata said that he is one of those who realize that the gap will remain and be even wider but the first thing to achieve is a minimum standard everywhere in the world, and thereafter one may talk about closing gaps.

Pierce after having listened to Tata reminded the participants that this symposium is about the place of value in a world of facts. Pierce felt that value means value to human beings. The facts of science can certainly have value if they are of use to man. In order for science to be valuable in the way that Tata suggested it must help to solve a problem, and for this to happen in a meaningful way you must have two things. First of all, the problem to be solved must be important. Otherwise it is not worth invoking science. Secondly, the problem must be tractable. Now, as Tata said, among us here there are some very fine scientists from different disciplines. Can the people here figure out one or a small number of problems which they deem to be extremely valuable and which they deem to be tractable in terms of present science, including social science? Can they point these out to whoever is listening and can they suggest practical means for a solution? Can we not only point out the goal and the general means but can we say: "Lift your right foot and put it there as the next step!".

King said to Monod that there are no good statistics for the need of fundamental research among the European countries as yet. There are rough estimates from the figures presented during the first international geophysical year but the definitions of what is fundamental research, what is applied research and what is development, are becoming increasingly difficult with the increasing merge of fundamental and applied research and the difficulty of separating them. There are no comparable international statistics on the social sciences whatsoever. There have been a few attempts to produce some figures but they are mainly speculations.

Presently, in OECD, there is a rather basic study concerning the place and functions of fundamental research in relation to the future need of society which will be posing some of the very questions which Monod raised, but to which I cannot give any answer now. One of these questions of course is: "Will the type of universities foreseen at the moment be compatible with research as we know it now?" King thought that most of us agreed that the university environment is probably better for research than most other artificial environments. At least we know that it functions as a creative source very strongly now. If this will be possible in the future we do not know. The second part of Monod's question is very important, namely science teachers in relation to the number of scientists. There are statistics beginning to be available on that. There is a study just completed on university expansion since the last decade and there will probably be a continuation with key studies of university innovation, in which these matters will be dealt with. It seems that this is particularly important, because if we can get really away from the two-cultures-approach—which King thought is inevitable—and recognize that science is part of contemporary culture and not *a* contemporary culture, then we need more and better science teaching everywhere and not in terms of chemistry, physics, botany and biology specificly, but as illustrations of their broad and deep connection with our culture as a whole. For this, science teachers in much larger numbers and of a much more civilized type are necessary.

Then King took up some aspects of what Pierce said. King felt that we are up against very big problems, and he could not be more sympathetic with the approach which Tata took in his intervention. King meant that the problem of the third world is immediate, overwhelming and is necessary to attack with great priority with consideration to the needs of the societies and the world as a whole and to basic humanity. But he was also himself convinced that the accumulating problems of the highly industrialized and affluent societies with their interrelations with the social disturbance they are breeding, threaten to undermine the whole fabric of the industrialized societies within the next decade. He thought that these two problems, which are interrelated are both enormous and he thought that they are both of equal priority, because if we do not attempt to attack the kind of problems he had presented in his paper, namely the interrelated socio-economical-political-technological problems, then we will not have the sustained growth and the continued possibility of the advanced countries leading the others. These things are inextricably connected, and he thought that unless we understand the nature of these multi-variant complex problems, we shall be continually attacking short term problems, which are symptoms, instead of understanding the real causes and getting down to the curing of the disease rather than removing its symptoms. But unless we realize that with these two great complexes of problems for the industrialized societies and for the less developed societies interrelated with one another in relation to the common destiny of man and unless we analyze, relate, interrelate and understand basic causes of the basic problems, unless we learn to master multidisciplinary approaches to multivariant problems, then we shall continue to muddle along and probably muddle into a situation which is increasingly difficult.

Tata, when listening to Salam, was reminded once again of how many things that have been said at this symposium that he wished could be said to the whole world, and particularly his lesson to us ethnocentrics about the way in which the scientific center of the world was seen at one time and how we and the West looked upon it. Tata hoped that something more then just a Nobel volume with proceedings would come out of this. Some of the things that have been said during the symposium might well have tremendous implications for the education of humanity.

Myrdal thought that the talk about a world university is only a big model. What the Americans want is to reform the American universities. And this is very natural. Myrdal had the same feeling when he recently went to Canada and found a very large number of young Americans there. One of the main reasons why they were there was their dissatisfaction with the atmosphere in America and at the universities. What they are up to, of course, is a situation where traditionally the professors do not have the same importance and the same power over the universities as they have in the old countries. Also they are up against things which they dislike very much. Much of the research—not only in natural sciences but also in social sciences—is paid for by the state department, the defense department and sometimes by CIA, even at such an institution as MIT. Myrdal made a comparison with his own field of research. In America very fine colleagues of his, prominent international lawyers and international political scientists, want to have a world government. This is not unrelated to the fact that America is so nationalistic, it is not unrelated to the fact that for instance the declaration of human rights have not been ratified by the Senate, in spite of the fact that Americans played a very important role in bringing them forward. And then, there is a sort of jump into the world government. Myrdal had given some thought to this, and by the experience he had had as an international civil servant for 10 years, he knew that there will not be any world government on this side of the year 2000 at least, for a number of reasons.

Myrdal pointed out that he all his life had lived in a world university. He had not been working as a Swede but as a world citizen. This was the whole spirit he got from his teachers. He did not believe that what is true in Jena is false in Weimar. When he gives a lecture on a certain subject, he says the same thing in Moscow, Chicago and at Harvard University. Myrdal would like to see a good research institute—we can afford it—for oriental illnesses. It will have to work out there, and we shall pay for it. This is a real thing and he did not well understand the idea about the world university. Sometimes he had a feeling that Lasswell talked about all the universities. And sometimes he had the feeling that Lasswell meant some new institutional structure. Myrdal did not think we need an institutional structure at all. He rather thought that people like those present who understand the problems do want to have a redirection of research and do want to have these reforms made in our own universities and that can not be solved by some international structure. This must be solved by hard fighting in every country about power and money.

Lambo directed some remarks to Salam and Lasswell, whose ideas he found to be very good. First of all he would like to say that probably the question of intellectual contacts or intellectual intercourse which is so very much desired by scientists in developing countries is not the only problem which is waiting for a solution. The question of international institutes being built will not solve the problems which are facing the scientists working in developing countries. Take as an example the role of the intellectual women in the developing countries. This is a much more human problem than just ordinary intellectual intercourse, which is equally important. Then Lambo said that the international centers have had many problems in Africa. They worked very well, especially the United Nation's international centers and international institutes, but some of them have inherent weaknesses and the administrative and financial structure is usually only temporary. Salam himself mentioned this. Usually you have money only for three to five years, during which you stimulate the interest of the people, and after the expiration of the first period the project reverts to local government, which will not have the same aims and objectives. Consequently one runs into administrative difficulties in most of the international centers in the developing countries. This, of course, will have some political and social difficulties which may be unacceptable to certain governments and certain countries. Their sensitivity and responsiveness to look at scientific problems will not be of immediate priority. In South East Asia the institutes have been the major concern of the Rockefeller and Ford Foundations but in some other places or on some other occasions the sensitivity is not there and you may find that you will not be able to influence the priorities of research and teaching of the international institutions. Lambo thought that the World University as presented by Lasswell is a very good idea. He would like to suggest that when concerning the developing countries it may be necessary to think in terms of pieces and steps of development. He was sure that if he went back to Nigeria and told his colleagues in Africa that the next institute will be a World University, they would think that he was crazy, because there are so many local problems with regard to the functioning capacity and effectiveness of existing universities. It may be necessary to formulate another strategy or method to impose to individualists and internationalize local universities so as to bring them to a common structure which can function not only locally but internationally and we can be very proud members of the future world university. Any proposal, any suggestion that will really sustain energy and impose and put more international spirit and international commitment into local universities and research centers is worth promoting by all means, said Lambo.

V. *Strategy for survival*

Hayashi expressed his opinion that one of the most difficult problems in bridging the gap between rich and poor countries is the distance between the economical measures and value systems.

However, Hayashi was optimistic about getting a change of the attitude towards conditions and environments in other countries. He thought that the advancement and international diffusion of telecommunication technology will contribute a great deal. According to Japanese experience a small child who cannot understand foreign languages has a considerable feeling and even understanding for customs in distant countries because of television programmes.

Hayashi then came to the gap between the older and younger generation. He felt that the lack of patriotism in the young generation which troubles the elders so very much, will show up but in another form than the traditional nationalistic or etnocentric patriotism. Hayashi said that when today's youngsters become prime ministers and university professors all programmes will be much more international. He was very optimistic about the progress of an international and more humanistic society.

Tinbergen commented on a direct question from one of the students why the Chinese system had not been considered in the work by the UN Development Planning Committee. Tinbergen said that our knowledge and information about China is very restricted and moreover, the present Chinese policy is only a few years old and history shows that great changes of fundamental nature will almost certainly take place. It is very difficult to say when the Chinese system will or will not function in all respects. No statistics from China is published and it is therefore impossible to draw objective conclusions about development or changes.

With regard to *Lederberg's* remark on the necessity to eliminate shocks of new, practicable developments, Tinbergen fully agreed. In particular, it has been proposed in the report of the UN Development Planning Committee that synthetics, immediately competing with some natural products, will be taken into use also in developing countries, so as to gradually increase their production. And that might at the same time also redirect research, in the sense that it will not be so rewarding to do research on products which can only be sold in limited quantities. In this way it may serve two ends at the same time. Tinbergen meant that there is also another possibility, namely, that through taxation it will be possible to diminish the shock. He thought that this should always be practiced because it is always a wise policy not to allow things to happen suddenly.

On a remark by *Tata*, Tinbergen added that in the report by the UN Development Planning Committee had also been suggested that the criteria according to which financial transfers—Tinbergen preferred that term— are being apportioned should be less governed by purely political considerations than had been the case in the past.

Tinbergen was interested to hear from Guth that at least on one point there was full agreement between the UN Committee and the Pearson Commission, namely, that efforts, or rather performance, should be one of the criteria. But the UN Committee had actually proposed three criteria. More money to countries whose income per capita is very low. But then the efforts should be made by the country itself and it would report about its success. These two things are not equivalent which is rather important. The UN Committee is working on a further elaboration of how precisely to practice these criteria and some calculations have provisionally been made.

Tinbergen was encouraged by the fact that the two Committees had independantly come to very similar conclusions in spite of their different composition and way of working. The Pearson Commission was set up by the World Bank and focused its attention on ways and means for economical transfer. In the UN Committee half of the members are from developing countries. Three of the members are from official communist countries and there is one Jewish and one Japanese member. Tinbergen thought that if we want to have things done in a short time—and many are really urgent— it would not be very helpful if very different suggestions were made.

Lambo thought that the theory presented by Koestler, that massenthusiasm or group-loyalty is one of the main self-destructive forces in the human mind, is very debatable. Koestler had drawn parallels between Hitler Jugend and Maoists in China. Lambo said that it would follow from this that a country like India would be healthier than a country like China, because they haven't got this enthusiasm among the people. The second thing which would follow is that the United States, which has not got this kind of enthusiasm, would be less aggressive in world politics than, for instance, China, which is not right, Lambo meant. One of the countries is at war at the present time. And it has been for quite a few years.

The comparison between Hitler and Mao is a very superficial one because it refers only to the forms of enthusiasm, not to the contents of what people are enthusiastic for, Lambo said. The reason why he brought up this point was that it has political implications and Lambo thought that Koestler was not aware of the values that are debated for his theory. A scientific theory should in an ideal case be free from valuation if it is objective. But of course this is impossible. You have to put in values, and you have to be aware of which value is objective and which is subjective. You may use axiomatic values, but then you have to present your axioms.

It seemed to Lambo, although he was not quite sure about it, that Koestler speaking about Maoism speaks about things which he has not studied. Lambo thought that his source of information had not been the Chinese press but rather the press of Western scholars, or even Western newspapers. Lambo then read the following quotation from Koestler's paper: "People must devote critical senses to resist onesided propaganda, oversimplified information and, above all, their own privileged feelings and group feelings." Lambo meant that this was a substantial point. He thought that Koestler was a victim of one of the aspects which may be defined as self-destructive, namely egocentricity. Koestler speaks about we and they. We are the good, they are the bad. What they do is very strange, what we do is the proper way of behaving.

Mead took up three points, one of which was related to our long biological heritage and which Koestler did not mention at all. The first point was the long period called "latency" before puberty during which man develops physically to reach the same level as the brain. This period gives us an interval which permits the kind of learning characterized by attempts with our brains.

The age of puberty drops on the average by four months every decade and this change has taken place since the time of improved nutrition. Unless this trend is halted for some reason we will—in a short time from now—have children reaching physical puberty at the age of ten. We will have to short-cut the tremendous biological gain caused by the postponement of puberty and create a longer period of reasonably conflict-free learning.

The second point Mead brought up was the long period of dependence for the infant on the adult authority. This will probably cause an excess of socialization.

The third point was related to Koestler's assumption about human sacrifice. He had assumed that this must be regarded as some innate flaw in our nature if it recurs over and over again.

However, Mead said, there is the possibility of frequent misunderstanding which is implicit in the whole nature of Man. Think about all myths made about the sun. And Man has repeatedly made the mistake to believe that blood produces fertility. This mistake is easy to understand, because childbirth is always accompanied with blood and we also have the phenomenon of menstruation. Primitive peoples who did not understand the mechanics of the birth process and of conception, instead overemphasized the importance of blood. This we find over and over again in primitive societies. And if blood meant fertility, which was good, then human sacrifice to make the fields fertile, to make the country strong, to make everything grow becomes and understandable misconception. This does not necessarily mean any inherent defect in our nature or any neural-schizoid break but simply that Man can make the same mistake over and over again. If we take cultural features like this in an attempt to read them into Man's innate nature, Mead believed we would produce an unusually discouraging and intractable picture.

Málek thought that there exists some semantic confusion about rationalism and irrationalism. The word rational is sometimes taken to designate the rational way of thinking that has been prevailing since the twelfth century. A religion, for instance, can be entirely logical, self-consistent and therefore rational. But we cannot use the same word, or we have to qualify it, if we mean the same as reason. This is the scientific meaning since rationality is the consultation of reason.

Klineberg was very much interested and fascinated by Koestler's attempt to find the specifically human as the basis for understanding some of the ills from which we are suffering. However, Klineberg thought that there are other things that seem to be as specifically human as the phenomena Koestler spoke of, for instance the fact pointed out many times by many people that man is the only animal that can build upon the experience of previous generations, and continue to learn through experimentation and through mistakes of previous generations. As a matter of fact, the tremendous flexibility of behaviour, again the difference in degree with animals, is certainly much more proof of human being than any other.

Klineberg thought it was Lorenz who said that both ways can make anything right, in other worlds, can make any system of morals acceptable.

If we have a possibility of learning from previous generations and if we are flexible and malleable in our behaviour, which is also essentially human, don't these possibilities—and there may be others—counteract somewhat the rather negative picture which Koestler gave, Klineberg asked. Then he added to what Mead said that he too was a little worried about regarding or accepting phenomena that occur with great frequency among human beings as necessarily having a kind of almost genetic species identification. He thought that very often similar phenomena can be explained by similar social situations and similar cultural combinations rather than necessarily being biological in their character.

Bruner was disturbed by the reasoning about our problems as if they were nothing but bad engineering in the evolution. He thought that in a sense this point of view is equivalent with assuming that evolution is working for the perfection of Man. This gets us into a very peculiar kind of trouble. One can deny it and yet make it seem as if failure of engineering of a proper organism is a difficulty. It puts us in a position which can be explained as follows. What we have got to do is to compensate for those bad features of engineering that didn't produce a fully rational man and Bruner meant that it is far better to take a realistic look at what in fact developed and how it developed in terms of Man's involvement.

For example, we talk about the long period of immaturity in human infancy. The best estimate now is that at the same time as evolution was selecting bi-pedalism and giving Man a larger brain, we learned to use the hands and a stronger pelvic girdle was required. To get a pelvic girdle that was stronger evolution selected a smaller birth canal. The only way in which a larger brain could get through a smaller birth canal and a stronger pelvis was to let Man be born immature.

Evolution was not thinking about the problem of how Man would cope with culture. However, Bruner wanted to bring up this when we talk about schizo-neurological patterns or something similar. We have a system which, looked at reasonably, is one that can be supported. We have strong midbrain mechanisms, we have a strong lymphic system that compels a lot of behaviour. There is also operative a cortical factor that can correct for wrong or odd impulses. Once we accept that this is one of the characteristics of Man, we can deal with it from the point of view of designing communities, as Doxiadis was talking about, designing educational systems, and so on. Bruner finally proposed that, rather than looking either at the successes or failures of evolution, we must look at how Man *is* and see what we can do about providing an environment that might strengthen those things which we think he has to cope with.

Koestler answered Lorenz who had criticized his paper for being over-simplified and a crude presentation. Koestler fully agreed. What he wanted to do was to compress a long book into a short paper, and he paid for it with brevity. Koestler then came to the question of rationality and meant that there is a complex, a complex of centering around rationality and its uses. He meant that we can have incompatible belief systems and logical systems side by side in agonized co-existence in our brains. The belief systems are based on emotional commitments, conscious or unconscious.— Metaphorically speaking, but only metaphorically, for a process analogous to imprinting we have on the one side something like a sort of steam-bath and on the other side we have a refrigarator of reason. Koestler guessed that they can co-exist. He thought that the scholastic statement that Monod had given was a method upon which was built the method of rationalization.

On Mead's points about "latency" and advances of the puberty, Koestler agreed fully and he thought it was very important. The over-all period of suggestibility—dependence he thought was absolutely species specific. Human sacrifice is not a proof of bad engineering in evolution, but human sacrifice together with a number of other things is nevertheless symptomatic of biased historical thinking against a blood fertilization. To cut the throat or cut the hearts out of living beings does not seem to be a very reasonable method of using blood fertilization. There is an element of devotional cruelty involved which certainly seems to be a pathological symptom. In one of the first chapters of Genesis the all-loving God ordered Abraham to cut the throat of his son, and Abraham gladly and happily was prepared to obey.

To Bruner, Koestler said that he never meant that evolution fails to conform with a perfect teleological blueprint. The narrow pelvis to let the head through, that is very bad engineering. Koestler emphasized that he did not mean to find any philosophical implications from Nature's bad engineering.

Lastly, Koestler, very firmly believed that modern pharmacology is almost within the reach to eliminate certain blockages and certain blood strains. The tranquillizers are stone-age implements compared to what in the next twenty years we shall be able to do, not in the sense of Huxley's coma and tranquillizers, but harmonizers. Koestler believed that Waddington's genetical assimilation might help—if we have sufficient time, through generations and generations, to use these artificially stimulated mutations.

Brown was very much impressed by Doxiadis' view of the future of urban development, particularly as he himself lives in an area which is growing very rapidly in the State of California. Bordering Washington it is expected in the next fifty years that urban areas which do not exist now and which are only country-side now will occupy something like fifteen times the present area.

For this reason it is terribly important that we think very seriously about what the formal structure of those cities is. Brown wanted to bring to the attention one very important point.

One of the main limiting factors as to what can be done is water, and looking at Doxiadis' maps we noticed that, quite correctly, he placed very high concentrations around the coastal areas. Brown believed that this is inevitable because we must have close proximity to water from the point of view of waste disposal, and in particular, heat disposal. Our per-capita energy use is something that is running up quite rapidly. Already now the amount of energy generated in many of our cities is equal to, or larger than, what falls on it through sunlight.

Brown believed that in the central regions of the country we will not in the future be able to support very high concentrations of population. He also believed that for the most part—and this will be a world-wide phenomenon—the central parts of our country will be used for agriculture, but not for high concentration of people engaged in industrial activities.

Doxiadis was glad to see the great concern about the questions brought up by Koestler because the key also for the problems with which we are dealing in city building is Man's attitude in all these affairs. Unless we manage to deal with Man in some way we'll never deal reasonably with his cities. So Doxiadis hoped that the main progress that humanity is going to make will have to be in this direction.

Here he thought that the city can help because the modern city by bringing people together as they want to come together, but allowing them to be together without any reasonable control and organization, increases their problems. The most inhuman characteristic of the modern city is that it does not help people to develop on the basis of the third principle of protecting one another's distances when they talk, when they walk, when they make noise and when they have relationships in space.

We need the green areas badly because we like to live on a farm but also want to be in an urban system, and there are those who need some green areas around them, even if they don't own them. But unless we take the big cities for granted and we understand this urban system, we'll never be able to protect private land or farms. If we allow a highway to be built, very soon the land values are going up, and very soon people in the surrounding are going to press the nearby city to change the regulations to allow high density building. It is by forecasting such a development that we can help to avoid crises.

Pierce had said that it is television and mechanical communication systems that keep him in touch with others. Doxiadis thought that we need more and more of these means if we want everyone to live in his own way.

But others will select the areas of high density, others the areas of very low density.

Doxiadis was also very much interested in the observations of Brown. As he rightly said, our main concentrations—and this is where all our predictions lead—are going to be around the coastal areas, near the rivers, and mostly around the great lakes. Water is going to be the deciding factor and the areas inside our continents are going to look very much like the mountains. The Appalachian mountains for instance which people are now abandoning, or most of the mountains of France, where the studies have been carefully done and we can see over the last hundred and twenty years people abandoning them more and more. The density is dropping continuously and this is going to happen all over our continents.

Doxiadis was also interested in the broader discussions and about research and the advancement of society. This question of the menace and promise is very characteristic, he meant. We face it in our profession, in our action everywhere. If we take the attitude "let us stop research in some directions", then we are not only unscientific but we are inhuman. Man wants to find out more and more about things, and this is what he needs to progress. Our choice is not to start acting as a police force for mankind, believing that we know better than common man. People will make progress from science in order to make sense out of the progress. This does not mean to carry on only in some directions and to lead this system to an imbalance but, by illuminating the whole system, to show where we need to make more progress.

It is for this reason, Doxiadis said, that six of us here have met in the past years, not in Delphi where Apollo the Oracle lives, but on the island of Delos, where Apollo the God of harmony lives. If anything is missing today, it is the same thing that the ancient Greeks discovered when they developed their agriculture and their warfare: Harmony.

The Place of Value in a World of Facts

Report to the Nobel Foundation on Symposium 14
by a reporting group appointed by the Organizing Committee

Södergarn 20 September 1969

This symposium, attended by scholars from a broad variety of disciplines, assisted and stimulated by a group of students, was the occasion for discussion of major problems of the contemporary world. These problems, relating to both industrialized societies and to the underdeveloped world, are of a degree of complexity requiring the combined attack of many disciplines. The symposium achieved a high degree of communication and interaction between the participants. It should be the precursor of many other occasions of multidisciplinary study.

1. *Values and human needs*

A human society without a system of values shared by its members is highly unstable, but conflicting values operate in our world, and impede progress towards a global society. In addition to ideological differences the basis of traditional value systems is shaken by the discoveries of modern science, especially in biology (Monod), and by technological change (Lambo, Hayashi). There may even be a basic conflict between the biological utility of subjective purpose in man, as illustrated by neurological editing of sensory inputs, and the striving of scientists for control of bias (Bruner).

We may have to supplement traditional value systems with new axiomatic values analogous to the axioms of geometry (Monod). The choice of axioms is limited by biological realities (Lorenz, Waddington, Chagas). But such values as we know in art, poetry and science which transcend the concerns and the actions of the individual have come into being in the slow process of cultural evolution. They are far more easily destroyed than replaced (Gombrich, Auden, Pauling, Lorenz, Lambo). Still, while moral values may be called true or false, according to what their principle means to the welfare of mankind, they cannot be termed logically correct or incorrect (Castberg). As a consequence of these fundamental difficulties, the actual value systems of our present world show marked variation, as illustrated by the generation gap at a time when young people are better informed than ever before (Hayashi, Lorenz, Aiken, and others).

In particular, one of the greatest threats to human survival is the supremacy of the national ideal, at a time when advances in transport and communications have unified the world in a practical sense (Mead, Salam, Doxiadis, and others). Nationalism maintains unnecessary inequality and conflict in the world, and also the weapons systems which threaten catastrophe (Pauling and many others). It is sustained by the excessive indoctrinability, group loyalty and ethnocentric outlook of man (Monod, Lederberg, Koestler, Klineberg).

One of the moral responsibilities now falling heavily upon men and women of learning is that of strenuously cultivating in practical affairs, the international ideal already present in science (Salam and many others). Another is to repudiate politically opportunistic values, while making clear, in research, what value systems have been adopted, so that there is no deception (Myrdal, Mead and others). A third is to defend freedom of individual expression, which is essential for human wellbeing and intellectual advance (Engelhardt). Fourthly there is the obligation to ensure the diffusion of knowledge to all nations (Chagas). A fifth is the responsibility to assess the world resources and to strive for their national and equitable use (Brown).

2. *Knowledge and human needs*

The conspicious problems relating to human welfare and survival include armaments, poverty, overpopulation, oppression, waste of resources, pollution, cities unfit for people, and the unthinking introduction of new technologies (diverse speakers, e.g. Pauling). Confronting these problems, knowledge is the greatest form of capital (Seaborg). Occasionally, technology provides quasi-miraculous, temporary solutions to particular problems, for example in the new improved grains and birth control techniques (Tiselius, Chagas, Salam). More typically, however, the problems are global, complex and interconnected, and approaches to their solution require a pooling of expertise from many fields. Hitherto, national science policymaking has been naive and segregated; we must now relate science to policy in all fields and secure collaboration between natural scientists and experts of other kinds (King, Tiselius).

We cannot expect smooth advance in human affairs, but should instead strive to reduce "roughness" and "turbulence" (Millionshchikov). Pluralistic rather than "tidy" policies will be common (Lederberg, Hayashi, Tiselius).

Concerted intellectual leadership is needed for our technological civilization (Seaborg). Experts must identify and publicize foreseeable social consequences of innovations (Lederberg, Mead, Tiselius and others). For example, recent and current biological advances make possible profound changes in personal life and raise issues about liberty in parenthood (Lederberg). Systematic efforts to forecast the future, and changes in family life, education and work, should be an interdisciplinary and international activity (Segerstedt). Moreover laymen and experts must find new ways of sharing responsibility for the uses of science (Seaborg).

Knowledge is propagated by education, but in an inequitable way, and techniques of education must be sought which do not suppress the creativity of either the exceptional or the unexceptional pupil (Málek, Engelhardt, Bruner). New modes of communication offer remarquable opportunities for disseminating knowledge (Pierce). Not only techniques, but also the values underlying education, need thorough reappraisal (Bruner and others). An aspect of knowledge that merits much greater emphasis in education is the ecological view of man in nature (Chagas). A more acute sense of both environment and of human equality is also necessary if the giant cities of the future are not to be thoroughly dehumanizing (Doxiadis).

Opportunities exist in the world of learning for cultivating the international ideal, in particular by institutionalizing the existing exchange between leading academic centres in the conception of a World University. Such a network would emphasize interdisciplinary opportunities and concern for social implications and priorities (Lasswell, Pregel).

3. *World poverty*

Whether one takes as a simple working principle the maximization of human welfare (Tinbergen) or the minimization of human suffering (Pauling), the impoverished condition of two-thirds of the world's population, living mainly in the developing countries, should be a great burden on the conscience of the rich countries and a challenge to the man of learning. The disparity in wealth is appalling, and growing. Here, above all others, is a problem for the solution of which the improvement and strengthening of international institutions becomes urgent (Tinbergen, Guth).

Local cultivation of knowledge through education and indigenous research, generously supported from the rich nations, is essential for advancement in the poorer regions of the world (Chagas). Particular courses of action open to the academic world include the creation of international institutes and provision for associates coming at intervals from the developing countries (Salam). For young volunteers from the rich countries, 25,000 of whom already go annually to work in the developing countries, greater opportunities should be created for them to serve in this manner as teachers and technicians (Guth, Monod). Research workers in the rich countries should devote more attention to problems of the developing countries, in the scientific, technological, social and psychological spheres (Tata, Chagas, Salam, Lambo).

Plans for the second UN Development Decade, due to start in 1971, and also the aims of the Pearson Commission, demand unprecedented and imaginative efforts by all countries to reduce existing disparities and inequities in the world (Tinbergen, Guth). For the sake of all our children, whether in rich or poor nations, the mutuality and interdependence of human life and creativity, everywhere in the world, should be ever-present in our consciousness (Monod, Lasswell, Doxiadis).

Because of their special knowledge, responsibility falls on scientists and other experts in the rich countries to lead political and public opinion towards urgent dedication of resources to world development (Mead and others). *Sagesse oblige.* (WUSG tape.)

References to speakers indicate only a few of the speakers on particular points, as recalled by the reporting group, and should not be interpreted as necessarily establishing priority or exceptional concern.

95, 94, 100, 10,